D1573468

GERMANY AT ITS BEST
NORDRHEIN-WESTFALEN
DEUTSCHLAND VON SEINER BESTEN SEITE

KLARTEXT

Herausgeber / Publisher:
NRW.INVEST GmbH
Economic Development Agency
of the German State of North Rhine-Westphalia (NRW)
Völklinger Straße 4
40219 Düsseldorf, Germany

Verantwortlich (V.i.S.d.P.) / Responsible according to German Press Law:
Petra Wassner
Vorsitzende der Geschäftsführung / Chief Executive Officer

www.nrwinvest.com

Gestaltung und Produktion / Design and Production:
DIE PR-BERATER Agentur für Kommunikation GmbH
Worringer Straße 22
50668 Cologne, Germany

www.dieprberater.de

Bibliografische Information der Deutschen Bibliothek

Die Deutsche Bibliothek verzeichnet diese Publikation in der Deutschen Nationalbibliografie. Detaillierte bibliografische Daten sind im Internet über http://dnb.ddb.de abrufbar.

Druck und Bindung:
Himmer, Augsburg
1. Auflage Mai 2013
© Klartext Verlag, Essen 2013
ISBN 978-3-8375-0172-8

Alle Rechte der Verbreitung, einschließlich der Bearbeitung für Film, Funk, Fernsehen, CD-ROM, der Übersetzung, Fotokopie und des auszugsweisen Nachdrucks und Gebrauchs im In- und Ausland sind geschützt.

www.klartext-verlag.de

Bibliographic information of the German National Library

The German National Library records this publication in the German National Bibliography. Detailed bibliographic data can be called up on the internet via http://dnb.ddb.de.

Printing and Binding:
Himmer, Augsburg
1st edition May 2013
© Klartext Verlag, Essen 2013
ISBN 978-3-8375-0172-8

All rights to distribution, including processing for film, radio, television, CD-ROM, translation, photocopy and printing and use in extracts in Germany and abroad are protected.

www.klartext-verlag.de

ENTDECKEN SIE DEUTSCHLAND VON SEINER BESTEN SEITE: NORDRHEIN-WESTFALEN

Bei ihrer Wahl nach dem bestmöglichen Standort entscheiden sich ausländische Unternehmen am häufigsten für Nordrhein-Westfalen. Zahlreiche Bestleistungen zeigen auf beeindruckende Weise, wie viel Faszination in Deutschlands wirtschaftlich stärkstem Bundesland steckt.

Wirtschaft, Wissenschaft, Forschung, Kultur, Sport, Kunst – die Bestleistungen sind in Nordrhein-Westfalen allgegenwärtig und das in allen Bereichen. Einer der größten Märkte Europas überrascht immer wieder mit einer Vielfalt, die ihresgleichen sucht.

ENTDECKEN SIE DIE WIRTSCHAFTSKRAFT

Nordrhein-Westfalen liegt mitten in Europa. An Belgien und die Niederlande grenzend ist es mit 17,8 Millionen Einwohnern das bevölkerungsreichste aller 16 deutschen Bundesländer. In einem Umkreis von 500 Kilometern rund um die Landeshauptstadt Düsseldorf leben fast 150 Millionen Menschen. Ein riesiger Markt, der Unternehmen aus aller Welt anzieht. Die hervorragende Verkehrsinfrastruktur bietet beste Verbindungen in alle Welt. Und: Zahlreiche Industrie- und Gewerbeflächen in unterschiedlichsten Regionen lassen ausreichend Raum für neue Investitionen – und Chancen.

DISCOVER GERMANY AT ITS BEST: NORTH RHINE-WESTPHALIA

In their search for the best possible location, foreign companies most frequently opt for North Rhine-Westphalia. Numerous top achievements impressively demonstrate what makes Germany's economically strongest federal state so fascinating.

Business, science, research, culture, sports, art – top achievements are to be found in all fields throughout North Rhine-Westphalia. The unparalleled diversity of what is one of Europe's biggest markets never fails to surprise.

DISCOVER ECONOMIC STRENGTH

North Rhine-Westphalia lies in the heart of Europe, bordering on Belgium and the Netherlands. With 17.8 million inhabitants, it is the most populous of Germany's 16 federal states. Almost 150 million people live within a 500-kilometre radius of Düsseldorf, the state's capital. A huge market that attracts companies from all over the globe. The outstanding transport infrastructure offers excellent connections to destinations around the world. In addition, numerous industrial and commercial sites in a wide variety of regions allow ample space for new investments – and opportunities.

ENTDECKEN SIE WISSENSCHAFT UND FORSCHUNG

Nordrhein-Westfalen ist die Heimat für Innovationen. Wissenschaft und Forschung sind quantitativ und qualitativ weit vorn: Rund 100 Technologiezentren und hochschulexterne Forschungseinrichtungen bilden das dichteste Forschungsnetzwerk Europas – und damit bestmögliche Voraussetzungen für den Technologietransfer. Das breite Angebot der 69 Universitäten und Fachhochschulen versorgt Unternehmen aller Branchen mit qualifizierten Arbeitnehmern. Kein Wunder, dass viele der ansässigen Unternehmen nicht zuletzt dank des Know-how ihrer Mitarbeiter zum Marktführer ihrer Branche aufgestiegen sind. Ein Rundgang über die mehr als 100 internationalen, in Nordrhein-Westfalen beheimateten Leitmessen zeigt zudem Jahr für Jahr ein beeindruckendes Maß an Innovation.

ENTDECKEN SIE KULTURELLE VIELFALT

Nordrhein-Westfalen ist ein abwechslungsreiches Land. Dicht besiedelte Ballungsräume wechseln sich mit Naturlandschaften und ländlichen Gebieten ab. Jenseits der Topografie stehen die nordrhein-westfälischen Regionen mit ihrer jeweils spezifischen Identität für kulturelle Vielfalt. Eine Vielfalt, die auch durch die Menschen geprägt wird, die heute hier ihre Heimat haben. Rund ein Viertel der Bevölkerung hat internationale Wurzeln – für viele Unternehmen ein weiterer Grund, sich hier niederzulassen. Und die Lebensqualität?

Nordrhein-Westfalen bietet eine der reichsten Kulturlandschaften Europas: Viele renommierte Theater und Museen, vier UNESCO-Welterbestätten, Sportwettkämpfe und Kulturfestivals bieten für jeden Geschmack etwas.

DISCOVER SCIENCE AND RESEARCH

North Rhine-Westphalia is home to innovation. Quantitatively and qualitatively it is at the very forefront of science and research: some 100 technology centres and non-university research facilities form the densest research network in Europe, thereby providing ideal conditions for technology transfer. The broad spectrum covered by the 69 universities and universities of applied sciences provides companies from all fields with qualified employees. So it comes as no surprise that many of the companies based here have risen to the rank of market leaders in their respective fields, due in no small measure to the know-how of their employees. Moreover, a tour of the more than 100 leading international trade fairs held in North Rhine-Westphalia reveals an impressive scope of innovation, year after year.

EXPERIENCE CULTURAL DIVERSITY

North Rhine-Westphalia stands for diversity. Densely populated urban centres alternate with natural landscapes and rural areas. Beyond their topography, the regions of North Rhine-Westphalia with their individual identities represent cultural diversity. A diversity that is also characterised by the people who now call it their home. A quarter of the populace has roots abroad – yet another reason for many companies to settle here. And what about the quality of life?

North Rhine-Westphalia offers one of Europe's richest cultural landscapes: dozens of renowned theatres and museums, four UNESCO World Heritage Sites, sports competitions and cultural festivals – there is something to cater for every taste.

ENTDECKEN SIE DIESES BUCH

Bestleistungen aus Nordrhein-Westfalen gibt es unzählige. Dieses Buch stellt Ihnen 100 der Besten vor. Es ist die Auswahl einer hochrangig besetzten Jury. Rund 500 unterschiedliche Bestleistungen hatten sich hierfür über das Portal www.germany-at-its-best.de beworben, bewertet wurden unter anderem ihre Einzigartigkeit und Innovationskraft. Im Folgenden können Sie nun diese 100 entdecken – und damit auch Deutschland von seiner besten Seite: Nordrhein-Westfalen.

Münsterland
Ostwestfalen-Lippe
Metropole Ruhr
Niederrhein
Region Düsseldorf
Südwestfalen
Region Aachen
Region Köln/Bonn
Bergisches Städtedreieck

DISCOVER THIS BOOK

North Rhine-Westphalia has any number of top achievements. This book presents 100 of the best, selected by a jury of distinguished panel members. Around 500 different top performers competed for a place via the portal www.germany-at-its-best.de. Among other things they were judged for their uniqueness and innovative strength. You can now discover these 100 top achievements – and at the same time discover Germany at its best: North Rhine-Westphalia.

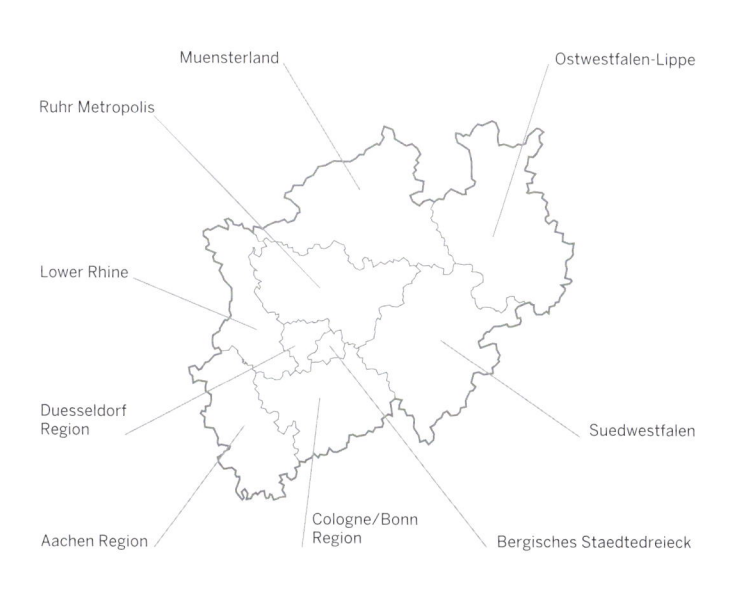

Muensterland
Ostwestfalen-Lippe
Ruhr Metropolis
Lower Rhine
Duesseldorf Region
Suedwestfalen
Aachen Region
Cologne/Bonn Region
Bergisches Staedtedreieck

100 BESTLEISTUNGEN AUS NORDRHEIN-WESTFALEN

100 TOP ACHIEVEMENTS FROM NORTH RHINE-WESTPHALIA

DER WELTREKORD IM KLEBEN
A WORLD RECORD FOR ADHESIVES

3M DEUTSCHLAND. Eine Stunde lang schwebt der LKW einen Meter über der Erde. Gehalten wird das zehn Tonnen schwere Fahrzeug einzig über eine Klebeverbindung von nur sieben Zentimeter Durchmesser. Diese spektakuläre Szene spielte sich auf dem Außengelände der 3M-Hauptverwaltung in Neuss ab. Dort stellte das internationale Technologieunternehmen 2012 gemeinsam mit der Rheinisch-Westfälischen Technischen Hochschule (RWTH) Aachen einen neuen Weltrekord im Kleben auf.

Das Herzstück der von einem Kran getragenen Hängevorrichtung bestand aus zwei Stahlbolzen. Diese wurden zuvor im Institut für Schweißtechnik und Fügetechnik der RWTH unter Aufsicht des Guinnessbuchs der Rekorde geklebt. Zum Einsatz kam mit dem Konstruktionsklebstoff 3M Scotch-Weld DP 760 ein handelsübliches Produkt.

In Deutschland ist 3M an 18 Standorten vertreten. Den größten Teil des weltweiten Produktspektrums vertreibt das Unternehmen von Neuss aus – dort, wo unlängst der über dem Boden schwebende LKW die Leistungskraft moderner Klebstoffe eindrucksvoll unter Beweis stellte.

3M GERMANY. Consider a ten tonne truck swaying for an hour one meter above the ground, held merely by a glued joint just seven centimetres in diameter. This amazing feat was carried out in the grounds of the 3M headquarters in Neuss. The international technology company set this new world record for adhesives in 2012, in conjunction with RWTH Aachen University.

The nub of the hanging contraption held by a crane consisted of two steel bolts. These had been stuck together earlier on using the structural adhesive 3M Scotch Weld DP 760, a standard commercial product, at the Department for Welding and Joining Technology of RWTH, under the supervision of the Guinness Book of World Records.

3M operates from 18 sites in Germany. The lion's share of its product range is marketed worldwide by the company from Neuss – the same place where, just recently, a truck swaying above the ground gave an impressive demonstration of the sheer capacity of modern adhesives.

Bestleistung: Weltrekord im Kleben
Region: Niederrhein
Ort: Neuss

Best performance: World record in adhesion
Region: Lower Rhine
Place: Neuss

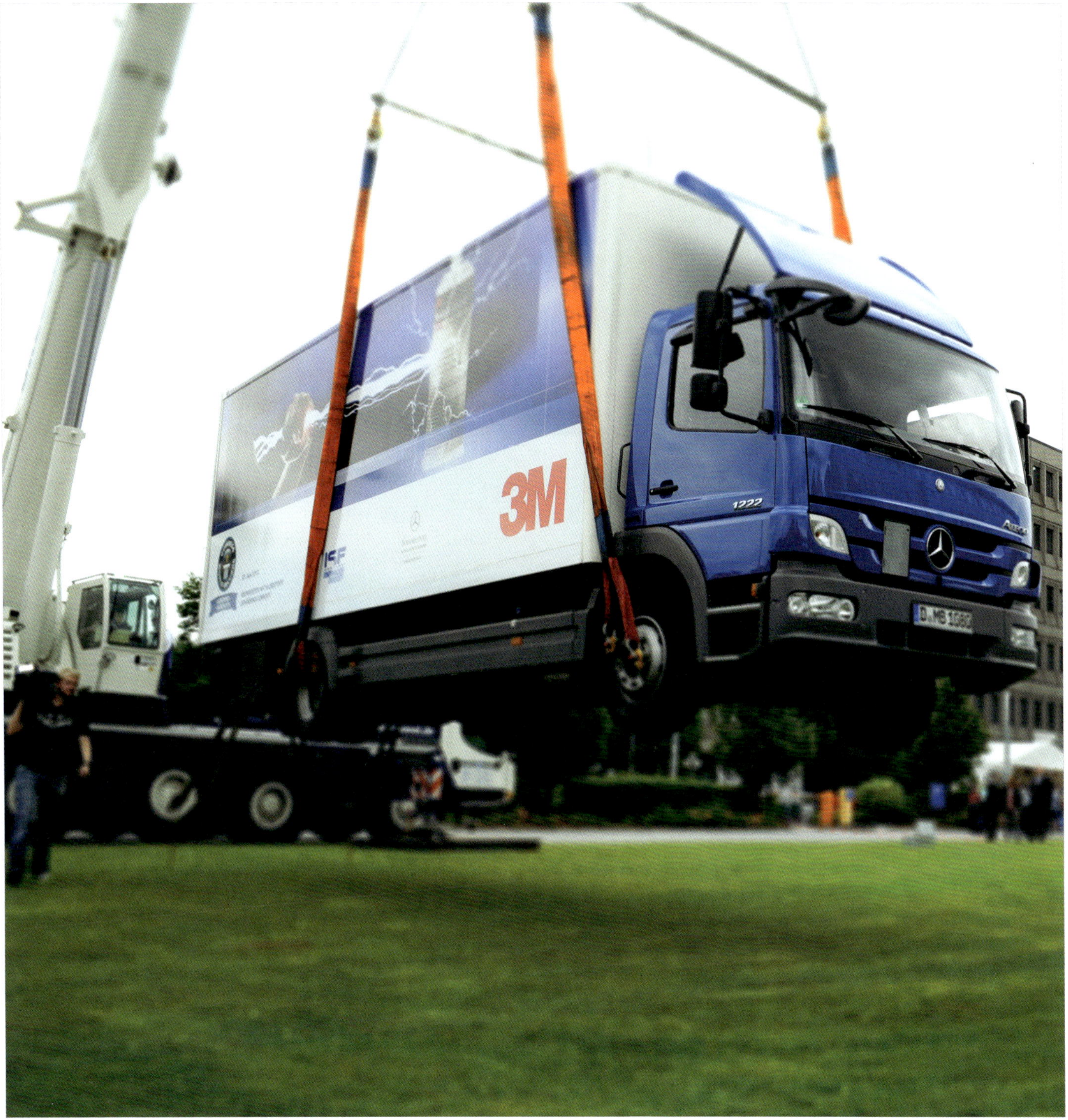
3M
1222

FÄLSCHUNGSSICHER DANK FARBCODES
TAMPER-PROOF BY COLOUR CODES

3S SIMONS SECURITY SYSTEMS. Angesichts weltweit vernetzter Produktions- und Lieferketten wird der Fälschungsschutz für Industrie, Handel und Verbraucher immer bedeutsamer. Einen rechtssicheren Schutz vor Plagiaten bietet die Mikro-Farbcodetechnologie SECUTAG® der 3S Simons Security Systems GmbH aus Nottuln in Westfalen.

Die Mikro-Farbcodes bestehen aus bis zu zehn verschiedenen Farbschichten. Diese sind für das bloße Auge unsichtbar, können aber mit einem handelsüblichen Stabmikroskop identifiziert werden. Mit dem System, das seit über 15 Jahren fälschungssicher im Einsatz ist und als gerichtliches Beweismittel anerkannt wird, lassen sich unter anderem Produkte, Verpackungen, Etiketten, Dokumente und Warenwirtschaftsdaten sichern.

Mehrere Branchenlösungen für die Bereiche Maschinenbau, Automotive, Pharma, Kosmetik, Fashion und für den Kunsthandel runden die Angebotspalette von 3S ab. Damit jedes Produkt von jedermann jederzeit zweifelsfrei und rechtssicher als Original identifiziert werden kann.

3S SIMONS SECURITY SYSTEMS. Globally interlinked production and supply chains make anti-forgery measures for industry, trade and consumers increasingly relevant. 3S Simons Security Systems GmbH from Nottuln in Westphalia offers legally binding counterfeit protection in the form of the micro colour code technology SECUTAG®.

The micro colour codes consist of a maximum of 10 different layers of colours. These are invisible to the naked eye but can be seen using a conventional pen microscope. The system has been counterfeit-proof for over 15 years now and is accepted as evidence by courts. It provides protection for products, packaging, labels, documents and merchandise management data.

Protection solutions for several sectors such as the mechanical engineering, automotive, pharmaceutical, cosmetics and fashion industries, and art trade complete the 3S range of products. This ensures a legally binding and definitive identification of originality for each product, by anyone, at all times.

Bestleistung: Kleinste Mikro-Farbcodepartikel zum Schutz vor Plagiaten
Region: Münsterland
Ort: Nottuln

Best performance: Smallest anti-forgery micro-colour code particles
Region: Muensterland
Place: Nottuln

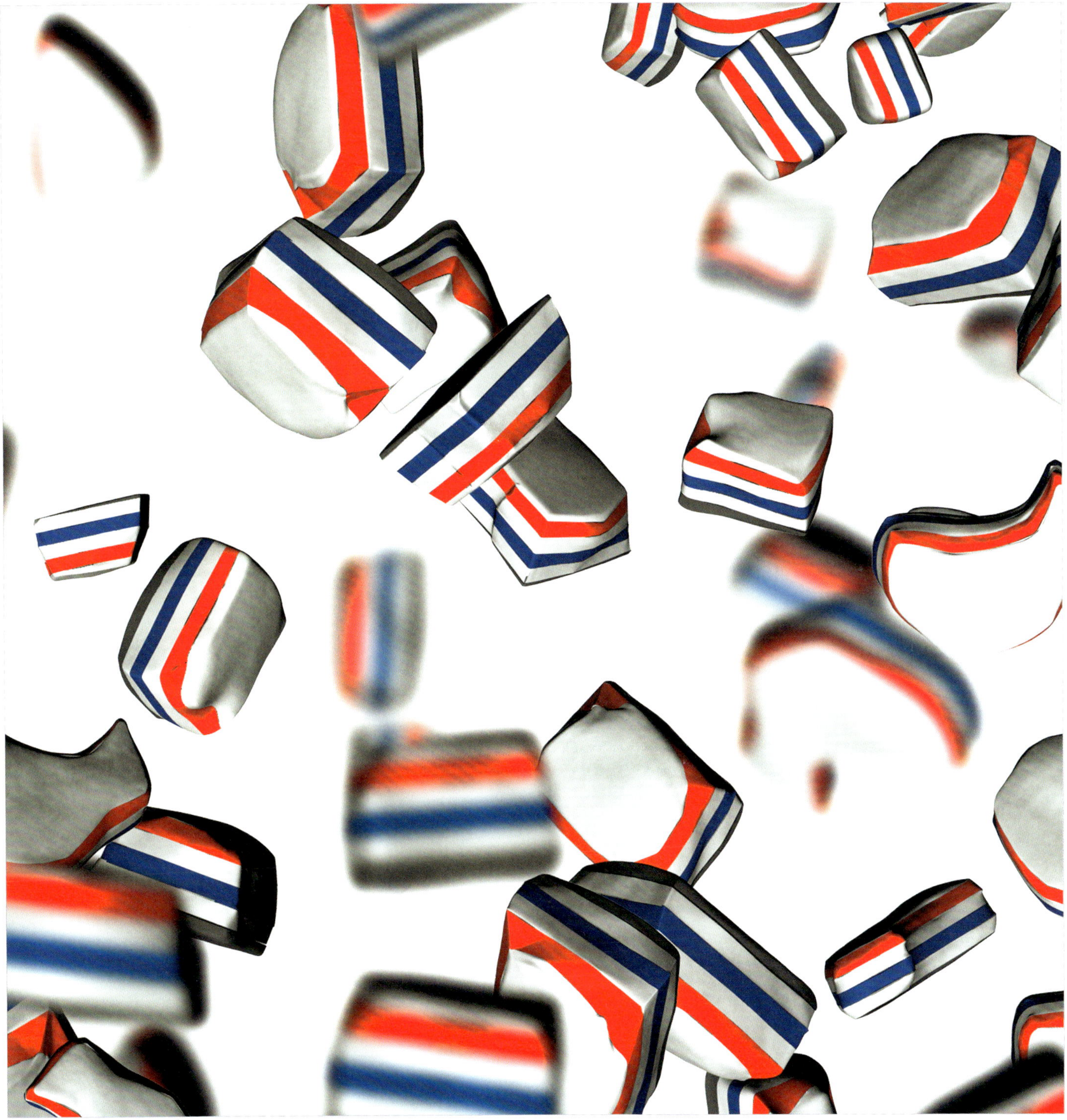

AUF DEN SPUREN KARLS DES GROSSEN
ON THE TRAIL OF CHARLES THE GREAT

AACHENER DOM. Die Geschichte des Aachener Doms beginnt als Kapelle: im Mittelalter regierten Könige nicht von einer Hauptstadt aus, sondern pendelten zwischen ihren Herrschaftsgebieten, um vor Ort den Kontakt zu ihren Gefolgsleuten halten zu können. Weil Kaiser Karl der Große besonders gern Aachen besuchte, ließ er dort einen architektonischen Prachtbau errichten – heute bekannt als Aachener Dom. Und 1978 wurde das Bauwerk – fast 1200 Jahre später – zum ersten deutschen UNESCO-Welterbe ernannt.

814 wird Karl hier in einem antiken Sarkophag beigesetzt – seit 1215 ruhen seine Gebeine im goldenen Karlsschrein. Seinen Königsthron aus kostbaren Marmorplatten besteigen zur Krönung in 600 Jahren mehr als 30 römisch-deutsche Könige. So viel Prominenz hinterlässt Spuren: Der Kirchenschatz samt Reliquien wächst, die Kirche wird zur europaweit beliebten Wallfahrtsstätte. Seit 1349 ziehen Pilgerscharen alle sieben Jahre nach Aachen, um die Reliquien zu verehren. Dann gibt der Marienschrein aus dem 13. Jahrhundert seine Schätze preis, etwa das Lendentuch Christi oder das Marienkleid – 2014 ist es wieder so weit.

AACHEN CATHEDRAL. Aachen Cathedral started out as a chapel. Mediaeval kings did not rule from a capital city, but shuttled between their dominions to meet with their subjects on site. As King Charlemagne liked visiting Aachen a lot, he had an architectural marvel built there, known today as Aachen Cathedral. Nearly 1,200 years later, in 1978, this was the first German edifice to be declared a World Heritage Site by UNESCO.

Charlemagne was interred here in 814 in an ancient sarcophagus; since 1215 his remains have rested in the golden shrine of Charlemagne. In 600 years his prized marble throne saw the coronation of over 30 Roman-German kings. Such eminence is bound to leave its mark: the church treasury and its relics swelled, it became one of Europe's most popular pilgrimage sites. Every seven years since 1349, the devout have been thronging Aachen to worship the relics. The 13th century shrine of the Virgin Mary then puts its treasures on view, like the swaddling-cloth of the Infant Jesus or cloak of the Virgin Mary ("Marienkleid"). The next date with history is set for 2014.

Bestleistung: UNESCO-Welterbe
Region: Aachen
Ort: Aachen

Best performance: UNESCO World Heritage Site
Region: Aachen
Place: Aachen

SIC DEUS HOC TUTUM STABILI... ...ACIS COMPAGE LIGANTUR
...OD CAROLUS PRINCEPS CONDIDIT ESSE VE...

DAS SCHNELLSTE FLÜSSIGGASAUTO
THE FASTEST LPG CAR

AC SCHNITZER. Er ist das weltweit schnellste Konzeptfahrzeug mit Straßenzulassung in seiner Klasse: der GP3.10 der Aachener Firma AC Schnitzer. Ein BMW 3er Coupé mit leistungsgesteigertem M5-Motor, 522 PS und von null auf hundert in 4,5 Sekunden – allein dies wäre schon spektakulär genug. Wirklich beeindruckend an der Konzeptstudie ist die Höchstgeschwindigkeit: fast 320 Kilometer pro Stunde – Weltrekord, denn der umgerüstete V10-Motor fährt mit Flüssiggas (LPG).

Der GP3.10 kann jederzeit auf den umweltschonenden Treibstoff umgestellt werden, er verfügt auch noch über einen herkömmlichen Benzintank. Bei Gasbetrieb spart das Auto rund 15 Prozent Kohlenstoffdioxid-Emissionen ein.

Im Motorsport ist das AC Schnitzer Motorsport-Team das erfolgreichste Tourenwagenteam weltweit. Materialien und Erfahrungen aus dem Rennsport setzt AC Schnitzer in Lösungen für den täglichen Gebrauch in Straßenfahrzeugen um. Alle Spezialteile des Tuningprogramms werden in Aachen entwickelt und von dort in die ganze Welt vertrieben. Mit Erfolg: AC Schnitzer ist der weltweit führende Anbieter für BMW- und MINI-Zubehör.

AC SCHNITZER. Made by Aachen-based company AC Schnitzer, the GP3.10 is the world's fastest street-legal concept car of its class. A BMW 3-series coupé equipped with a high-performance M5 engine, capable of producing 522 hp and accelerating from 0-100 in just 4.5 seconds alone would have sufficed to make it a spectacular car.

The really impressive bit about the concept study, however, is the top speed of almost 320 kilometres per hour, a world record considering that the converted V10 engine runs on liquid petrol gas (LPG).

The GP3.10 can be switched to this eco-friendly fuel at any time and is also fitted with a standard petrol tank. In gas mode, the car reduces CO_2 emissions by around 15 per cent.

The AC Schnitzer team is the most successful touring car team in the world of motorsports. The materials and experience gained in motor sporting are employed to create solutions for daily use in road vehicles. All special parts for the tuning programme are developed in Aachen and marketed from there all over the world. And with some success! AC Schnitzer is the world's leading supplier of BMW and MINI accessories.

Bestleistung: Schnellstes Flüssiggasauto der Welt
Region: Aachen
Ort: Aachen

Best performance: The fastest LPG car of the world
Region: Aachen
Place: Aachen

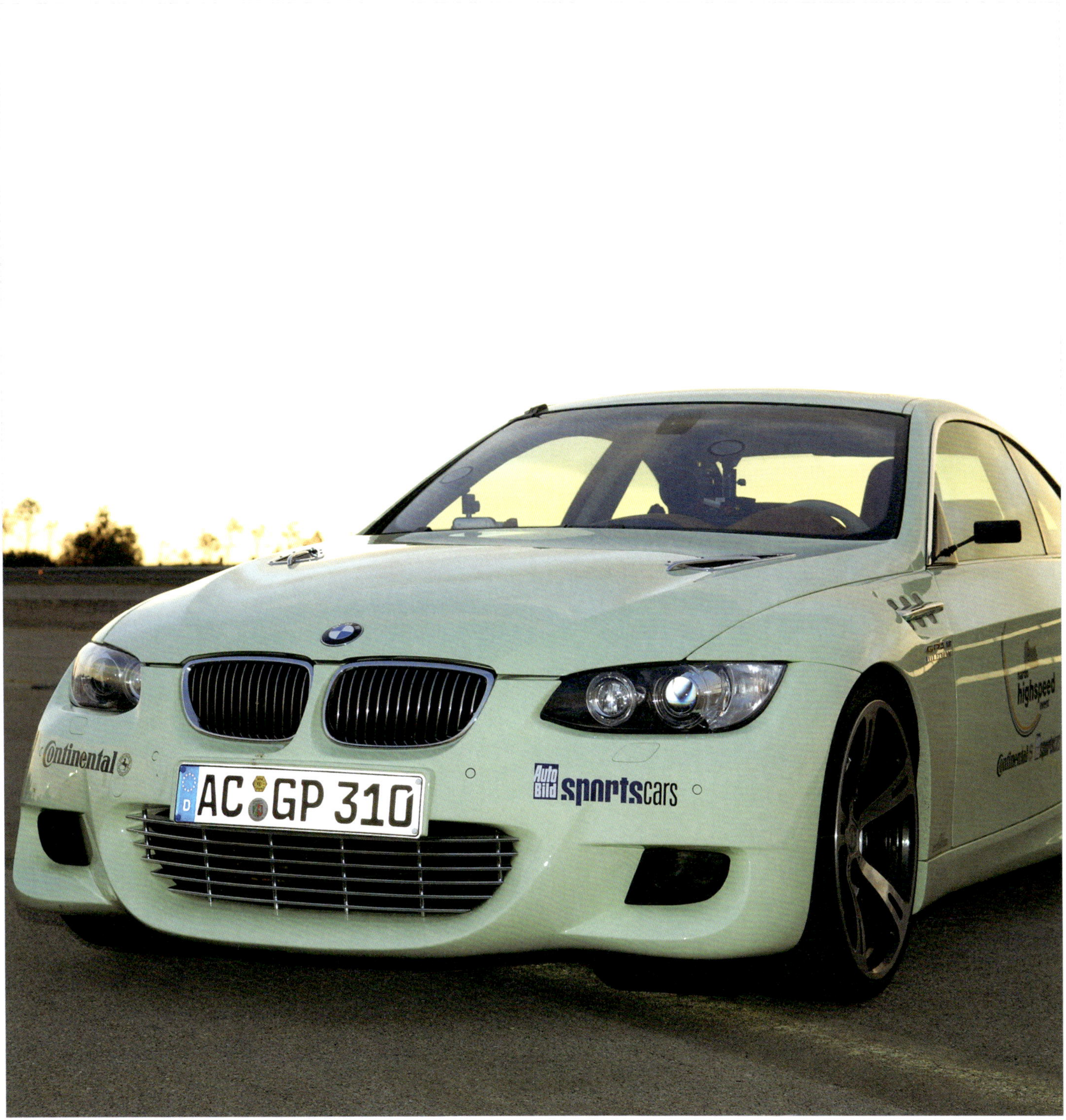
Continental
AC GP 310
Auto Bild
sportscars
highspeed

TIEF – TIEFER – AKER WIRTH
DEEP – DEEPER – AKER WIRTH

AKER WIRTH. Im Jahr 1990 entwickelte das Unternehmen Aker Wirth im Auftrag des weltgrößten Diamantenproduzenten De Beers ein spezielles Bohrsystem, um diamanthaltige Schichten abtragen und auf Bohrschiffe transportieren zu können. Das innovative System funktioniert sowohl auf unebenen Böden als auch in Wassertiefen bis zu 200 Metern. Bis heute hat das Unternehmen aus dem niederrheinischen Erkelenz seine Expertise in diesem Bereich weiter verfeinert und sich den inoffiziellen Titel „Weltmarktführer bei Bohrsystemen für die Diamantengewinnung auf hoher See" gesichert.

Mit mehr als 700 Mitarbeitern weltweit fertigt Aker Wirth darüber hinaus Bohrsysteme für Öl- und Gasindustrie sowie Berg- und Tiefbau – zu den Technologieführern gehört das 1895 gegründete Unternehmen auch im Tiefseebergbau. Aus diesem Grund entwickelte Aker Wirth im Auftrag der Bundesanstalt für Geowissenschaften und Rohstoffe ein Konzept für den ökologischen Rohstoffabbau aus Meerestiefen von bis zu 4.500 Metern.

AKER WIRTH. In 1990 the company Aker Wirth developed a special drilling system commissioned by the largest diamond producer of the world, De Beers, to enable the stripping of diamond-bearing layers and for their transportation on drilling vessels. The innovative system worked on uneven floors as well as in water depths of up to 200 metres. This company from Erkelenz of the Lower Rhine region to date continues honing its expertise in this field and has clinched the unofficial title of "the global market leader in drilling systems for diamond extraction on the high seas" for itself.

With more than 700 employees worldwide Aker Wirth also manufactures drilling systems for the oil and gas industry and for mining and underground civil engineering – the company founded in 1895, for deep-sea mining as well, belongs to these leaders of technology. On account of this, Aker Wirth on behalf of the Federal Institute of Geosciences and Natural Resources is developing a concept for the ecological mining of resources from the sea depths of up to 4,500 metres.

Bestleistung: Marktführer für Bohrsysteme
Region: Niederrhein
Ort: Erkelenz

Best performance: Market leader in drilling systems
Region: Lower Rhine
Place: Erkelenz

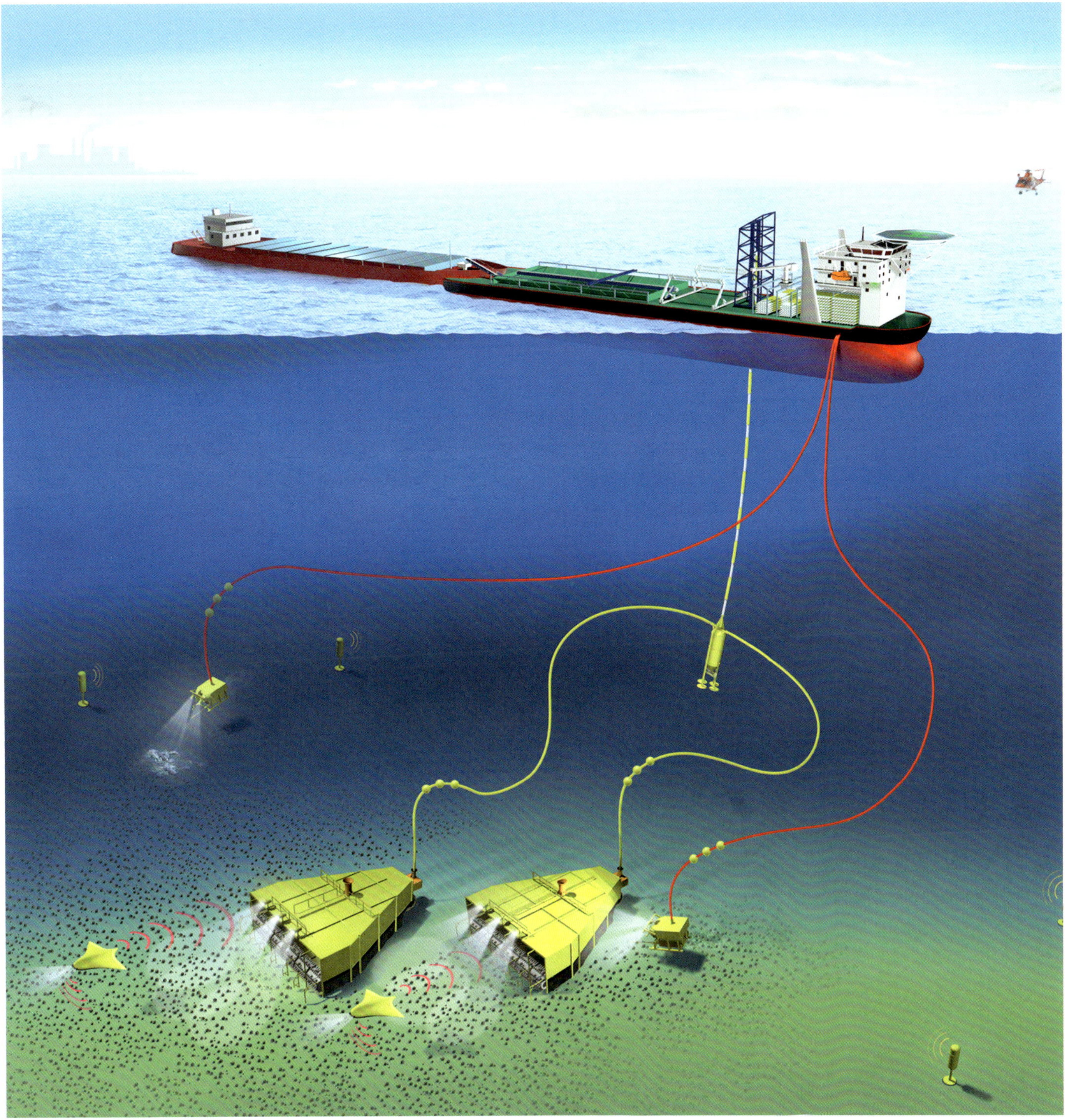

IM LIEGEN DUSCHEN UND ENTSPANNEN
RECLINE, BATHE, RELAX

ALOYS F. DORNBRACHT. Vor über 60 Jahren tüftelten Aloys F. Dornbracht und sein Sohn Helmut nach Feierabend in einer Garage an ihrem ersten Patent: einer Armatur mit ausziehbarem Auslauf für die Küche – damals die einzige Wasserstelle im Haus. Mit großem Einsatz bauten sie so ihr Geschäft auf. Heute ist die Aloys F. Dornbracht GmbH & Co. KG mit Hauptsitz in Iserlohn Weltmarktführer bei der Herstellung von Premiumarmaturen. Seit der Gründung hat Dornbracht den Stellenwert von Design und Architektur in Küche und Bad wesentlich beeinflusst. Davon zeugen unzählige renommierte Auszeichnungen der Dornbracht-Produkte. Als Innovationsführer der Branche treibt das Familienunternehmen zudem Technik und Produktion kontinuierlich voran.

So hat Dornbracht mit der Ambiance Tuning Technique (ATT) ein völlig neuartiges Duscherlebnis geschaffen. Erstmals lassen sich verschiedene Wasserstrahlarten zu Choreografien mit unterschiedlicher Wassertemperatur und -menge kombinieren. Diese wirken nach Wunsch belebend oder entspannend und lassen sich mit der Horizontal Shower sogar im Liegen genießen.

ALOYS F. DORNBRACHT. 60 years back Aloys F. Dornbracht and his son Helmut worked painstakingly in their free time in a garage on their first patent: a tap with a detachable nozzle for the kitchen; at the time the only water outlet in the house. A lot of hard work went into establishing their business. Now headquartered in Iserlohn, Aloys F. Dornbracht GmbH & Co. KG is an international leader in the manufacture of premium fittings. Since its inception, Dornbracht has greatly contributed to the role of design and architecture in the kitchen and bathroom realm. The many prestigious awards its products have attracted speak for themselves. As leaders of innovation in the segment, this family business also strives to continually push the boundaries of technology and production.

For example, Dornbacht's Ambiance Tuning Technique (ATT) creates an entirely new bathing experience, combining different water jets into choreographies of varied temperatures and quantities that invigorate or relax in sync with your bathing needs. The Horizontal Shower indulges its user even in the reclined position.

Bestleistung: Führender Hersteller von Premiumarmaturen
Region: Südwestfalen
Ort: Iserlohn

Best performance: Leading manufacturer of premium taps
Region: Suedwestfalen
Place: Iserlohn

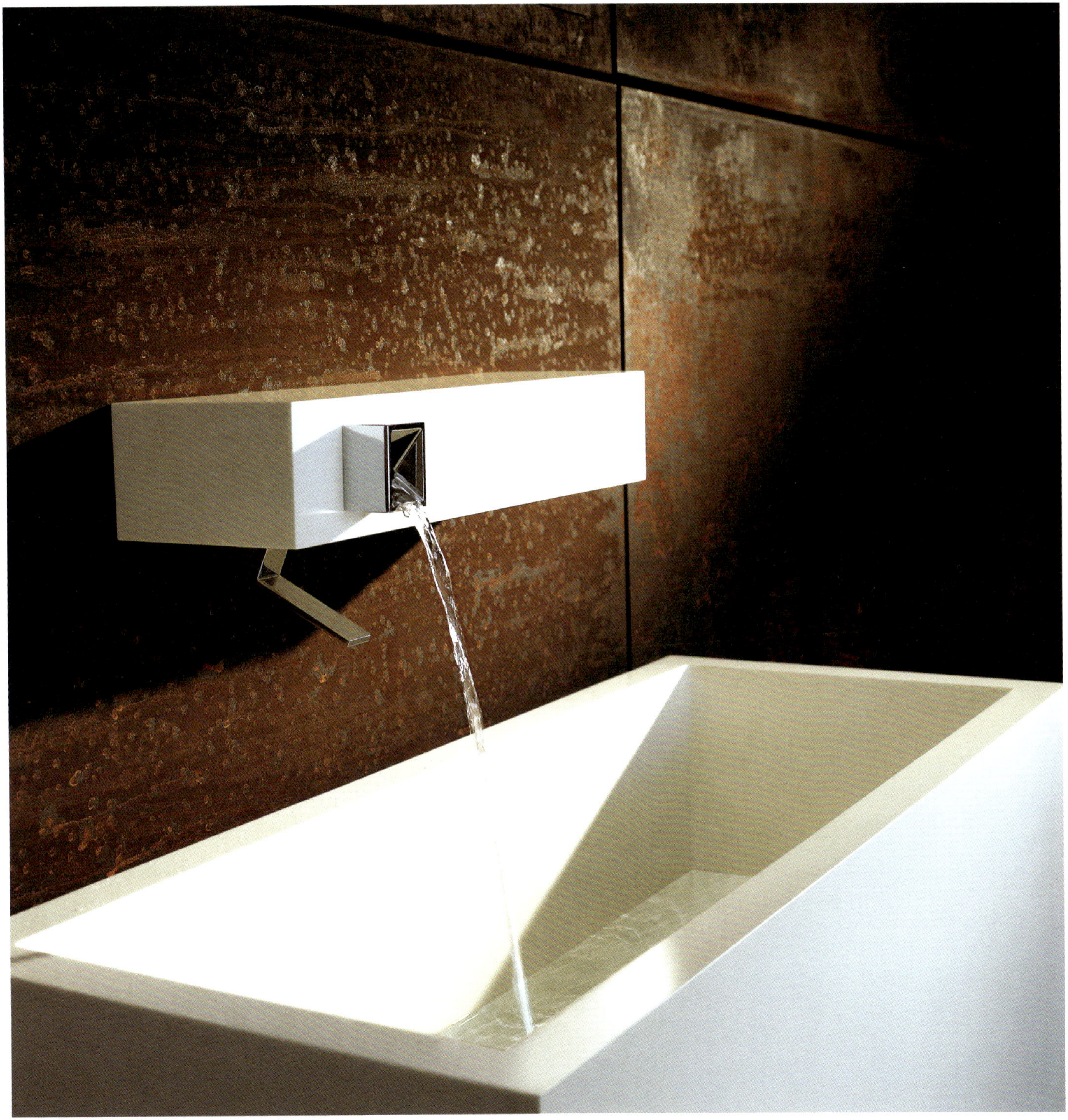

WALZWELTMEISTER AUS NEUSS
CASTING AND ROLLING EXPERTS OF NEUSS

ALUMINIUM NORF. Das Gelände südlich von Neuss fasst eine Fläche von mehr als 60 Fußballfeldern und beherbergt das weltweit größte Schmelz- und Walzwerk für Aluminium. Rund um die Uhr, sieben Tage die Woche, 365 Tage im Jahr sind hier 2.100 Mitarbeiter damit beschäftigt, Aluminium zu recyceln, zu gießen und zu walzen. Jahr für Jahr kommen so 1.500.000 Tonnen des Leichtmetalls in den Produktionskreislauf – und dank unendlichem Recycling immer wieder zurück.

Recyclingschrott und weiteres Kaltmetall werden eingeschmolzen, zu Walzbarren gegossen und dann – weltweit einzigartig – auf gleich zwei Warmwalzstraßen zu zwei bis zehn Millimeter dickem, rollbarem Band gepresst. Schöner Nebeneffekt: Die Abluft der Gießerei versorgt einen ganzen, in der Nähe liegenden Stadtteil mit Fernwärme.

Betrieben wird Aluminium Norf je zur Hälfte von den Gesellschaftern Hydro und Novelis. Im Verbund mit den weiteren Werken der beiden Gesellschafter sowie der größten deutschen Aluminiumhütte – in unmittelbarer Nachbarschaft – ist so in der Region Neuss ein europaweit einzigartiger Spitzenstandort der Aluminiumverarbeitung entstanden.

ALUMINIUM NORF. The site south of Neuss has an area measuring larger than 60 football fields and is home to the world's biggest aluminium smelting and rolling plant. 2,100 workers recycle, cast and roll aluminium around the clock, seven days a week, 365 days a year. Year after year 1,500,000 tonnes of this light metal are fed into the production cycle, over and over again thanks to endless recycling.

Recycling scrap and other cold metals are melted and cast into ingots before, in a step that is unique in the world, being immediately compressed into rollable bands with a thickness of two to ten millimetres in two hot-rolling mills. As a great spin-off, the air discharged from the foundry supplies district heating to a whole township close by.

Aluminium Norf is operated jointly by two companies, Hydro and Novelis. Combined with their other factories and the biggest German aluminium smelting plant – located immediately adjacently – a top location for aluminium processing, unique in Europe, has emerged in the Neuss region.

Bestleistung: Das weltgrößte Walz- und Schmelzwerk
Region: Niederrhein
Ort: Neuss

Best performance: World's biggest rolling and smelting plant
Region: Lower Rhine
Place: Neuss

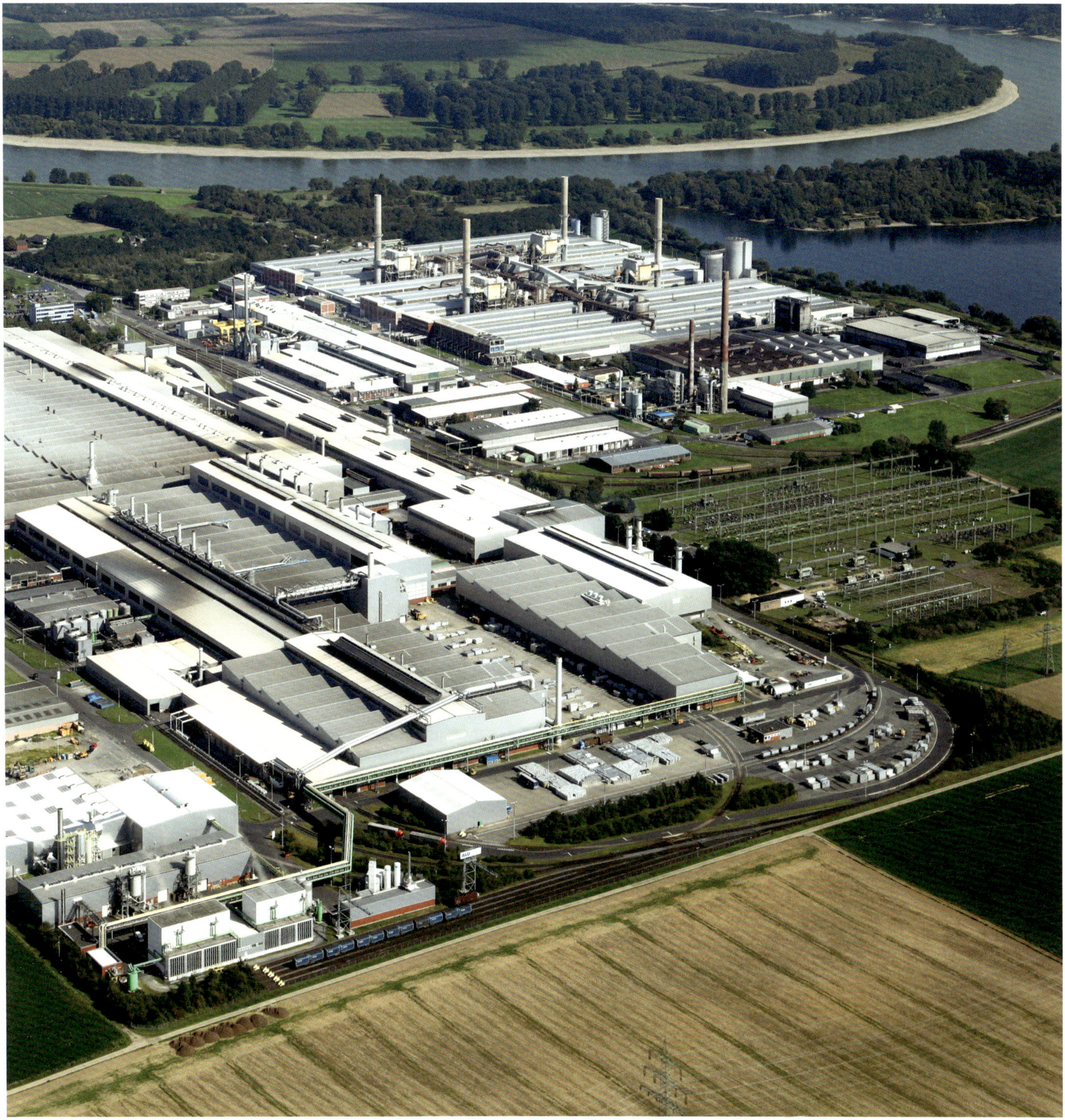

RÖMISCHE ZEITREISE IN 3-D
ROMAN TIME TRAVEL IN 3D

ARCHÄOLOGISCHER PARK XANTEN (APX). Für eine kleine Stadt hat Xanten viel zu bieten: eine hübsche Altstadt samt Dom, schöne Seen und dank Siegfried von Xanten eine Rolle in der Nibelungensage. Aber der größte Publikumsmagnet ist sicher das archäologische Freilichtmuseum. Und dieses verdankt die Stadt am unteren Niederrhein – einem Glücksfall!

Die Colonia Ulpia Traiana, eine der größten römischen Städte nördlich der Alpen, wurde nach dem Untergang des Römischen Reiches nie überbaut. Ein Eldorado für Forscher und Entdecker! So entstand die Idee eines einmaligen archäologischen Parks, der Forschung und Museum vereint. Heute ist der APX Deutschlands größtes archäologisches Freilichtmuseum und mit jährlich mehr als 600.000 Gästen auch das bestbesuchte.

Römische Geschichte, Kultur, Alltag und Handwerk werden hier und im zugehörigen, preisgekrönten RömerMuseum anschaulich präsentiert, wissenschaftlich begleitet und unterhaltend vermittelt. Hafentempel, Amphitheater, Stadtmauer, Wohnhäuser und Badeanlagen bieten einen lebendigen Eindruck vom römischen Leben in Germanien. Viele Veranstaltungen laden zum Mitmachen und Zuschauen ein. „Salve, Xanten!"

ARCHAEOLOGICAL PARK XANTEN (APX). For a small town, Xanten has a lot to offer: a charming city centre with a cathedral, scenic lakes and, thanks to Siegfried von Xanten, its role in the Nibelungen tales. But it is the archaeological open air museum that is the biggest public attraction. It is a sheer stroke of luck for this city in the Lower Rhine region.

The Colonia Ulpia Traiana, one of the biggest Roman cities north of the Alps, was never built over after the fall of the Roman empire, making it a virtual gold mine for researchers and explorers! This fuelled the concept of a unique archaeological park, as both a place for research and a museum. Today, APX is Germany's biggest open air archaeological museum and 600,000 visitors annually mean that it is also the most visited one.

The prized RömerMuseum at the site depicts Roman history, culture, daily life and crafts supported by compelling scientific facts. Harbour temple, amphitheatre, city wall, houses and baths provide a vivid impression of Roman life in Germania. Myriad events beckon you to participate and witness them with a "Salve Xanten" on your lips!

Bestleistung: Deutschlands größtes Freilichtmuseum
Region: Niederrhein
Ort: Xanten

Best performance: Germany's biggest open air museum
Region: Lower Rhine
Place: Xanten

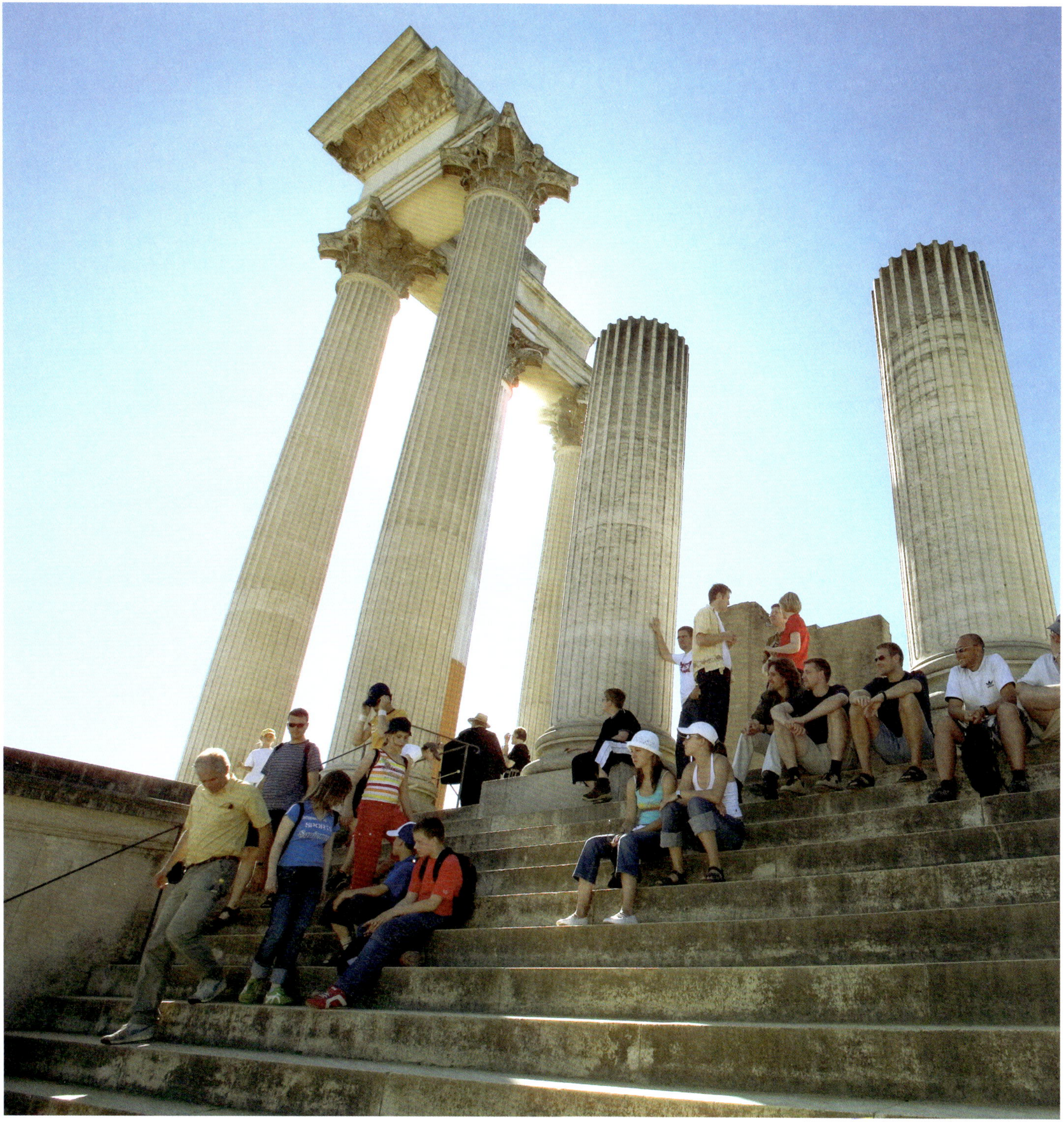

KÖLNS GLOBALE KUNSTMESSE
COLOGNE'S GLOBAL ART FAIR

ART COLOGNE. Rund 200 Galerien bieten jährlich an die 2.000 Werke der modernen Kunst, der Nachkriegs- und zeitgenössischen Kunst auf über 33.000 Quadratmetern in den Kölner Messehallen an – eine anregende Mischung aus jungen Wilden und etablierten Größen. 60.000 Interessierte und Sammler tummeln sich hier: Willkommen auf der ART COLOGNE, der ältesten Kunstmesse der Welt!

1967 kamen zwei Kölner Galeristen auf die Idee, eine Verkaufsmesse für progressive Kunst zu etablieren. Schon der erste „Kunstmarkt Köln '67" war ein Erfolg – auch dank der wieder dynamischen deutschen Künstlerszene nach dem Krieg sowie der vielen Mäzene und Sammler an Rhein und Ruhr. Und nun feiert die ART COLOGNE bald ihren 50. Geburtstag.

Doch nicht ihr Alter oder ihre Größe machen den Unterschied: Die globale Kunstszene entscheidet sich aufgrund ihrer Qualität und ihres internationalen Renomees für die Mutter aller Kunstmessen. Deswegen zählt sie zu Recht zu den Topmessen weltweit – auf Augenhöhe mit Basel, London, Hongkong und New York.

ART COLOGNE. On show in over 33,000 square metres of area at the Cologne fair pavilion annually are around 2,000 works of modern art, post-war and contemporary art from about 200 galleries; an inspiring mix of works by young bohemians and established greats. Welcome to ART COLOGNE, the world's oldest art fair bustling with 60,000 art enthusiasts and collectors.

In 1967 two gallery owners from Cologne came up with the idea of starting a trade fair for progressive art. At its very birth in 1967, what is now ART COLOGNE was a success, as much for the revived dynamism of the German art scene after the war as the many patrons and collectors of the Rhine and Ruhr regions. The event will soon be celebrating its 50 years of existence!

Yet it is hardly its vintage or scale that bring distinction. The global art scene values this mother of all art fairs for its quality and universal contemporaneity. Not without reason then that it should rank among the top international fairs, on a par with Basel, London, Hong Kong and New York.

Bestleistung: Älteste Kunstmesse der Welt
Region: Köln / Bonn
Ort: Köln

Best performance: World's oldest trade fair on art
Region: Cologne / Bonn
Place: Cologne

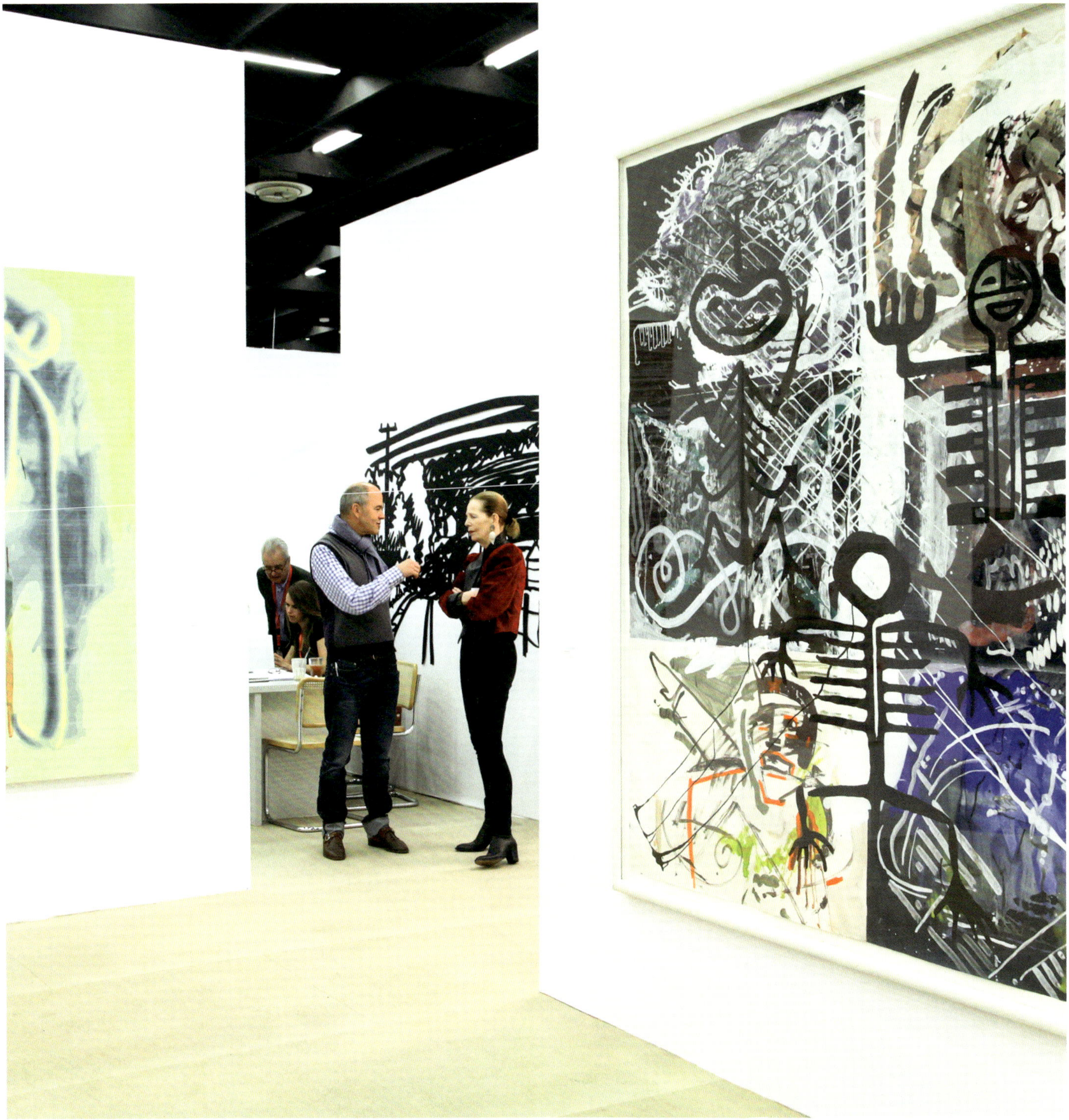

EDLER ZWIRN FÜR AUTOMOBILE
CLASSY YARNS FOR CARS

AUNDE GRUPPE. Mit zwölf Webstühlen startete das Unternehmen Achter & Ebels 1899 in Mönchengladbach seine „mechanische Weberei in Herrenstoffen nebst dazugehörenden Vorarbeiten, wie Zwirnerei und Spulerei". Bis 1927 entwickelte sich die Weberei zur Volltuchfabrik mit 500 Beschäftigten und galt als größtes in Privatbesitz befindliches Textilunternehmen in der Region Mönchengladbach. Bereits zu dieser Zeit begann das Unternehmen mit der Entwicklung und Produktion von Polsterstoffen sowie technischen Textilien für die Automobilindustrie. Seitdem ist viel passiert: Aus Achter & Ebels ist in den letzten 25 Jahren die Unternehmensgruppe AUNDE geworden, zu der die Marken AUNDE und ISRINGHAUSEN gehören. Sie beschäftigt mittlerweile 13.000 Mitarbeiter und zählt zu den 100 größten Automobilzulieferern der Welt. Weitere Highlights: AUNDE gehört zu den Weltmarktführern für Automobiltextil, Sitzbezüge aus Textil und Leder für Fahrzeuginnenräume. ISRINGHAUSEN ist Weltmarktführer für Nutzfahrzeugsitze und liefert zudem komplette Sitzsysteme für PKWs, Jeeps, Vans und Minibusse sowie Passagiersitze für Busse und öffentliche Transportmittel. Produziert wird in 86 Werken in 25 Ländern.

AUNDE GROUP. In 1899 the firm Achter & Ebels started its "mechanical weaving mill for men's clothing materials and related preparatory work like spinning and winding" with twelve looms in Moenchengladbach. By 1927 the mill had become a vertically integrated textile mill with 500 employees and was regarded as the biggest privately owned textile company in the Moenchengladbach region. It was as long ago as then that the company began developing and producing upholstery materials and technical textiles for the automotive industry. A lot has happened since: Achter & Ebels has grown into the AUNDE Group in the last 25 years with the flagship brands AUNDE and ISRINGHAUSEN under its wings. It now employs 13,000 people and figures among the 100 largest suppliers to the automotive industry in the world. Other highlights: AUNDE ranks among the global market leaders for automotive textiles, cloth and leather seat covers for car interiors. ISRINGHAUSEN is the global market leader for commercial vehicle seats and besides this supplies complete seating systems for passenger cars, jeeps and mini buses, as well as passenger seats for buses and public transport. Production is carried out in 86 factories spread over 25 countries.

Bestleistung: Führender Hersteller von Automobiltextilien
Region: Niederrhein
Ort: Mönchengladbach

Best performance: Leading manufacturer of automobile textiles
Region: Lower Rhine
Place: Moenchengladbach

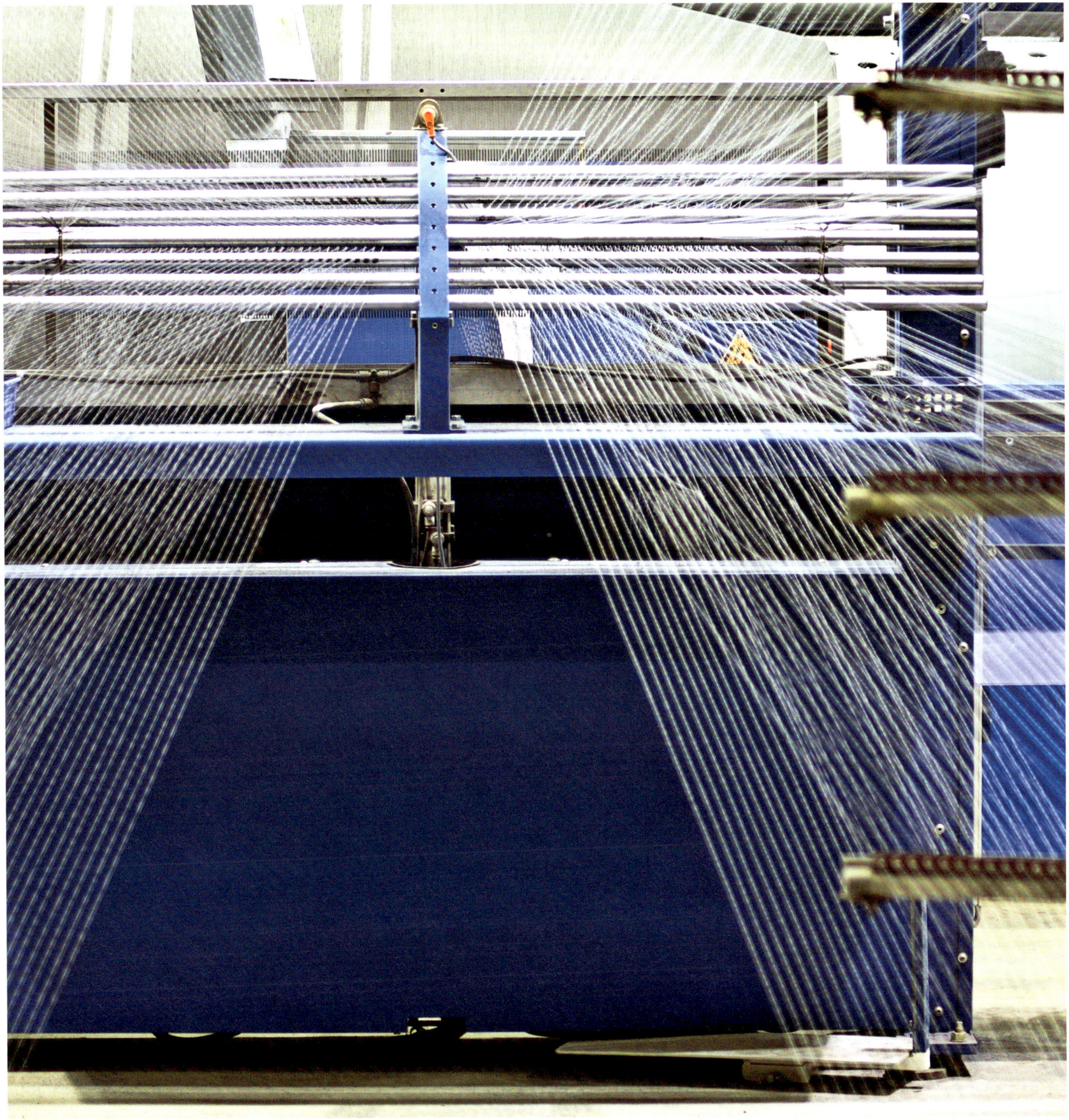

ROBOTERANZUG ALS THERAPIEHILFE
ROBOT SUIT AS THERAPY AID

BAYER MATERIALSCIENCE. Nach einer Operation oder einer schweren Krankheit erwartet den Betroffenen zumeist eine langwierige und kräftezehrende Rehabilitation – speziell bei neurologischen Schäden oder Beeinträchtigungen des Bewegungsapparats ist eine vollständige Heilung oft ungewiss. Hier kommt ein neuartiger Roboteranzug mit innovativen Materialien von Bayer MaterialScience ins Spiel. Das Exo-Skelett HAL® (Hybrid Assistive Limb) bietet eine erfolgreiche Hilfe im Therapiebereich. Die Idee dazu stammt von dem japanischen Forscher Yoshiyuki Sankai. Seine Firma Cyberdyne produziert auch die künstlichen Gliedmaßen, wobei das spezielle Polycarbonat für das Gehäuse vom Chemiespezialisten aus Leverkusen kommt.

Reha-Patienten wird HAL® um Arme und Beine gegurtet. Ein Computer übersetzt dann Nervensignale in unterstützende Bewegungsabläufe, sobald der Träger etwa ans Gehen oder Treppensteigen denkt. In Japan findet der Roboteranzug bereits in über 100 Rehabilitationseinrichtungen Verwendung, seit 2012 wird er auch in Deutschland eingesetzt. Zukünftig könnte das Exo-Skelett zudem im Katastrophenschutz zum Einsatz kommen.

BAYER MATERIALSCIENCE. Long drawn-out, energy-sapping rehabilitation is usually the norm after an operation or serious illness. Complete recovery is often uncertain, especially where there is neurological damage or impairment of the musculoskeletal system. A new kind of robot suit made from innovative materials by Bayer MaterialScience can be of help in such cases. The HAL® (Hybrid Assistive Limb) exoskeleton serves as a successful therapy aid. The concept comes from the Japanese researcher Yoshiyuki Sankai. His company, Cyberdyne, also manufactures the artificial limbs. The special polycarbonate used here for the casing is supplied by specialists in chemistry at Leverkusen.

The HAL® is strapped to the arms and legs of the rehab patients. Once the wearer thinks of, say, walking or climbing steps, a computer translates nerve signals into supportive limb movements. The robot suit is already in use at over 100 rehabilitation centres in Japan and has likewise been put into service in Germany since 2012. In future, the exoskeleton could well be used also for civil protection at disaster sites.

Bestleistung: High-Tech-Kunststoff für innovativen Roboteranzug
Region: Köln / Bonn
Ort: Leverkusen

Best performance: High-tech synthetic material for innovative robot suit
Region: Cologne / Bonn
Place: Leverkusen

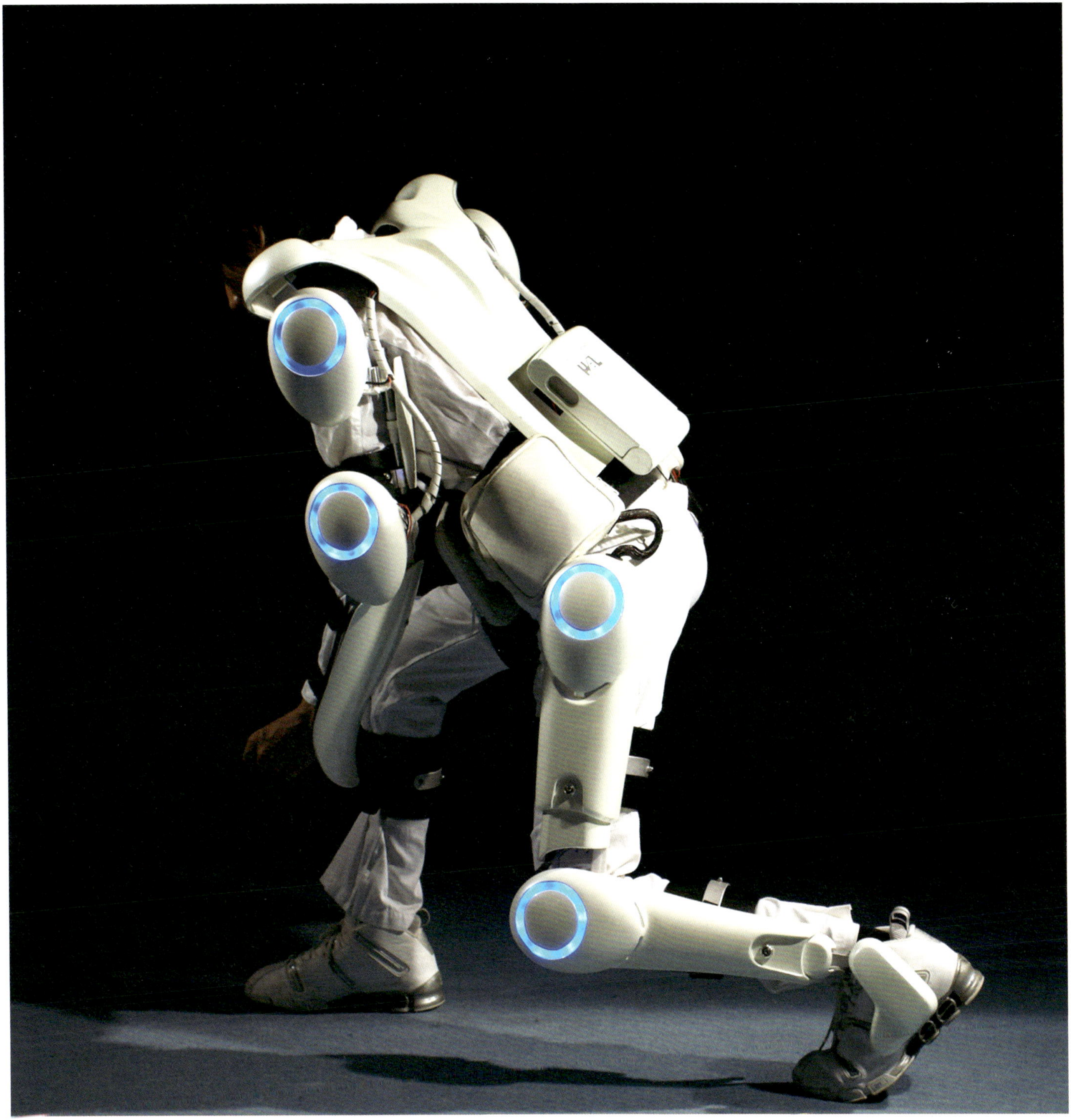

WELTREKORDFAHRT IM E-MOBIL
WORLD RECORD JOURNEY IN AN E-MOBILE

BEA-TRICKS. Am 17. Oktober 2011 startete ein zum Elektromobil umgerüsteter Citroën Berlingo in Flensburg eine Rekordfahrt. Ziel des mit spezieller Akkutechnik versehenen Fahrzeugs war das 1.000 Kilometer entfernte München. Nach 17 Stunden traf der Wagen, der mit 50 bis 80 Kilometern pro Stunde auf Landstraßen und Autobahnen unterwegs war, in der südlichen Metropole ein. Die gesamte Strecke legte das Elektromobil auf öffentlichen Straßen – und damit unter realen Verkehrsbedingungen – sowie mit lediglich einer Batterieladung zurück: ein neuer Reichweiten-Weltrekord.

Hinter der Spitzenleistung steht das Herner Unternehmen BEA-tricks, das Kleinwagen mit einem eigens dafür entwickelten Umrüstkit zu umweltfreundlichen und effizienten E-Mobilen umbaut. Schon eine ganze Reihe von Fahrzeugen, vor allem solche mit Motorschaden, konnten so „recycelt" und vor dem Schrottplatz gerettet werden. Mit dem Konzept des modernen Fahrzeugrecyclings hat sich das Unternehmen europaweit einen Namen gemacht. Und sogar bis nach China hat es die smarte Lösung bereits geschafft.

BEA-TRICKS. A Citroën Berlingo converted into an e-mobile began its world record-breaking journey on 17th October 2011 in Flensburg. The destination of the car equipped with special battery technology was Munich, located 1,000 kilometres away. After a 17-hours journey on country roads and highways at speeds of 50 to 80 kilometres per hour the car reached the southern metropolis. The e-mobile covered the entire stretch on public roads and therefore under actual traffic conditions, and with just one battery recharge, to set a new range record.

BEA-tricks, the company based in Herne, is at the helm of this outstanding achievement. It carries out the modification of sub-compact cars into eco-friendly and efficient e-mobiles with a conversion-kit specially designed for this. As a result, a great many cars, especially those with engine troubles, have already been recycled and saved from being relegated to the junkyard. The company owes its reputation across the length and breadth of Europe to this concept of modern automobile recycling. This smart solution has in fact even reached the distant shores of China.

Bestleistung: Größte Reichweite eines E-Mobils
Region: Metropole Ruhr
Ort: Herne

Best performance: The biggest cruising range for an electric car
Region: Ruhr Metropolis
Place: Herne

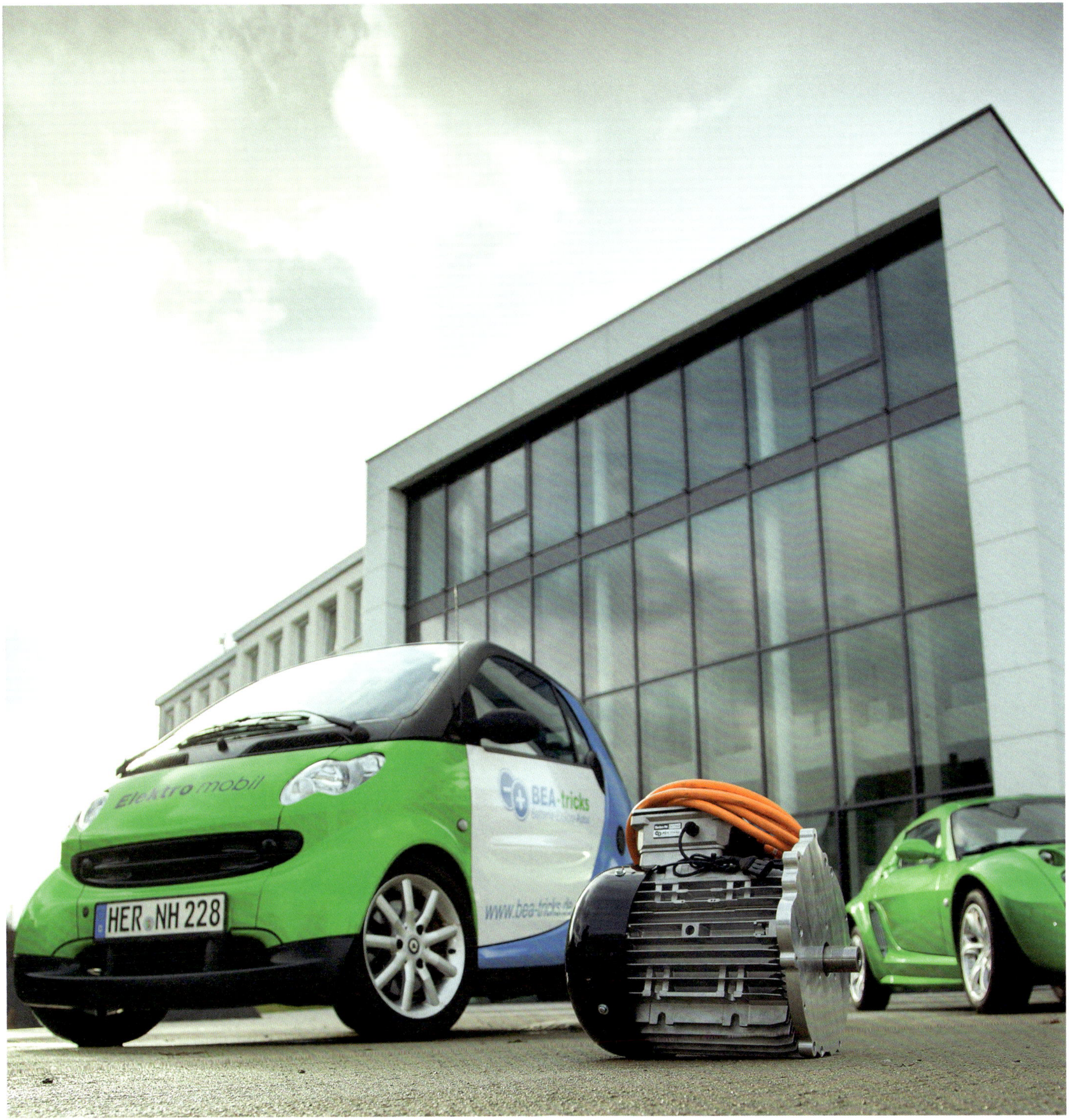
Elektro mobil
BEA-tricks
HER NH 228
www.bea-tricks.de

WUPPERTALER TEILCHENSUCHER
PARTICLE EXPLORERS OF WUPPERTAL

BERGISCHE UNIVERSITÄT WUPPERTAL. Existiert das Higgs-Teilchen tatsächlich? Es ist das noch fehlende Puzzleteil des Standardmodells der Elementarteilchenphysik – und seit 50 Jahren wird danach intensiv gesucht. Seine Existenz könnte eine der fundamentalen Fragen der Natur beantworten: Wodurch entsteht Masse? Im Sommer 2012 wurde am Europäischen Zentrum für Teilchenphysik CERN in Genf ein Kandidat gefunden – unter wesentlicher Mitarbeit aus Wuppertal.

Das Standardmodell beschreibt die grundlegenden Bausteine unseres Universums. Zu bestätigen ist es nur mit modernster Technologie. Am größten Teilchenbeschleuniger der Welt, dem Large Hadron Collider (LHC) des CERN, steht der Teilchendetektor ATLAS, mit dem das Standardmodell präzise getestet werden kann. Eine Forschergruppe der Bergischen Universität hat wichtige Komponenten für ATLAS entwickelt. Sie beteiligt sich auch mit einem großen Computing-Cluster an der weltweit durchgeführten Berechnung der Daten und sucht in den Billionen von Ereignissen nach neuen Teilchen.

UNIVERSITY OF WUPPERTAL. Does Higgs boson really exist? It is the missing piece in the Standard Model of particle physics. An intensive search for this holy grail of particle physics has been going on for the past 50 years. Its existence holds the key to one of the most fundamental questions of nature: how is mass formed? Experiments at the European Centre for Particle Physics CERN in Geneva, with sizeable co-operation from Wuppertal, discovered a likely candidate in 2012.

The Standard Model describes the fundamental building blocks of our universe. Only the most advanced technology can validate this. The Large Hadron Collider (LHC) of CERN, the world's largest particle accelerator facility, has the particle detector ATLAS, which can test the Standard Model with precision. A research group from the University of Wuppertal has developed important components for ATLAS. The group is also associated with a large computing cluster involved worldwide in computing the data, and is on the quest for new particles among the billions of cosmic events.

Bestleistung: Entdeckung des Higgs-Teilchens
Region: Bergisches Städtedreieck
Ort: Wuppertal

Best performance: Discovery of the Higgs particle
Region: Bergisches Staedtedreieck
Place: Wuppertal

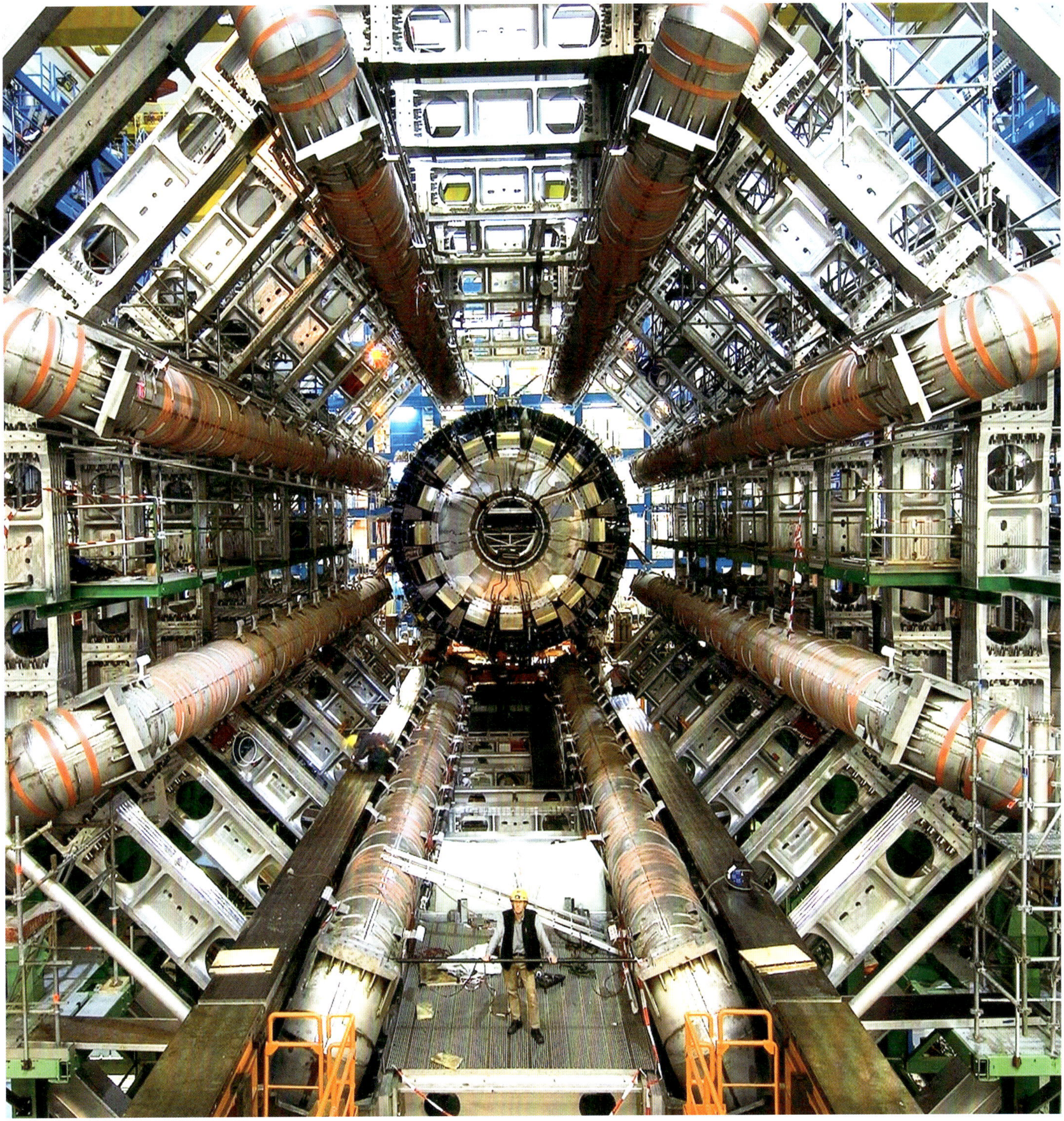

DAS INTELLIGENTE STROMNETZ
THE SMART GRID

BERGISCHE UNIVERSITÄT WUPPERTAL. Die Wende hin zu den alternativen Energien bringt viele Veränderungen mit sich: Immer mehr kleine, regenerative und dezentrale Erzeuger wie Sonnen- und Windenergieanlagen oder sogenannte Blockheizkraftwerke speisen ihren Strom ins Netz ein. Gleichzeitig steigt der allgemeine Grundbedarf kontinuierlich, da sich immer mehr Verbraucher für Elektroautos oder Wärmepumpen entscheiden. Dies hat zur Folge, dass die deutschen Stromnetze stark schwankenden Belastungen unterliegen, für die sie nie geplant und gebaut wurden.

Um diese kritischen Netzsituationen auszugleichen, wurde am Lehrstuhl für Elektrische Energieversorgungstechnik der Bergischen Universität Wuppertal die intelligente Netzstation (iNES) konzipiert – und gemeinsam mit Partnern aus der Wirtschaft bis hin zur Marktreife weiterentwickelt. Eingebaut in die örtlichen Verteilerkästen, reguliert die kleine Wunderbox den eingespeisten Strom auf das richtige Maß und verhindert damit Stromausfälle. iNES ist damit die erste konkrete Anwendung für das deutsche Stromnetz der Zukunft und sorgt bereits in Ratingen und Frankfurt für das richtige Strommaß.

UNIVERSITY OF WUPPERTAL. The switchover to alternative energy sources is bringing many changes with it. An increasing number of small, renewable and decentralised sources of power generation, such as solar and wind energy plants or so-called block heat and power plants, are feeding the electricity they generate into the grids. At the same time, as more and more consumers opt for electric cars or heat pumps, the basic requirement in general is on the rise. Consequently, grids in Germany are becoming subject to severe load fluctuations, something they were neither planned nor equipped for.

In order to resolve this critical situation in the grids the Intelligent Grid Station (iNES) has been conceived by the Research Group for Electrical Energy Supply Technology of the University of Wuppertal and brought to market readiness in collaboration with industry stakeholders. Built into local junction boxes, this tiny wonder-kit regulates the amount of electricity fed in, preventing power outages and making it the first concrete application for the next generation German grid. iNES is already in operation in Ratingen and Frankfurt to regulate electricity levels.

Bestleistung: Wunderbox gegen Stromausfall
Region: Bergisches Städtedreieck
Ort: Wuppertal

Best performance: Wonder kit to prevent outages
Region: Bergisches Staedtedreieck
Place: Wuppertal

⊗ Mess-, Kommunikations- und Regelpunkt für PLC (Power Line Communication)
Control, communication and regulator station for Power Line Communication (PLC)

---- Kommunikation zur Zentrale des EVU´s (Elektrizitätsversorgungsunternehmen)
Communication channel to the energy provider

PLC

iNES

EXZELLENTE ROBOTERSCHULE
AN EXCELLENT SCHOOL FOR ROBOTS

CITEC. Greifen und begreifen – was wir von Kindesbeinen an spielerisch lernen, haben die Roboter bei CITEC, dem Exzellenzcluster Kognitive Interaktionstechnologie der Universität Bielefeld, noch vor sich. Die Wissenschaftler möchten künstlichen Systemen kognitive und sensorische Fähigkeiten „beibringen". Roboter und Alltagsgeräte von morgen sollen leichter verstehen, was wir von ihnen wollen und wie sie uns hilfreich zur Hand gehen können.

Sie sollen natürlich mit Menschen kommunizieren und sich individuell auf ihr Gegenüber einstellen. Dazu müssen die Forscher Wahrnehmung, Gedächtnis und Lernen bis hin zu sozialer Kompetenz in ihren künstlichen Systemen nachbilden – eine gewaltige Aufgabe. Dennoch ist man schon weit gekommen. 2007 als Teil der deutschen Exzellenzinitiative gestartet, ist CITEC heute ein international vernetzter Cluster mit rund 40 Arbeitsgruppen.

2013 beziehen in Bielefeld rund 250 Wissenschaftler den Neubau des weltweit einzigartigen Kompetenz- und Forschungszentrums für Interaktive Intelligente Systeme. Ziel der interdisziplinären Forschung: Eine Technik der Zukunft, die sich am Menschen orientiert.

CITEC. Gripping and grasping are things we have all learnt by play from an early age; the very tasks set before robots at CITEC, the Center of Excellence Cognitive Interaction Technology, Bielefeld University. Scientists here are seeking to "instil" cognitive and sensory abilities in artificial systems.

The aim is to make next generation robots and everyday devices know what we need from them easily, and how they can be of help to us.

They should obviously communicate with humans and adjust to them individually. To achieve this, researchers will need to simulate cognition, memory and learning capacity right down to social skills in their synthetic systems – a tall order. The progress made so far has, nevertheless, been promising. Introduced in 2007 as part of the German excellence initiative, CITEC has grown today to a globally interactive cluster consisting of around 40 working groups.

In 2013, 250 scientists will move into a new building: the globally unique Centre of Excellence and Research for Interactive Intelligent Systems. Interdisciplinary research here is designed to produce technology for tomorrow, shaped around human needs.

Bestleistung: Entwicklung der intelligentesten künstlichen Systeme
Region: Ostwestfalen-Lippe
Ort: Bielefeld

Best performance: Development of the most intelligent artificial systems
Region: Ostwestfalen-Lippe
Place: Bielefeld

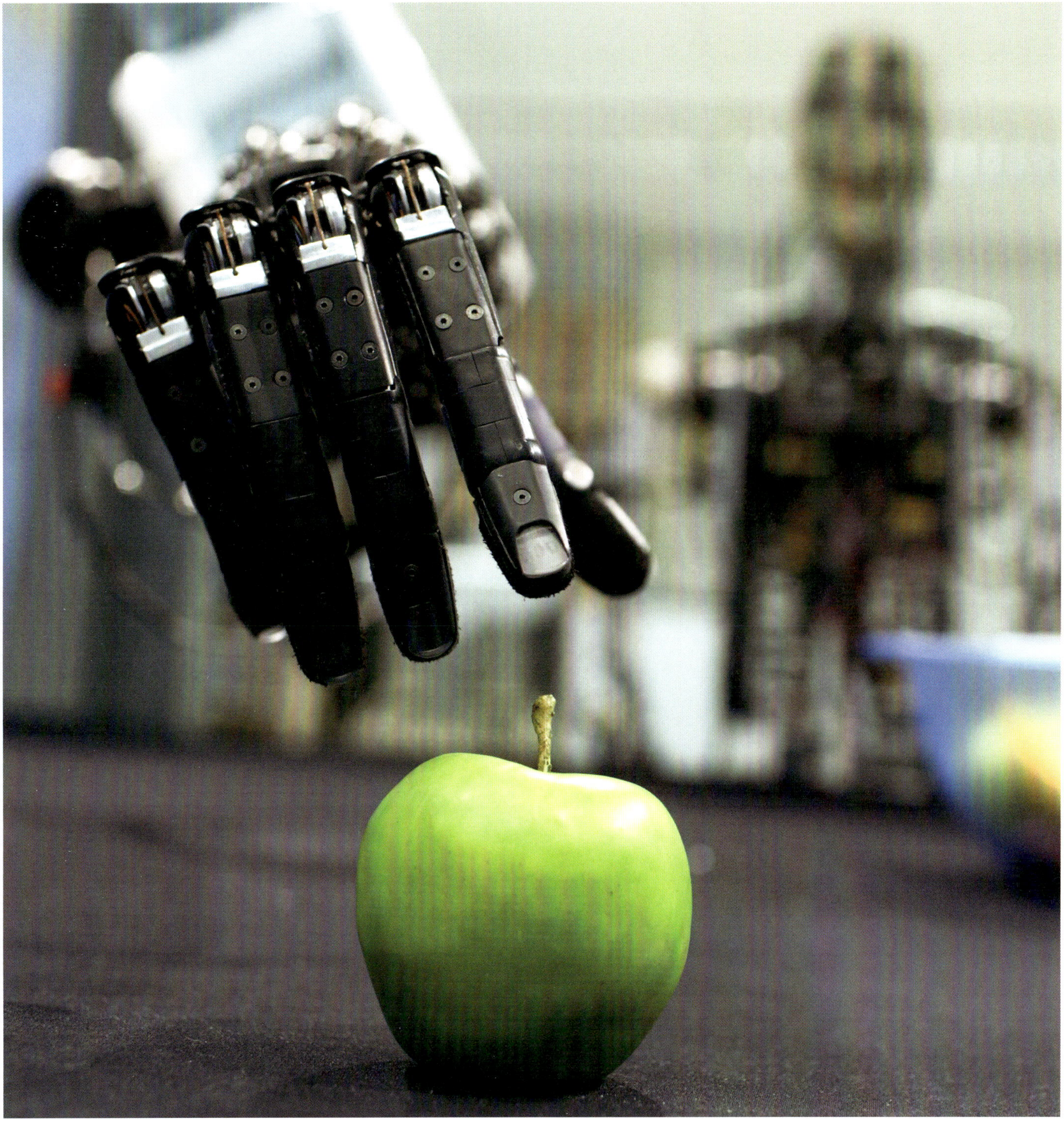

DER PERFEKTE ERNTEHELFER
THE PERFECT HARVEST AID

CLAAS. Ist das Korn erntereif und trocken, muss der Landwirt schnell und effizient ernten können – oft bleibt dafür nur ein kleines Zeitfenster. Zudem soll die größtmögliche Menge an Weizenkorn in kurzer Zeit vom Feld in den Speicher gelangen. Bei der sogenannten Durchsatzleistung hat der CLAAS LEXION 770 deutlich die Nase vorn: knapp 676 Tonnen Weizen konnte der riesige Präzisionsmähdrescher in acht Stunden ernten – gut 84,5 Tonnen pro Stunde: Weltrekord und verdienter Eintrag ins Guinness-Buch der Rekorde! Dies war im September 2011, und gleich im Anschluss hatte der High-Tech-Mähdrescher des Landmaschinenkonzerns aus Harsewinkel noch eine Nachtschicht im englischen Lincolnshire: Nach insgesamt 20 Stunden Dauereinsatz waren 1.361 Tonnen Weizen geerntet: wobei der sparsame Rekordhalter nur 1,15 Liter Diesel pro Tonne verbrauchte.

100 Jahre Erfahrung stecken in diesem perfekten Erntehelfer: 1913 übernahm der Maschinenschlosser August Claas das kleine väterliche Unternehmen und legte damals mit seinen Brüdern den Grundstein für den Erfolg: Claas ist der europaweit führende Hersteller von Mähdreschern.

CLAAS. No sooner the grain ripens and dries than the farmer needs to harvest it quickly and efficiently, often left with only a very small window of time to achieve this. Besides, maximum amounts of grain need to reach the granary from the fields as soon as possible. Thanks to its throughput rate, the CLAAS LEXION 770 is clearly a nose ahead in this respect. This huge precision combine harvester reaped nearly 676 tonnes in just eight hours or 84.5 tonnes per hour – a world record and well-deserved entry into the Guinness Book of Records.

This happened in September 2011 and, following that, this high-tech harvester from the agro machines company of Harsewinkel did a night shift at Lincolnshire in England, reaping 1,361 tonnes of grain in a total of 20 hours of non-stop operation and consuming just 1.15 litres of diesel per tonne. A hundred years of experience has gone into perfecting this harvesting aid. Mechanic August Claas took over the reins of this small concern owned by his father in 1913. He and his brothers then laid the foundations for what is today the leading combine harvester manufacturer in Europe.

Bestleistung: Weltrekord in Mähdrusch
Region: Ostwestfalen-Lippe
Ort: Harsewinkel

Best performance: World record in threshing
Region: Ostwestfalen-Lippe
Place: Harsewinkel

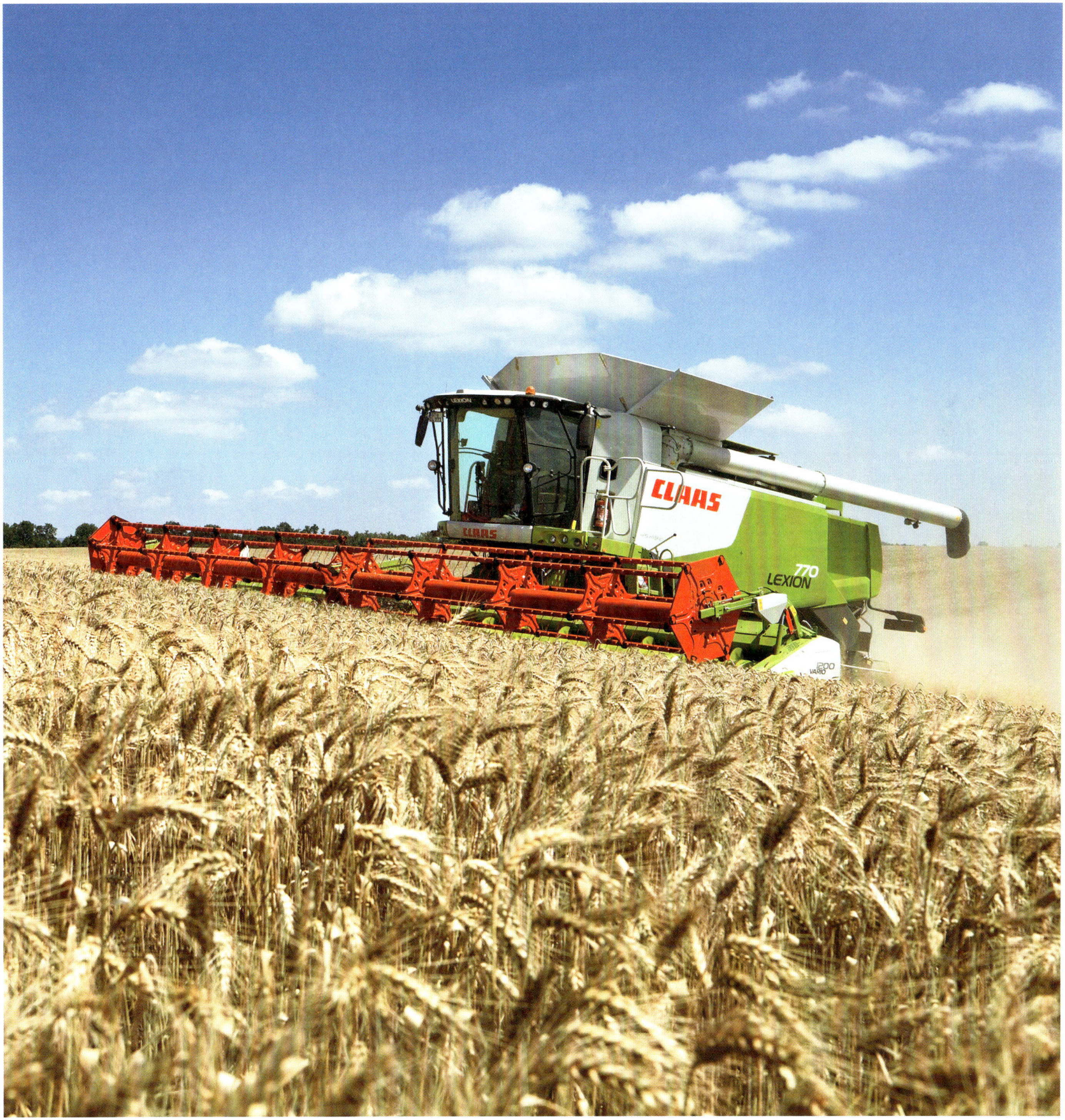
CLAAS
LEXION
770

HIER KOMMT DIE MAUS
HERE COMES THE MOUSE

DIE SENDUNG MIT DER MAUS. Mit freundlichem „Klack Klack" beim Augenzwinkern erklärt sie uns die Welt: Die Maus spricht nicht, aber seit ihrem ersten TV-Auftritt 1971 gibt „Die Sendung mit der Maus" vom Westdeutschen Rundfunk Antworten auf Kinderfragen. Die Lach- und Sachgeschichten bringen Kleine und Große zusammen vor den Fernsehschirm.

Mit ihren besten Freunden, dem kleinen blauen Elefanten und der frechen gelben Ente, ist die Maus das Herz der Sendung. Zu den regelmäßigen Gästen zählen beispielsweise Shaun das Schaf und Käpt'n Blaubär sowie andere ausgezeichnete Trickfilme. Rätsel des Alltags sind die Themen in den Sachgeschichten. Hier gibt das Maus-Team Antworten auf Fragen wie „Warum ist der Himmel blau?" oder „Wie kommt die Miene in den Bleistift?" Besonders komplexen Themen widmet die Maus eine ganze Sendung: Wer einmal die „Atom-Maus" gesehen hat, wird nicht wieder vergessen, dass sich die atomare Kettenreaktion mit Tischtennisbällen und Mausefallen erklären lässt.

Die Maus erhielt bisher mehr als 100 Auszeichnungen, darunter viele internationale. Ihre Beiträge werden in rund 100 Ländern ausgestrahlt. Rekordverdächtig!

THE PROGRAMME WITH THE MOUSE. With a friendly "click-clack" and a twinkle in the eye the mouse decodes the world for us. It does not speak but ever since its TV debut in 1971 "The Programme with the Mouse" by WDR (German TV) has answers for kiddies' queries. The "Laugh and Learn" programme has both kids and "grown-ups" glued to TV screens.

The mouse is the star of the programme, bringing its best friends the tiny blue elephant and the cheeky yellow duck along. "Shaun the Sheep", "Captain Bluebear" and other first-rate cartoon characters are among its regular guests. Documentaries tackle the mysteries of everyday life. Here the mouse team answers questions like "Why is the sky blue?" or "How does lead find its way into a pencil?" The mouse devotes a whole show to highly complex topics. Once you see the "atom mouse" you will never forget that mere table tennis balls and mouse traps can explain an atomic chain reaction.

This programme has to date won over 100 awards, many of them international awards. The Mouse clips are aired in about a 100 countries. Simply record breaking!

Bestleistung: Bekannteste und beliebteste Kindersendung Deutschlands
Region: Köln / Bonn
Ort: Köln

Best performance: Germany's most renowned and most popular children's programme
Region: Cologne / Bonn
Place: Cologne

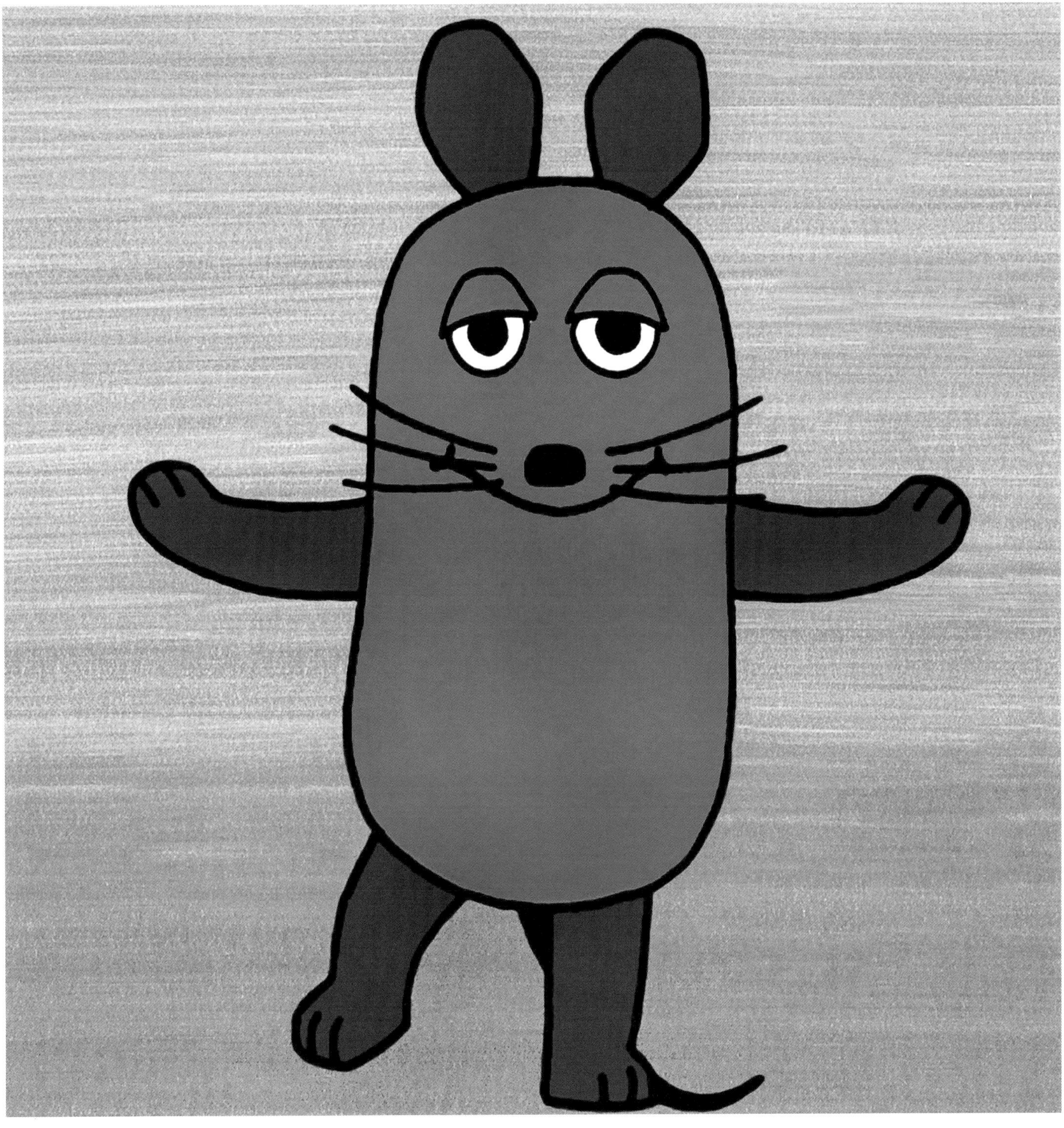

ABGAS WIRD ZUR RESSOURCE
TURNING A POLLUTANT INTO A RESOURCE

DREAM PRODUCTION. Das gibt es so nur hier: Im CHEMPARK in Leverkusen testet Bayer MaterialScience in einer Pilotanlage, das Abfallprodukt Kohlendioxid in eine wertvolle Ressource zu verwandeln. Das Ziel: aus dem Schadstoff hochwertige Kunststoffe zu produzieren – und den knappen Rohstoff Erdöl einzusparen.

Möglich wurde das neue Verfahren durch eine innovative Katalysetechnik: So lässt sich das reaktionsträge Kohlendioxid ohne zu großen Aufwand in eine Chemikalie einbauen, aus der Polyurethan hergestellt wird. Dieser Schaumstoff ist fester Bestandteil im Alltag – er findet sich etwa in Matratzen, Sitzmöbeln oder Sportschuhen wieder.

„Dream Production" heißt das gemeinsame Projekt von Wirtschaft und Wissenschaft: Von dem Energiekonzern RWE stammt das eingesetzte Kohlendioxid, und gemeinsam mit Forschern des CAT Catalytic Center in Aachen ist der Durchbruch in der Katalysetechnik gelungen. Die Chancen liegen auf der Hand: Gelingt es, das klimaschädliche Abgas nachhaltig als Rohstoff und Erdöl-Ersatz einzusetzen, könnten zwei Fliegen mit einer Klappe geschlagen werden – und das wäre dann wirklich eine Traumproduktion!

DREAM PRODUCTION. A unique project is underway at the CHEMPARK in Leverkusen. At a pilot plant here, Bayer MaterialScience is running tests to turn the waste product CO_2 into a valuable resource. The aim is to obtain high grade synthetic materials from the pollutant to save on the limited resource, crude oil.

This new process, made possible by innovative catalysis technology, integrates inert CO_2 into a chemical precursor, which is processed into polyurethane at no great expense. This foam material is an integral part of our daily lives, be it in mattresses, sofas or sports shoes. This project combining economy and science is called "Dream Production". The CO_2 used is supplied by the power company RWE and this breakthrough in catalysis technology has been made in collaboration with researchers of the CAT Catalytic Center in Aachen. The potential is obvious. Using CO_2, harmful for the climate, as a sustainable raw material and fossil fuel substitute successfully, would be killing two birds with one stone. Now, that truly would be a dream production!

Bestleistung: Erste Pilotanlage zur Herstellung von Kunststoff aus CO_2
Region: Köln / Bonn
Ort: Leverkusen

Best performance: The first pilot plant for production of synthetic material from CO_2
Region: Cologne / Bonn
Place: Leverkusen

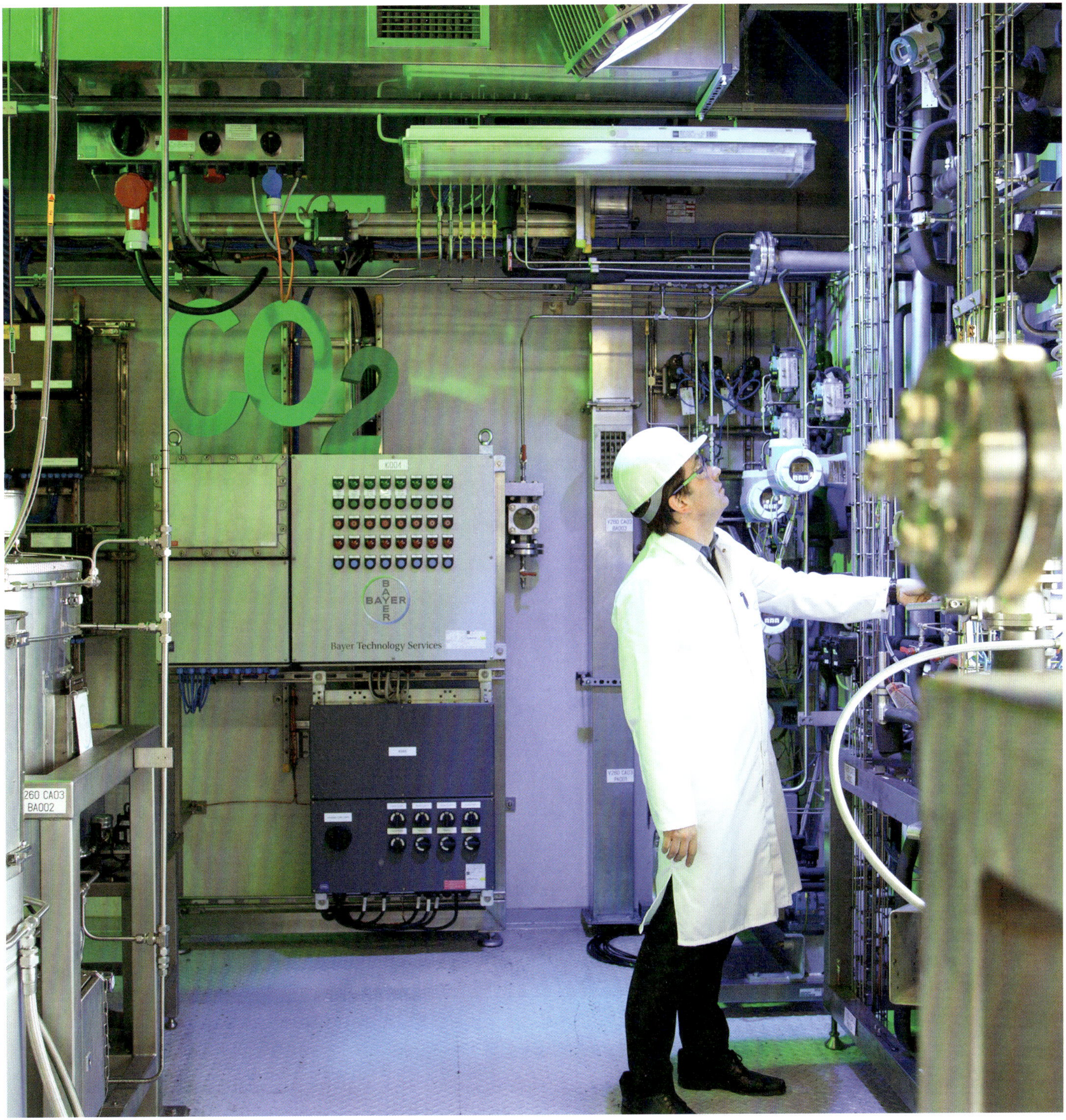
CO2
BAYER
Bayer Technology Services
260 CA03
BA002

BUSINESS MEETS LIFESTYLE

DÜSSELDORF. Ein Amerikaner, der in Düsseldorf schnell heimisch geworden ist, brachte es auf den Punkt: „We make money, where the money is, but we don't live here just to work." Mit dieser Balance aus Lebensqualität und hervorragenden Standortfaktoren sicherte sich Düsseldorf einen Superlativ: Platz 1 in Deutschland bei ausländischen Neuinvestitionen – so die Ergebnisse einer Studie von Ernst & Young.

Mit 52 Investitionsprojekten im Jahr 2011 liegt die Landeshauptstadt an der Spitze vor allen anderen deutschen Städten. Investoren aus dem Ausland zieht es demnach ins Wirtschaftszentrum Düsseldorf, weil sie hier finden, was sie zum erfolgreichen Arbeiten brauchen: die zentrale Lage im Herzen Europas mit einem internationalen Flughafen sowie ein riesiges Kunden- und Absatzpotenzial – zudem internationale Schulen und gut ausgebildete Fachkräfte in ausreichender Zahl.

Hier stimmt die Mischung aus Business und Lifestyle: Düsseldorf bietet ein Metropolenprogramm bei Kultur, Events oder Sport und bleibt dennoch eine entspannte, eine lebens- und liebenswerte Stadt. Weltoffen – auch nach Feierabend eben!

DUESSELDORF. An American who within no time at all felt at home in Duesseldorf put it succinctly, "We make money where the money is, but we don't live here just to work." This balance between quality of life and terrific location factors has earned Duesseldorf a superlative, with a study by Ernst and Young declaring the city to be the no. 1 place in Germany for new foreign investments.

Among all other German cities, this state capital made it to the top of the heap with 52 investment projects in 2011. Foreign investors are drawn to this commercial centre as it gives them what is needed to work effectively: a central location in the heart of Europe with an international airport, huge customer and marketing potential, not to speak of the international schools and ample skilled labour.

Here, the blend of business and lifestyle is just right. Be it culture, events or sports, Duesseldorf offers you a range worthy of an international metropolis, yet retains an air of ease, making it worth living in. A delightful city that is cosmopolitan even beyond working hours!

Bestleistung: Die meisten ausländischen Neuinvestitionen in einer deutschen Stadt
Region: Düsseldorf
Ort: Düsseldorf

Best performance: The highest number of new investments made in a German city
Region: Duesseldorf
Place: Duesseldorf

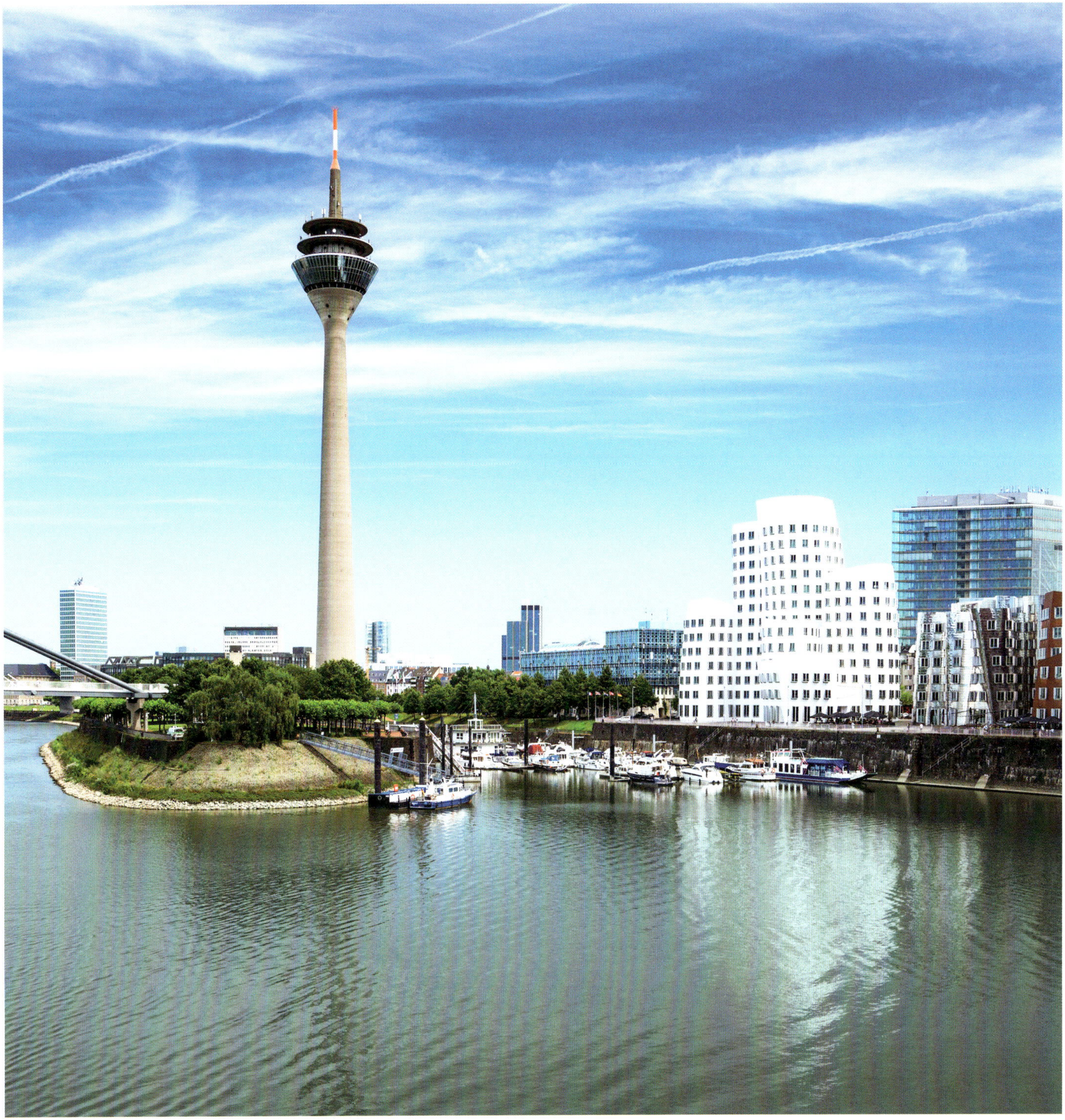

MEHR ALS 190 FLUGZIELE WELTWEIT
OVER 190 DESTINATIONS WORLDWIDE

DÜSSELDORF AIRPORT. Abu Dhabi, Los Angeles oder Peking – welche Destination darf es sein? Über 190 Ziele weltweit fliegen 70 Airlines vom Düsseldorfer Flughafen aus an. Mit Lufthansa und Air Berlin nutzen gleich die beiden größten deutschen Fluggesellschaften Düsseldorf als Drehkreuz – das ist deutschlandweit einmalig. Gemeinsam mit den Partnern der Star Alliance und der oneworld Alliance bieten die beiden Gesellschaften jede Menge Langstreckenverbindungen vom Rhein aus an.

Bei seinen jährlich über 20 Millionen Fluggästen punktet Nordrhein-Westfalens größter Airport nicht nur durch kurze Wege unter einem Terminaldach und kurze Umsteigezeiten, sondern auch mit exzellentem Service: Bei den Skytrax World Airport Awards 2011 belegte Düsseldorf Airport den ersten Platz in der Kategorie „Servicequalität der Flughafenmitarbeiter". Für die Reduzierung der CO_2-Emissionen – der Düsseldorfer Airport betreibt unter anderem im Sicherheitsbereich eine große Photovoltaikanlage – gab es zudem 2012 das Gütesiegel des Klimaschutzprogramms „Airport Carbon Accreditation".

DUESSELDORF AIRPORT. Abu Dhabi, Los Angeles, Beijing – where do you want to go today? 70 airlines depart for over 190 destinations around the globe from the Duesseldorf Airport. It is the chosen hub of the two country's biggest airlines, Lufthansa and Air Berlin, making it unique in Germany. These airlines and their partners, Star Alliance and Oneworld, offer any number of long-haul connections from this Rhine location.

For its 20 million passengers every year, the biggest airport in North Rhine-Westphalia scores not only as an "airport of short distances" under a single terminal building and for short transfer times, but for excellent service as well. Duesseldorf Airport won first prize in the "Service Quality of Airport Employees" category at the Skytrax World Airport Awards 2011. Its efforts to reduce CO_2 emissions, not least through the operation of a huge photovoltaic plant within the security area, also secured it the seal of approval of the "Airport Carbon Accreditation" climate protection programme in 2012.

Bestleistung: Drehkreuz der beiden größten deutschen Fluggesellschaften
Region: Düsseldorf
Ort: Düsseldorf

Best performance: Hub of Germany's two biggest airlines
Region: Duesseldorf
Place: Duesseldorf

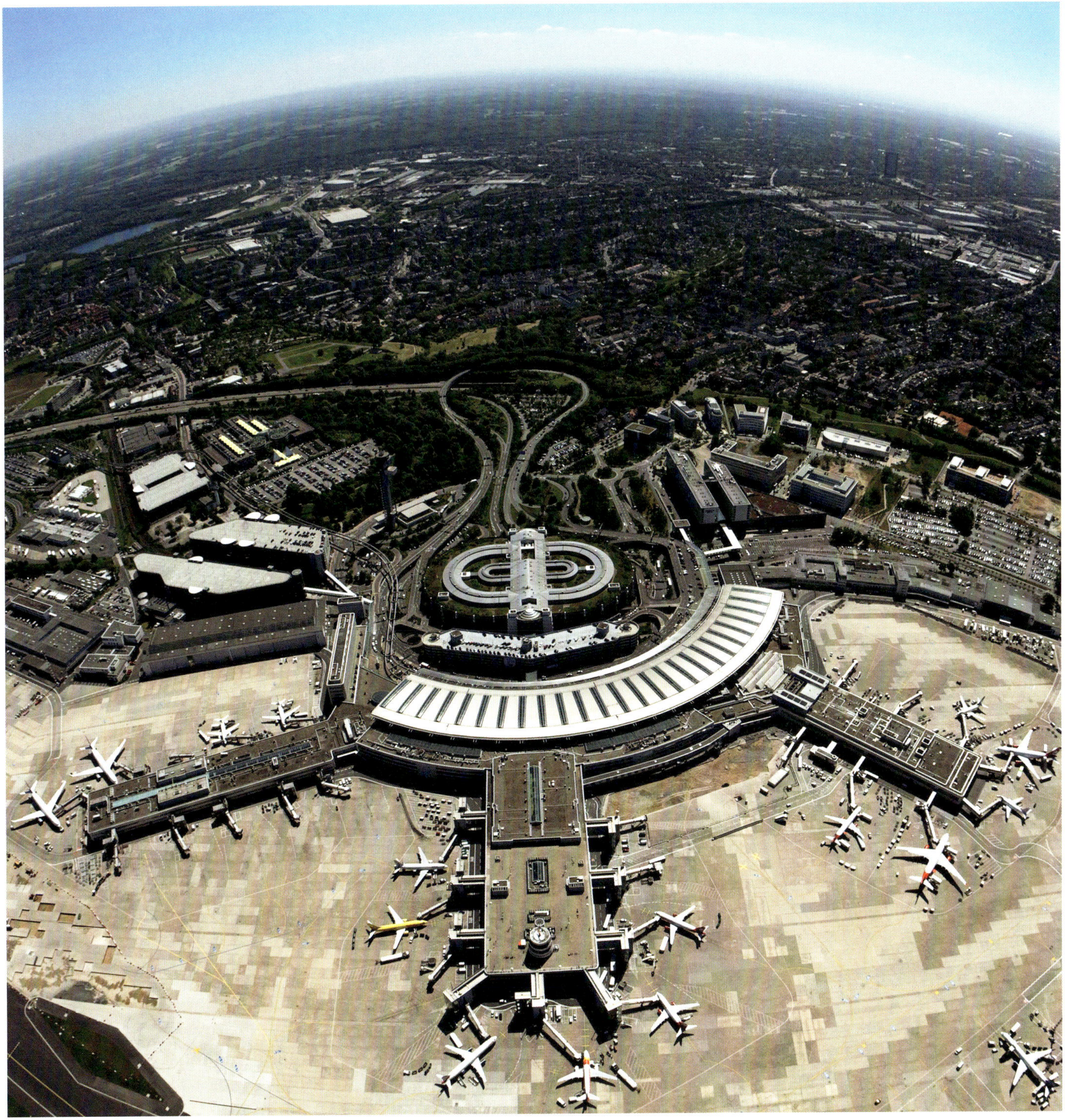

KLIMAANLAGE AUS DER TIEFE
SUBTERRANEAN AIR CONDITIONING SYSTEM

E.ON WESTFALEN WESER. Das ostwestfälische Paderborn wird auch die Stadt der Quellen genannt. Denn 200 Brunnen aus der Tiefe speisen zusammen den Fluss Pader, waren Anziehungspunkt für die frühen Siedler und sorgen bis heute für ein reichhaltiges Grundwasservorkommen. Doch das ist noch nicht alles: Der regionale Energieversorger E.ON Westfalen Weser realisiert hier in Kooperation mit der Stadt Paderborn eine ganz neue Form der Energienutzung.

So wird in der Paderborner Innenstadt das Grundwasser zur umweltschonenden Kühlung und Beheizung von inzwischen 15 Gebäudekomplexen genutzt. Das Wasser hat je nach Jahreszeit eine Temperatur zwischen neun und dreizehn Grad und gelangt über Brunnen an die Oberfläche. Im Winter entziehen spezielle Pumpen dem Wasser die Wärme – die so aus dem Grundwasser erzeugte Energie beheizt die Gebäude. Im Sommer nutzt man das Grundwasser für deren Kühlung.

Grundlage für dieses Projekt ist die spezifische hydrogeologische Situation in Paderborn: ein Übermaß an oberflächennahem Grundwasser mit konstanter Temperatur.

E.ON WESTFALEN WESER. Paderborn in Ostwestfalen-Lippe is also called the City of Springs. 200 underground springs feed the river Pader, drawing the early settlers and to this day providing a rich supply of groundwater. But that's not all. Regional power supplier E.ON Westfalen Weser is now working with the city of Paderborn to make use of an innovative form of energy.

Groundwater is being used in Paderborn city centre for the eco-friendly cooling and heating of a current total of 15 building complexes. Depending on the time of the year, the temperature of the water ranges between nine and thirteen degrees, making its way to the surface by the springs. Special pumps extract warmth from the water in winter, with the energy they harness being used to heat the buildings. In summer, groundwater is put to use for cooling them.

The hydrogeological conditions intrinsic to Paderborn – an abundance of shallow subsurface groundwater with a constant temperature – form the basis for this project.

Bestleistung: Nutzung von Grundwasser zur Energieerzeugung
Region: Ostwestfalen-Lippe
Ort: Paderborn

Best performance: Harnessing energy from ground water
Region: Ostwestfalen-Lippe
Place: Paderborn

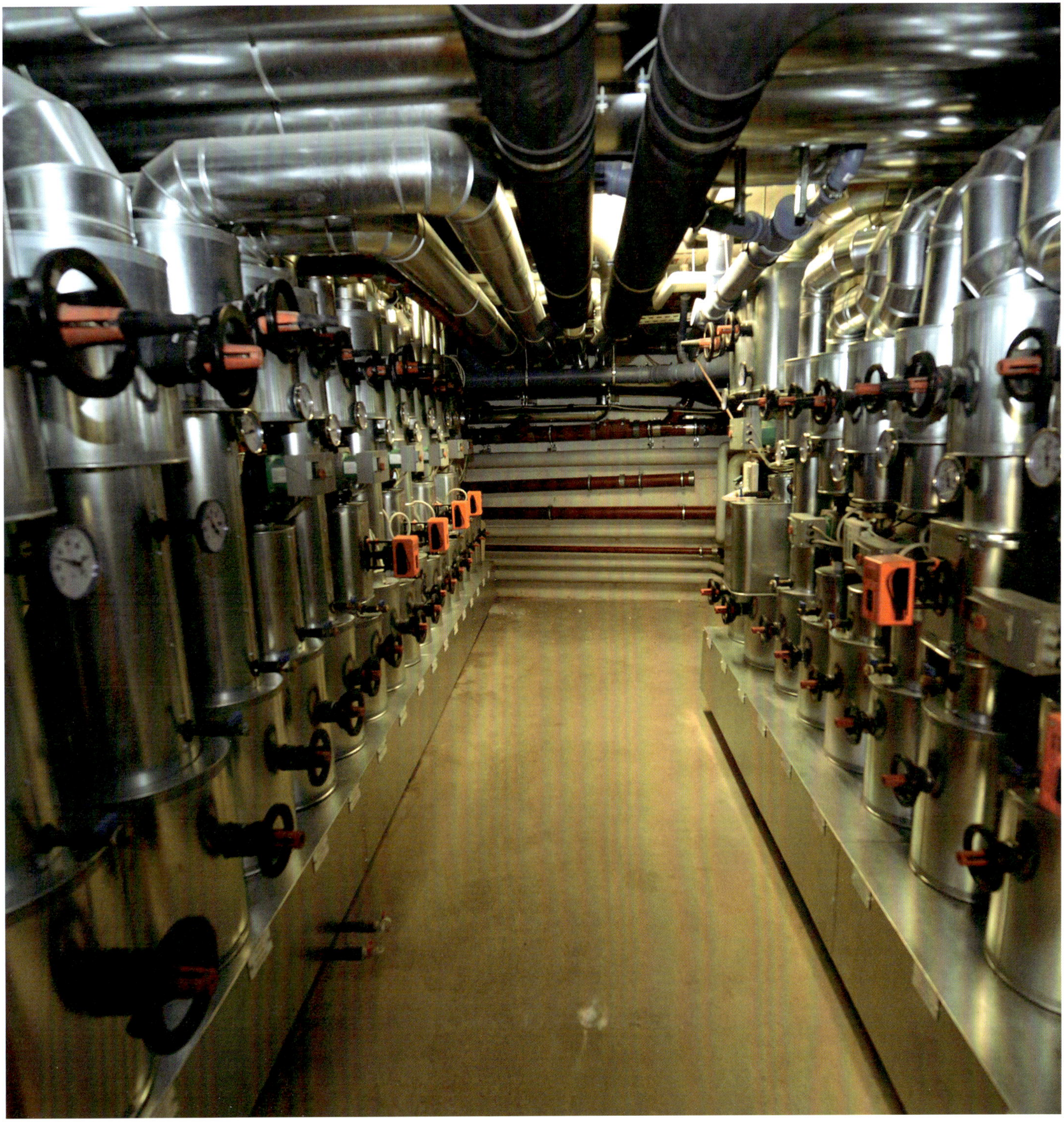

MEILENSTEIN DER MUSIKEDITION
MILESTONE IN MUSIC EDITION

EDIROM. Für einen Physiker besteht Musik aus Tönen, und Töne sind Schwingungen. Für einen Musiker sind Töne auch Notenmaterial. Forscher und Softwareprogrammierer der Universität Paderborn denken bei Musik seit 2006 an Edirom, ihre gemeinsam an der Detmolder Hochschule für Musik entwickelte digitale Musikedition – ein weltweit einzigartiges Projekt.

Edirom soll die Entstehung musikalischer Werke rekonstruierbar machen und Wissenschaftlern wie Musikern eine Hilfestellung bieten. Jede Komposition hinterlässt Spuren – dazugehörige Manuskripte, Notizen oder sogar Briefe, die mit Edirom erschlossen und gedeutet werden. Die Musikedition setzt alle Zeugnisse einer Komposition anschaulich in Beziehung zueinander. Eine eigene Website und eine Software sind Produkte des Projekts. Sie bieten Musikhandschriften, Notendrucke und Skizzen.

Das Paderborner Team arbeitet auch an einem internationalen Standard zur Kodierung von Notationen mit. Damit kann künftig das Potenzial digitaler Musikeditionen besser ausgeschöpft werden.

EDIROM. For a physicist, music consists of sounds and sounds are vibrations. To a musician sounds also mean sheet music. Since 2006 researchers and software programmers from the University of Paderborn have been associating music essentially with Edirom. The only project of its kind in the world, "Digital Music Editions" – or Edirom – has been jointly developed by them at the Academy of Music Detmold.

Edirom has been conceived with a view to reconstructing the creation of musical works, meaning it can be of assistance to scientists and musicians alike. Each composition leaves behind traces in the form of related manuscripts, notes and even letters that can be accessed and interpreted by Edirom, which then places all reference materials of a composition visually in interrelation to each other. A dedicated website and software are the fruits of this project, providing music manuscripts, printed music and sketches.

The team from Paderborn is also collaborating on a universal standard for the coding of notations. This should help maximise the potential of digital music editions in future.

Bestleistung: Einzigartige Software zur Indizierung von Musikkompositionen
Region: Ostwestfalen-Lippe
Ort: Paderborn

Best performance: Unique software to index music compositions
Region: Ostwestfalen-Lippe
Place: Paderborn

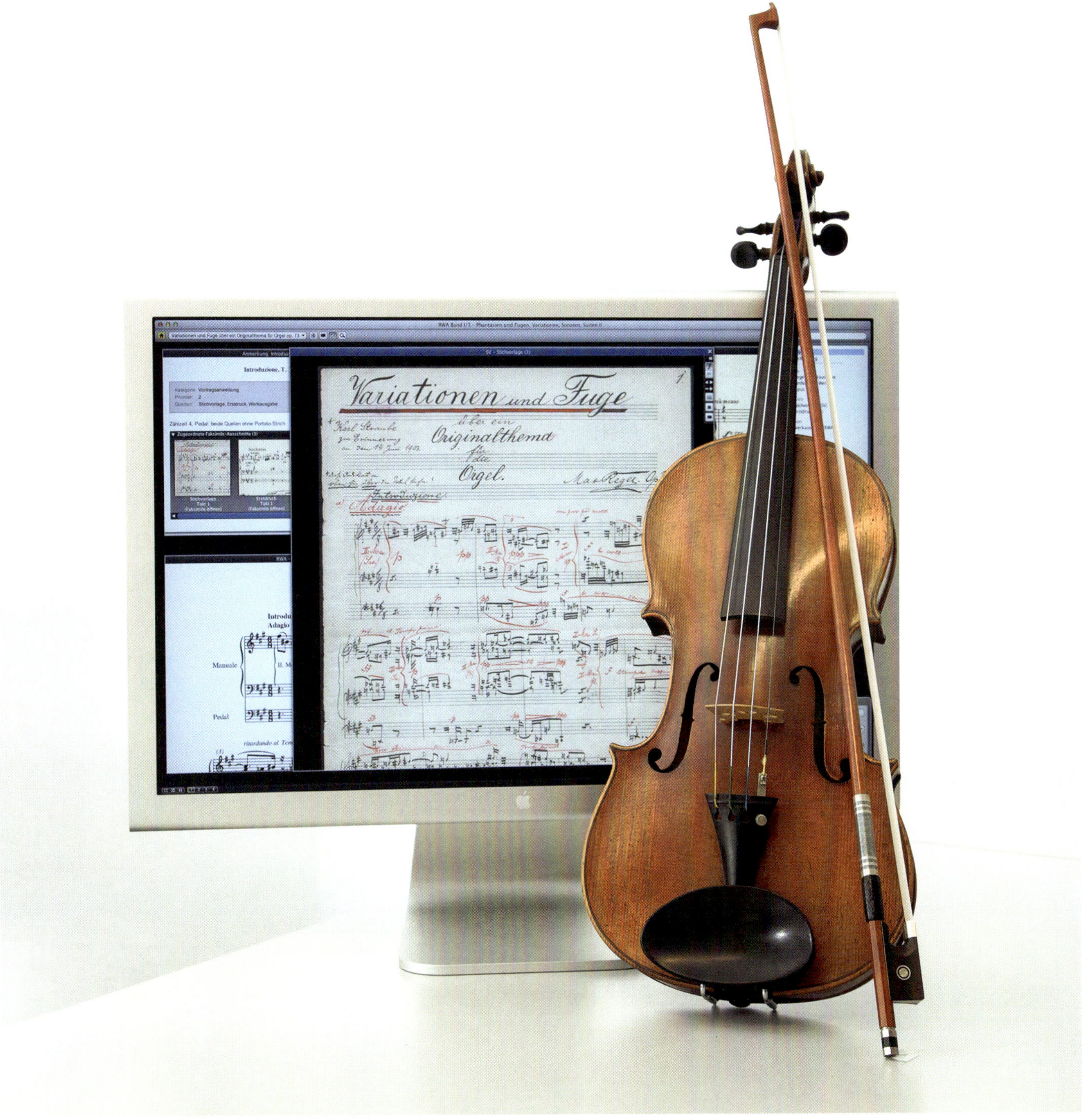
Variationen und Fuge
Originalthema
Orgel.
Manuale
Pedal

SPARLAMPEN OHNE QUECKSILBER
ENERGY-EFFICIENT BULBS WITHOUT MERCURY

EMIL SPARLAMPEN. „Experiment trifft Theorie" lautet das Motto von Prof. Dr. Anja-Verena Mudring. Die Spezialistin für anorganische Chemie untersucht an der Ruhr-Universität Bochum strukturelle Eigenschaften von Materialien. Ziel ist es, neue umweltverträgliche Lösungen zu entwickeln. Im Rahmen ihres Projekts EMIL (exceptional materials from ionic liquids) wird erforscht, wie mithilfe von ionischen Flüssigkeiten quecksilberfreie Energiesparlampen hergestellt werden könnten.

Solche bei Raumtemperatur noch flüssigen Salze stoßen auf großes Interesse bei Forschung und Wirtschaft. Auch deshalb wird EMIL seit 2007 mit ungefähr einer Million Euro vom European Research Council (ERC) gefördert.

Prof. Mudring und ihr Team entwickeln diese leuchtenden Nano-Materialien und möchten sie zur Marktreife führen. Anwendung finden sie in Plasmabildschirmen sowie Solarzellen und bald auch in Energiesparlampen. Die flüssigen Salze brennen und verdampfen nicht, sie lassen sich einfach handhaben und recyceln. In Zeiten sinkender Ressourcen, steigender Energiepreise und wachsenden Umweltbewusstseins wäre das ein Coup.

EMIL ENERGY EFFICIENT BULBS. "Experiment meets Theory" is Prof. Dr. Anja-Verena Mudring's maxim. This expert in inorganic chemistry is studying the structural features of materials at Ruhr University Bochum with a view to developing new eco-friendly solutions. Named EMIL (exceptional materials from ionic liquids), her project provides the framework for research on the production of mercury-free energy-efficient bulbs using ionic liquids.

Ionic salts that retain their liquid form at room temperature are of great interest to science and industry. Thus EMIL has been supported by a grant of approximately one million Euros from the European Research Council (ERC) since 2007.

Prof. Mudring and her team are developing these luminescent nano-materials, seeking to harness them for marketable products. They are used in plasma screens and solar cells and soon also for energy-efficient bulbs. Liquid salts are non-flammable and do not vaporise, easy to handle and recyclable. In this age of dwindling resources, rising energy prices and growing ecological awareness, it would well be a coup!

Bestleistung: Umweltfreundlichste Energiesparlampe
Region: Metropole Ruhr
Ort: Bochum

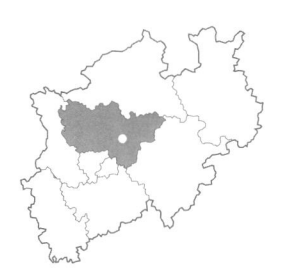

Best performance: The most eco-friendly energy efficient bulbs
Region: Ruhr Metropolis
Place: Bochum

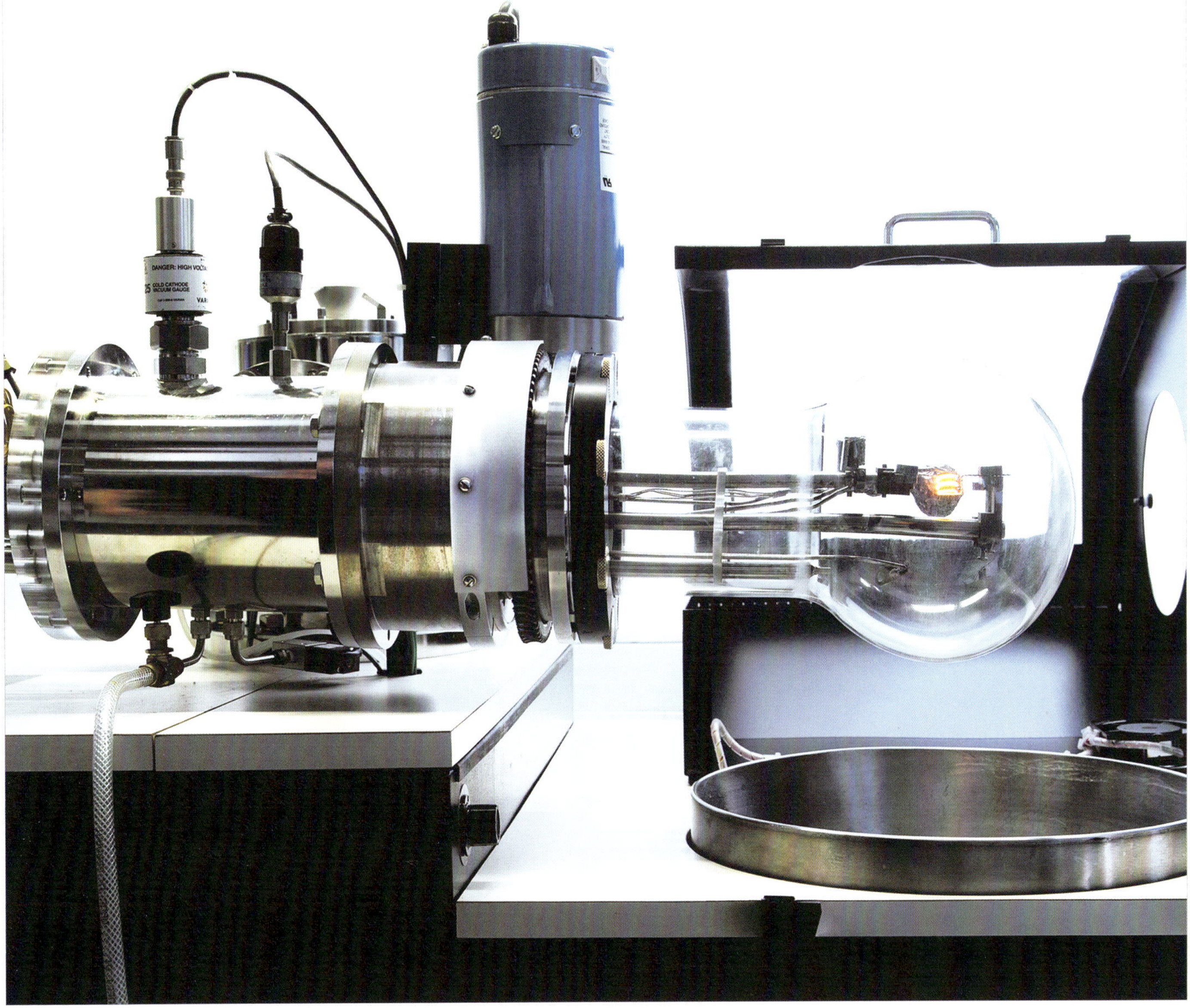
COLD CATHODE
VACUUM GAUGE

MIT WINDENERGIE DURCHS OUTBACK
ACROSS THE OUTBACK ON WIND ENERGY

EVONIK INDUSTRIES. Mit dem Wind Explorer hat erstmals ein durch Windkraft angetriebenes Elektrofahrzeug Australien durchquert. Dabei stellte es gleichzeitig einen Weltrekord auf: Das Leichtbaufahrzeug legte die längste Strecke zurück, die jemals mit einem per Windenergie gespeisten E-Mobil an einem Tag bewältigt wurde: 493,5 Kilometer.

Zwei deutsche Extremsportler und ein Plan: per Elektrofahrzeug den australischen Kontinent von West nach Ost zu durchqueren – und das komplett mit der Energie des Windes.

Ausgestattet mit Lithium-Ionen-Batterietechnik von Evonik Industries, dem Essener Spezialchemiekonzern, konnten die beiden Fahrer Dirk Gion und Stefan Simmerer die per Windgenerator gewonnene Energie zwischenspeichern. Bei guten Wetterverhältnissen zog der Wind zusätzlich an einem Kitesegel.

All dies gelang unschlagbar ressourceneffizient – fast ohne Kohlendioxidausstoß. Nur bei Windstille wurde Strom aus der Steckdose bezogen – mit nur zehn Euro Stromkosten konnte der 200 Kilogramm leichte Wind Explorer so fast 5.000 Kilometer zurücklegen. Für das ökologische Konzeptfahrzeug bekam Evonik den internationalen Umweltpreis „ÖkoGlobe 2011".

EVONIK INDUSTRIES. For the first time, Australia has been crossed by an electric vehicle powered by wind. In doing so, "Wind Explorer" also set a world record. The lightweight vehicle travelled the longest distance ever covered by a wind-powered electric car in a day, i.e. 493.5 kilometres.

Two German extreme-sport buffs, one plan: to cross the Australian continent from West to East in an electric car, powered by wind energy alone.

Lithium-ion batteries provided by the Essen-based speciality chemicals company, Evonik Industries, enabled the drivers, Dirk Gion and Stefan Simmerer, to store energy generated by a wind turbine. On days with good weather conditions the Wind Explorer was also propelled by kite sails.

All this worked in an unbeatable resource-efficient manner with almost zero CO_2 emissions. Electricity was drawn from a plug-in connection only when the wind dropped. Weighing merely 200 kilogrammes, the Wind Explorer thus ran up a power bill of just ten Euros in covering almost 5,000 kilometres. The ecological concept car earned Evonik the "ÖkoGlobe 2011" international environmental award.

Bestleistung: Längste Strecke eines Windkraft-Fahrzeugs
Region: Metropole Ruhr
Ort: Essen

Best performance: The longest distance covered by a wind powered vehicle
Region: Ruhr Metropolis
Place: Essen

Stefan Simmerer
Dirk Gion
EVONIK
INDUSTRIES
Separion® Litarion® ROHACELL®
STOKO
Continental
ERDINGER
ALKOHOLFREI
502
ZBT

DIE NACHT DER INDUSTRIEKULTUR
THE NIGHT OF INDUSTRIAL HERITAGE

EXTRASCHICHT. Es wird gigantisch, wenn diese spezielle Spätschicht im Ruhrgebiet einfährt. Sie fördert etwas, was es nur hier geben kann: Kunst und Kultur inmitten beeindruckender Industriedenkmäler. Die ExtraSchicht präsentiert und feiert die Metropole Ruhr und ihr industrielles Erbe. Für eine Sommernacht wird Europas drittgrößter Ballungsraum zum ganz besonderen Erlebnis – mit Konzerten, Ausstellungen, Museumsführungen, Theater, Lichtkunst und vielem mehr.

Ein einzigartiges Konzept: 2012 präsentierten 1.000 Künstler vor 230.000 Besuchern 450 Events an 53 Spielorten in 23 Städten! Der Clou dabei: Eine Nacht, ein Ticket – auch für den Shuttle-Service, der alle Spielstätten verbindet. Die Kulturangebote werden als Einheit mit den monumentalen Industriekulissen inszeniert: Kokereien und Zechen werden erleuchtet, beschallt und zu Bühnen der Kultur. Es gibt viel zu erleben, aber auch zu lernen. Stahlwerke und Hochöfen können besichtigt werden. Das breit gefächerte Programm dieses Festivals für Industriekultur zieht bereits seit 2001 immer mehr Gäste an. ExtraSchicht verdichtet Faszination, Energie und Vielfalt einer ganzen Region in einer Nacht.

EXTRASCHICHT. Things take on a mega dimension when this special late shift begins in the Ruhr Metropolis. ExtraSchicht promotes what is inimitably typical of this region: art and culture, against a backdrop of striking industrial monuments, taking over the Ruhr Metropolis to showcase it and celebrate its industrial legacy. For one summer's night Europe's third largest megalopolis takes off to an explosion of experience with concerts, exhibitions, museum tours and much more besides.

A unique stage: 2012 saw 1,000 artists, 230,000 visitors, 450 events at 53 venues in 23 cities! The one night, one ticket concept is an added attraction, including shuttle service connections to all venues. Cultural events are choreographed to incorporate the gigantic industrial monuments in their performance. The use of light and sound in coking plant and coal mine spaces leaves you with a lot to experience and learn too. Try visiting the steel mills and furnaces! The wide choice of programmes at this festival of industrial culture has been attracting evermore visitors since 2001. ExtraSchicht packs in all the allure, dynamism and diversity of an entire region in a single night.

Bestleistung: Kulturfestival der Superlative
Region: Metropole Ruhr
Ort: Oberhausen

Best performance: A cultural festival of superlatives
Region: Ruhr Metropolis
Place: Oberhausen

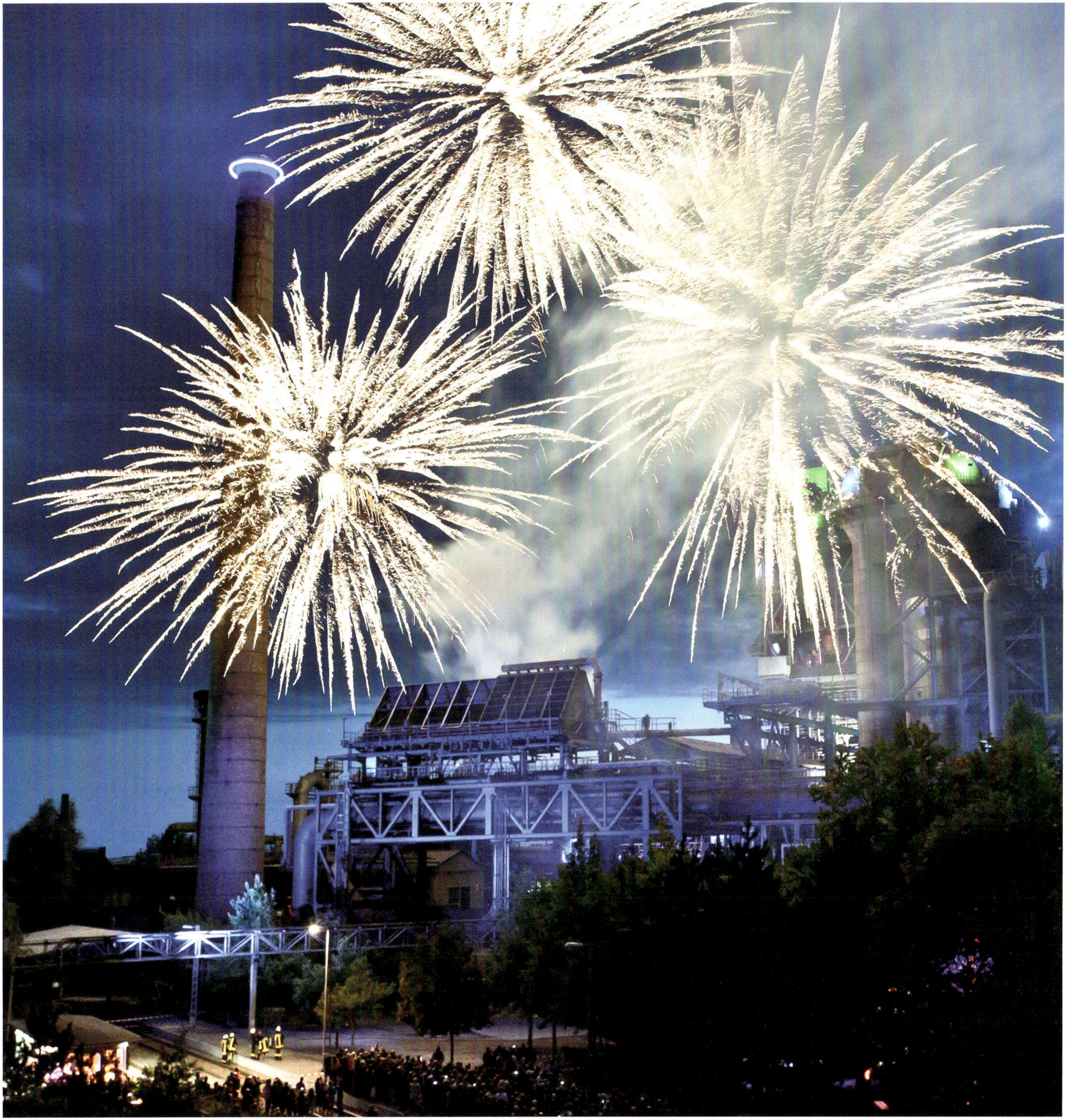

SPITZENSOCKEN AUS DEM SAUERLAND
TOP-QUALITY SOCKS FROM SAUERLAND

FALKE. Die Cousins Paul und Franz-Peter Falke leiten seit 1990 – als Doppelspitze und in vierter Generation – den gleichnamigen Familienbetrieb. Der 1895 in Schmallenberg gegründeten Falke Gruppe bekommt dies sehr gut: Trotz starker Konkurrenz haben die beiden Sauerländer eine international gefragte Marke aufgebaut – und seit 2008 gehört sogar die Traditionsmarke Burlington dazu.

Hohe Qualität und anspruchsvolles Design – dafür ist Falke weltweit bekannt, etwa durch Pullover oder funktionale Sportkleidung. Allem voran steht die Qualitätsmarke jedoch für Strumpfware. Von eleganten Feinstrumpfhosen über luxuriöse Businessstrümpfe bis hin zu High-Tech-Socken: Modische Kreativität ergänzt sich mit Funktionalität – und so bilden diese beiden Faktoren die tragenden Säulen in der Produktentwicklung des Unternehmens.

240 Millionen Euro Umsatz hat die Falke Gruppe 2011 erwirtschaftet – davon 43 Prozent im Ausland. Jeder Zweite der weltweit 3.100 Beschäftigten arbeitet übrigens in Deutschland – und das ist in der Textilindustrie wirklich eine Seltenheit.

FALKE. Since 1990 cousins Paul and Franz Peter Falke have been running a family business as joint managers. The business goes by the family name and is in its fourth generation. Formed in 1895 in Schmallenberg, Germany, the Falke Group has done well down the ages. In the face of stiff competition the duo from Sauerland has built up a brand that is much sought after internationally. Year 2008 even saw the traditional brand "Burlington" come under the wings of this group.

Falke products are internationally renowned for their top-quality and superior design, for instance of pullovers or functional sportswear. A leading premium brand, it actually stands for a mark of quality, primarily in hosiery products. Whether elegant tights, luxury business socks or high-tech socks, functionality complements fashionable creativity. These two features form the mainstay of product development for the company.

The Falke Group generated a turnover of 240 million Euros in 2011 – 43 per cent of this overseas. Incidentally, out of the 3,100-strong global workforce every second employee works in Germany – truly a rarity in the textile industry!

Bestleistung: Führender Hersteller von Markenstrumpfwaren
Region: Südwestfalen
Ort: Schmallenberg

Best performance: Leading manufacturer of branded hosiery
Region: Suedwestfalen
Place: Schmallenberg

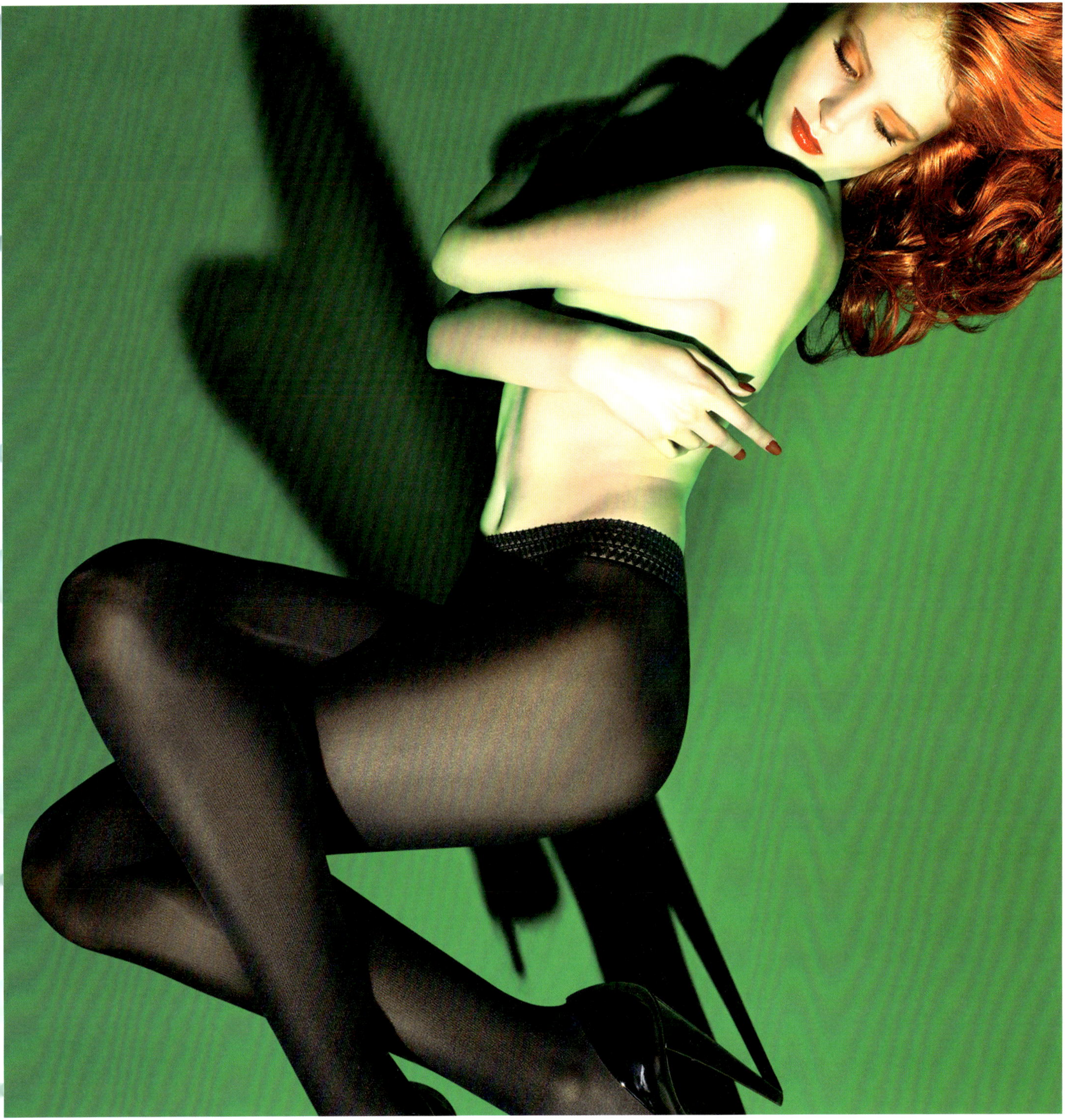

EDELBRAND DANK ALTER EICHE
FINE BRANDY THANKS TO OLD OAK

FEINBRENNEREI SASSE. Ist das ein Korn? Rein und klar ist die typische deutsche Spirituose, ein aus Getreide gebrannter Schnaps. Doch dieser ist goldbraun. Rüdiger Sasse schwenkt sein Glas, atmet die feinen Aromen ein, nippt und nickt zufrieden.

Der Münsterländer Lagerkorn ist ein Topprodukt des seit 1707 bestehenden Familienbetriebs, den der 43-Jährige bereits in zwölfter Generation führt. Vier Jahre Lagerung in alten Eichenfässern gibt der hochprämierten Spirituose die kräftige Farbe und den milden Charakter mit leichter Fruchtnote. Das Geheimnis liegt in der Veredelung.

Das Konzept der Traditionsbrennerei aus Schöppingen reicht weiter: Frische Bio-Zutaten aus der Region im Münsterland werden in sorgfältiger Handarbeit verarbeitet. Hinzu kommt ein 140 Jahre alter Kupferkessel, der wie ein Katalysator wirkt und dem Alkohol Schadstoffe entzieht. Die so entstehenden Edelbrände, etwa der Himbeergeist oder der Brand Cigar Special, sind ausgezeichnete Produkte. Außerdem wurde die Feinbrennerei bei den World Spirits Awards 2012 zur World Class Distillery ernannt – als einzige in Deutschland und als eine von nur 19 Betrieben weltweit.

FEINBRENNEREI SASSE (SASSE DISTILLERY). Is that Korn? German liquor is typically white and clear, a brandy made from grains. However, this one is golden brown. Rüdiger Sasse swirls his glass, inhales the fine aromas, sips and nods with satisfaction.

Muensterland Korn stored over time (Lagerkorn) is the premium product of a family business. This business, which has been in existence since 1707 and is run by the 43-year-old, is now in its twelfth generation. Storing it for four years in old oak casks lends the prize-winning spirit its strong colour and mellow character with light fruity notes. The mystery lies in the ageing.

The concept of traditional distillation from Schoeppingen lives on: fresh bio-ingredients from the Muensterland region are carefully processed by hand. Added to this is the 140-year-old copper cauldron, which acts as a catalyser and removes harmful substances from the alcohol. The high-quality brandy thus extracted, like Himbeergeist (raspberry spirit) or the Cigar Special brand, are exceptional products. What's more, the distillery was nominated a World Class Distillery at the World Spirits Awards 2012, the only one from Germany and one of only 19 companies worldwide to receive this award.

Bestleistung: Einzige deutsche „World Class Distillery"
Region: Münsterland
Ort: Schöppingen

Best performance: The only German "World Class Distillery"
Region: Muensterland
Place: Schoeppingen

Theo Sasse
MÜNSTERLÄNDER
LAGERKORN
aus Malzdestillaten
Barriqueausbau
V.S.O.P.
SASSE
Feinbrennerei Sasse
Schöppingen/Westf.
SASSE

KLEINER ANTRIEB, GROSSE WIRKUNG
TINY ACTUATOR, BIG IMPACT

FG-INNOVATION. Selbst der Antrieb einer Tankklappe kann den Energieverbrauch eines Autos positiv beeinflussen: Wo bisher schwere Elektromotoren benötigt wurden, können heute sogenannte Aktorsysteme von FG-INNOVATION eingesetzt werden. Diese Antriebselemente sind die leichtesten und leistungsstärksten auf der ganzen Welt und bringen einen Gewichtsvorteil von bis zu 95 Prozent. Und das geringere Gewicht des Automobils reduziert den Kraftstoffverbrauch.

Auch andere mechatronische Systeme in Fahrzeugen, zum Beispiel für Tankklappe oder Rückbank, können mit Aktoren des Bochumer Unternehmens betrieben werden. Diese arbeiten mit intelligenten Materialien, sogenannten Formgedächtnislegierungen (FGL). Dabei wird ein FGL-Draht elektrisch erwärmt. Dieser verformt sich und löst einen Stellmechanismus aus: Die Tankklappe öffnet sich. Kühlt der Draht ab, kehrt er in seinen Ursprungszustand zurück.

FG-INNOVATION ist eine Ausgründung der Ruhr-Universität Bochum und mittlerweile Teil der weltweit agierenden EGELHOF-Gruppe. Die innovative FGL-Technologie wird nicht nur in der Automobil, sondern auch in der Luftfahrt- und Gebäudetechnik eingesetzt.

FG-INNOVATION. Who would have thought that even a fuel filler door actuator could have a positive effect on energy consumption? Heavy electric motors that were once used can now be replaced by the so-called actuator systems from FG-INNOVATION. They are the lightest and most powerful drive elements in the world, bringing down weight by up to 95 per cent. A reduction in the weight of an automobile lowers fuel consumption.

Actuators made of intelligent materials, the so-called shape memory alloys (SMA) produced by this company from Bochum, also operate other mechatronic systems in vehicles, for example fuel filler doors or rear seats. When electrically heated an SMA actuator will deform, releasing an actuation mechanism that opens the fuel filler door. Upon cooling, this wire returns to its original state.

FG-INNOVATION is a spin-off company founded by the Ruhr University Bochum and now part of the internationally established EGELHOF Group. The pioneering SMA technology finds application not only in automotive engineering but also in aeronautics and building technology.

Bestleistung: Weltweit leichtestes Aktorsystem
Region: Metropole Ruhr
Ort: Bochum

Best performance: The lightest actuator of the world
Region: Ruhr Metropolis
Place: Bochum

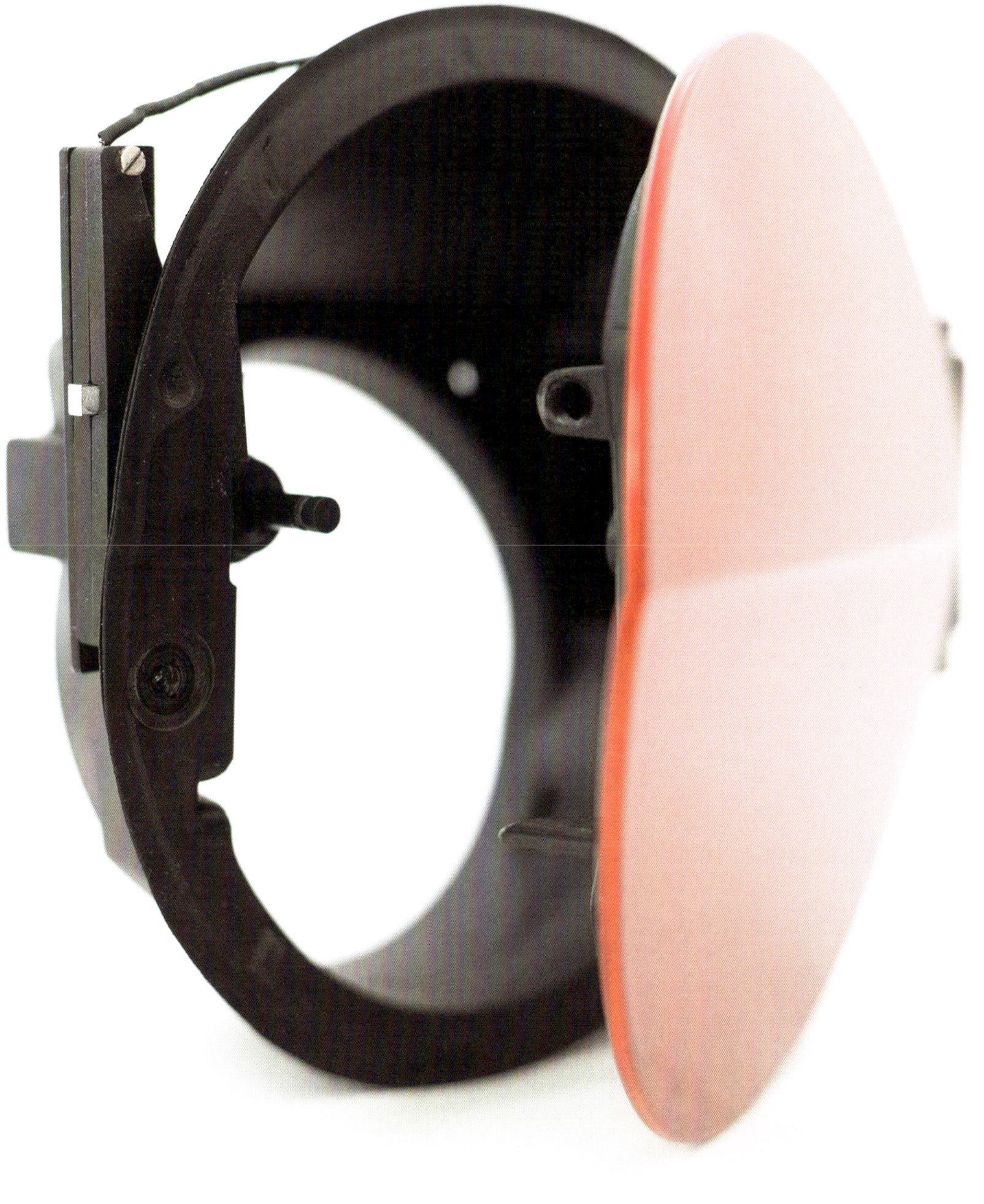

FORSCHEN FÜR DIE GUTE LUFT
QUEST FOR GOOD AIR

FORSCHUNGSVERBUND „THE REACTING ATMOSPHERE". Luftqualität und Klimawandel sind gravierende Probleme für die Menschheit zu Beginn des 21. Jahrhunderts. Der Forschungsverbund „The Reacting Atmosphere – Understanding and Management for Future Generations" versucht, nachhaltige Lösungen zur Verbesserung der Luftqualität zu erarbeiten.

Unter Führung der Bergischen Universität Wuppertal wollen Wissenschaftler renommierter nordrhein-westfälischer Forschungseinrichtungen gemeinsam ein grundlegendes Verständnis erarbeiten: Wie funktionieren die chemischen und physikalischen Prozesse in der Atmosphäre? Wie kann man Maßnahmen zur Verbesserung der Luft sinnvoll bewerten?

Zusammen mit der Industrie entwickelt der Forschungsverbund auch neue Techniken, um Luftschadstoffe selbst in kleinsten Mengen nachzuweisen. Bislang eindrucksvollstes Ergebnis ist das weltweit empfindlichste Messgerät zum Nachweis von Stickstoffdioxid in der Atmosphäre: Das giftige Gas kann nun erstmals isoliert von anderen Luftschadstoffen erforscht werden – ein wichtiger Schritt in Richtung langfristiger Steigerung der Luftqualität.

RESEARCH ASSOCIATION "THE REACTING ATMOSPHERE". At the advent of the 21st century, air quality and climate change pose serious problems for mankind. The Research association "The Reacting Atmosphere – Understanding and Management for Future Generations" is trying to develop sustainable solutions to improve air quality.

Under the leadership of the University of Wuppertal scientists from leading North Rhine-Westphalian research institutions are seeking to jointly come to a basic understanding of the way in which chemical and physical processes function in the atmosphere, and how measures to improve air quality can be reliably evaluated.

This association, together with industry, is developing new techniques to identify even minimal amounts of pollutants. The most impressive breakthrough so far has been the world's most sensitive device to detect nitrogen dioxide in the atmosphere. For the first time ever, this poisonous gas can be researched upon in isolation from other pollutants; an important step towards the long-term enhancement of air quality.

Bestleistung: Innovatives Stickstoffdioxid-Messgerät
Region: Bergisches Städtedreieck
Ort: Wuppertal

Best performance: Innovative device to gauge nitrogen dioxide
Region: Bergisches Staedtedreieck
Place: Wuppertal

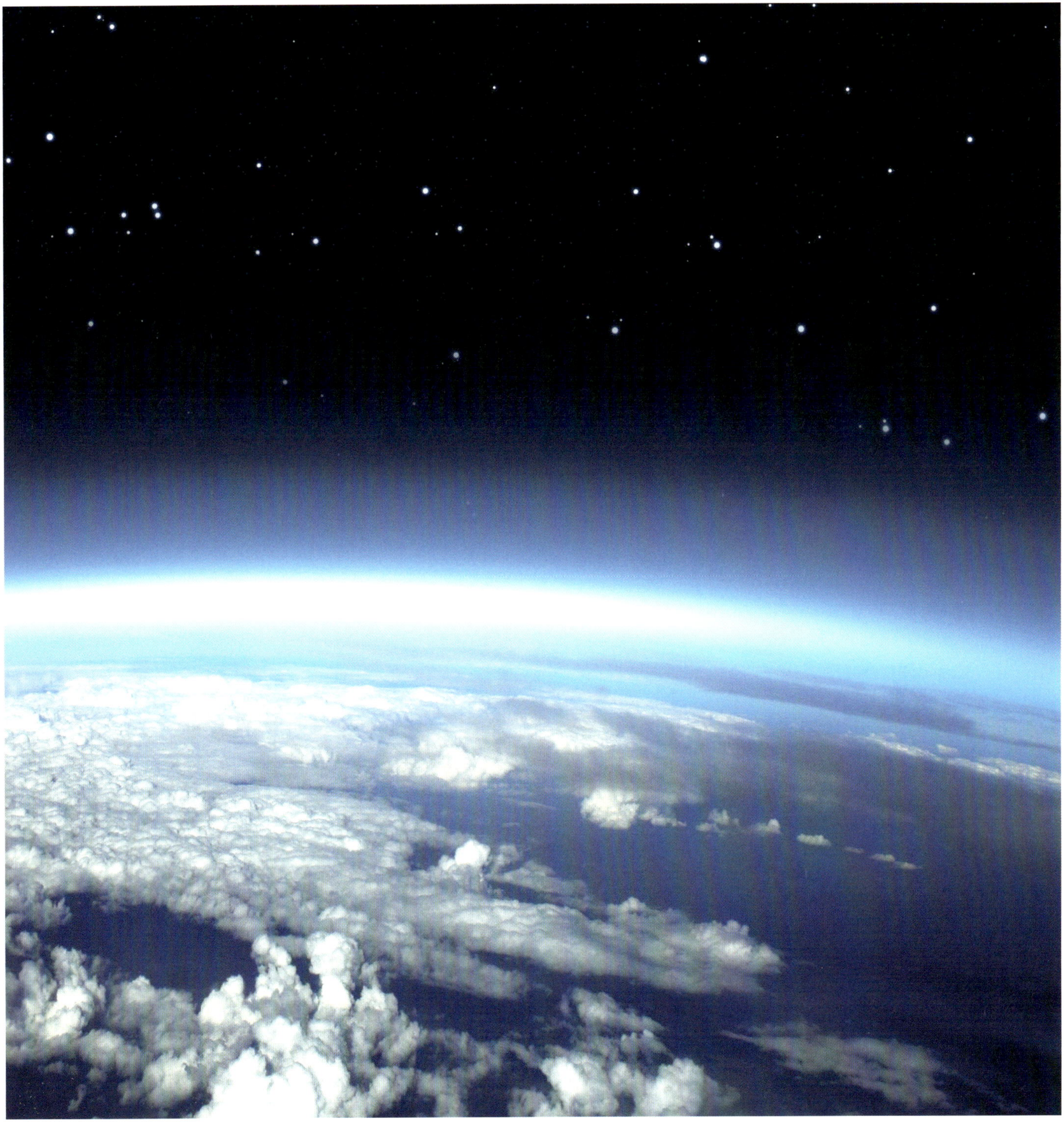

PICO SIEHT FAST ALLES
PICO SEES NEARLY EVERYTHING

FORSCHUNGSZENTRUM JÜLICH & RWTH AACHEN. PICO sieht alles, fast alles. Mit dem stärksten Elektronenmikroskop Europas dringen Wissenschaftler in unvorstellbar kleine Bereiche vor und studieren Details, die winziger sind als ein Atom. Das auf dem Gelände des Forschungszentrums Jülich betriebene Hochleistungsmikroskop verbessert die Auflösung und die Genauigkeit, mit der sich Abstände und Verschiebungen elementarer Teilchen messen lassen – und schafft ein schärferes Bild als je zuvor.

Die Superlupe ermöglicht, den Zusammenhang von Atomstrukturen und physikalischen Eigenschaften sowie die Beschaffenheit einzelner Materialien zu analysieren. Auf dieser Basis lassen sich Werkstoffe verbessern oder völlig neue Komponenten entwickeln. Dies ist bereits bei noch leistungsfähigeren Solarzellen oder Mikrochips gelungen.

Mit PICO haben die Betreiber, das Forschungszentrum Jülich und die Rheinisch-Westfälische Technische Hochschule (RWTH) Aachen, ihre internationale Spitzenposition in der ultrahochauflösenden Elektronenmikroskopie weiter ausgebaut.

RESEARCH CENTER JUELICH & RWTH AACHEN UNIVERSITY. PICO can see everything, well, almost everything. Scientists foray into inconceivably small areas and study details more minuscule than an atom, with the help of Europe's most powerful electron microscope. The high-precision microscope used at the campus of the Forschungszentrum Juelich improves the resolution and increases the precision in measuring interatomic distances and atomic displacements, producing a sharper picture than ever before.

The high-tech loop enables analysis of the correlation between atomic structures and physical features as well as the properties of individual materials. It forms the basis for improving materials or developing completely new elements. This has already been put to test in high-performance solar cells or microchips successfully.

PICO helps the operators, the Research Center Juelich and the RWTH Aachen University, to further strengthen their global position at the forefront of ultra high-resolution electron microscopy.

Bestleistung: Stärkstes Elektronenmikroskop Europas
Region: Aachen
Ort: Jülich

Best performance: Europe's most powerful electron microscope
Region: Aachen
Place: Juelich

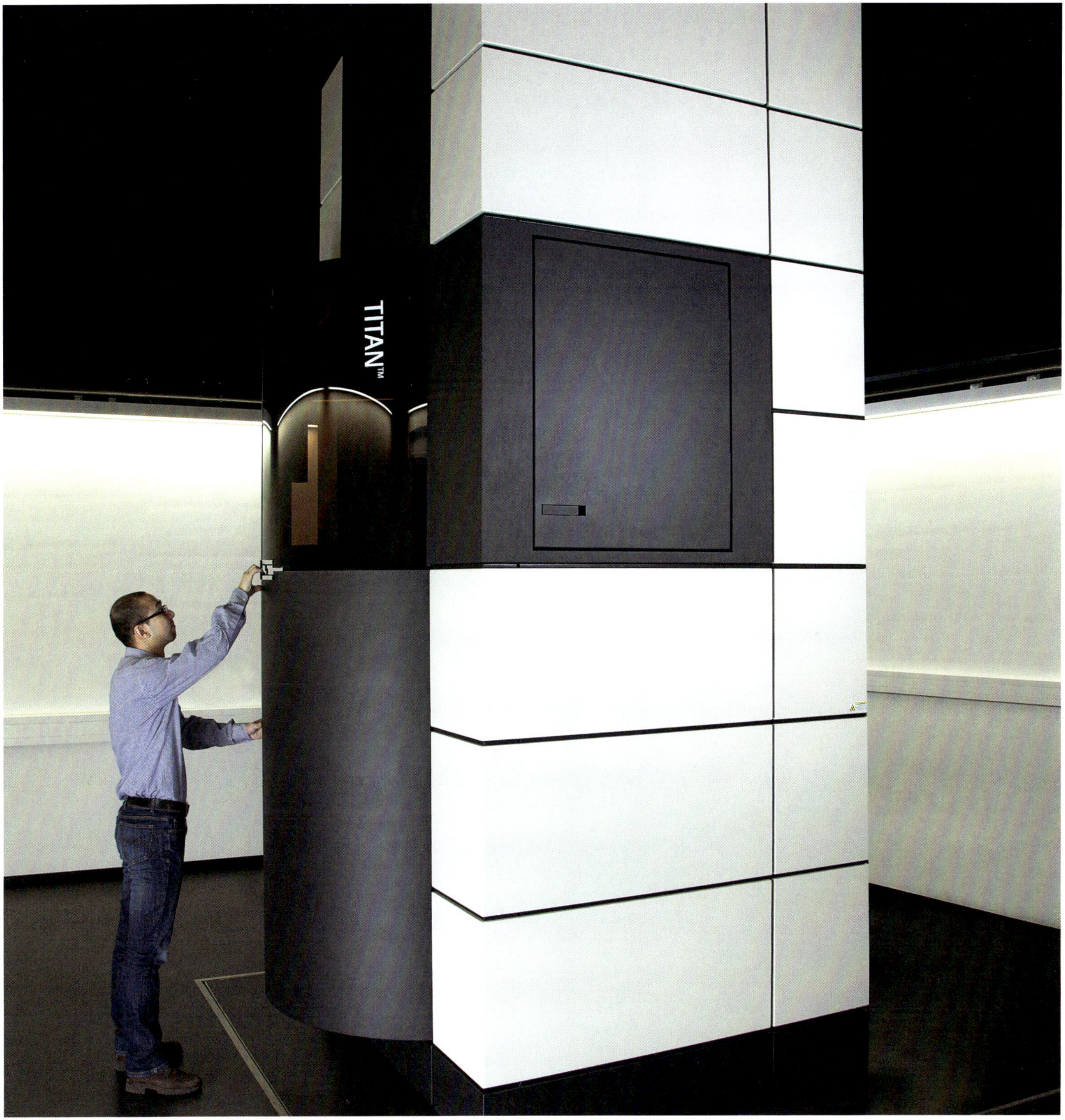
TITAN™

MASCHINENBAUER HAT DEN DREH RAUS
MACHINE MANUFACTURERS WITH A FLAIR

GILDEMEISTER. Das Jahr 1928 ist für Gildemeister aus Bielefeld ein entscheidendes Jahr: Geschäftsführer Wilhelm Berg erhält das Patent Nr. 544 604 für die „Entwicklung einer Maschine mit freiem Spänefall und für die Ausführung von Automaten in Portalformat", einem Vorgänger der heutigen Dreh- und Fräsmaschinen. Damit beginnt für das Unternehmen ein anhaltender Aufschwung.

Heute ist Gildemeister einer der größten Werkzeugmaschinenhersteller in Deutschland und ein weltweit führender Produzent von CNC-gesteuerten Dreh- und Fräsmaschinen, ebenso bei den spanenden Werkzeugmaschinen in den Technologien Drehen und Fräsen sowie Ultrasonic/Lasern. Mit 93 Vertriebs- und Servicestandorten im In- und Ausland und über 6.000 Mitarbeitern ist Gildemeister ein global tätiger Anbieter.

Zudem arbeitet das Unternehmen mit Partnern der Universität Paderborn an der Weiterentwicklung sogenannter Intelligenter Technischer Systeme: Ziel ist eine vollständig digitale Produktionsplanung. Dies bedeutet, dass Maschinen noch während des Betriebs für darauffolgende Produktionen programmiert werden – und so ohne Unterbrechung viel effizienter arbeiten.

GILDEMEISTER. 1928 marks a watershed year in the history of Gildemeister from Bielefeld. Its director, Wilhelm Berg, was awarded patent no. 544 604 for "making a machine with free chip fall and automatic machines in the portal format", a forerunner to the present day lathes and milling machines. The company has never looked back since.

Today, Gildemeister is one of the biggest machine tool manufacturers in Germany and world's leading producer of CNC lathes and milling machines, cutting machine tools related to turning and milling technology, as well as ultrasonic and laser technology. With 93 national and international sales and service locations and 6,000 employees, Gildemeister ranks as a global supplier.

Furthermore, its collaboration with partners at Paderborn University in the development of "Intelligent Technical Systems" is designed to allow for the complete digitalisation of production planning, meaning that machines can be programmed for the next production process while still in operation, thus optimising efficiency by running without a break.

Bestleistung: Weltweit führender Hersteller von Dreh- und Fräsmaschinen
Region: Ostwestfalen-Lippe
Ort: Bielefeld

Best performance: World's leading manufacturer of lathes and milling machines
Region: Ostwestfalen-Lippe
Place: Bielefeld

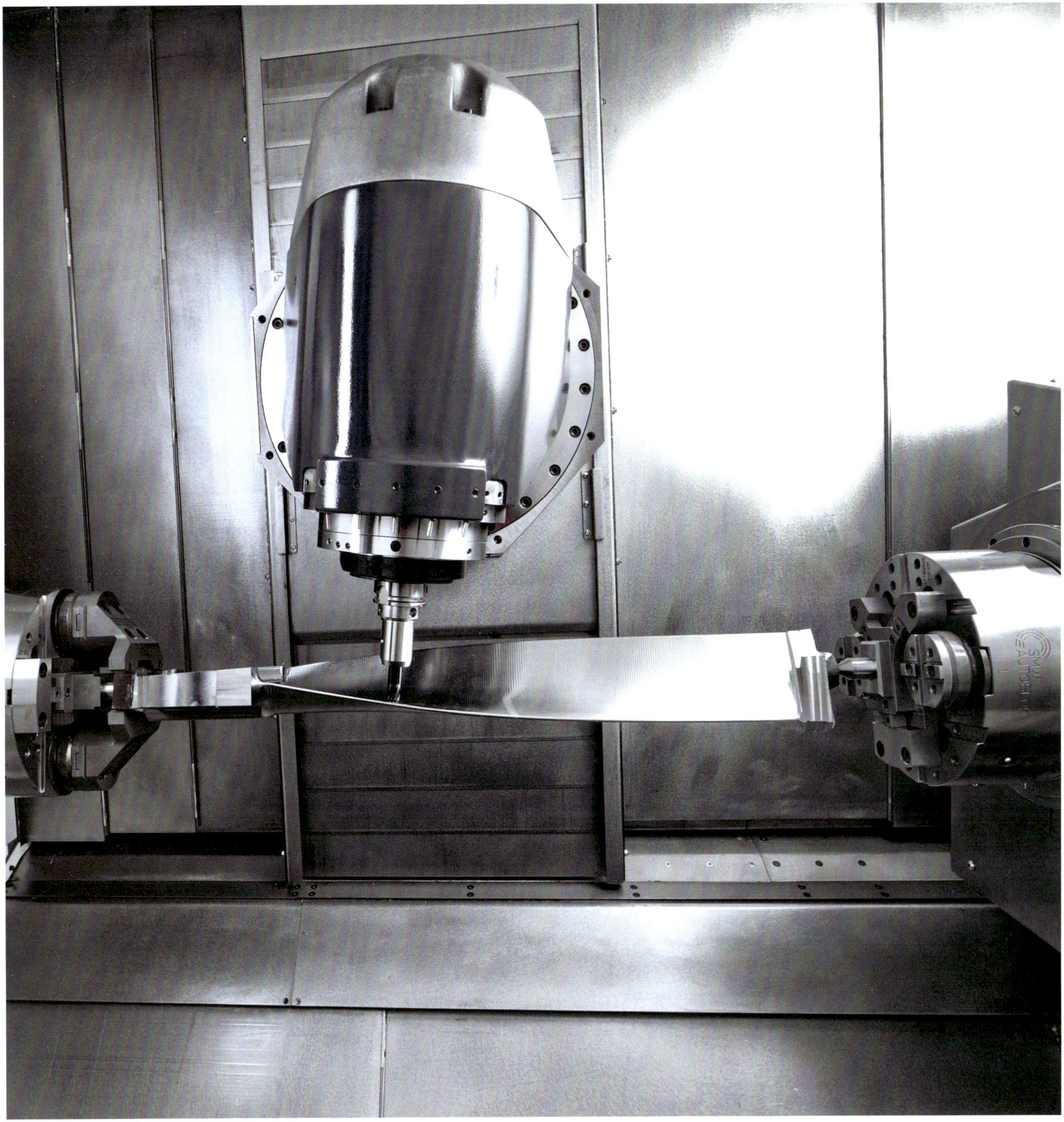
SMW
AUTOBLOK

BARRIEREFREIHEIT FÜR ALLE
FREEDOM FROM BARRIERS FOR ALL

GÜTESIEGEL RAL BARRIEREFREI. Die elektrische Drehtür sollte eigentlich für Rollstuhlfahrer geeignet sein – und stellt dennoch ein Hindernis dar, da der Bodenbelag Rollstühle ausbremst. Alltag für die Tester von EUKOBA, dem Euregio Kompetenzzentrum für Barrierefreiheit in Aachen. Sind alle Barrieren beseitigt, erhält ein Objekt, ein Produkt oder eine Dienstleistung das sogenannte RAL-Gütezeichen. 1925 wurde RAL gegründet, seit 1980 steht das Deutsche Institut für Gütesicherung und Kennzeichnung hinter RAL. Es gibt gut 170 Gütezeichen aus allen Bereichen, und über 11.000 Unternehmen in 30 Ländern nehmen teil.

Beraten und Lösungen finden: EUKOBA unterstützt Behörden, Gemeinden und Unternehmen. Das standardisierte Prüfverfahren wurde mit behinderten Menschen entwickelt – und diese prüfen auch aktiv vor Ort. Das Motto lautet: „Für alle heißt für alle!" Und von Barrierefreiheit profitiert am Ende wirklich jeder, auch Senioren oder Mütter mit Kinderwagen. 2012 wurde das „RAL barrierefrei"-Prüfverfahren selbst von der „Initiative Mittelstand", der Interessengemeinschaft der deutschen Wirtschaft, ausgezeichnet.

RAL CERTIFICATE BARRIER-FREE. Electric revolving doors should actually be friendly to people in wheelchairs, but their floors obstruct access. For testers at EUKOBA, the Euregio Centre of Excellence for Barrier-Free Systems in Aachen, this is a routine issue. An object, product or service that is barrier-free gets so-called RAL certification. RAL was formed in 1925 and has been supported since 1980 by the German Institute for Quality Assurance and Certification. It certifies fully 170 objects from all fields, with the participation of 11,000 companies from 30 countries. EUKOBA supports government agencies, communities and companies through consultation and solutions. People with disabilities have helped develop the standardised testing methods, including by actively participating in on-site tests. The motto is "For everyone means for absolutely everyone!". After all each one stands to gain from this freedom from barriers, even senior citizens or mothers with prams. In 2012 the "RAL without barriers" testing method was awarded the "Initiative Mittelstand", a prize for innovation for medium-sized business initiatives sponsored by the German Association of SMEs.

Bestleistung: Ältestes Gütesicherungsverfahren in Europa
Region: Aachen
Ort: Linnich

Best performance: Europe's oldest system of quality control
Region: Aachen
Place: Linnich

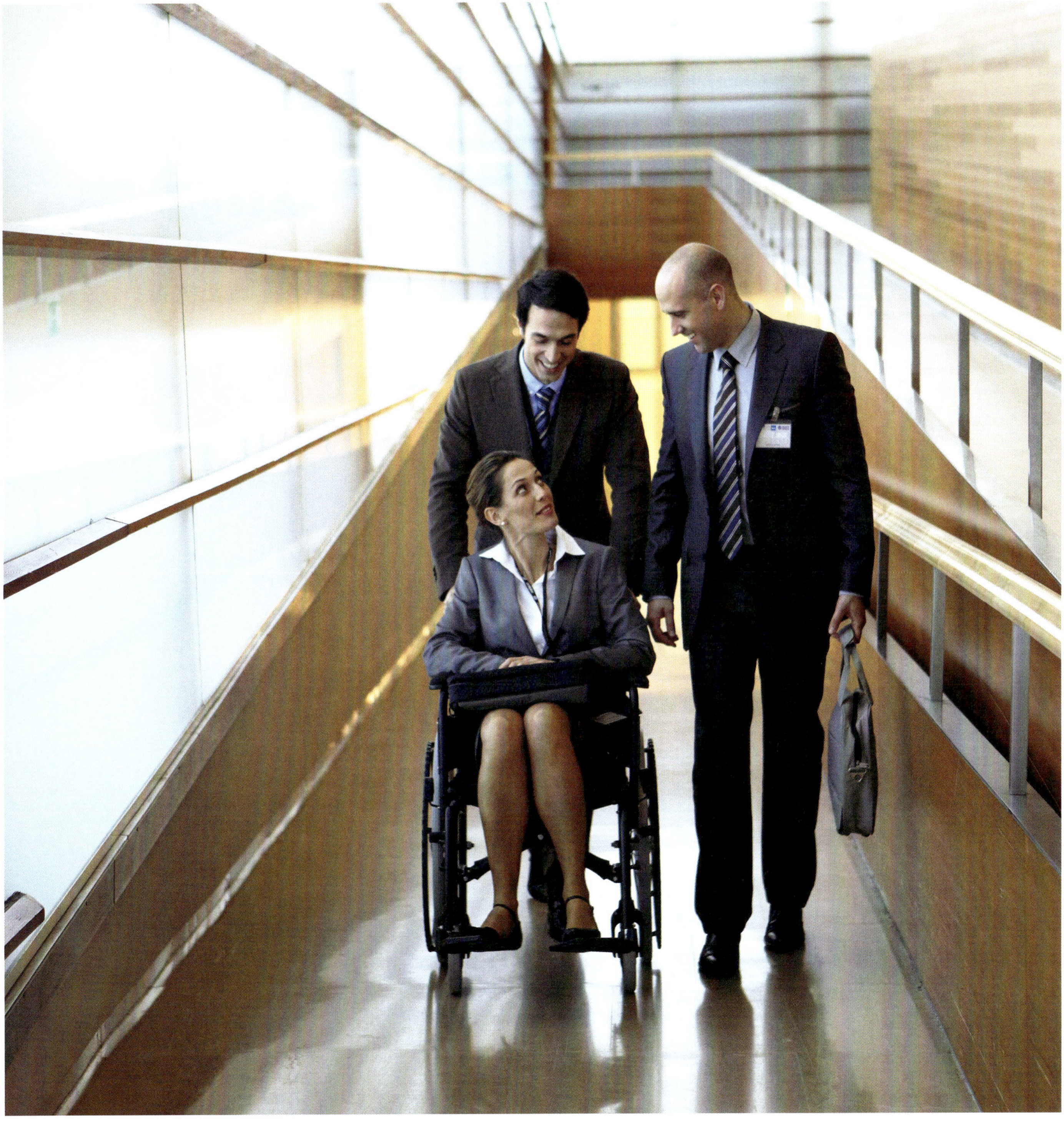

HÖREN WIE EIN MENSCH
HEARING LIKE HUMANS

HEAD ACOUSTICS. Mikrofone statt Ohren – Kunstköpfe sind komplexe Messgeräte, die Geräusche genauso „hören" wie das menschliche Ohr. Rund um diese Spezialdisziplin ist das Herzogenrather Unternehmen HEAD acoustics einer der weltweit führenden Anbieter von Produkten und Lösungen in den Bereichen Geräuschanalyse und -optimierung.

Der Kunstkopf „HMS IV" liefert alle akustisch relevanten Daten, um Produkte hinsichtlich ihrer Geräuschqualität und ihres Sounddesigns analysieren und optimieren zu können – zum Beispiel im Autoinnenraum. Kunstköpfe sind für die Geräuschoptimierung sehr wichtig, denn „normale" Mikrofone können das Hören mit menschlichen Ohren nicht gut nachbilden. Der HMS IV berücksichtigt jedoch die akustischen Filtereigenschaften von Kopf und Ohren – somit werden dem menschlichen Gehör entsprechende Aufnahmen möglich.

Innovative Forschung an der Rheinisch-Westfälischen Technischen Hochschule (RWTH) Aachen führte 1986 zu der Ausgründung des Unternehmens, sein Gründer und Inhaber Prof. Dr.-Ing. Klaus Genuit hatte zunächst selbst an der Aachener Hochschule promoviert.

HEAD ACOUSTICS. Can microphones replace ears? Almost. The artificial head is a complex apparatus that "hears" sounds, i.e. perceives them just as a human ear would. A leading global supplier of products and provider of solutions for the analysis and optimisation of sound, HEAD acoustics, based in Herzogenrath, is all about this specialised branch.

The "HMS IV" artificial head provides the acoustic data required to analyse and optimise products with regard to their sound quality and sound design, say, in the interior of a car. Artificial heads are very important for sound optimisation since "normal" microphones cannot simulate human hearing very well. The HMS IV, however, takes the acoustic filter characteristics of the head and ear into account, enabling aurally accurate recordings to be made that are true to the holistic impression of sound perceived by the human ear. Ground-breaking research conducted at RWTH Aachen University led to the formation of the company in 1986. In fact, founder Prof. Dr.-Eng. Klaus Genuit himself gained his doctorate from the very same university.

Bestleistung: Führender Anbieter für Geräuschoptimierung
Region: Aachen
Ort: Herzogenrath

Best performance: Leading suppliers of sound optimisation devices
Region: Aachen
Place: Herzogenrath

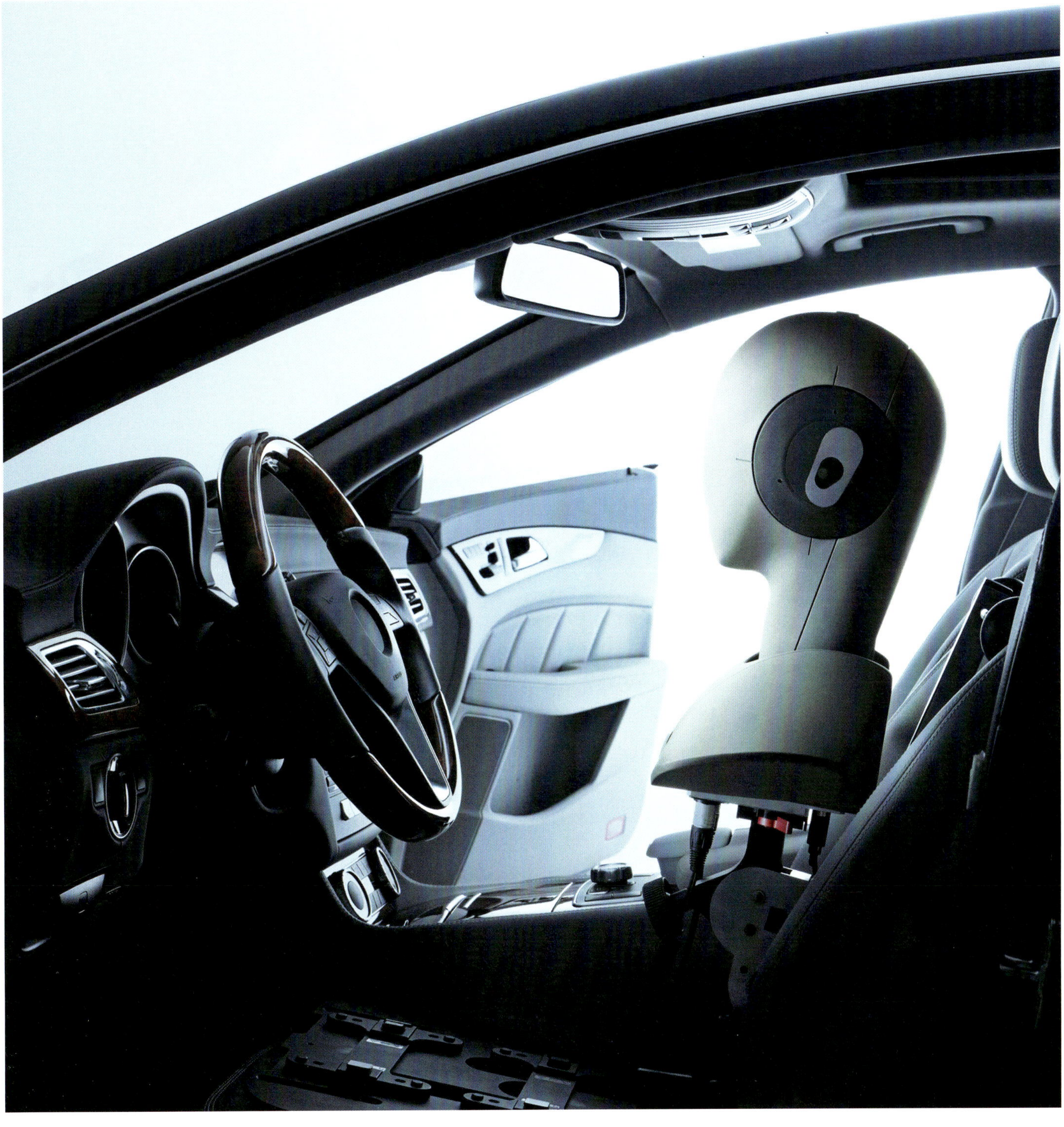

DER POLITISCHE ROMANTIKER
THE POLITICAL ROMANTICIST

HEINRICH HEINE. Er hat die deutsche Alltagssprache lyrikfähig gemacht, hat bis heute gültige Maßstäbe im Journalismus gesetzt, seine Reiseprosa, Essays und Polemiken waren ebenso berühmt wie gefürchtet, für seine literarischen Attacken auf die Herrschenden wurde er am Ende per Haftbefehl gesucht. Und der als Harry Heine 1797 in Düsseldorf geborene Schriftsteller jüdischer Abstammung hat Gedichte geschrieben, die häufiger vertont worden sind als die jedes anderen Dichters weltweit.

Schon 30 Jahre nach seinem Tod im Jahr 1856 existierten tausende von Kompositionen zu Texten von Heine; bis heute sind mehr als 7.000 bekannt. Besonders populär wurde die „Lorelei"-Vertonung Friedrich Silchers von 1837. Alle berühmten deutschen Liederkomponisten des 19. Jahrhunderts wie Franz Schubert, Felix Mendelssohn Bartholdy, Robert Schumann und Johannes Brahms haben Heine vertont. Und Musiker aus aller Welt bemühen sich bis heute darum, das Spezifische seines Tons in Musik zu bannen.

Heine zählt zu den letzten großen romantischen Schriftstellern. Zugleich ist er mit seinen Themen und seiner Sprache ein wichtiger Wegbereiter der Moderne.

HEINRICH HEINE. He made colloquial German worthy of verse and set a benchmark for journalism that applies even today. His travel writing, essays and polemics were as famous as they were feared until finally a warrant was issued on him for his literary attacks on the rulers. This writer of Jewish origin was born in 1797 in Duesseldorf as Harry Heine. More of his poems have been set to music than of any other writer in the world.

Within 30 years of his death, in 1856, there were 1,000 compositions on Heine's lyrics, today over 7,000 of them are known to exist. "Lorelei", set to music by Friedrich Silchers in 1837, was exceptionally well-received. All famous German art song composers of the 19th century, such as Franz Schubert, Felix Mendelssohn Bartholdy, Robert Schumann and Johannes Brahms, chose to set his works to music. Musicians across the world assay till today to capture the idiosyncrasy of his tone in music.

Heine was one of the last great romantic writers. Equally, his language and choice of themes made him a significant precursor to modernism.

Bestleistung: Meistvertonter Dichter der Weltliteratur
Region: Düsseldorf
Ort: Düsseldorf

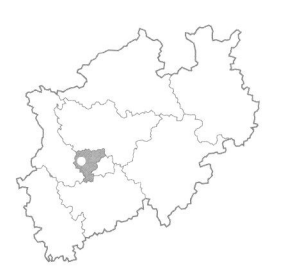

Best performance: The maximum number of works by an author set to music in the literary world
Region: Duesseldorf
Place: Duesseldorf

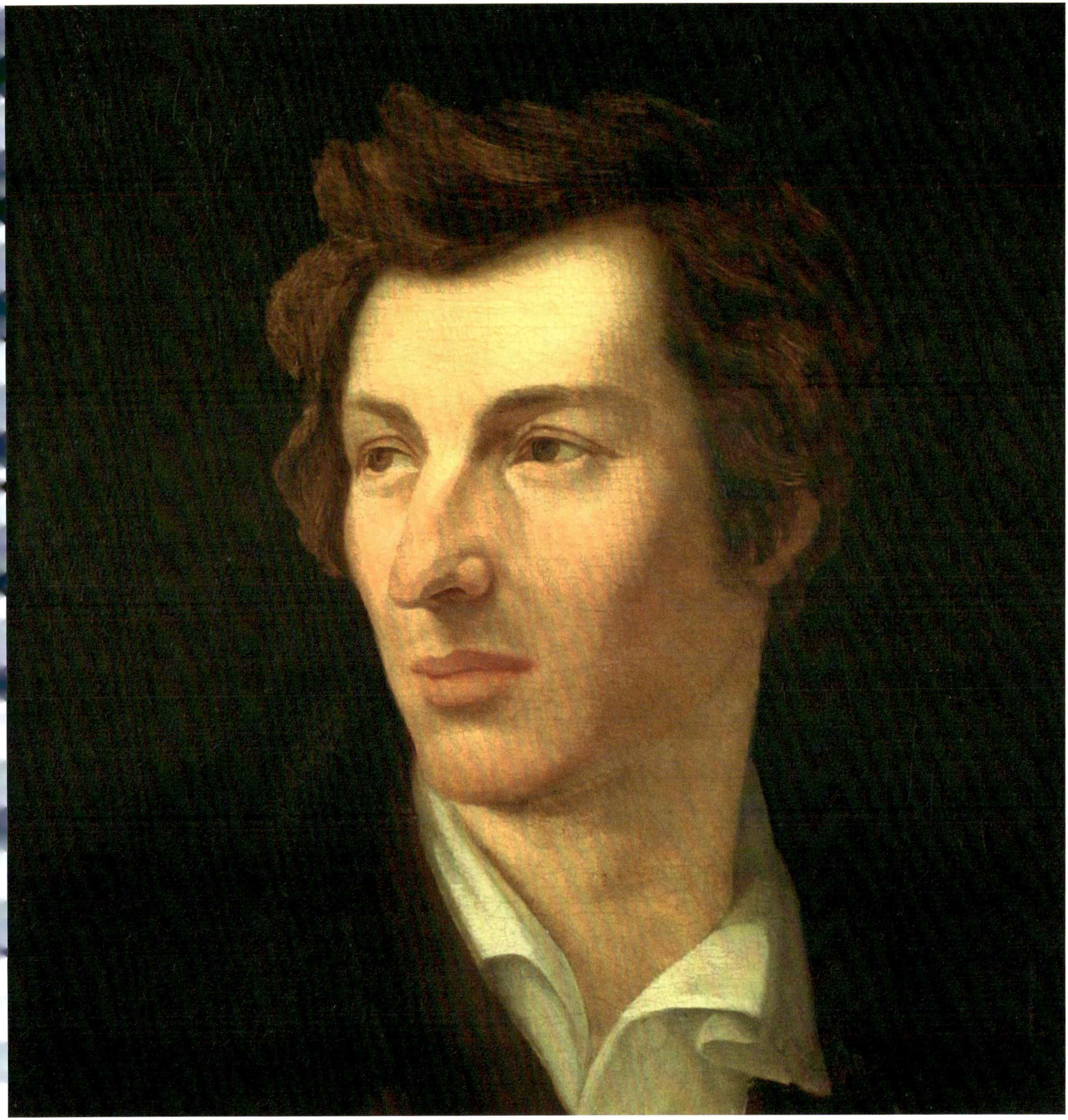

INTELLIGENTE LICHTTECHNIK
INTELLIGENT LIGHTING TECHNOLOGY

HELLA. Moderne Autoscheinwerfer sind heutzutage mehr als Lampen – besonders, wenn sie aus dem westfälischen Lippstadt stammen. Hier sitzt das weltweit erfolgreiche Familienunternehmen HELLA, hier werden Innovationen und Lösungen für die Automobilindustrie entwickelt und produziert: etwa der weltweit erste kamerabasierte Autoscheinwerfer mit automatischer Leuchtweitenregulierung, der erste Voll-LED-Scheinwerfer in Großserie oder der erste Xenon-Scheinwerfer mit blendfreiem Fernlicht.

Auch das von HELLA entwickelte Kurvenlicht ist ein weiteres leuchtendes Beispiel für die Innovationskraft des Unternehmens. Bereits 1899 wurde die Firma gegründet – inmitten der Automotive-Region Südwestfalen führt das Unternehmen heute auch den Markt für elektronische Fahrpedale mit an und ist mit seiner Radarsensorik für Spurwechselassistenten weltweit die Nummer eins.

HELLA ist zudem eine der global größten Handelsorganisationen für Kfz-Teile, Zubehör, Diagnose- und Serviceleistungen. Insgesamt zählt HELLA weltweit zu den Top 50 der Automobilzulieferer sowie den Top 100 der größten deutschen Industrieunternehmen.

HELLA. Nowadays, headlights are more than just lamps, even more so if they happen to be made in Lippstadt in Westphalia, home to the internationally successful family-run company HELLA, which develops innovations and solutions for the automotive industry. The company has many firsts to its credit: camera-based automatic headlight range control, mass-produced full-LED headlights, or Xenon headlights with anti-glare beams.

The bend lighting developed by HELLA is a further shining example of the company's inventive skills. Founded in 1899 in the heart of the automotive manufacturing region of South Westphalia, HELLA continues to this day to lead the market in electronic accelerators and is the world's number one in radar sensors for lane change assistant systems.

Furthermore, it has the world's largest dealership network of automobile parts, accessories, diagnostic services and services. Taken together, this places HELLA among the world's top 50 automotive suppliers and top 100 German industrial concerns.

Bestleistung: Innovativstes Unternehmen für Kfz-Lichttechnologie
Region: Südwestfalen
Ort: Lippstadt

Best performance: A pioneering company for automobile lighting technology
Region: Suedwestfalen
Place: Lippstadt

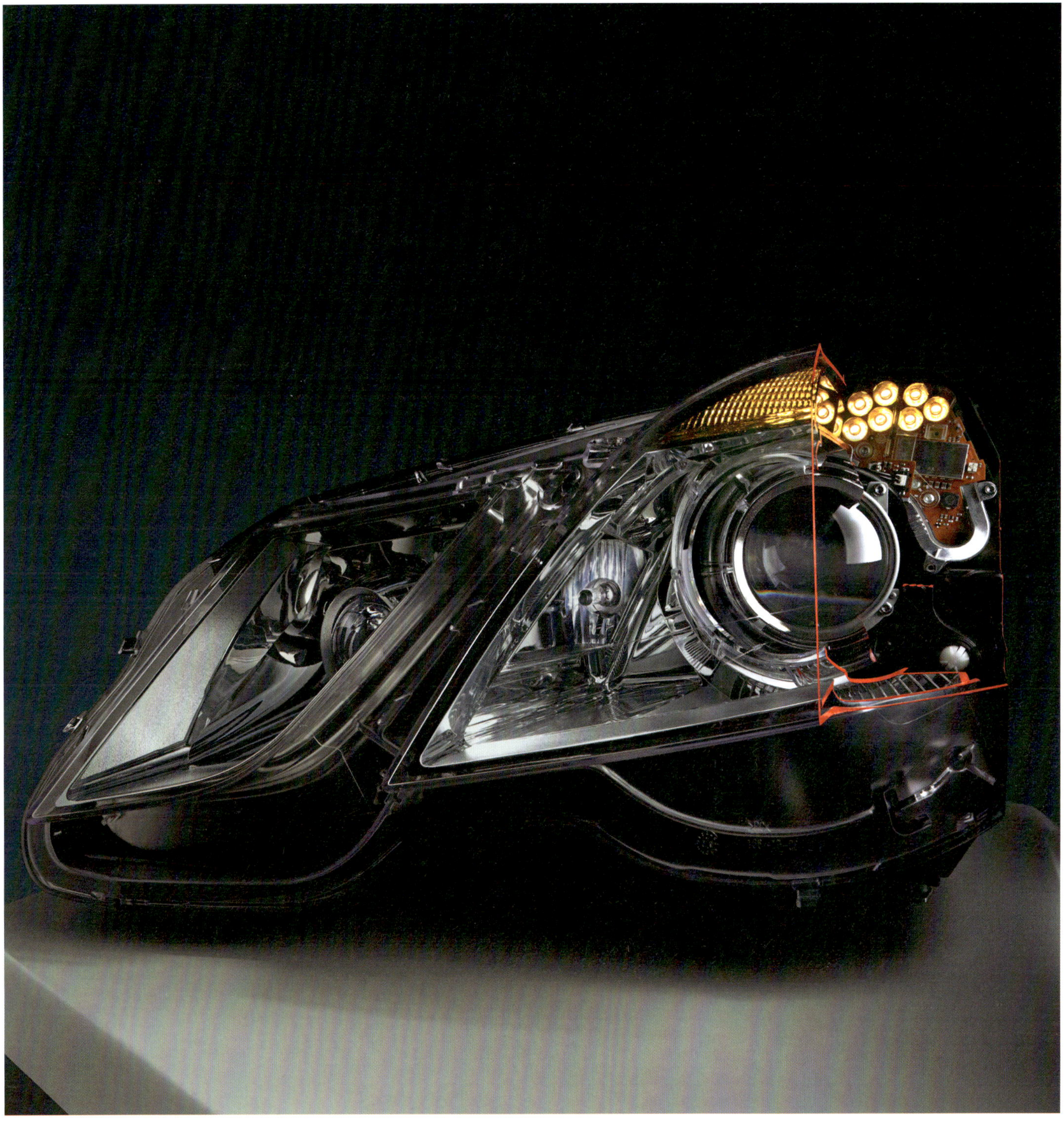

FABRIKANT UND FREIGEIST
INDUSTRIALIST AND FREE THINKER

HISTORISCHES ZENTRUM WUPPERTAL. Bei unerträglichen 35 Grad, inmitten ratternder, ölverschmierter Maschinen stehen die Arbeiter einer Textilfabrik. Eine beeindruckende Erfahrung: Willkommen im Erlebnisraum des größten deutschen Museums für Frühindustrialisierung! Auf dem Gelände des Museums befindet sich zudem eine Industriellenvilla, die einst ein berühmter Sozialrevolutionär bewohnte: der Fabrikantensohn Friedrich Engels, Pionier der empirischen Soziologie.

Das Gebäudeensemble des Zentrums zeigt den Arbeitsalltag in Spinnereien oder Webereien – und die verheerenden Folgen der industriellen Revolution für die Menschen. Unterschwellig schwingt eine historische Ironie mit: Das Weltbuch „Das Kapital" wurde von Friedrich Engels mitfinanziert, denn dieser unterstützte seinen Freund, Mitstreiter und Autor Karl Marx im Londoner Exil.

Das Patrizierhaus des Großvaters, in dem Engels aufwuchs, zeigt heute eine große Dokumentation über den Mitbegründer einer neuen, kommunistischen Gesellschaftstheorie. Er prangerte die Diktatur von „König Dampf" an – und wurde doch selbst Fabrikant. Dafür war Marx ihm zeitlebens dankbar – für Engels' Geduld.

HISTORICAL CENTRE WUPPERTAL. To see workers toiling at an unbearable 35 degrees Celsius amid the roar of greasy machines in a textile factory is an amazing experience. Welcome to this hall of graphic experience at Germany's biggest museum for early industrialisation. The son of an industrialist, Friedrich Engels, a famous social revolutionary who pioneered scientific socialism once lived in the industrialist villa in the museum grounds.

The buildings that make up the centre depict a typical day in spinning and weaving mills and the ravages of the industrial revolution on people. The epochal work "Das Kapital" echoes of historically ironic underpinnings. Engels co-financed it in support of his friend, comrade-in-arms and author in exile in London, Karl Marx.

The grandfather's patrician villa, where Engels grew up, now presents copious documentation on the co-founder of a new communist social theory. This man who denounced the tyranny of the "The Steam King" (Edward Mead poetry – used by Engels as "König Dampf"), a symbol of the industrial revolution, himself later became an industrialist. A reason for Marx's eternal gratitude – Engels' indulgence!

Bestleistung: Größtes Museum für Frühindustrialisierung
Region: Bergisches Städtedreieck
Ort: Wuppertal

Best performance: The biggest museum for early industrialisation
Region: Bergisches Staedtedreieck
Place: Wuppertal

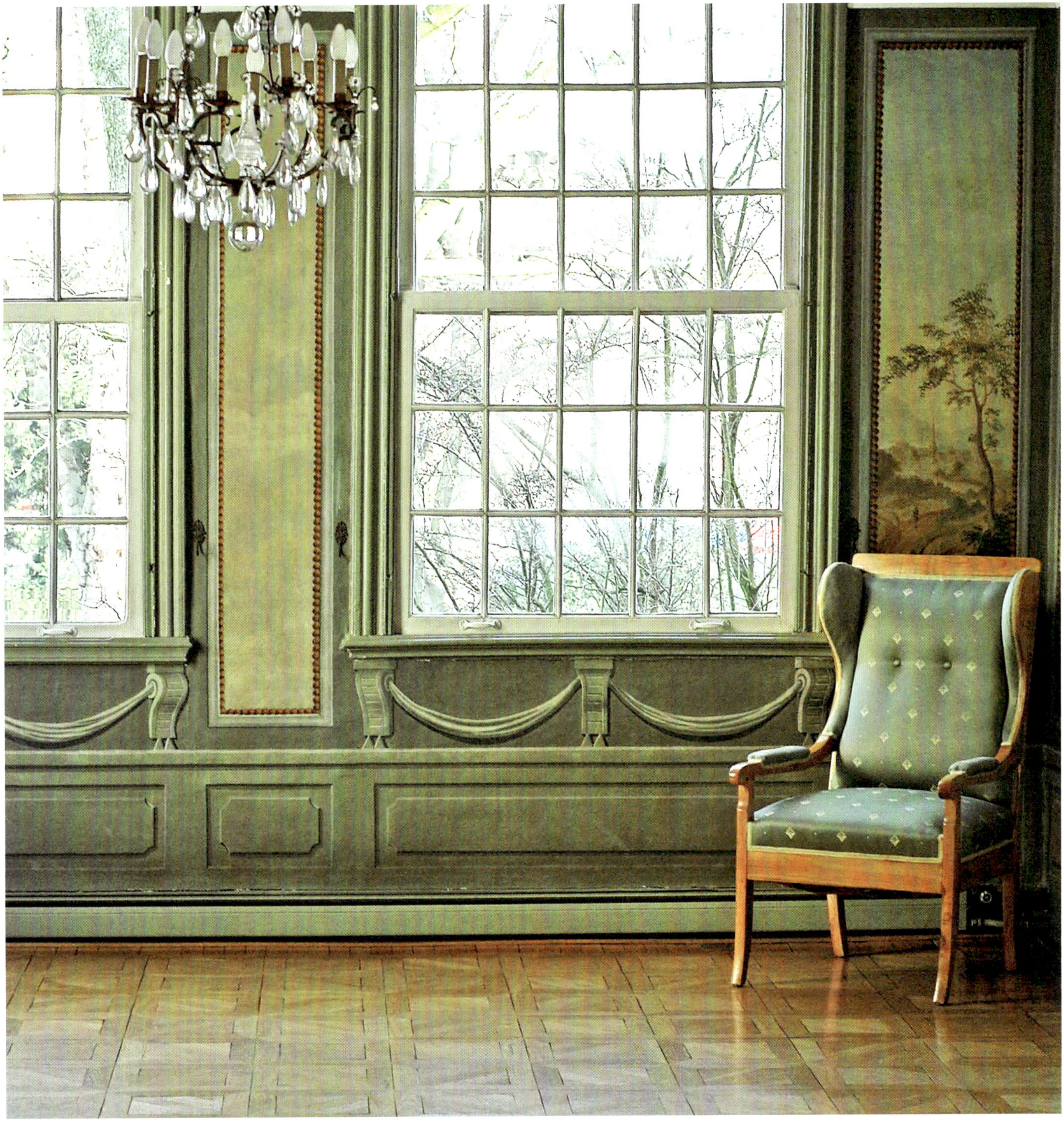

ALUMINIUM DÜNNER ALS EIN MENSCHENHAAR
ALUMINIUM FINER THAN HUMAN HAIR

HYDRO ALUMINIUM. Neun Meter lang und 30 Tonnen schwer sind die Aluminiumbarren vor ihrer Verarbeitung im Hydro-Walzwerk Grevenbroich. Nach vielen Warm- und Kaltwalzvorgängen haben die Barren eine wahrhaftige Metamorphose hinter sich: Aus ihnen entstehen rund 660 Kilometer Folie, aufgerollt zu großen sogenannten Coils, mit einer Dicke von unglaublich dünnen sechs Mikrometern.

Nirgendwo weltweit wird so viel dieser High-Performance-Folien produziert wie hier. Aus Grevenbroich kommen auch die weltweit meisten Aluminiumbänder für Offset-Druckplatten, die beispielsweise im Zeitungsdruck Anwendung finden. Seit 1922 wird zwischen Köln und Düsseldorf Aluminium verarbeitet. Heute fertigen rund 2.000 Mitarbeiter im Hydro-Walzproduktewerk jährlich bis zu 120.000 Tonnen Folie. Die Serie 2, die größte vollautomatisierte Produktionslinie der Welt, walzt pro Minute über 2.500 Meter Aluminiumfolie – dünner als Menschenhaar.

Die Folien finden vielfältig ihren Weg in den Alltag: als Joghurtbecherdeckel, bei Tablettenverpackungen oder als Getränkekarton. Richtig recycelt, kann Aluminium unbegrenzt wiederverwendet werden.

HYDRO ALUMINIUM. The aluminium ingots at the rolling mills of Hydro in Grevenbroich are nine metres long and weigh 30 tonnes before processing. After a series of hot and cold rolling processes, the ingots undergo true metamorphosis, transformed into 660 kilometres of foil rolled into huge so-called coils with an incredible thinness of six micrometres.

More high-performance foils are made here than anywhere else in the world. Grevenbroich also accounts for the highest number of aluminium strips for offset printing plates produced worldwide. Uses to which these are put include newspaper printing. Since 1922, the areas between Cologne and Duesseldorf have been home to aluminium processing. Around 2,000 employees at the Hydro Aluminium Rolled Products GmbH now turn out up to 120,000 tonnes of foil annually. The biggest fully automatic production line in the world, Series 2 rolls out over 2,500 metres of aluminium foil finer than a human hair each minute.

Aluminium foils blend into daily life in many forms: as lids on yogurt containers, in tablet blister packs or as drinks cartons. If properly recycled, aluminium can be re-used endlessly.

Bestleistung: Walz-Weltmeister bei Aluminiumfolien
Region: Niederrhein
Ort: Grevenbroich

Best performance: A champion in the field of rolling aluminium sheets
Region: Lower Rhine
Place: Grevenbroich

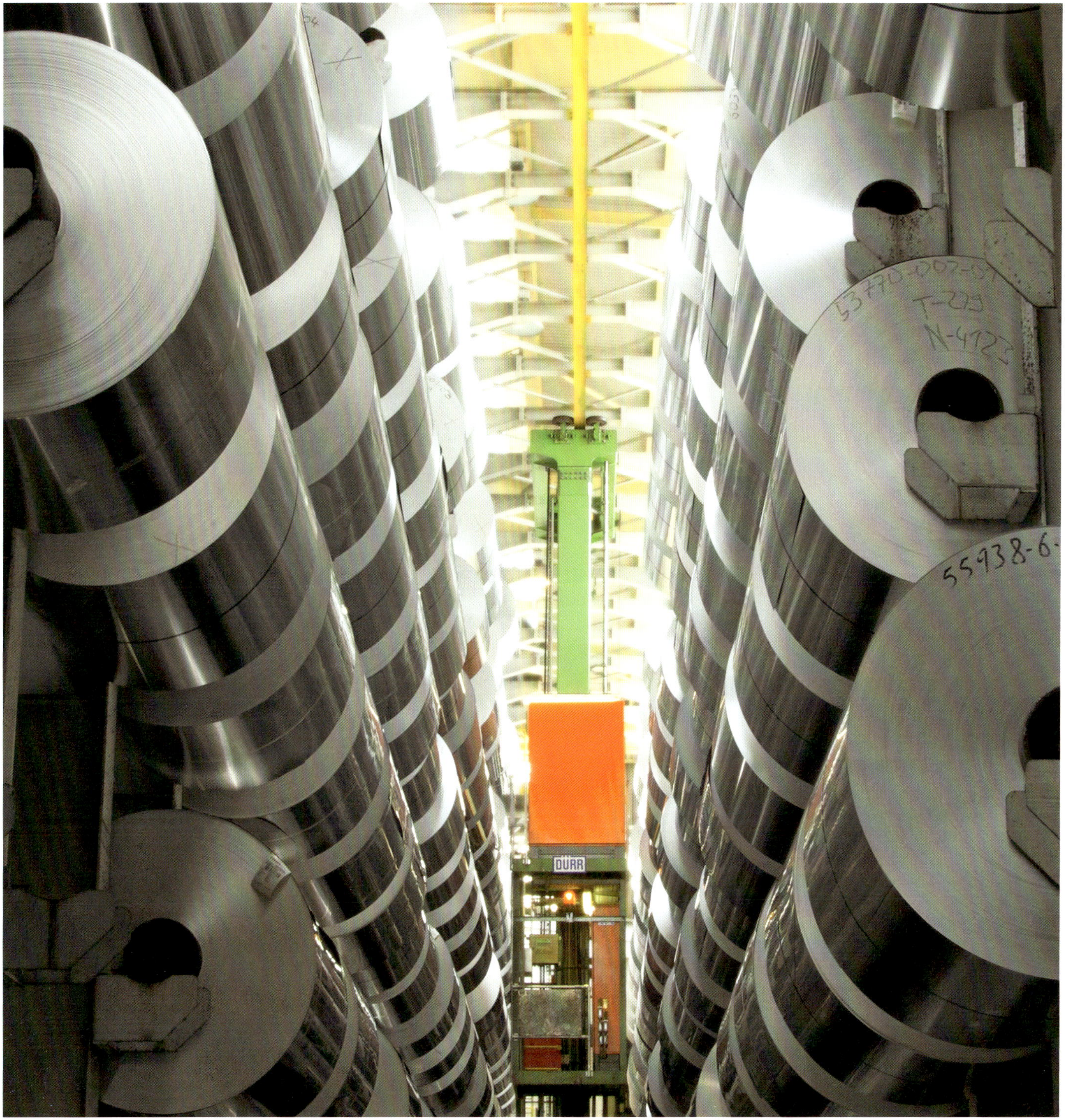
DÜRR
55938-6-

GEMEINSAM INNOVATIV
INNOVATION THROUGH CO-OPERATION

INNOVATIONSALLIANZ. Ein weitreichendes Hochschulnetzwerk dient nicht nur der Forschung, sondern kann auch der Wirtschaft eine besondere Hilfestellung bieten. 2007 haben 23 Universitäten und Fachhochschulen auch deshalb die Innovations-Allianz der nordrhein-westfälischen Hochschulen gegründet. Deutschlands größtes Hochschulbündnis bietet sich Hochschulen, Unternehmen, Kommunen und sozialen Einrichtungen als gemeinsame Plattform für Kooperationen an.

Das Netzwerk dient dem Transfer von wissenschaftlicher Expertise in die Praxis. Kleine und mittlere Unternehmen aus Nordrhein-Westfalen erhalten von der InnovationsAllianz Gutscheine, mit denen das Bündnis Forschungsaufträge durch Landesmittel mitfinanziert. Viele Veranstaltungen zu Forschungsthemen bringen künftige Partner zusammen, alle zwei Jahre findet der „InnovationsDialog NRW" statt. Auch stärkt die InnovationsAllianz vernetzte Forschung und Wissenstransfer unter den beteiligten Hochschulen. Weiterhin vertritt das Bündnis aktiv und kompetent die Leistungen des Forschungsstandorts Nordrhein-Westfalen überregional und international.

INNOVATIONSALLIANZ (ALLIANCE FOR INNOVATION). An extensive network of universities doesn't just serve to promote research, but can also be of particular assistance to the economy. Realising this, 23 universities and polytechnics formed the InnovationsAllianz of North Rhine-Westphalia in 2007. Germany's biggest alliance of universities offers a common platform of co-operation for universities, companies, communities and social institutions.

The network helps put scientific expertise into practice. Small and medium-sized enterprises in North Rhine-Westphalia get credit notes from the InnovationsAllianz, with which the alliance co-finances research assignments through state funding. Potential partners can interface at the various fora on research topics; the "InnovationsDialog NRW" is held every two years. InnovationsAllianz also consolidates interactive research and knowledge transfer among the participating universities. Additionally, the alliance actively and efficiently promotes North Rhine-Westphalia's achievements beyond regional and national borders.

Bestleistung: Größtes Hochschulbündnis in Deutschland
Region: Düsseldorf
Ort: Düsseldorf

Best performance: Germany's biggest alliance of universities
Region: Duesseldorf
Place: Duesseldorf

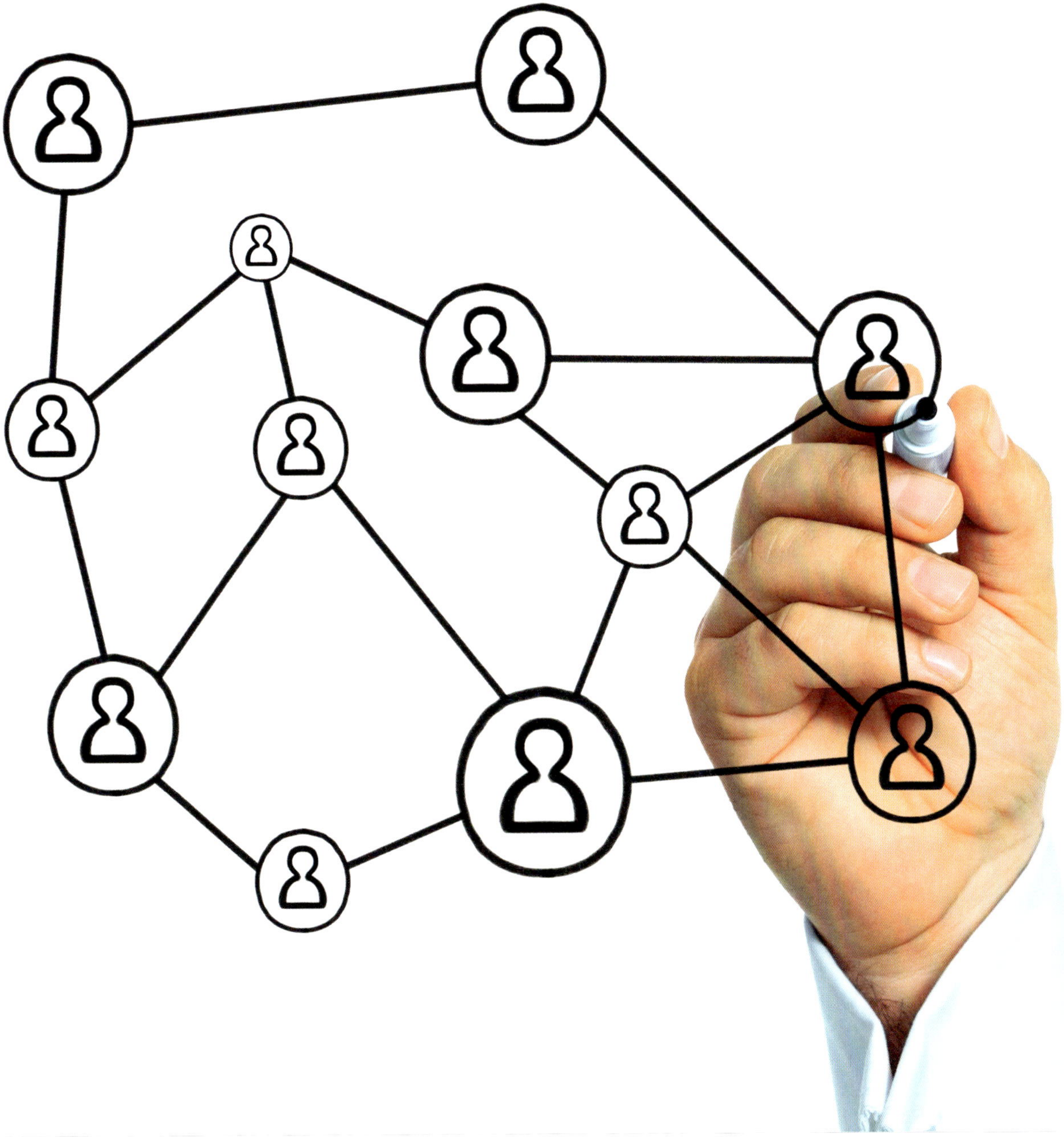

AUSZEICHNUNG FÜR GROSSE EUROPÄER
AWARD FOR GREAT EUROPEANS

INTERNATIONALER KARLSPREIS ZU AACHEN. Als Karl der Große mit Anfang 20 den Thron bestieg, war Europa in Aufruhr. Nach 47-jähriger Herrschaft wurde er am 28. Januar 814 in Aachen beigesetzt – und hat ein besseres Europa hinterlassen. Der Kaiser des „Heiligen Römischen Reiches deutscher Nation" herrschte über ein riesiges Imperium, oft wird er auch „Vater Europas" genannt.

Zu Recht prangt sein Konterfei deshalb auf der Medaille des neuen Preises, den Aachener Bürger Ende 1949 ins Leben riefen. Nach dem Zweiten Weltkrieg hatten diese genug von Schrecken, Diktatur und geistiger Manipulation. Es sollte ein Freiheitspreis wie auch eine ethische Verpflichtung werden – für herausragende Persönlichkeiten, die sich um Europa verdient gemacht haben. Der Internationale Karlspreis zu Aachen zählt längst zu den bedeutendsten europäischen Auszeichnungen.

Von Angela Merkel über Bill Clinton, François Mitterrand und Helmut Kohl bis hin zu Winston Churchill: Über 50 Menschen wurde bereits die Medaille verliehen – für ihre besonderen Verdienste im Zeichen eines friedlichen und vereinten Europas.

INTERNATIONAL CHARLEMAGNE PRIZE OF AACHEN. Europe was in turmoil when Charles the Great ascended the throne in his early twenties. After a 47 year reign he was interred on 28th January 814 in Aachen leaving behind a better Europe. The emperor of the "Holy Roman Empire of the German Nation" ruled over a vast empire: he is often also called "The Father of Europe".

It is only befitting then that his portrait be emblazoned on the medal of the new prize, instituted by the citizens of Aachen at the end of 1949. By the end of the Second World War they had had enough of the horror, dictatorship and psychological manipulation. This was to be both a peace prize and be an ethical obligation for towering personalities, who had rendered outstanding services to Europe. The International Charlemagne Prize of Aachen has long been among the most significant European prizes.

From Angela Merkel to Bill Clinton, Francois Mitterrand to Helmut Kohl right back to Winston Churchill, over 50 people have been awarded this medal for their exceptional services in the cause of a peaceful and united Europe.

Bestleistung: Eine der bedeutendsten europäischen Auszeichnungen
Region: Aachen
Ort: Aachen

Best performance: One of Europe's most significant awards
Region: Aachen
Place: Aachen

DER INTERNATIONALE
KARLSPREIS
ZU AACHEN
DER INTERNATIONALE
KARLSPREIS
ZU AACHEN
DER INTERNATIONALE
KARLSPREIS
ZU AACHEN

BÜROSTUHL SPART ENERGIE
AN OFFICE CHAIR THAT SAVES ENERGY

IQFY. Wenn ein Mitarbeiter des Iserlohner Bauamts sein Büro verlässt, geht das Licht aus. Kurz darauf sinkt die Heizungstemperatur um vier Grad Celsius. Alles ganz automatisch und ohne Zutun des Mitarbeiters – wie von Geisterhand. Doch dahinter steckt der IQfy Funkstuhl – eine bahnbrechende Erfindung, mit der sich über den Bürostuhl Energie sparen lässt. Alle Arbeitsplätze der Abteilung sind damit ausgestattet.

Die innovative Sitzgelegenheit ist der weltweit einzige kabellose Präsenzmelder zur Energieeinsparung: Ein batterie- und wartungsfreier Drucksensor, der sich in das Polster fast aller gängigen Bürostühle integrieren lässt, registriert, ob der Mitarbeiter an seinem Arbeitsplatz sitzt oder nicht und reguliert dementsprechend Beleuchtung, Heizung, Stromgeräte und Lüftung.

Mit dem IQfy Funkstuhl lassen sich 40 Prozent der Heiz- und Stromkosten einsparen, erfunden wurde er 2005 im sauerländischen Balve von Klaus Kleine. Der Tüftler vertreibt die mehrfach ausgezeichnete Lösung mittlerweile europaweit – denn die Aussicht, per Bürostuhl Energie zu sparen, begeistert über die deutschen Grenzen hinweg.

IQFY. When an employee of the Building Inspection Bureau of Iserlohn leaves his office, the lights switch off. Heating is then soon reduced by four degrees Celsius. All this takes place fully automatically and unassisted by any employee, as if by magic. Not so! What performs this miracle is actually the IQfy chair – a groundbreaking invention that uses integrated wireless technology to save energy. All workplaces in the department are now equipped with the system.

This innovative seating is world's only wireless presence detector for the conservation of energy. A battery- and maintenance-free pressure sensor that can be integrated into the cushion of almost any modern office chair, it registers whether an employee is sitting on it or not and adjusts lighting, heating, electrical appliances and air conditioning to suit.

Invented in 2005 by Klaus Kleine of Balve in Sauerland, IQfy chairs deliver savings on heating and power costs of up to 40 per cent. This innovator now markets his multi award-winning concept all over Europe. The prospect of saving energy via the office chair clearly inspires many beyond the German borders.

Bestleistung: Innovative Energiesteuerung im Büro
Region: Südwestfalen
Ort: Meinerzhagen

Best performance: Innovative energy control in an office
Region: Suedwestfalen
Place: Meinerzhagen

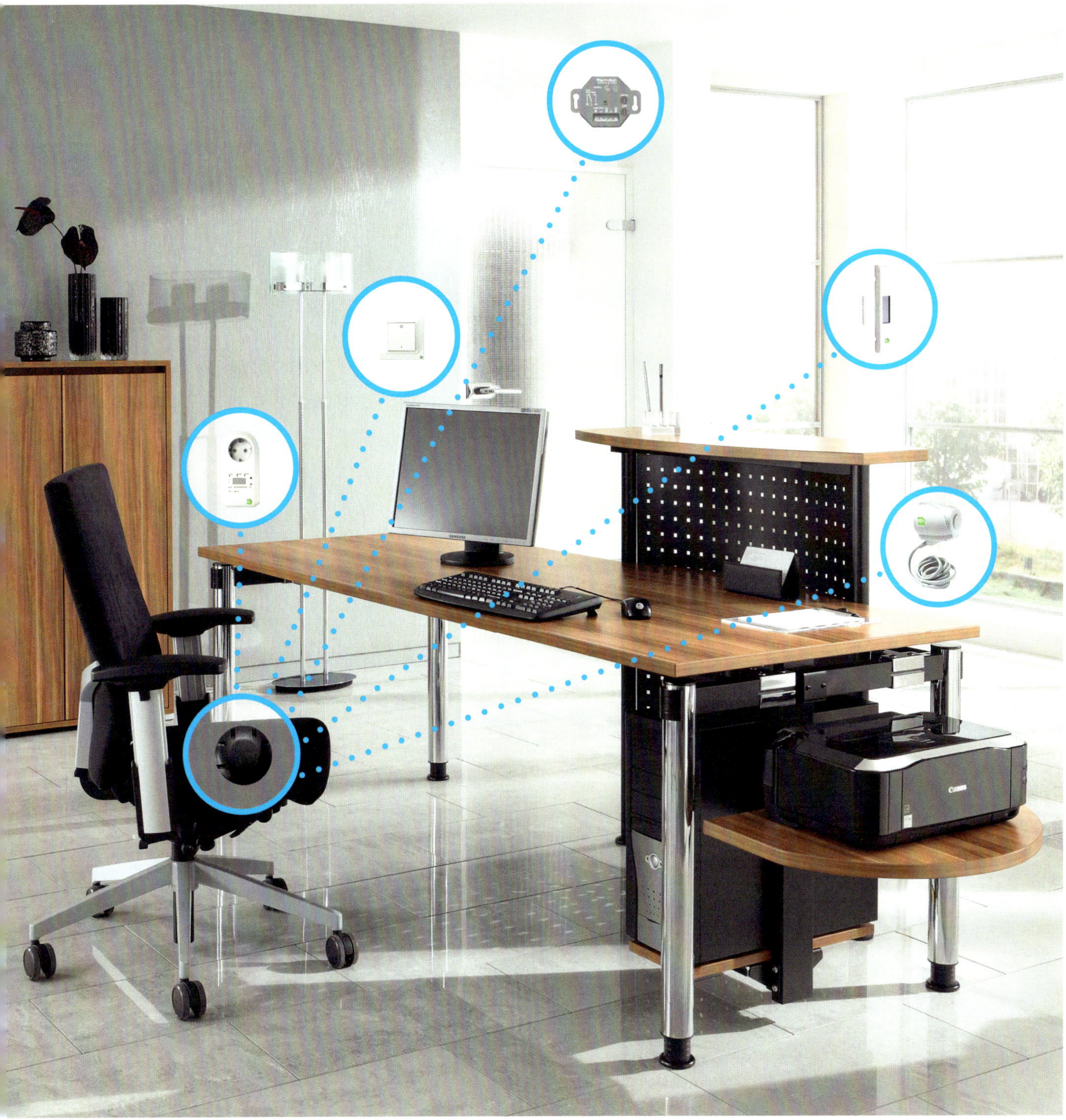

EIN IRRES SPIELFELD
A MIND-BOGGLING PLAYGROUND

IRRLAND. Am Eingang stehen Bollerwagen für Getränke, Grillgut und Gepäck. Damit ziehen die Familien los ins Pflanzenlabyrinth, auf der Suche nach Freizeitspaß und Erholung. Sie befinden sich in einer riesigen, grünen Oase mit über 300.000 Quadratmetern – überdachte Sitz- und Grillplätze stehen überall bereit. Haben die Eltern ein gutes Plätzchen gefunden, flitzen die Kleinen los. Für sie ist Irrland ein Paradies: die weltgrößte, frei bespielbare Fläche.

Überall wird getobt, geklettert und gestaunt: Mehr als 80 Attraktionen, 28 Abenteuerrutschen und viele streichelbare Tiere wollen entdeckt werden. Irrland ist Abenteuerspielplatz, Bauernhof und Erlebnislabyrinth zugleich. 500.000 Besucher zieht es jährlich aufs Land in die Nähe von Kevelaer und der niederländischen Grenze. Dies liegt sicher auch an der konsequenten Familienfreundlichkeit mit niedrigen Eintrittspreisen und erwünschter Selbstverpflegung.

Die neueste Attraktion: Irrland International, der erste bespielbare Flughafen der Welt mit echten Flugzeugen, Feuerwehrautos und einem Tower. Abenteuerpilot für einen Tag – Ihre Kinder werden begeistert sein.

IRRLAND. There are trolleys at the entrance for drinks, barbecue items and baggage. Families set off with them into the shrub labyrinth in pursuit of recreation and relaxation. They enter an immense oasis of greenery, 300,000 square metres to be precise; canopied seating areas and inviting barbecue areas all over the place. Once parents settle down in a spot, children begin to play around. Irrland is a paradise for them. The biggest playground in the world.

Watch the children climb and jump around, sense the wonderment everywhere: over 80 attractions, 28 adventure rides and a pets zoo with a lot of animals are waiting to be discovered. Irrland is an adventure playground, barnyard and exciting leisure-labyrinth all rolled into one. It attracts 500,000 visitors annually to the countryside close to Kevelaer and the Dutch border. Clearly geared towards families, the low entry fees and desired self-catering facilities certainly speak for the numbers.

The latest attraction: Irrland International, the first make-believe airport in the world to play in, with real aeroplanes, fire engines and a control tower. The very idea of being an adventure pilot for a day is sure to make your children all agog.

Bestleistung: Größte Spielfläche Deutschlands
Region: Niederrhein
Ort: Kevelaer

Best performance: Biggest playground of Germany
Region: Lower Rhine
Place: Kevelaer

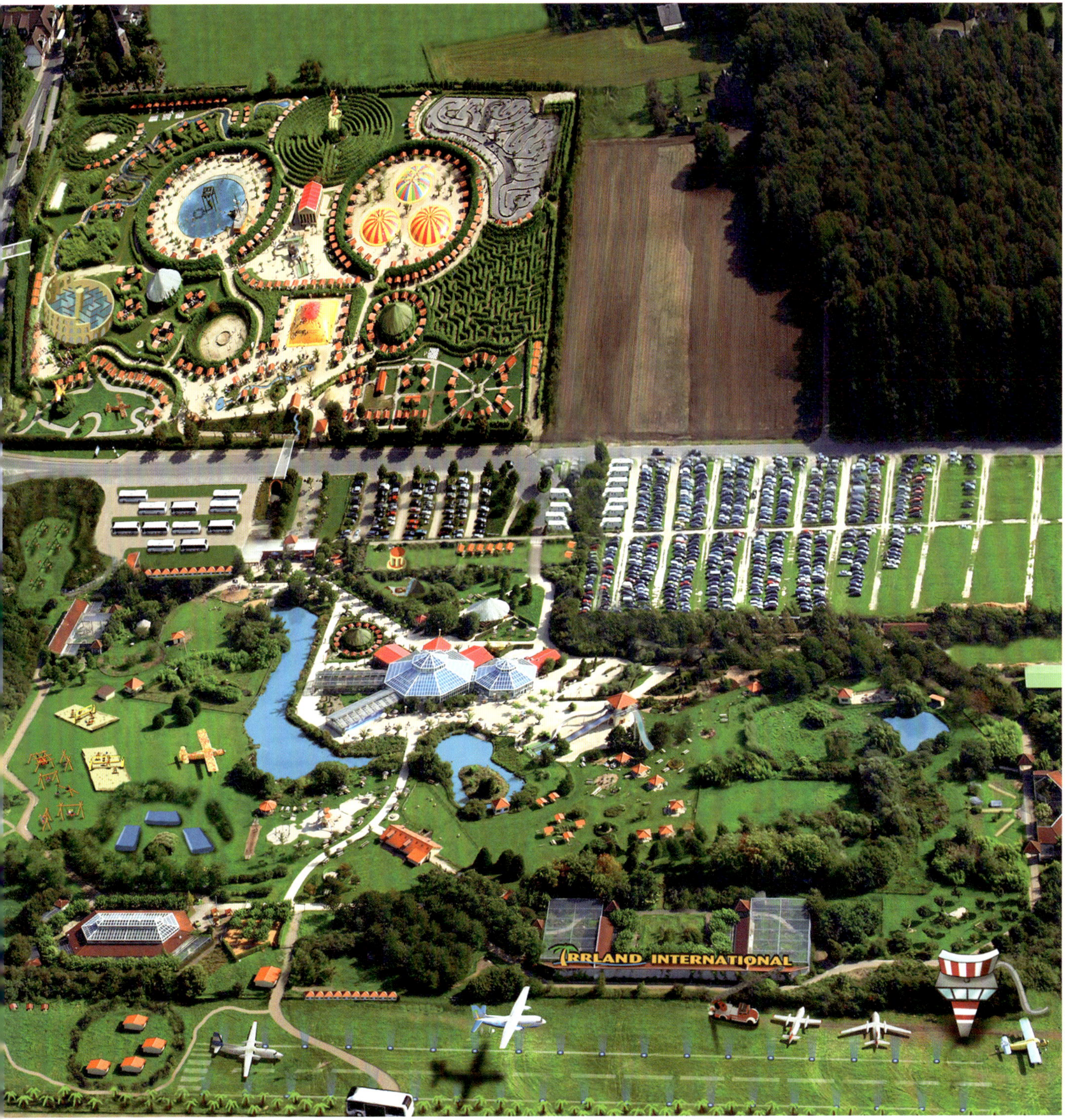
IRRLAND INTERNATIONAL

GESAMTKUNSTWERK MIT HUT
ONE GREAT WORK OF ART WEARING A HAT

JOSEPH BEUYS. Fettstuhl, Honigpumpe am Arbeitsplatz, Filzdecke auf Schlitten, 7.000 Eichen, verstörende Darbietungen mit totem Hasen und ausgesperrtem Publikum. Doch der Mensch steht bei ihm im Zentrum, ist selbst Ästhetik, Material, Kunstwerk. „Jeder Mensch ein Künstler" – und mittendrin, als Gesamtkunstwerk und stets mit Filzhut: Joseph Beuys (* 1921 in Krefeld, † 1986 in Düsseldorf), einer der weltweit bedeutendsten Künstler der Nachkriegszeit.

Er ist starker Symboliker, Provokateur, mit zunehmendem Alter stark politisch Engagierter. Seine Themen sind klar erkennbar, etwa Freiheit, Energie oder Geheimnisse, doch alle Referenzen schlagen fehl. Seine Werke sind Sinn-Generatoren: Sie stellen Fragen, bieten aber keine platten Botschaften – die muss der Betrachter selbst finden. Dafür liebt Beuys den Dialog: Über sein Werk, seine Aktionen, als Kunstprofessor und durch seine sozial-politischen Aktivitäten. Er entwirft das Konzept der sozialen Plastik, tritt streitbar ein für seinen Anspruch auf gesellschaftliche Veränderung. So ist seine Relevanz vor allem aus der Gesamtsicht zu erkennen – als sein größtes Kunstwerk gilt vielen dabei er selbst: Joseph Beuys.

JOSEPH BEUYS. Installations like Fat Chair, Honey Pump at the Workplace, Felt-Blanket on Sled, 7,000 oak trees and edgy performances with a dead hare and debarred audience – yet the human being was central to him. "Everyone is an artist"; humans beings form the very aesthetics, material and work of art. Amidst all this as one great work of art was the man sporting a trilby at all times: Joseph Beuys (* 1921 in Krefeld, † 1986 in Duesseldorf), one of world's most influential artists of the post-war era.

He was a fervent symbolist, provocateur and with age engaged intensely with politics. His themes are clearly discernible like freedom, energy or mysteries, yet all points of reference fall short. His works trigger the quest for meaning, ask questions but have no banal messages to offer. The viewer has to figure it out on his own. Instead Beuys loved dialogue, be it on his works, his actions, as art professor or through his socio-political pursuits. He crafted the concept of social architecture, acrimoniously claiming a participatory role in changing society. His relevance can thus be culled primarily from an overarching perspective and for many his greatest work of art is Joseph Beuys, the man himself.

Bestleistung: Einer der bedeutendsten Künstler
Region: Düsseldorf
Ort: Düsseldorf

Best performance: One of the most distinguished artists
Region: Duesseldorf
Place: Duesseldorf

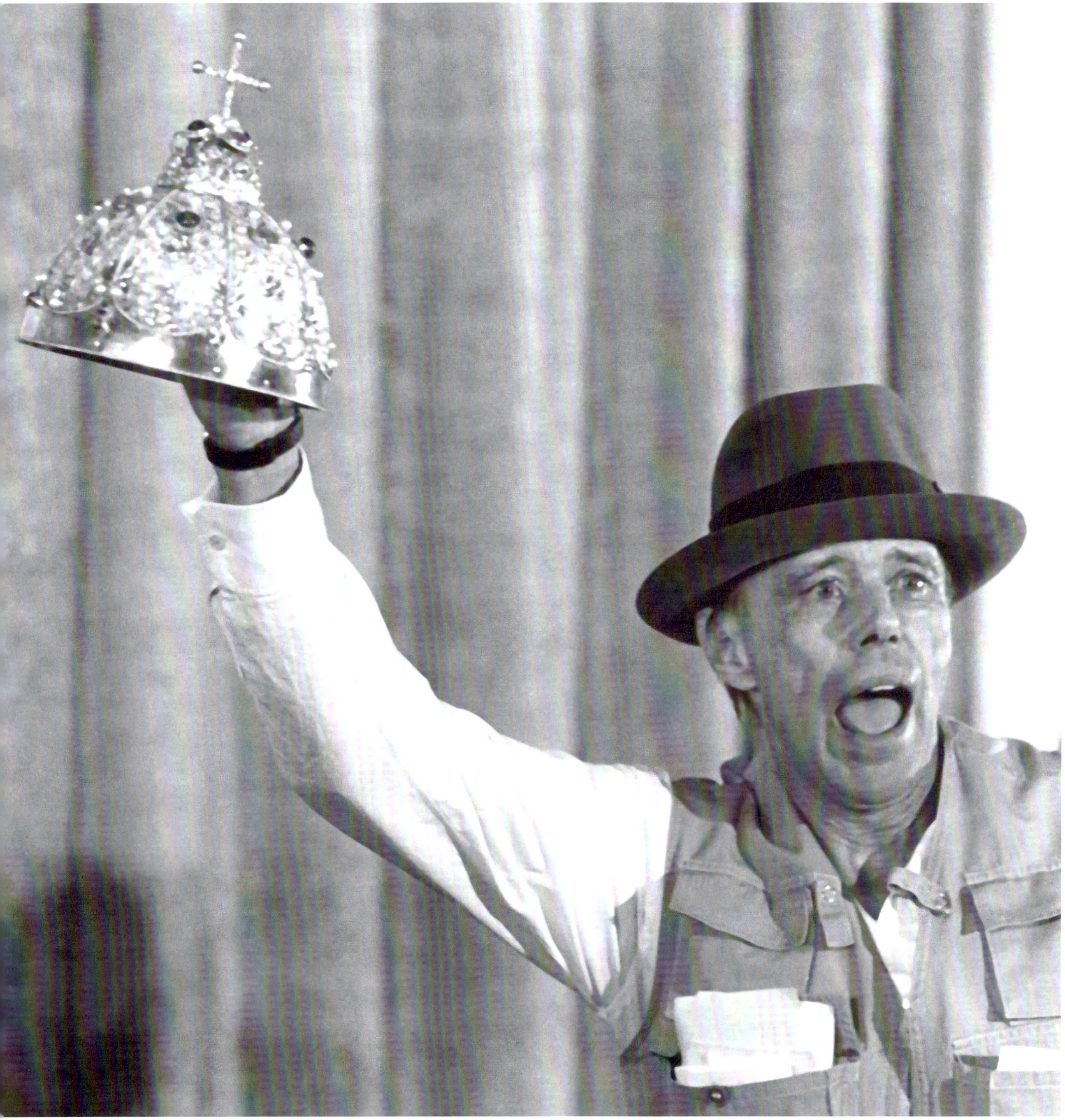

BAGGER-KÖNIGE IM SAND
VOLLEYBALL KINGS IN THE SAND

JULIUS BRINK UND JONAS RECKERMANN. London, im Sommer 2012: Sie sind gerade erneut Europameister geworden, sind mehrfache deutsche Meister und Weltmeister von 2009. Nun steht das Duo im Finale der Olympischen Sommerspiele und tritt nach sechs Vorrundensiegen immer noch als klarer Außenseiter auf dem acht mal acht Meter großen Sandfeld an. Emanuel Rego und Alison Cerrutti heißen ihre Gegner. Ausgerechnet die amtierenden Weltmeister aus dem traditionell starken Brasilien, das zusammen mit den USA seit Jahren den Beachvolleyball dominiert.

Bis jetzt: Aufschlag, Block, Zuspiel – vier Jahre sind die beiden Münsterländer und Wahlkölner bereits ein Team. Julius Brink und Jonas Reckermann ergänzen sich perfekt. Das Duo kämpft auf Sand, vor 15.000 Zuschauern auf der Horse Guards Parade. Sie pritschen, baggern und schlagen, kämpfen bis zum Schluss. Und gewinnen am Ende eines dramatischen Spiels olympisches Gold – dies ist das erste für ein deutsches wie auch ein europäisches Beachvolleyball-Team überhaupt.

JULIUS BRINK AND JONAS RECKERMANN. They recently regained the title of European Champions, have been frequent German Champions and were World Champions in 2009. Yet despite the six victories in the preliminaries, here were the duo in London, summer 2012, clearly competing as underdogs. Of all people, the reigning Brazilian world champions, Emanuel Rego and Alison Cerrutti, were to be their opponents on the 8 x 8 m sand court at the Summer Olympic finals. Traditionally a strong side, Brazil has dominated beach volleyball along with USA for years.

Until now, that is. Serve, block, pass: Julius Brink and Jonas Reckermann both from Muensterland have played as a team for four years now and complement each other perfectly. The duo is fighting on the sands in front of a crowd of 15,000 at the Horse Guards Parade. Passing, serving and striking they battle to the end, to emerge as winners of the Olympic Gold from a thrilling match. A first not only for a German team but a European one too!

Bestleistung: Erste deutsche Olympiasieger im Beachvolleyball
Region: Münsterland
Ort: Münster

Best performance: The first Olympic winners in beach volleyball from Germany
Region: Muensterland
Place: Muenster

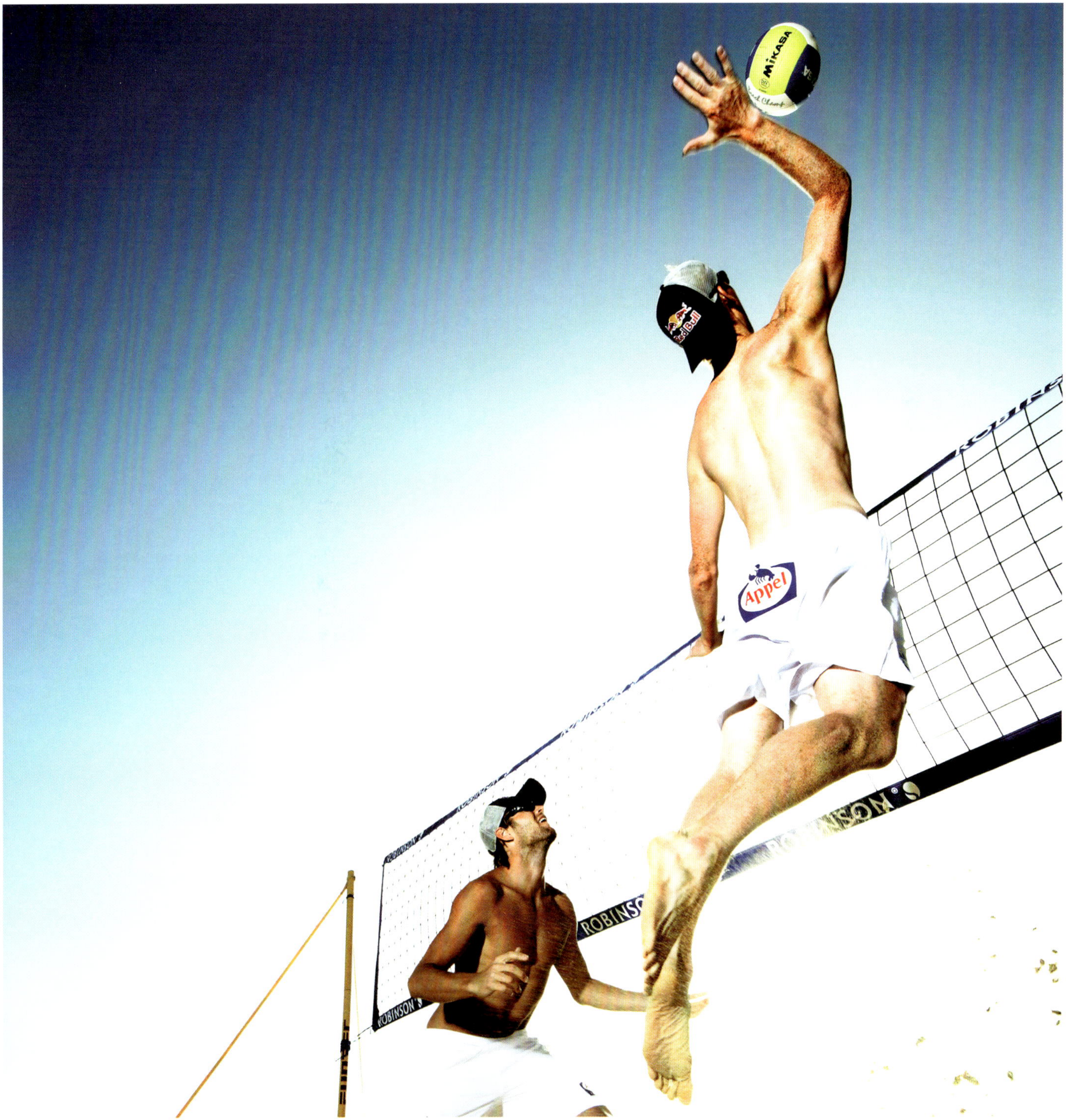
MIKASA
Red Bull
Appel
ROBINSON
ROBINSON
ROBINSON

DAS GOTISCHE MEISTERWERK
THE GOTHIC MASTERPIECE

KÖLNER DOM. Traditionell liebt der Kölner sein Kölsch, seinen Karneval und natürlich – seinen Dom. Doch nicht nur der heimatverbundene Stadtbürger gerät beim Anblick der beiden Domspitzen in Verzückung: Der Kölner Dom ist mit jährlich sechs Millionen Besuchern aus aller Welt die meistbesichtigte Sehenswürdigkeit Deutschlands.

Die „Hohe Domkirche zu Köln" war noch bei ihrer Vollendung 1880 das höchste Gebäude der Welt, heute gilt die gotische Kathedrale mit ihren 157,38 Metern als zweithöchster Kirchenbau Europas. Trotz der über 600-jährigen Bauzeit entspricht die Architektur größtenteils den Plänen des Mittelalters. Die Westfassade des Doms verfügt zusammen mit den beiden Türmen über eine Gesamtfläche von 7.100 Quadratmetern und ist somit die größte Kirchenfassade der Welt.

1996 wurde der Kölner Dom als europäisches Meisterwerk gotischer Architektur in die Liste des UNESCO-Weltkulturerbes aufgenommen. Zu den Besuchermagneten im Innern der katholischen Kirche zählen der Reliquienschrein mit den Gebeinen der Heiligen Drei Könige und seit 2007 das vom renommierten deutschen Künstler Gerhard Richter gestaltete Fenster im Südquerhaus.

COLOGNE CATHEDRAL. A native of Cologne is known by his love of Kölsch (beer), carnival and of course the cathedral. The sight of the two cathedral spires enthrals not just the natives but six million visitors from all corners of the world annually, making the Cologne Cathedral the most visited landmark of Germany.

When completed, in 1880, the "High Cathedral of Cologne" was the highest building in the world. At 157.38 metres, the Gothic cathedral is currently Europe's second-tallest church building. The architecture kept to the mediaeval plans for the most part, despite 600 years of construction. The West face of the cathedral, including the two towers, has a surface area of 7,100 square metres making it the largest church facade in the world.

A European masterpiece of Gothic architecture, the cathedral was declared a World Heritage Site by UNESCO in 1996. The reliquary of the remains of The Three Kings inside the Catholic church draws scores of visitors, as does the stained glass in the southern transept window, created by the famous German artist, Gerhard Richter, in 2007.

Bestleistung: Meistbesuchte Sehenswürdigkeit Deutschlands
Region: Köln / Bonn
Ort: Köln

Best performance: The most visited monument of Germany
Region: Cologne / Bonn
Place: Cologne

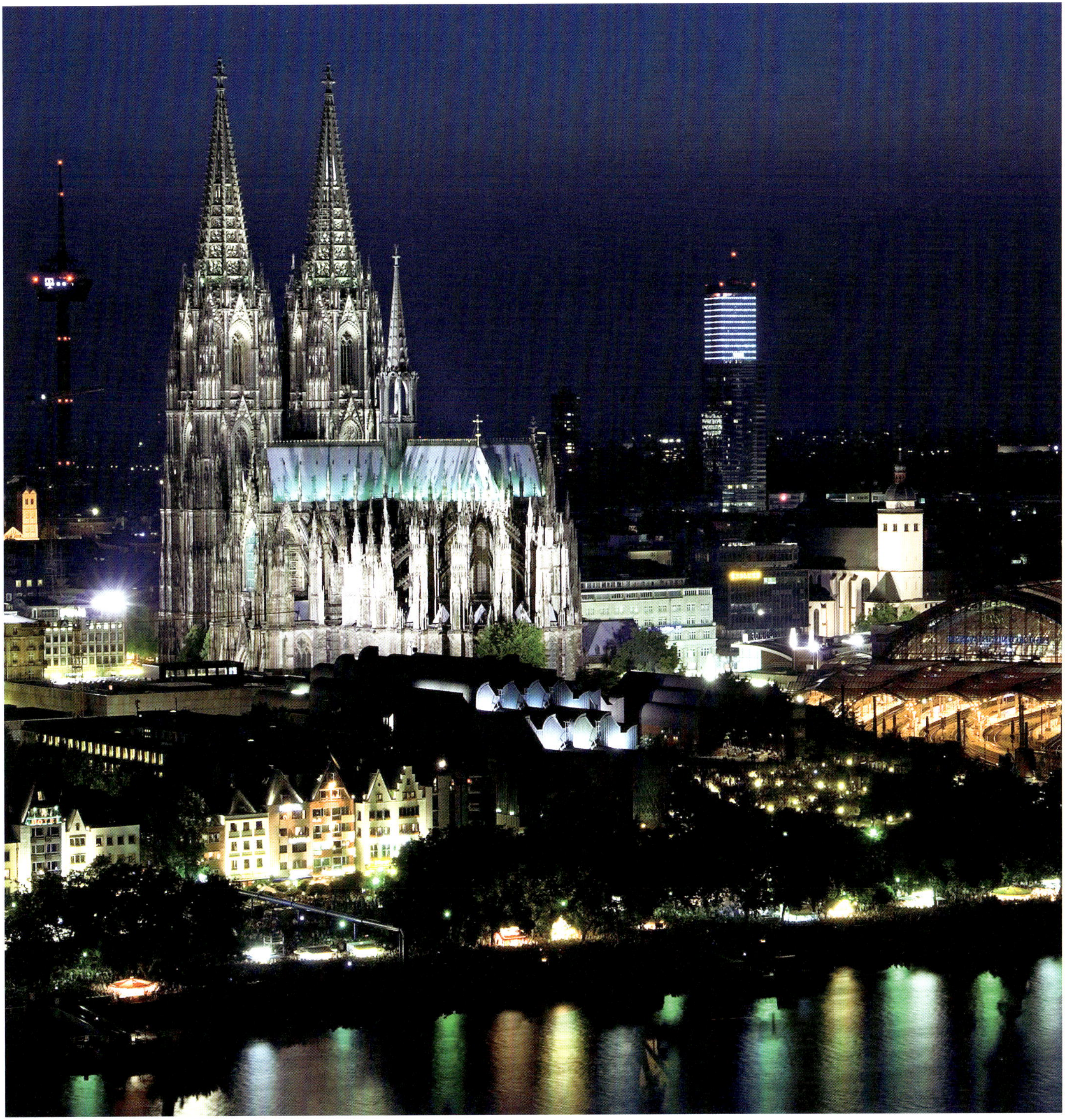

MEHR ALS EIN KARNEVALSZUG
MORE THAN A CARNIVAL PARADE

KÖLNER ROSENMONTAGSZUG. Der kunterbunte Karnevalszug, fast sieben Kilometer lang, schlängelt sich durch die Innenstadt, vorbei an einer Million Zuschauer. Ein Zug, der verbindet: Köln mit seinen Bürgern und Gästen, aber auch mit seiner Tradition: Deutschlands größter Rosenmontagszug und Europas größter Volksfest-Umzug bewegt seit 1823 die Kölner Herzen. Und die Kölner Wirtschaft: Rund eine halbe Milliarde Euro setzen Umzüge, Sitzungen und der Kneipenkarneval jährlich um. Tickets und Verzehr, aber auch Taxifahrten, Flugreisen und Kostüme lassen die ganze Region profitieren und sichern rund 5.000 Arbeitsplätze.

Doch der Karneval leistet viel mehr: 30.000 Kölner engagieren sich ehrenamtlich in über 160 Karnevalsgesellschaften – das ganze Jahr über! Netzwerke werden gebildet, Veranstaltungen organisiert, rund 1,5 Millionen Euro Spenden für soziale Projekte gesammelt. Die aktive Brauchtumspflege des Karnevals ist auch eine gesellschaftliche Brücke, offen für alle und alle Richtungen: Auf dem gesellschaftlichen Parkett hilft sie, Kunden zu pflegen, Mitarbeiter zu motivieren und Zugezogene zu integrieren. Von Alt bis Jung, von unten bis oben: Der Kölner Karneval bietet Menschen die schönsten Verbindungen an.

THE SHROVE MONDAY PARADE IN COLOGNE. The motley carnival parade winds almost seven kilometres through the inner city past a million spectators. A parade for natives and visitors to bond not just with Cologne, but also with its tradition. Since 1823 Germany's biggest Shrove Monday parade and Europe's largest folk festival procession has stirred hearts in Cologne, making its economy richer every year by about half a billion Euros from the processions, meetings and pub-hopping revelry. The entire region profits from ticket sales and consumption, cab rides and air travel, costume sales and creation of about 5,000 jobs.

And yet there is more to the carnival: 30,000 denizens of Cologne offer voluntary services all year round to 160 carnival societies! There is networking, organisation of events and about 1.5 million Euros collected in donations for social projects. Keeping alive the carnival tradition also means forming a social bridge open to all, in every sense. On the corporate front it helps cultivate clients, motivate employees and integrate newcomers. To old and young, from top to bottom the Cologne carnival offers people the best connections.

Bestleistung: Europas größter Rosenmontagszug
Region: Köln / Bonn
Ort: Köln

Best performance: Europe's biggest Shrove Monday parade
Region: Cologne / Bonn
Place: Cologne

SCHLECKER
Martinspförtchen
7
GRUPPE
Gougel
Street View
Schnüsse Tring
DIE JOHANNITER

SÜSSES FÜR DIE QUEEN
DESSERTS FIT FOR THE QUEEN

KONDITOREI HEINEMANN. Champagnertrüffel gibt es viele, doch ganz besondere findet man zum Beispiel in den Düsseldorfer Cafés von Heinemann: Die Konditorei erfand die weltbekannte Praline und fertigt noch heute die besten ihrer Art von Hand – das wissen sogar der Papst und die Queen. Herzlich willkommen in einem der führenden Familienbetriebe des europäischen Konditorhandwerks!

Hermann und Hanni Heinemann gründeten vor über 80 Jahren die erste Konditorei Heinemann im niederrheinischen Mönchengladbach, 1992 übernahm ihr Sohn Heinz-Richard den Betrieb. Der diplomierte Konditor- und Confiseurmeister lernte in Spitzenbetrieben in Paris, Lausanne und Zürich – heute betreibt er Konditoreien mit Café-Restaurant in Duisburg, Mönchengladbach, Krefeld, Neuss sowie Düsseldorf.

Vater Hermann gab seinem Sohn schon früh eine klare Anweisung mit auf den Weg: „Verwendet nur die besten Zutaten: frischeste Butter, erste Sahne und feinste Kakaobohnen. Bloß keine Konservierungsstoffe, sonst gibt's Ärger!" Daran hat sich Heinz-Richard Heinemann bis heute gehalten – und der Erfolg gibt ihm recht: 2012 zeichnete die Vereinigung Euro-Toques das Unternehmen mit dem „Pastry Award" aus.

KONDITOREI HEINEMANN. Champagne truffles are not uncommon but for really special ones you need to head for places such as the Heinemann cafés in Duesseldorf. Heinemann invented the world-famous praline and creates the best hand-made ones even today. Even the Pope or the Queen would endorse that! Meet one of Europe's first families in the business of handmade confectionery.

Hermann and Hanni Heinemann opened the first Heinemann pastry shop in Moenchengladbach, Lower Rhine, over 80 years ago. Their son Heinz-Richard took over in 1992. A qualified master confectioner, he honed his craft in top establishments in Paris, Lausanne and Zurich and now manages pastry shops with café-restaurants in Duisburg, Moenchengladbach, Krefeld, Neuss and Duesseldorf.

Hermann senior left his son with some sound early advice for the road ahead: "Use only the best ingredients: the freshest butter, premium cream and the finest cocoa beans. No preservatives ever, or else you'll have hell to pay!" Even now the son lives by those words and is crowned with success. In 2012, the association Euro-Toques honoured the company by awarding it its "Pastry Award".

Bestleistung: Die besten Champagnertrüffel der Welt
Region: Düsseldorf
Ort: Düsseldorf

Best performance: World's best champagne truffles
Region: Duesseldorf
Place: Duesseldorf

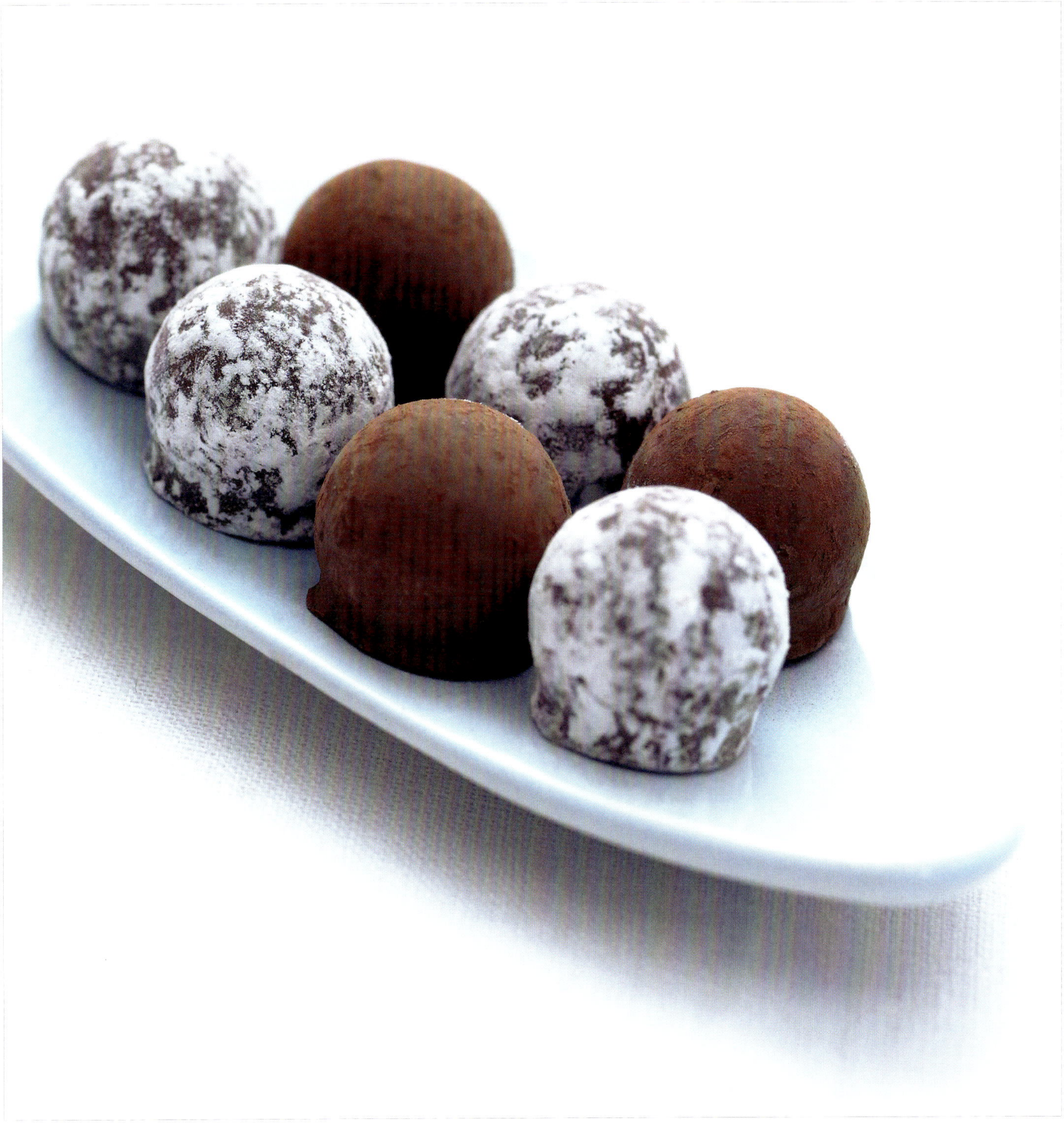

MEISTVERKAUFTES PILSENER BIER
THE TOP-SELLING PILSENER BEER

KROMBACHER BRAUEREI. Die Krombacher Brauerei, gegründet im gleichnamigen Ortsteil der Stadt Kreuztal, wird erstmals im Jahr 1803 urkundlich erwähnt. Zur damaligen Zeit holt Braumeister Johannes Haas das Wasser für die Hausbrauerei noch fassweise und mit dem Ochsenkarren von der Quelle im Westen des Dorfes zur Braustätte. Trotzdem hat die Brauerei schon einen beträchtlichen Erfolg. Bereits 1829 gibt es vertraglich fixierte Beziehungen zu den Veranstaltern des Olper Schützenfestes, das seitdem Jahr für Jahr mit Bier aus Krombach beliefert wird. Damals ging es um eine Lieferung von 25 Ohm, was nach heutiger Rechnung etwa 37,5 Hektolitern entspricht.

Mit einem Gesamtausstoß von 6,428 Millionen Hektolitern ist Krombacher heute eine der größten deutschen Privatbrauereien. Die Sorte Krombacher Pils ist mit 4,4 Millionen Hektolitern die meistgekaufte Pilsener Marke in Deutschland; das alkoholfreie Bier ist ebenfalls Marktführer in seiner Sparte. Die Brauerei ist einer der Hauptsponsoren in mehreren sportlichen Bereichen. Gesponsert werden unter anderem die Übertragungen der Formel 1, darüber hinaus ist man Partner der DFL und Sponsor der Bundesligisten Eintracht Frankfurt, VfB Stuttgart und VfL Wolfsburg.

KROMBACHER BREWERY. The brewery carrying the name of its birthplace, Krombach, a district of Kreuztal town, appears in official documents for the first time in 1803. In those days the master brewer, Johannes Haas, fetched water for this family-run brewery in barrels from a spring in the west of the village by ox carts. That notwithstanding the brewery met with substantial success. As early as 1829 a deal was made with the organisers of the Olpe Marksman's Festival to provide beer from Krombach. This contractual arrangement is still in place today. What was then a supply of 25 Ohm (an outdated German measurement for liquids) is the equivalent of 37.5 hectolitres today.

With a total production of 6.428 million hectolitres Krombacher ranks today among the largest privately owned German breweries. "Krombacher Pils" with a consumption of 4.4 million hectolitres is the top-selling Pilsener brand in Germany: the alcohol-free beer is likewise a market leader in its segment. The brewery is one of the main sponsors in various fields of sports, Formula 1 broadcasts being one of them. It is also the official partner of the DFL (German Football League) and sponsor of the Bundesliga football clubs Eintracht Frankfurt, VfB Stuttgart and VfL Wolfsburg.

Bestleistung: Meistverkauftes Pilsener Bier Deutschlands
Region: Südwestfalen
Ort: Kreuztal

Best performance: The largest selling Pilsener of Germany
Region: Suedwestfalen
Place: Kreuztal

MEISTERKUCHEN IN GROSSSERIE
LARGE-SCALE PRODUCTION OF CAKES BY MASTERS

KUCHENMEISTER. Mit dem Urgroßvater fing alles an: Kaum hatte Julius Trockels 1884 seine kleine Bäckerei in Soest eröffnet, erfand er einen neuartigen Ofen. Fast 130 Jahre und mehrere Generationen im Familienbetrieb später stellen 1.000 Mitarbeiter von Kuchenmeister an vier Standorten jährlich 92.000 Tonnen Konditorei- und Backwaren her. Die Kombination aus Bäckerhandwerk und Technik bestimmt auch heute das Unternehmen: eine ganze Abteilung mit 30 Ingenieuren und Spezialisten arbeitet an innovativen Fertigungsmethoden.

Kuchenmeister führt in Deutschland den Markt bei Fertigkuchen an, bei dem traditionellen Baumkuchen und bei Stollen ist man gar Weltmarktführer. Gebacken wird unter eigenem Namen oder als Handelsmarke. In 80 Länder wird geliefert, der Export steuert rund ein Drittel zum Unternehmensumsatz bei. Hans-Günther Trockels hat 1995 die Geschäftsführung von seinem Vater übernommen, gemeinsam mit seinen beiden Brüdern vermarktet er ein Sortiment mit ungefähr 40 Artikelgruppen und 450 Produkten.

Mitarbeiterverantwortung, schmackhafte Kuchen und innovatives Maschinen-Know-how – das sind die entscheidenden Zutaten für das Erfolgsrezept der Kuchenmeister GmbH.

KUCHENMEISTER. It all began with the great grandfather: barely had Julius Trockels opened his small bakery in Soest in 1884 when he devised a new kind of oven. Nearly 130 years later and down many generations of family business, 1,000 employees of Kuchenmeister join hands in producing 92,000 tonnes of confectionery and bakery products annually at four facilities. This mix of baking craft and technology continues to define the company today. An entire department of 30 engineers and specialists devotes itself to innovating manufacturing techniques.

Kuchenmeister dominates the market for ready-made cakes in Germany. It has, in fact, the largest share in the global market for traditional Baumkuchen (pyramid cakes) and Stollen (fruit loaf). Its products are sold both under its own name and as own label brands and supplied to 80 countries, with exports accounting for about a third of the company's turnover. Hans-Günther Trockels took over the reins from his father in 1995. Together with his brothers, he now markets an assortment of about 40 kinds of articles and 450 products.

Employee responsibility, delicious cakes and pioneering expertise in machinery – these are the vital ingredients of the recipe for success of Kuchenmeister GmbH.

Bestleistung: Führender Anbieter von Baumkuchen und Stollen
Region: Südwestfalen
Ort: Soest

Best performance: The biggest supplier of pyramid cakes and stollen
Region: Suedwestfalen
Place: Soest

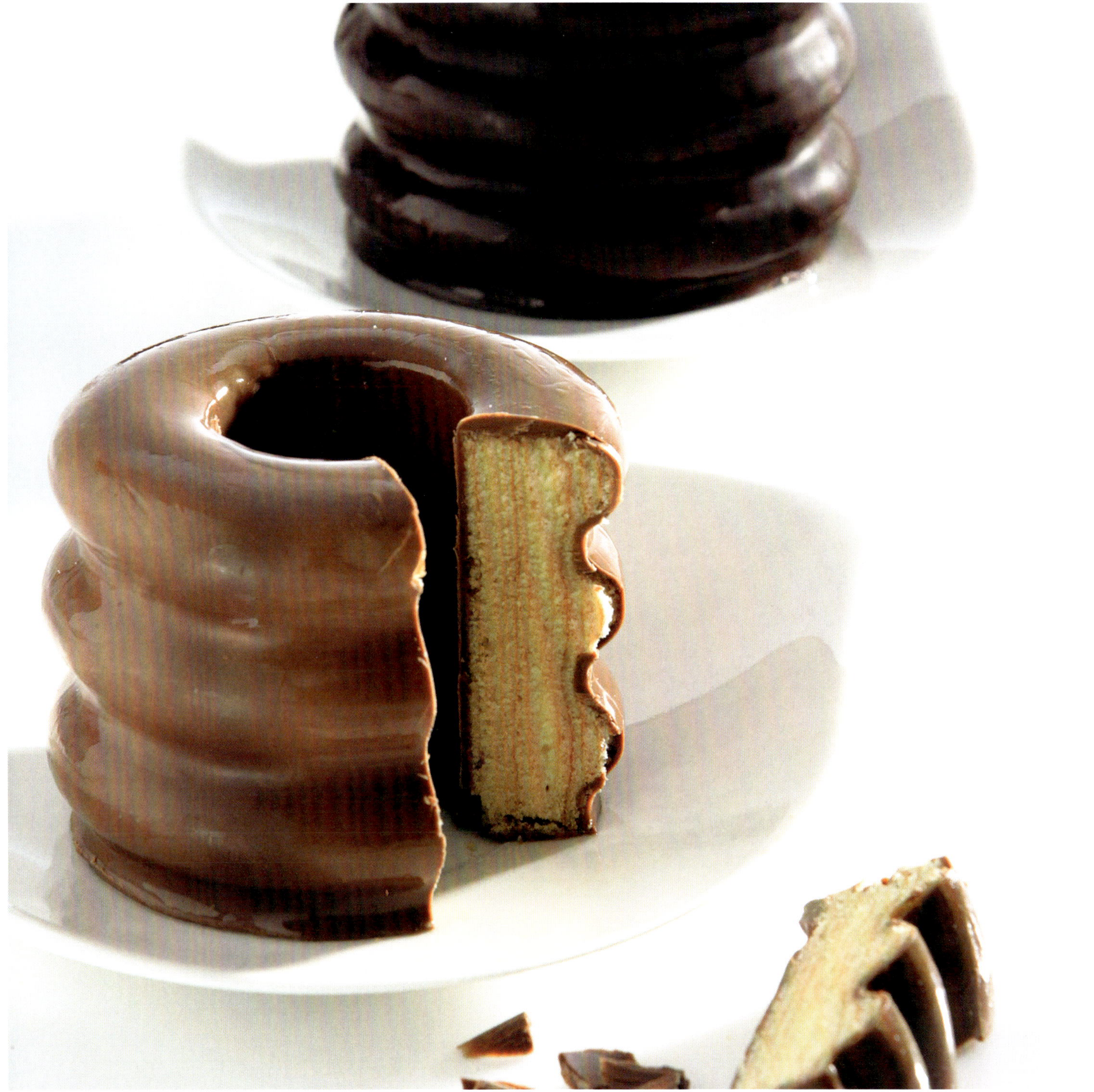

TALENTE SCHMIEDEN TALENTE
TALENTS SHAPE TALENTS

KUNSTAKADEMIE DÜSSELDORF. Vor 240 Jahren vom Kurfürsten Carl Theodor gegründet, ist die Hochschule der Kunst und der Künstler heute eine Einrichtung des Landes Nordrhein-Westfalen. Man setzt auf künstlerische Qualität, Vielfalt und Internationalität. Ihr Rektor Tony Cragg ist selbst ein bekannter Bildhauer. Im Geiste der freien Kunst gibt es diverse Fachbereiche, zum Beispiel Malerei, Bildhauerei, freie Grafik, aber auch Baukunst, Bühnenbild oder Fotografie sowie Video. Ein erfolgreiches Konzept – seit vielen Jahrzehnten.

Die Akademie wie auch ihre Künstler genießen international hohes Ansehen, schon im 19. Jahrhundert absolvierten viele berühmte Künstler die „Düsseldorfer Malerschule". Seit den 50er Jahren behauptet die Kunstakademie eine ähnlich bedeutende Stellung für die Gegenwartskunst. Die Künstler der Akademie repräsentieren die internationale Kunstszene, viele zählen zu ihren bekanntesten Protagonisten, etwa Joseph Beuys, Gerhard Richter, Katharina Grosse oder Jörg Immendorff. Zahlreiche der renommierten Professoren haben ursprünglich selbst an der Akademie studiert. Wenn Talente mit Weltniveau Talente schmieden ...

ART ACADEMY DUESSELDORF. This university for art and artists founded by Elector Carl Theodor 240 years ago is now a state institution in North Rhine-Westphalia. It is committed to artistic quality, range and transnational contemporaneity. Vice-chancellor Tony Cragg is a well-known sculptor in his own right. In the spirit of fine arts there is an array of disciplines including painting, sculpture, graphic arts, architecture, stage design and photography and video. The concept has been a proven success, for decades now, earning both the academy and its artists high international repute.

As early as the 19th century many famous artists graduated from the "Duesseldorf School of Painting". Since the 1950s, the academy has occupied a similarly prominent position in contemporary art. The artists of the academy represent the international art scene and many of them – such as Joseph Beuys, Gerhard Richter, Katharina Grosse and Jörg Immendorff – are its most celebrated trailblazers. A number of professors here are themselves alumni of this institution. When world-class talents shape talents, creativity reaches critical mass!

Bestleistung: Eine der renommiertesten Ausbildungsstätten für bildende Kunst in Europa
Region: Düsseldorf
Ort: Düsseldorf

Best performance: One of Europe's most renowned institution for instruction in fine arts
Region: Duesseldorf
Place: Duesseldorf

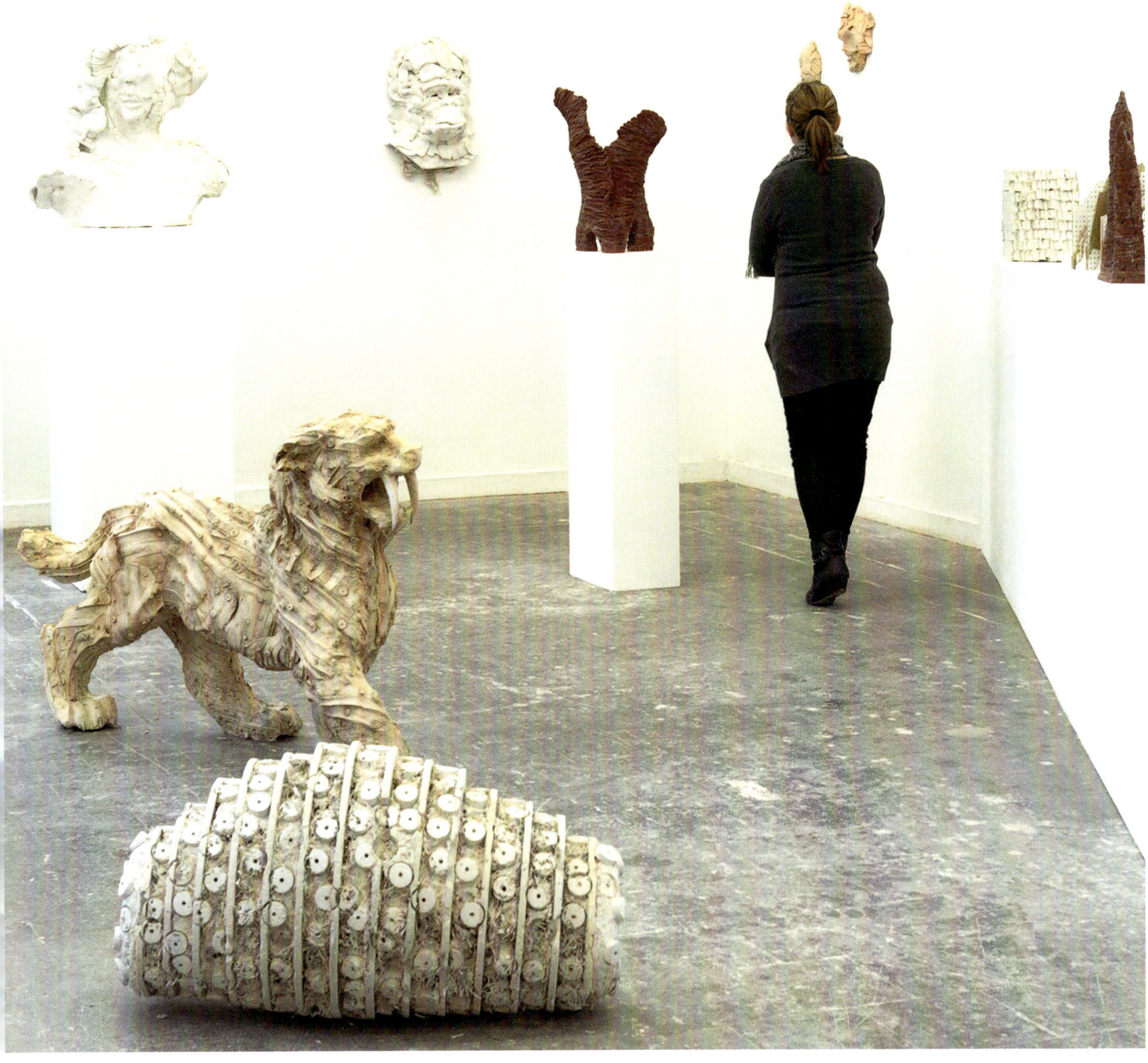

WENN KLEINES GANZ GROSS WIRD
WHEN TINY BECOMES TITANIC

LAVISION BIOTEC. Dreidimensionale Aufnahmen des Rückenmarks einer Maus oder detailreiche Ansichten menschlicher Zellen und Blutgefäße. Nicht möglich? Doch. Mit dem 3-D-Lichtblattmikroskop – entwickelt von LaVision BioTec und Experten des Instituts für Physikalische und Theoretische Chemie der Rheinischen Friedrich-Wilhelms-Universität Bonn. Die innovative Neuerung eröffnet ganz neue Perspektiven für die laserbasierte Mikroskopie.

Das Besondere an dem neuen Ansatz: Anders als bei herkömmlichen Mikroskopen beleuchtet ein Laser die Probe nicht von oben oder unten, sondern von der Seite. Dies geschieht mittels eines nur wenige Mikrometer dünnen Lichtblatts. Es entstehen bis zu 1.000 Bilder des Objekts, die dann im Computer zu einem 3-D-Datensatz zusammengesetzt werden. So können dreidimensionale Gewebe ab einem Volumen von ungefähr 0,5 Kubikmillimeter abgebildet werden.

Für das 3-D-Mikroskop erhielt das Bielefelder Biotech-Unternehmen, das 32 Mitarbeiter beschäftigt, den ZIM-Preis 2012. Das Bundesministerium zeichnet damit einmal im Jahr innovative mittelständische Unternehmen aus.

LAVISION BIOTEC. Think that 3D pictures of the spinal cord of a mouse or microscopic images of human cells and blood vessels are impossible? Then think again. LaVision BioTec and experts from the Institute for Physical and Theoretical Chemistry, University of Bonn, have developed a 3D light sheet microscope, an innovation that opens up brand new vistas for laser-based microscopy.

The novelty of the approach lies in illumination of the sample by laser, i.e. a thin light sheet measuring a few microns, from the side rather than the top or bottom as in conventional microscopes. Over 1,000 images of the object are generated. These are then compiled into a 3D dataset on a computer, making possible three dimensional imaging of tissue starting from a volume of about 0.5 cubic millimetres.

This biotech company from Bielefeld, which employs 32 people, received the ZIM award in 2012 for the 3D microscope. The award is given annually by the Federal Government to recognise innovation by medium-sized companies.

Bestleistung: Innovatives 3-D-Lichtblattmikroskop
Region: Ostwestfalen-Lippe
Ort: Bielefeld

Best performance: Innovative 3D light sheet microscope
Region: Ostwestfalen-Lippe
Place: Bielefeld

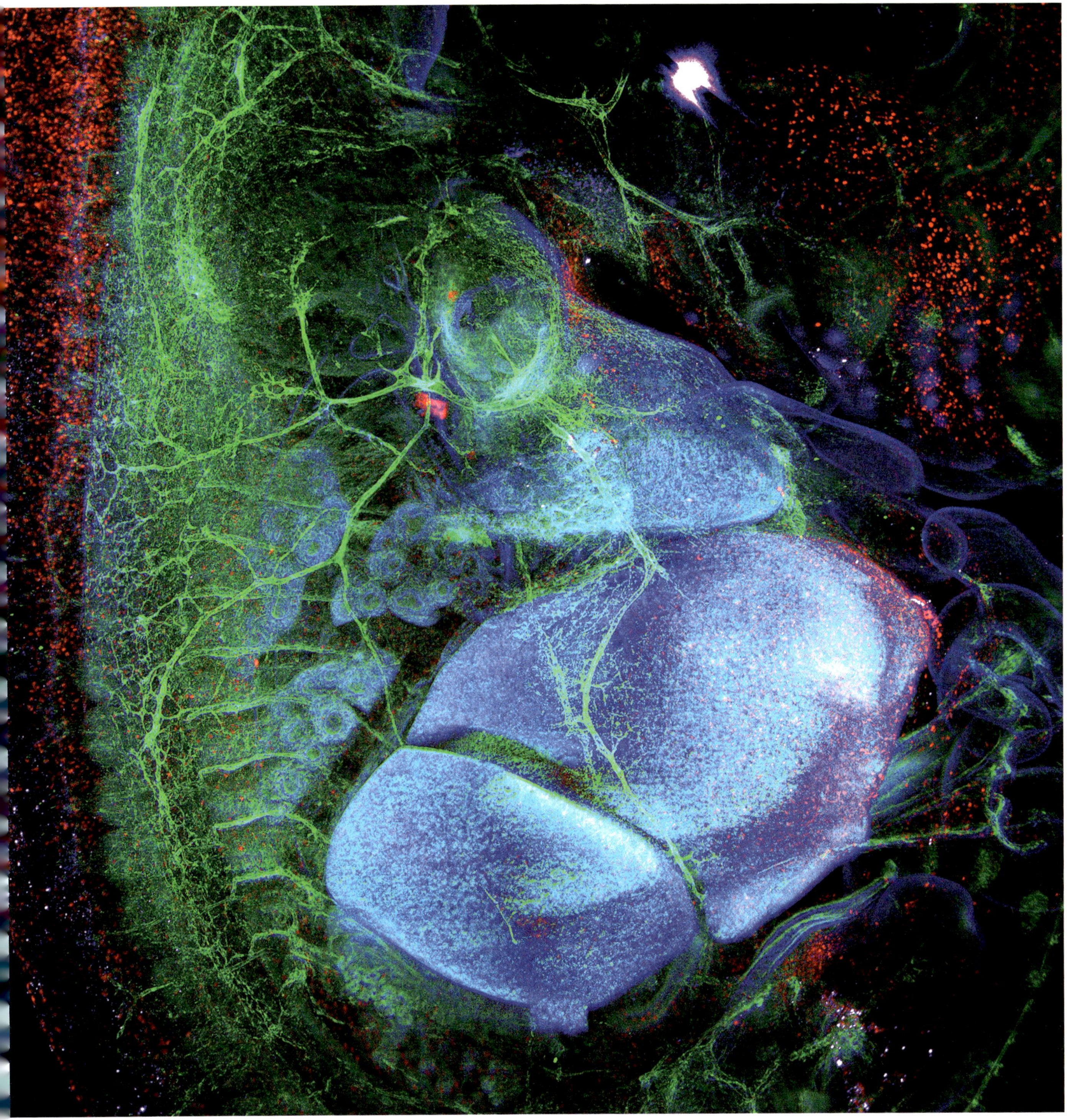

LOGISTIK-IT AUS DER CLOUD
LOGISTICS IT FROM THE CLOUD

LOGISTICS MALL. Erstmalig in der Logistik-IT erlaubt es eine Cloud-Computing-Lösung, Dienste, Prozesse und Programme als einzelne flexible und untereinander kompatible Bausteine zu mieten und nutzungsorientiert abzurechnen.

Willkommen in der Logistics Mall! Das virtuelle Kaufhaus bietet Softwareanbietern und -anwendern eine Onlineplattform für die Vermarktung und den Erwerb logistischer Software.

Hier findet der Kunde Lösungen für die verschiedensten Bereiche – von Kommissionierung, Verpackung und Umlagerung bis hin zu kompletten Supply Chains. Mithilfe der Cloud-Technologie kann der Nutzer die Programme via Internetbrowser nicht nur auswählen, sondern auch konfigurieren und steuern. Er muss sich nicht mehr um Installation oder Wartung kümmern.

Entwickelt wurde die Logistics Mall von den Fraunhofer-Instituten für Materialfluss und Logistik IML sowie für Software- und Systemtechnik ISST in Dortmund. Die Plattform wurde schon vielfach ausgezeichnet, unter anderem mit dem „Innovationspreis-IT 2011" und dem „elog@istics award 2012".

LOGISTICS MALL. For the first time in logistics IT, a cloud computing solution enables the hiring and user-oriented accounting of services, processes and programmes in the form of separate, flexible and mutually-compatible modules.

Welcome to the Logistics Mall! This virtual supermarket offers software suppliers and users an online platform to market and acquire logistics software.

Here clients can find solutions for a wide range of fields, starting with commissioning, packaging and relocation down to complete supply chains. Cloud technology helps the user not only to choose the programmes using their internet browser, but also to configure and manage them with no need to worry about installation or maintenance.

The Logistics Mall has been developed by the Fraunhofer Institutes for Material Flow and Logistics (IML) and Software and Systems Engineering (ISST) in Dortmund. The platform has already won many awards, among them the "Innovationspreis-IT 2011" and "elog@istics award 2012".

Bestleistung: Innovative Cloud-Computing-Software
Region: Metropole Ruhr
Ort: Dortmund

Best performance: Innovative Cloud Computing software
Region: Ruhr Metropolis
Place: Dortmund

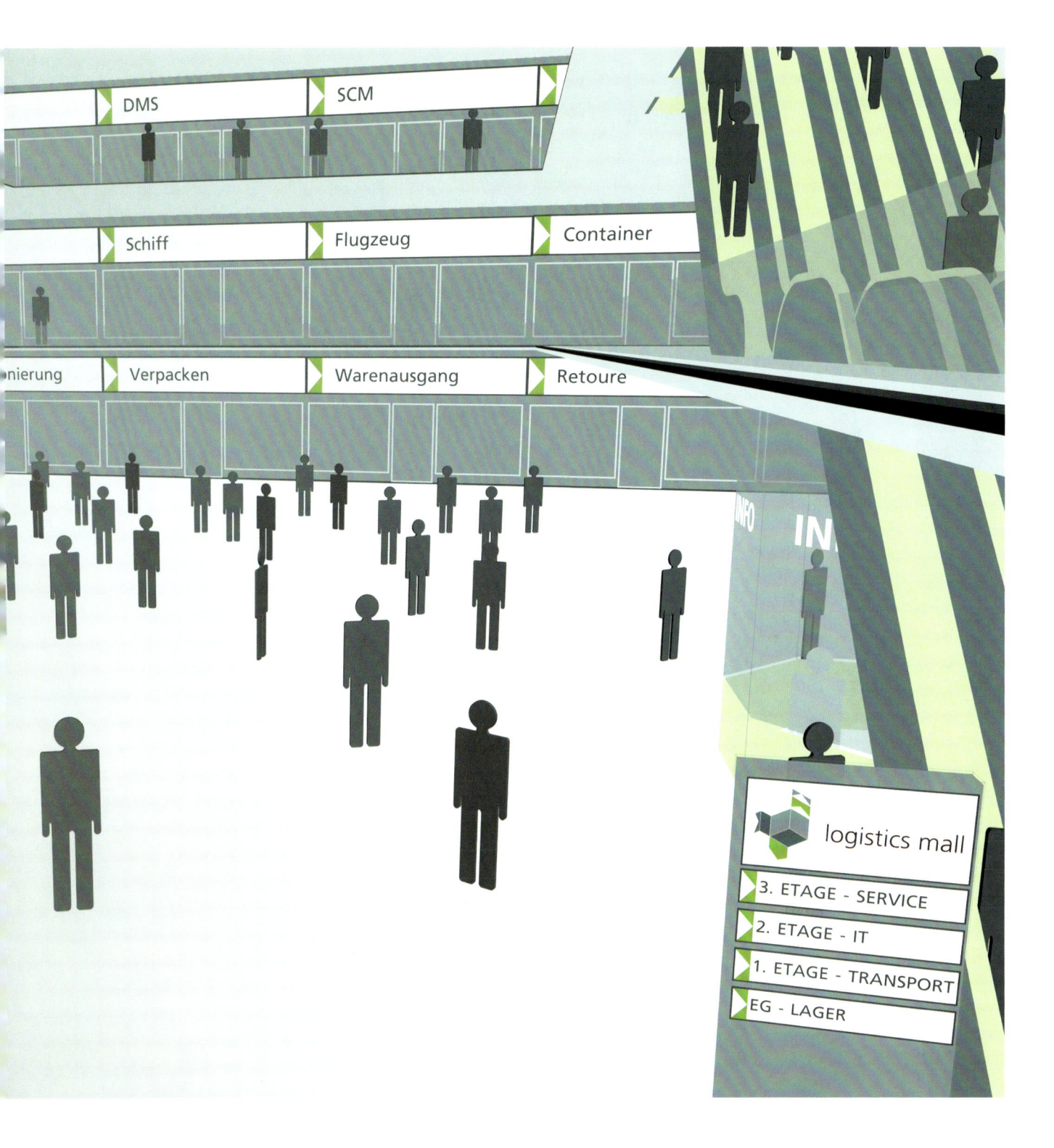

DMS	SCM
Schiff	Flugzeug	Container
nierung	Verpacken	Warenausgang	Retoure

logistics mall

- 3. ETAGE - SERVICE
- 2. ETAGE - IT
- 1. ETAGE - TRANSPORT
- EG - LAGER

DIE WISSENSQUELLE FÜR MEDIZIN
AT THE HUB OF THE MEDICAL WORLD

MEDICA. Seit ihren Anfängen im Jahr 1968 hat sich die MEDICA in Düsseldorf zur weltweit größten Messe für Medizinprodukte und -technik entwickelt. Jährlich pilgern rund 130.000 Fachbesucher an den Rhein – etwa die Hälfte davon aus dem Ausland. Sie informieren sich bei über 4.500 Ausstellern über neue Geräte und Verfahren für die ambulante wie stationäre Behandlung.

Die Messe Düsseldorf als Veranstalter der MEDICA setzt seit Langem auf eine Mischung aus technischer Innovation und anschaulicher Wissensvermittlung – in fachlicher Kooperation mit renommierten Partnern für die stattfindenden Kongresse und Foren. Jährlich werden im Rahmenprogramm der Messe ungefähr 1.000 Seminare, Kurse, Vorträge und Diskussionsrunden angeboten.

Das Interesse von Ausstellern und Besuchern ist ungebrochen, und die Macher suchen nach sinnvollen Ergänzungen des bestehenden Angebots: 2012 feierte das MEDICA ECON FORUM Premiere – ein Forum mit speziellem Fokus auf Themen für Führungskräfte der Krankenkassen und des Gesundheitswesens.

MEDICA. Since its inception in 1968, MEDICA in Duesseldorf has emerged as the world's biggest trade fair for medical products and technology. Around 130,000 people related to this field, about a half of them from abroad, set out on an annual quest to the Rhine. Visiting the 4,500 exhibitors helps them stay abreast of latest developments in equipment and procedures for ambulant and clinical treatment.

For the conventions and forums, the organiser of MEDICA, Messe Duesseldorf, has – in co-operation with eminent partners – long relied on a mix of technical innovation and demonstrable knowledge transfer. The trade fair offers about 1,000 seminars, courses, lectures and discussions in its programme every year. Never has the interest of exhibitors and visitors dropped and the planners constantly seek to make meaningful additions to the existing line-up. 2012, for example, saw the debut of MEDICA ECON FORUM, a forum with a special focus on issues facing executives from the health insurance and health care sectors.

Bestleistung: Weltgrößte Medizinfachmesse
Region: Düsseldorf
Ort: Düsseldorf

Best performance: The biggest trade fair on medicine in the world
Region: Duesseldorf
Place: Duesseldorf

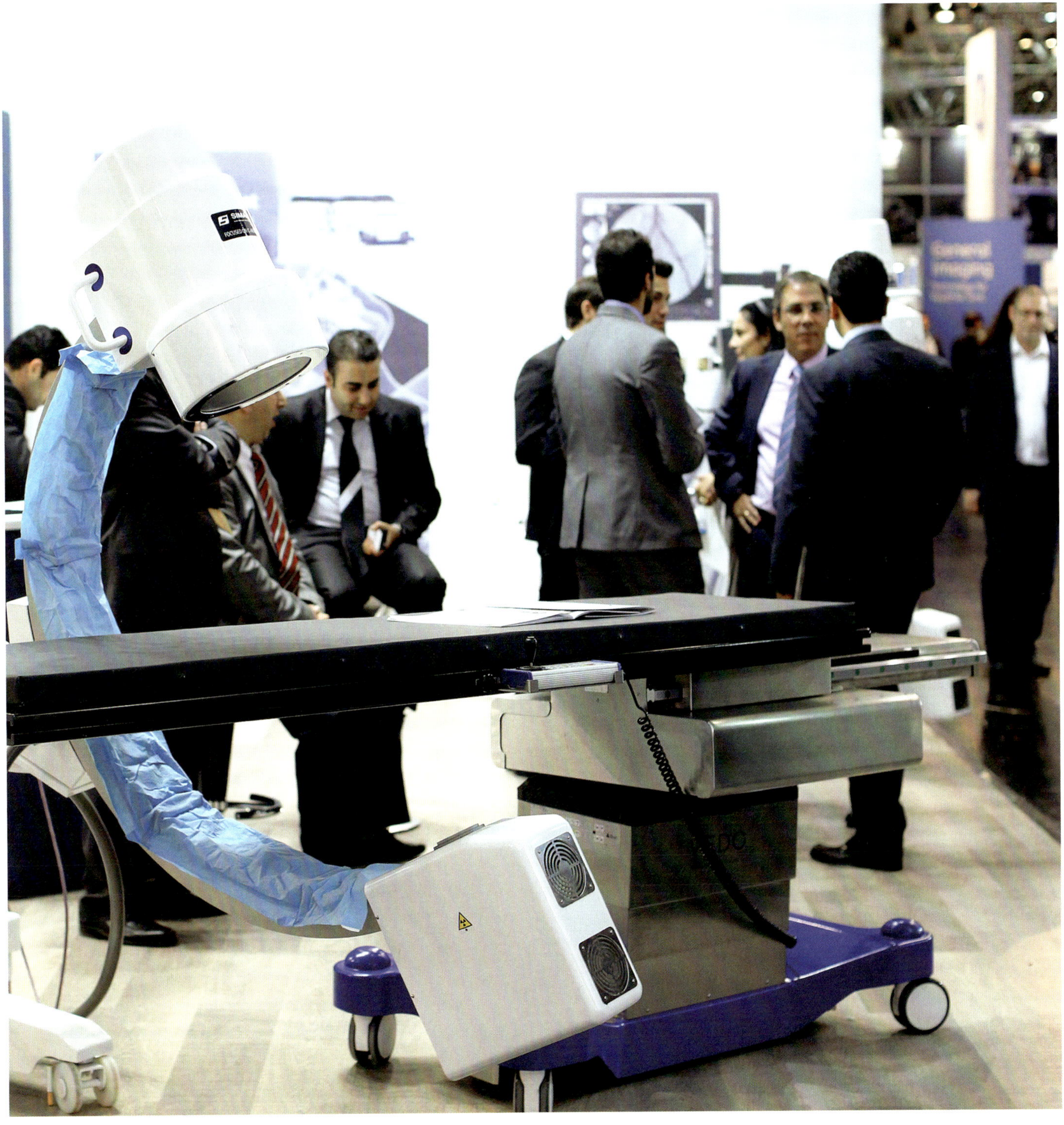

ENERGIESPEICHER FÜR DIE ELEKTROMOBILITÄT
ENERGY STORAGE FOR ELECTRIC MOBILITY

MEET – MÜNSTER ELECTROCHEMICAL ENERGY TECHNOLOGY. Anfang November 2012 war es soweit: Am MEET-Batterieforschungszentrum der Westfälischen Wilhelms-Universität Münster fiel der Startschuss für „MEET Hi-EnD": ein Forschungsverbund unter der Leitung von Prof. Dr. Hans-Dieter Wiemhöfer vom Institut für Anorganische und Analytische Chemie sowie Prof. Dr. Martin Winter vom MEET-Batterieforschungszentrum.

Die Forschergruppe arbeitet an Batterien mit deutlich höheren Energiedichten, um damit die Reichweiten von Elektrofahrzeugen zu steigern. Durch die Entwicklung neuer Zellkomponenten soll die Energiedichte der momentan verfügbaren Lithium-Batterien verfünffacht werden.

Dieses und viele weitere Projekte machen das MEET zu einer innovativen und international renommierten Forschungseinrichtung. Erstmalig werden hier Grundlagenforschung und Praxistransfer an einem Ort zusammengeführt. Das internationale Team aus 100 Spezialisten arbeitet stetig an der Verbesserung und Praxistauglichkeit von Energiespeichern – für die Nutzung in Elektroautos, aber auch bei der Zwischenspeicherung von regenerativ erzeugtem Strom.

MEET – MÜNSTER ELECTROCHEMICAL ENERGY TECHNOLOGY. The time had finally come: early November 2012 marked the kick-off for "MEET Hi-EnD" at the MEET Centre for Research on Batteries of the University of Muenster. "MEET Hi-EnD" is a research association led by Dr. Hans-Dieter Wiemhöfer of the Institute for Inorganic and Analytical Chemistry and Dr. Martin Winter of the MEET Centre for Research on Batteries. The research group is working on batteries with distinctly higher volume densities to increase the cruising range of electric cars. The development of new cell components is aimed at a fivefold increase in the volume density of the presently available lithium batteries.

This and many other projects make MEET an innovative research institution of international repute. For the first time pure research and practical application have been united under the same roof. The international team made up of 100 specialists is constantly working towards the improvement and viability of energy storage mediums. They will not only be of use to electric cars but also serve as intermediate storage mediums in the production of renewable energy.

Bestleistung: Innovative Batterieforschung
Region: Münsterland
Ort: Münster

Best performance: Innovative battery research
Region: Muensterland
Place: Muenster

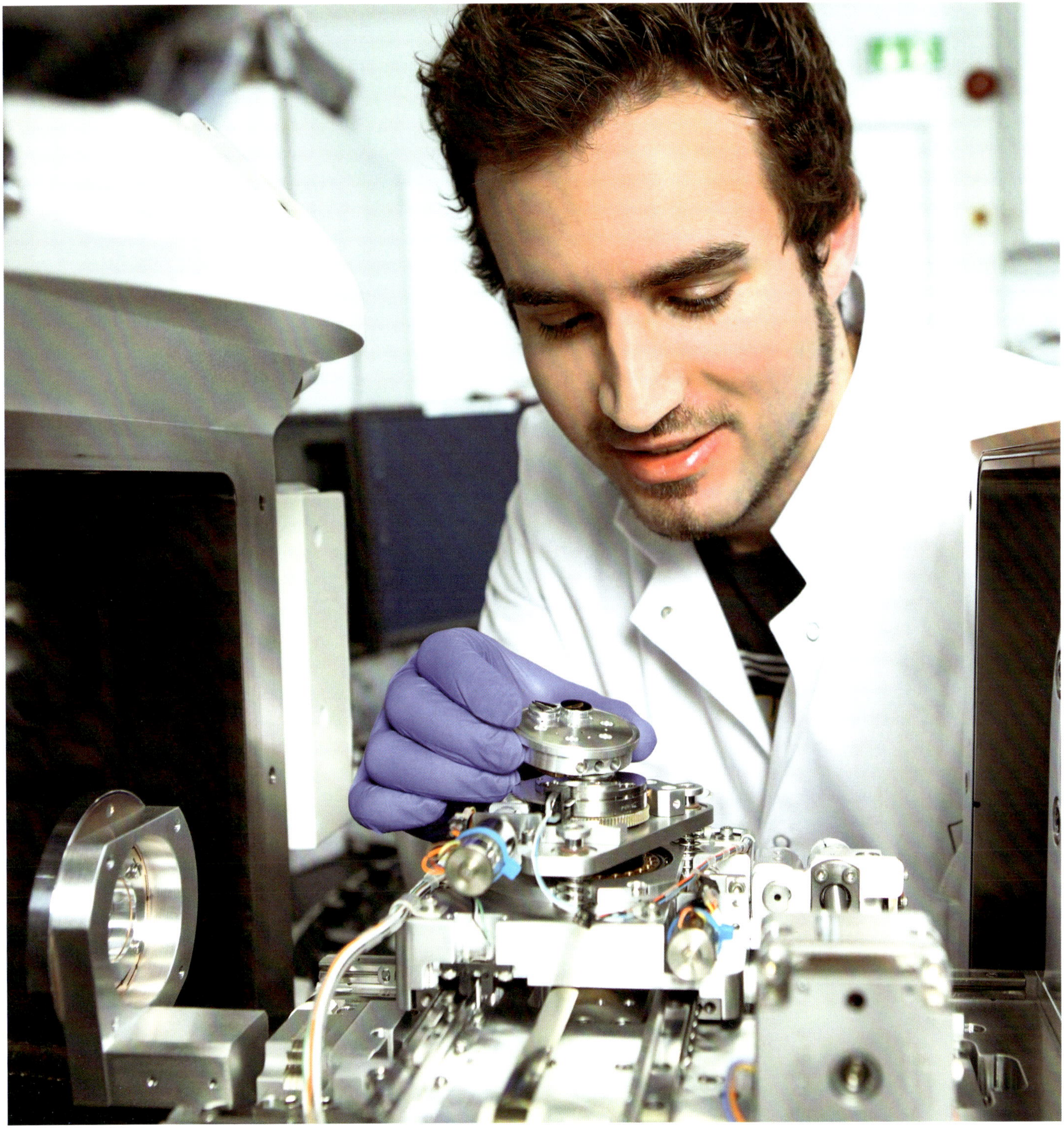

360 CROSSOVER MOVE UND DIE HALLE TOBT
360 CROSSOVER MOVE BRINGS THE HOUSE DOWN

MEHMETCAN ÖRÜCÜ. Der aus Neuss stammende Mehmetcan Örücü hält den Fußball einige Male hoch, springt und kreuzt die Beine. Er jongliert weiter mit der Lederkugel, schießt sie in die Luft, dreht sich um die eigene Achse, um dann den Ball direkt wieder in die Höhe zu befördern. Mit dem sogenannten 360 Crossover Move steht der Deutsch-Türke seit 2010 im Guinness-Buch der Rekorde. Kein anderer hat es bislang geschafft, den Trick in einer Bewegung viermal hintereinander und ohne Bodenberührung des Balls durchzuführen.

Zum Fußball-Freestyle kam der „King of 360" im Alter von 16 Jahren. Als ihm sein Cousin ein Freestyle-Video zeigte, packte ihn die Leidenschaft. Seitdem perfektioniert er seine Technik und trainiert mittlerweile mehrere Stunden täglich. Eine Ausdauer, die neben dem Weltrekord weitere Früchte trägt: So war Örücü türkischer Meister im Fußball-Freestyle und gilt heute als Deutschlands bester Straßenfußballer. Mittlerweile kümmert er sich auch aktiv um den Nachwuchs und trainiert an einer Neusser Realschule die jungen Trickser von morgen – mit dem 360 Crossover Move als Ziel.

MEHMETCAN ÖRÜCÜ. Mehmetcan Örücü from Neuss holds the football up a couple of times, jumps and crosses his legs. He continues juggling the leather ball, shoots it up into the air, spins around, only to send the ball shooting straight up again. The German-born Turk has been in the Guinness Book of Records since 2010 for the so-called 360 Crossover Move. No one else has since managed to perform the trick in a single move four times in a row without the ball touching the ground.

The "King of the 360" was initiated into freestyle football at the age of 16. He was seized by passion for this sport when his cousin showed him a video on freestyle. He has been perfecting his technique since then and in the meantime trains for several hours each day. This perseverance has borne fruit in other ways apart from the world record. Örücü reigned as the Turkish master in freestyle football and is considered today to be Germany's best street footballer. Meanwhile, he is actively involved in nurturing budding talent and trains the young, next-generation freestyle footballers in the 360 Crossover Move at a secondary school in Neuss.

Bestleistung: Weltrekordler im Fußball-Freestyle
Region: Niederrhein
Ort: Neuss

Best performance: World record holder in freestyle football
Region: Lower Rhine
Place: Neuss

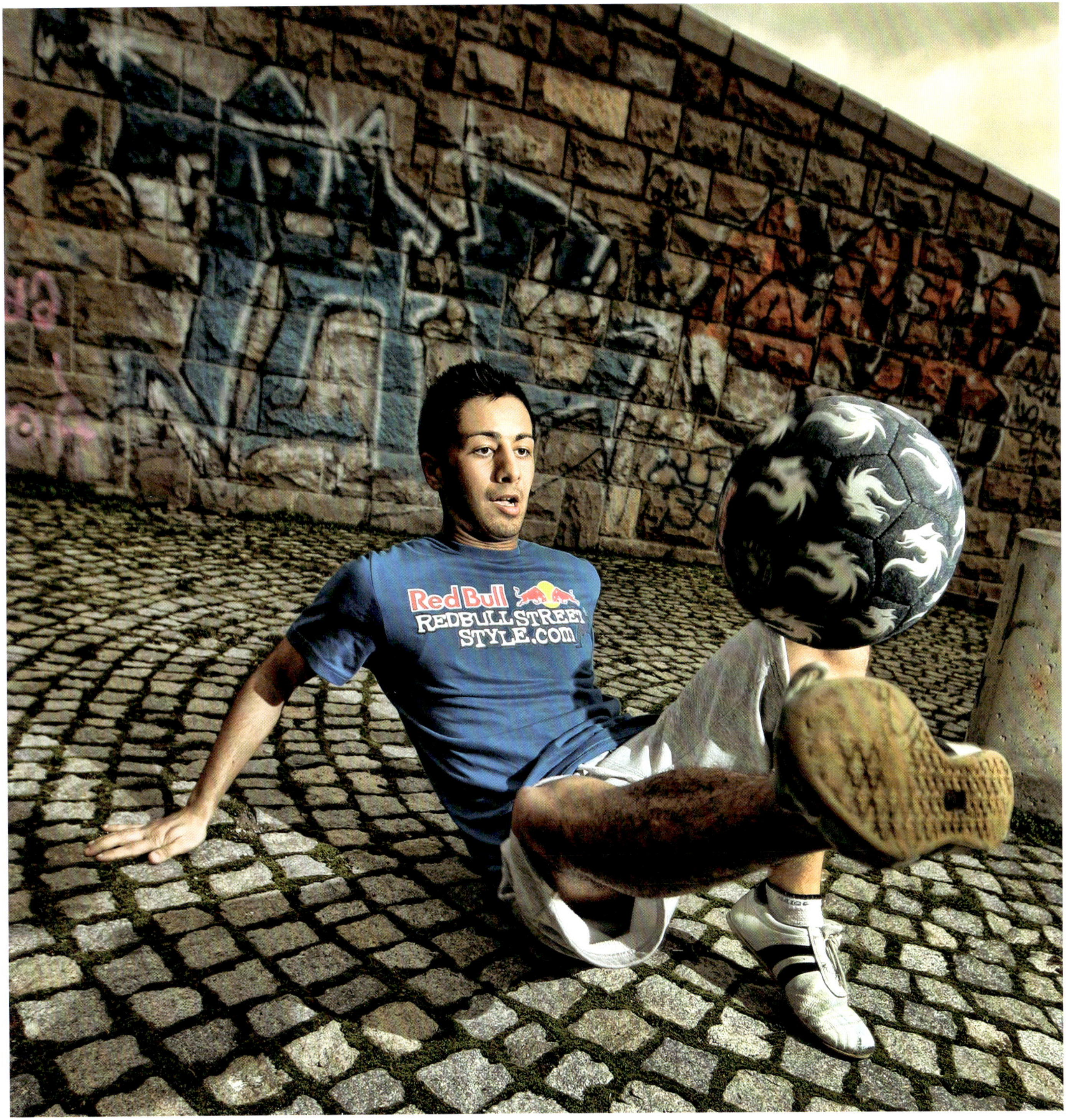
Red Bull
REDBULLSTREET
STYLE.com

STECKER FÜR DIE WELT
PLUGS FOR THE WORLD

MENNEKES ELEKTROTECHNIK. Bei einem Fußballspiel des FC Bayern München im Jahr 2008 überreichte Walter Mennekes, Geschäftsführer des gleichnamigen Unternehmens für Elektrotechnik, VW-Chef Martin Winterkorn den Prototypen eines Ladesteckers für Elektroautos. Winterkorn versprach, den Stecker seinen Ingenieuren in Wolfsburg zu zeigen – ein wichtiger Schritt.

Denn nur kurze Zeit später waren neben VW auch fast alle anderen führenden europäischen Autohersteller auf den sogenannten Typ 2 Stecker aus dem Hause MENNEKES aufmerksam geworden. Das Unternehmen wurde so nicht nur zum Entwickler des deutschen Normentwurfs für Ladesteckvorrichtungen bei Elektroautos – seit Januar 2013 ist der Typ 2 Stecker auch Norm in der Europäischen Union.

Die Produktpalette des 1935 gegründeten Unternehmens umfasst insgesamt über 11.000 verschiedene Industriesteckvorrichtungen – damit ist MENNEKES Weltmarktführer in diesem Bereich. Heute ist das Unternehmen aus Kirchhundem mit Tochtergesellschaften und Vertretungen in über 90 Ländern tätig und beschäftigt weltweit mehr als 900 Mitarbeiter, davon zwei Drittel in Deutschland.

MENNEKES ELECTRICAL ENGINEERING. At a football match of FC Bayern Munich in 2008 Walter Mennekes, director of the electrical engineering company bearing the same name, presented the prototype of a recharging connector for electric cars to VW chief Martin Winterkorn. Winterkorn promised to show the plug to his engineers in Wolfsburg – a significant step. Rightly so, since soon thereafter, the so-called Type 2 plug by MENNEKES caught the attention of almost all other leading European automobile manufacturers besides VW. Thus the company became the developer of the German draft standard for charging couplers meant for electric cars – since January 2013 the Type 2 plug has been standard throughout the European Union.

The product range of the company founded in 1935 covers 11,000 different industrial plugs and connectors in all, making MENNEKES the global market leader in this field. Today, this company from Kirchhundem along with subsidiaries and agencies operates in over 90 countries and employs more than 900 people, two thirds of them being in Germany.

Bestleistung: Führender Hersteller von Steckvorrichtungen
Region: Südwestfalen
Ort: Kirchhundem

Best performance: Leading manufacturer of plug connections
Region: Suedwestfalen
Place: Kirchhundem

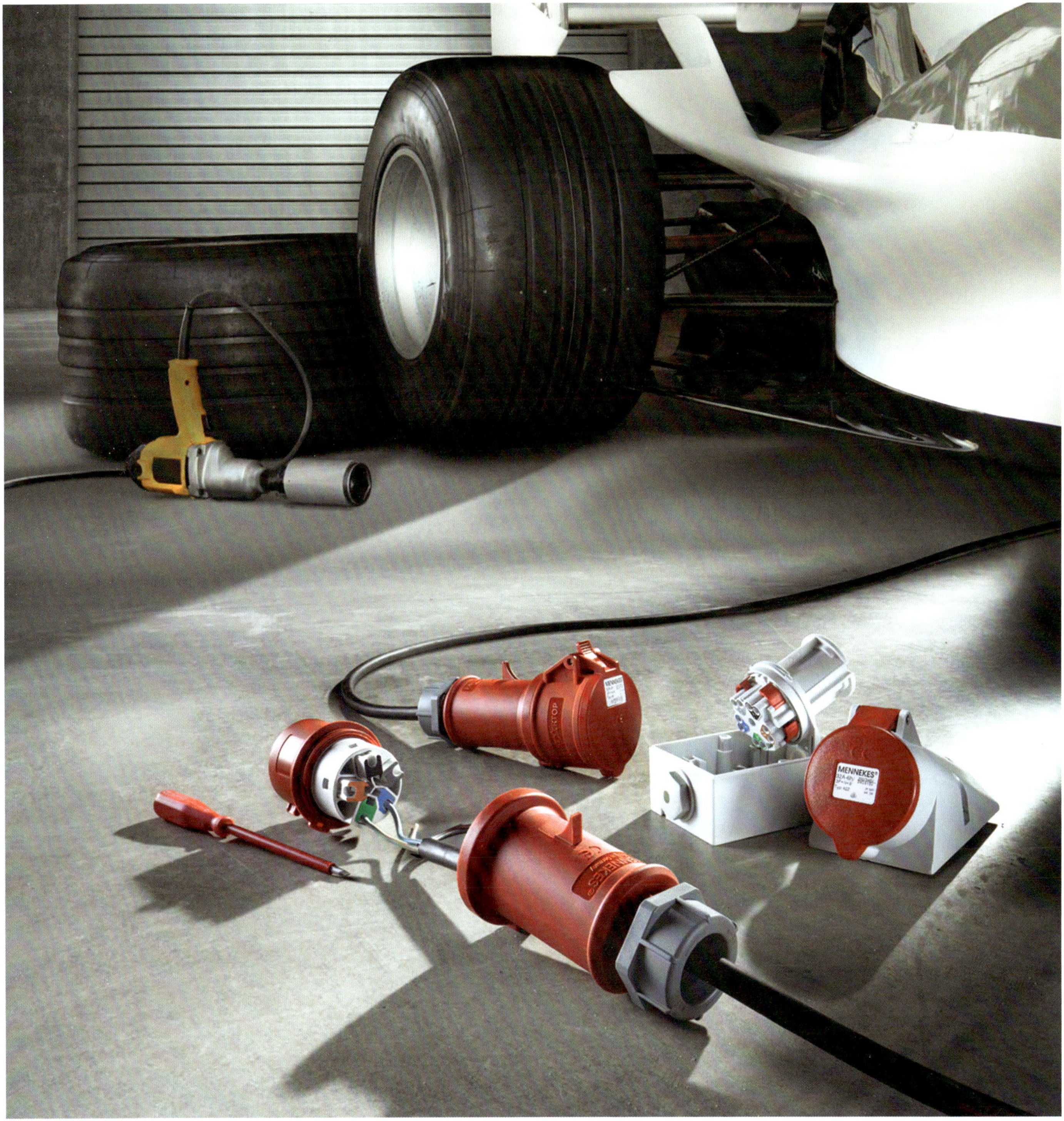
MENNEKES

AUS DEM KELLER ZUM WELTMARKTFÜHRER
FROM BASEMENT TO GLOBAL LEADER

MILTENYI BIOTEC. Mitte der 80er Jahre entwickelte Stefan Miltenyi im Rahmen seiner Diplomarbeit ein Verfahren zur Kennzeichnung und Sortierung von Zellen – ein großer Fortschritt in der damaligen Forschung. Nur wenig später gründete der Physiker mit 5.000 Euro Startkapital sein eigenes Unternehmen im Keller des elterlichen Hauses – heute beschäftigt die Miltenyi Biotec GmbH mehr als 1.300 Beschäftigte in 14 Niederlassungen weltweit. Die Produkte des Unternehmens werden in Forschung und medizinischer Praxis verwendet, in den Bereichen der Immunologie, der Krebsforschung, der Neurowissenschaft und der Stammzellentherapie.

Labore weltweit setzen die hier entwickelte und patentierte MACS-Technologie des Bergisch Gladbacher Weltmarktführers ein, um Zellen mithilfe kleinster Teilchen innerhalb eines magnetischen Feldes zu trennen und zu sortieren. Ungefähr 30 Prozent seines Umsatzes investiert Miltenyi Biotec in Forschung und Entwicklung. Nicht zuletzt deshalb wurde das Unternehmen im Rahmen der Initiative „Fortschritt NRW" als „Ort des Fortschritts" ausgezeichnet.

MILTENYI BIOTEC. In the mid 1980s while working towards his degree, Stefan Miltenyi developed a method of identifying and sorting cells; a leap in research for those times. Shortly thereafter, this physicist started his own company in the cellar of his parent's house with 5,000 Euros seed capital. Today, Miltenyi Biotec GmbH employs 1,300 people in 14 subsidiaries worldwide. Its products are used in research and medicine; in the fields of immunology, cancer research, neurosciences and stem cell therapy.

Laboratories all over the world use the MACS Technology, developed and patented by this global leader from Bergisch Gladbach, to separate and sort cells with the help of nanoparticles placed on a magnetic field. Miltenyi Biotec ploughs back about 30 per cent of its turnover into research and development, a fact which surely will have played a part in the company being awarded the "Place of Progress" ("Ort des Fortschritts") title in 2011 as part of the "Progress NRW" ("Fortschritt NRW") initiative.

Bestleistung: Führend bei Produkten zur magnetischen Zellsortierung
Region: Köln / Bonn
Ort: Bergisch Gladbach

Best performance: Leader in products for magnetic sorting of cells
Region: Cologne / Bonn
Place: Bergisch Gladbach

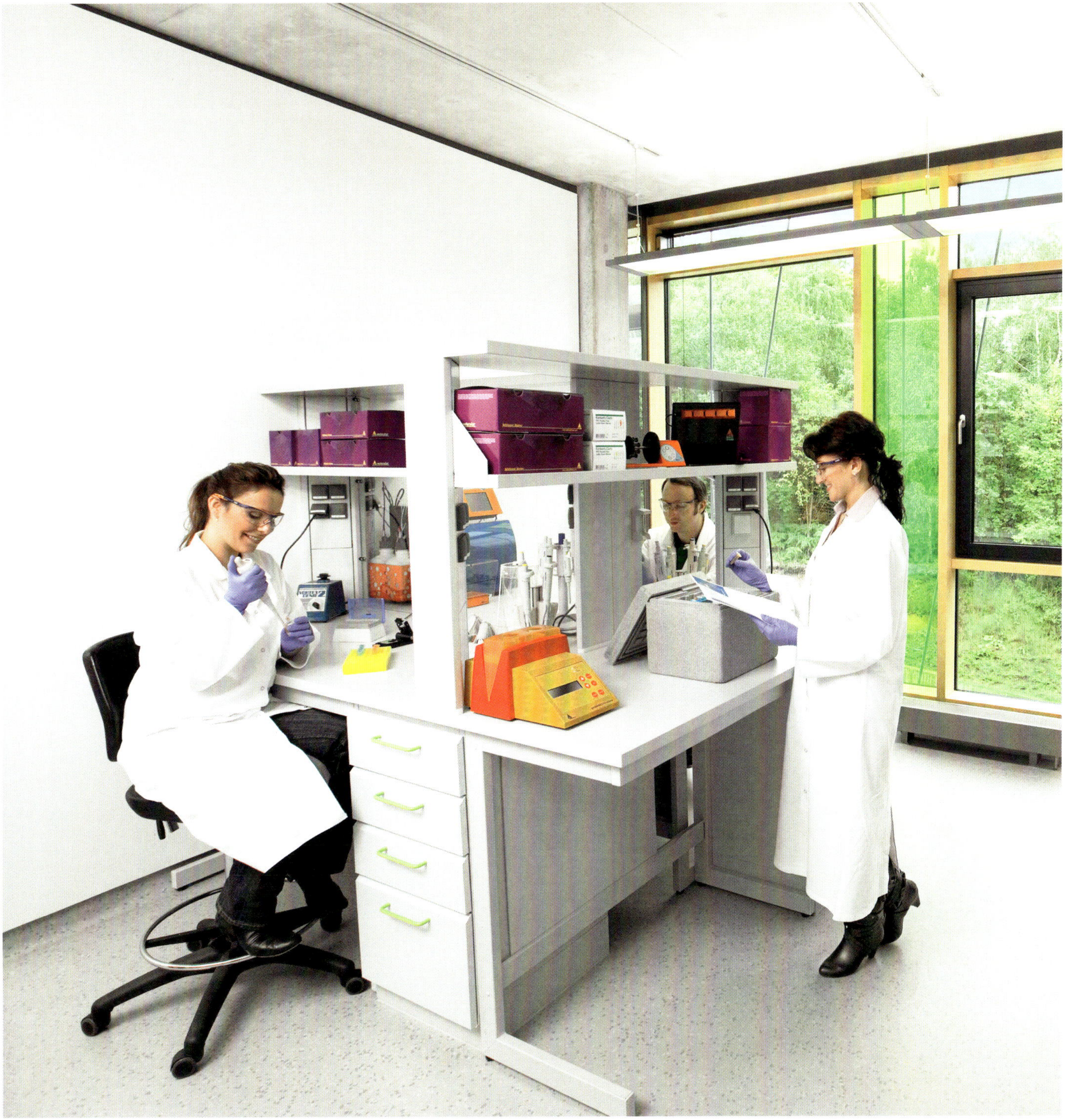

DAS WELTKULTURERBE IM KOFFER
WORLD CULTURAL HERITAGE IN A SUITCASE

MUSEUMSKOFFER. Kann heutzutage ein analoges, fast antiquiert wirkendes Angebot Klein und Groß beeindrucken, in Zeiten von Tablets und Smartphones? Museumskoffer, das einzigartige Kunst- und Pädagogik-Forschungsprojekt der Universität Paderborn, beweist es – seit über zehn Jahren. Alte Reisekoffer, zu Themenwelten ausgebaut, laden die Betrachter zum langen Verweilen ein, lassen sie lernen und staunen.

Denn hier wird eben nicht einfach schnell durchgeklickt wie beispielsweise bei einem Computer: Jeder Deckel dieser Museen im Kleinen öffnet eine eigene Themenwelt – zum Anfassen und Erleben. Es sind individuelle, mit Liebe zum Detail gestaltete Originale. Die Schöpfer der weit über 450 Koffer, Paderborner Kunststudierende, sind Verpackungskünstler: Wahre 3-D-Welten breiten sich aus, und alle Sinne werden angesprochen. Hier werden die Kunstwerke zum Lernmedium, und dies wird auch über die deutschen Grenzen hinaus honoriert: Als Kulturbotschafter für die UNESCO gehen Museumskoffer seit 2003 international auf Reisen.

SUITCASE MUSEUMS. Can an analogous, seemingly antiquated set of items impress young and old alike in this day and age of tablets and smartphones? Museumskoffer or "Suitcase museums" the unique research project of Paderborn University relating to art and education has borne testimony to this for more than ten years. Old suitcases showcasing realms through objects invite onlookers to dwell on them unhurriedly, leaving them to learn and marvel.

Here it is not just about of a quick click on the keys as with computers: every lid of these museums in miniature reveals an individual microcosm to experience hands-on. These are unique originals created with a love for detail.

The creators of the far more than 450 bags, Paderborn's art students, are wizards in packaging concepts. A veritable 3D world unfolds and appeals to all the senses. Here works of art transform into educational media and go beyond German borders to garner awards. Museumskoffer has gone international in its role of a cultural ambassador for UNESCO by becoming a travelling exhibition in 2003.

Bestleistung: Weltweit kleinstes Museum
Region: Ostwestfalen-Lippe
Ort: Paderborn

Best performance: The smallest museum of the world
Region: Ostwestfalen-Lippe
Place: Paderborn

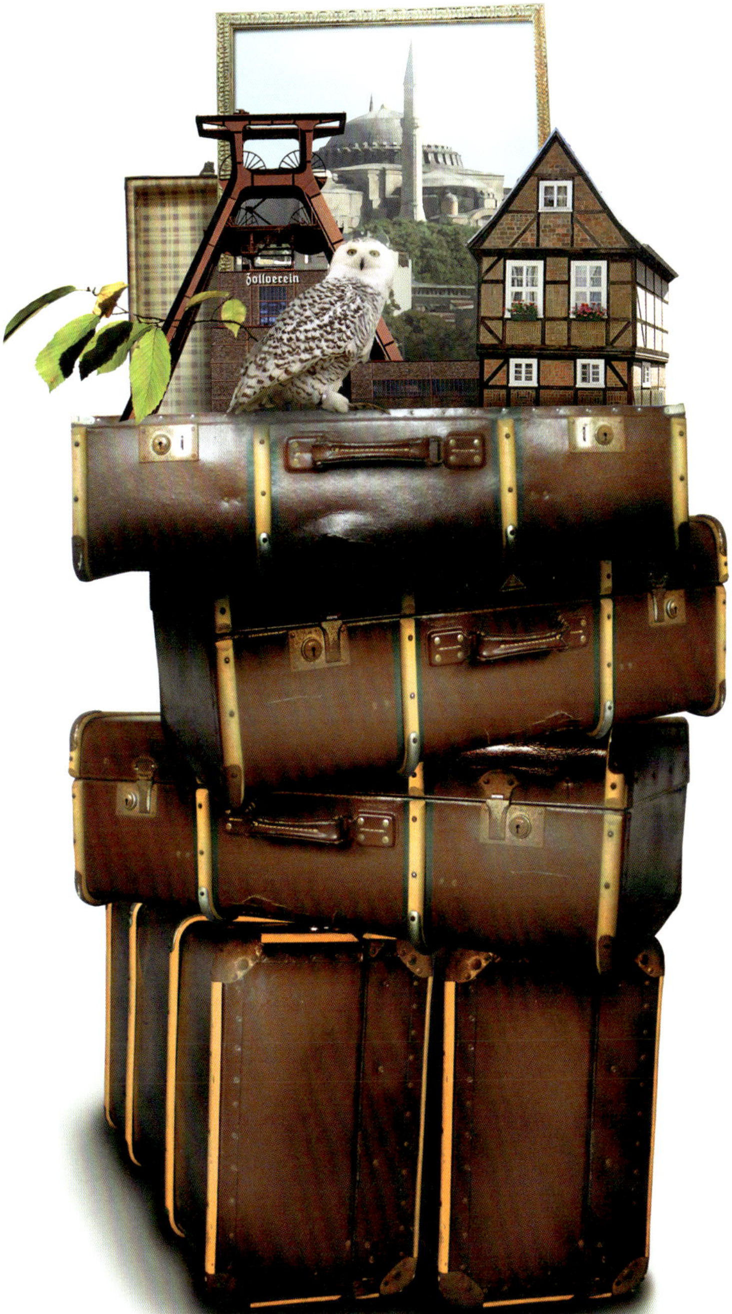
Zollverein

ANSTIFTUNG ZUM REKORD
RECORD ENDOWMENT

MUSEUM LUDWIG. Ein Kölner Ehepaar hat 1976 einiges angestiftet: Die leidenschaftlichen Kunstsammler Peter und Irene Ludwig schenkten der Stadt Köln rund 350 Werke – Grundstock für das zehn Jahre später eröffnete gleichnamige Museum.

Zentraler könnte es nicht liegen: eingerahmt von Rhein, Hauptbahnhof, Dom und Altstadt, direkt über der Philharmonie im gleichen Hause. Dieses war zunächst für zwei Museen konzipiert, seit 2001 stehen dem Ludwig durch einen Neubau für das Wallraf-Richartz-Museum die fast 9.000 Quadratmeter Ausstellungsfläche alleine zur Verfügung.

Umso mehr ist drin: Dank den Ludwigs, weiteren Stiftungen und Zukäufen ist die Sammlung moderner und zeitgenössischer Kunst immens gewachsen. Die umfangreichste Sammlung amerikanischer Pop Art außerhalb der USA – mit vielen Schlüsselwerken etwa von Andy Warhol, Jasper Johns und Roy Lichtenstein. Die europaweit größte Sammlung der Editionen Sigmar Polkes, die größte deutsche Kollektion mit Arbeiten Pablo Picassos, russischer Avantgarde, deutschen Expressionismus … Und das ist nur die ständige Sammlung – verpassen Sie nicht die spektakulären Sonderausstellungen.

MUSEUM LUDWIG. In 1976 a couple from Cologne sure set a lot in motion! Passionate art collectors Peter and Irene Ludwig gifted about 350 works to the city of Cologne, forming the basis for the creation of a museum of the same name ten years later.

Directly above the concert hall, framed by the Rhine, main station, cathedral and historic city centre, Museum Ludwig could not be more centrally located. Two museums were originally planned for the site, but since 2001 it has had almost 9,000 square metres exhibition space to itself, with the Wallraf Richartz Museum getting a new building.

So much the better to pack in more! The Ludwigs, other endowments and purchases have helped in acquiring a prolific collection of modern and contemporary art. The permanent exhibits alone comprise the largest collection of American pop art outside the USA with many seminal works by the likes of Andy Warhol, Jasper Johns and Roy Lichtenstein. Then there's Europe's biggest collection of Sigmar Polke's editions, the largest collection in Germany of works by Pablo Picasso, Russian avant-gardists, German expressionists… How could anyone miss out on seeing such amazing special exhibits?

Bestleistung: Größte Sammlung amerikanischer Pop Art außerhalb der USA
Region: Köln / Bonn
Ort: Köln

Best performance: Biggest collection of American Pop Art outside the USA
Region: Cologne / Bonn
Place: Cologne

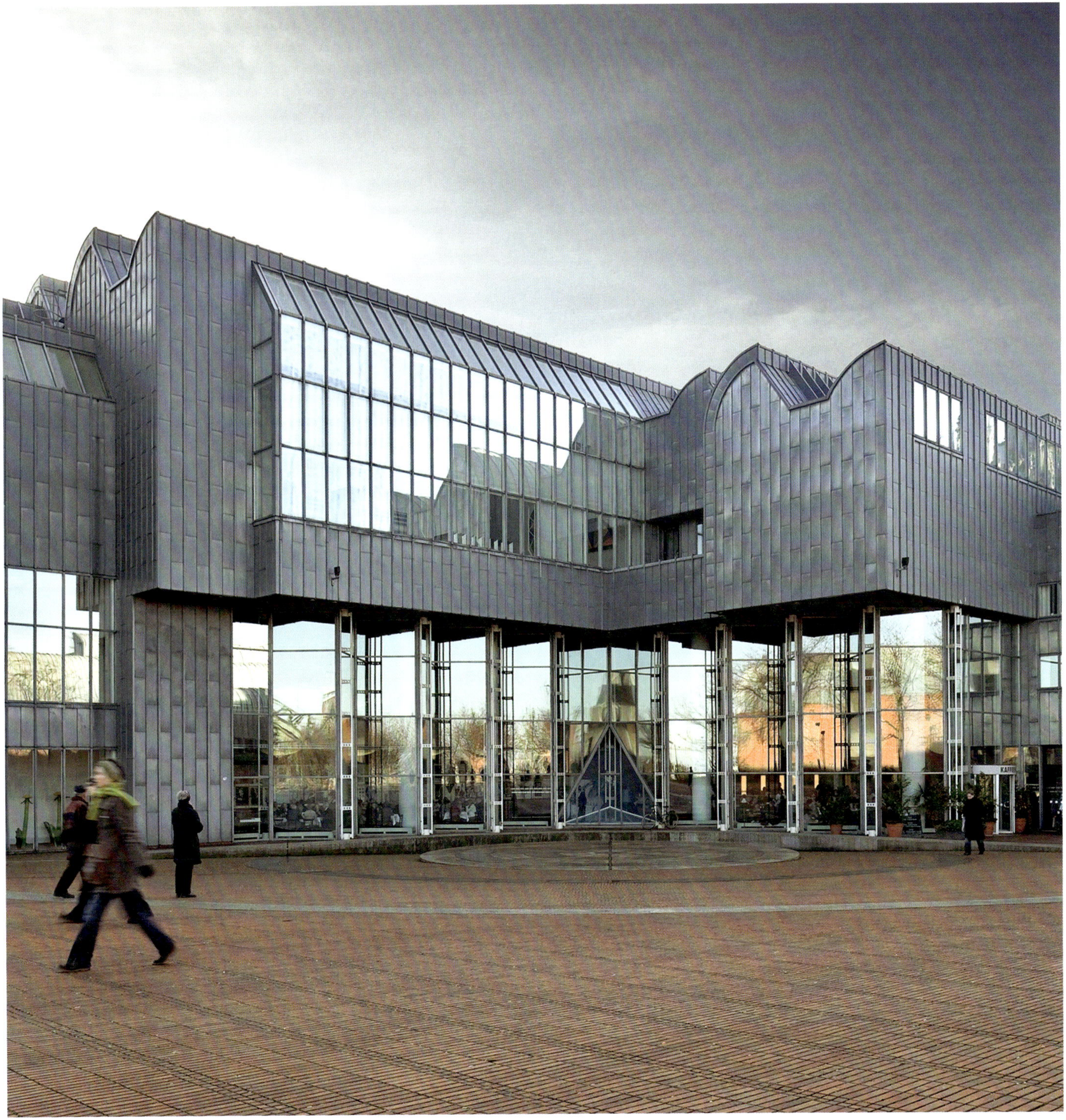

MODERNE PIRATENBEUTE
MODERN PIRATE LOOT

MUSEUM PLAGIARIUS. Überquellende Schatztruhen voll strahlenden Goldes und Geschmeides – so stellt man sich einen typischen Piratenschatz vor. Mitten in der Klingenstadt Solingen gibt es so etwas wirklich, nur viel moderner und ungefährlicher.

Moderne Piraten heißen heute Raubdesigner oder Markenpiraten. Sie klauen Ideen, fälschen oder kopieren beliebte Produkte. Ihr „Raubgold" zeigt das Museum Plagiarius in Deutschlands größter Sammlung von dreisten Kopien. Bei Vielfalt und Herkunft gibt es dabei keine Grenzen: Haushaltsgegenstand, Werkzeug oder Spielzeug – über 350 Paare bietet die Ausstellung, jeweils Original und Fälschung.

Es gibt jedoch nicht nur Ausstellungsstücke zu bewundern: Der jährlich verliehene Negativpreis „Plagiarius" – von Design-Professor Rido Busse 1977 ins Leben gerufen – stellt die dreistesten Plagiate öffentlich an den Pranger. Die Trophäe ist ein schwarzer Gartenzwerg mit goldener Nase – Letztere symbolisiert die unrechtmäßig eingestrichenen Gewinne der modernen Piraten.

MUSEUM PLAGIARIUS. Overflowing treasure troves full of gleaming gold and jewels – that is how one pictures a typical pirate treasure. Such a thing actually exists smack-bang in the middle of Solingen, the "City of Blades" (made famous for the manufacture of knives), only this version is far more modern and innocuous.

Designers of knock-offs or brand pirates are the modern pirates of our times. They steal ideas, create fakes or copies of goods that are in vogue. Their "illicit booty" is on display at the Plagiarius Museum (The Plagiarism Museum) together with Germany's largest collection of the most brazen copies. The range and sources of the products on display here: household articles, tools or toys, are boundless – the exhibition displays 350 pairs of original products with their imitations alongside.

However, it is not just the exhibits that are astonishing. The dubious honour of the "Plagiarius", the mock prize awarded annually, was initiated in 1977 by design professor Rido Busse to publicly shame the most flagrant knock-offs. The trophy is a garden gnome painted in black with a golden nose, the latter representing the illicit earnings of the modern pirates.

Bestleistung: Größte Plagiat-Sammlung
Region: Bergisches Städtedreieck
Ort: Solingen

Best performance: The biggest collection of copies
Region: Bergisches Staedtedreieck
Place: Solingen

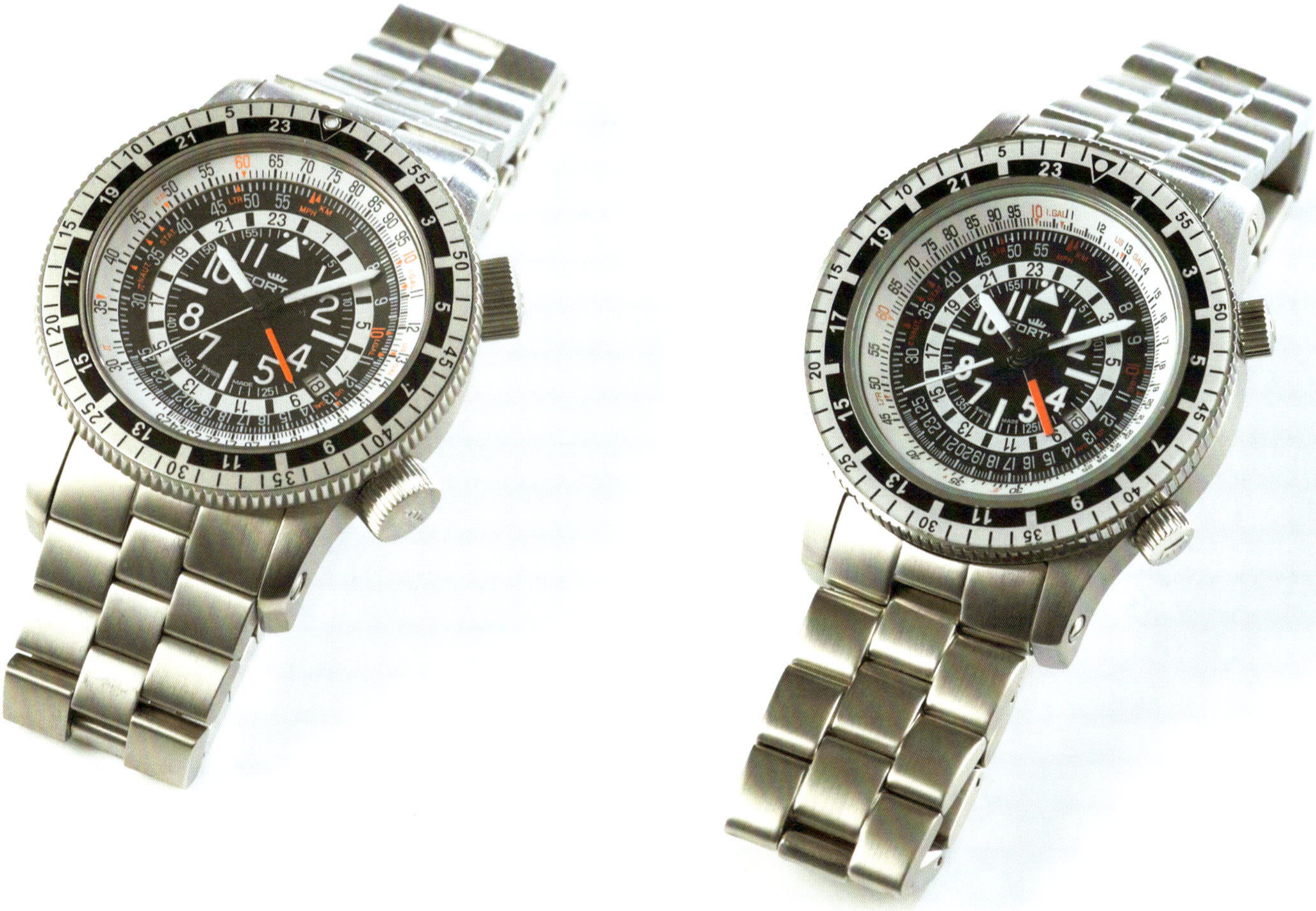

IMMER AUF DER SICHEREN SEITE
ALWAYS ON THE SAFE SIDE

NETZWERK ZUHAUSE SICHER. Nach einem Einbruch oder Wohnungsbrand kommt Betroffenen oft die Einsicht, dass sie durch bessere Vorbeugung die schlimmen Folgen des Verbrechens bzw. Brands hätten verhindern können.

Damit es nicht soweit kommt, hat die Polizei 2005 in Münster das innovative Netzwerk gegründet. Stichwort Prävention: Was kann jeder Einzelne tun, woher Informationen bekommen und wie seriöse Handwerker finden? Hier setzt das Netzwerk an – durch die Bündelung der Kompetenzen von Polizei, Handwerk, Industrie und Versicherern.

Drei Schritte führen zum sicheren Zuhause: Zunächst bieten Polizeiexperten eine persönliche Sicherheitsberatung an – wie Täter arbeiten, wie man sich richtig verhält oder welche Schlösser geeignet sind. Dann verweisen sie auf geschulte Fachbetriebe vor Ort, die die geprüfte Sicherheitstechnik zuhause installieren. Im dritten Schritt gibt es eine Präventionsplakette, für die es zum Beispiel bei Hausratversicherern Rabatte gibt. Ein überzeugendes Projekt – die Bundesregierung hat es als Best-Practice-Beispiel für Prävention ausgewählt.

NETWORK FOR HOME SECURITY. Victims of a break-in or house fire often find in hindsight that they could have averted the dire consequences of such incidents with better precautionary measures.

In 2005 the police authorities in Muenster created an innovative network to ensure this may never come to pass. The buzzword is prevention. It raises questions as to individual action plans, sources of information and reliable workers. In this context the network has the police join forces with craftsmen, industry stakeholders and insurance agencies.

Three steps lead to home security: firstly, experts in the police department provide counselling on safety and security – how culprits operate, how does one deal with this correctly or what are suitable locks. They then identify skilled specialists in the area dealing with installation of tested safety systems at home. In the third step, a prevention sticker is provided for which discounts are offered, say at agencies providing insurance cover for personal belongings. A credible project – the Federal Government has chosen this as a best practice model for prevention.

Bestleistung: Innovative Initiative für Einbruch- und Brandschutz
Region: Münsterland
Ort: Münster

Best performance: An innovative initiative to prevent break-ins and fires
Region: Muensterland
Place: Muenster

Zuhause sicher

MIT DEM SÄBEL ZUM SIEG
SUCCESS WITH THE SABRE

NICOLAS LIMBACH. Sein Säbel wiegt 500 Gramm – Hiebe und Stöße sind mit der spektakulären Klinge erlaubt. Fernab der Fechtbahn wirkt Nicolas Limbach sympathisch und zuvorkommend – auf der Planche wird er jedoch angriffslustig, selbstbewusst und ehrgeizig: Der Dormagener Vorzeigeprofi im Säbelfechten hat immer den Erfolg im Visier.

Der 27-Jährige hatte schon früh üben können: Mit 19 Jahren wurde er Junioren-Weltmeister. Spätestens 2009 dann, mit dem Gewinn der Herren-Weltmeisterschaft, sorgte Limbach für Aufsehen – es war das erste WM-Gold für einen deutschen Säbelfechter nach 15 Jahren. Auch 2012 war ein gutes Jahr für den Ausnahmeathleten: Für seinen Heimatverein TSV Bayer Dormagen erfocht er den Gesamtweltcupsieg, führte die Weltrangliste an, wurde bereits zum fünften Mal deutscher Einzelmeister und hat mit der Nationalmannschaft EM-Bronze erkämpft. Zudem errang er bei den Olympischen Spielen in London den fünften Platz. All das hat er in einem einzigen Jahr erreicht – und ist somit bestens gewappnet für die kommenden Olympischen Spiele.

NICOLAS LIMBACH. His sabre weighs 500 grammes and he is allowed to strike and thrust with its awesome blade. Off piste, Nicolas Limbach comes across as being amiable and courteous, but once on it, he is feisty, confident and ambitious. This exemplary professional fencer from Dormagen always sets out to win.

The 27 year-old started early. At the age of just 19, he was crowned Junior World Champion and, in 2009, caused a stir by winning the men's World Championship – the first gold for a German sabre fencer in 15 years. 2012 proved to be a good year for this exceptional sportsman, too. Fighting for his local club TSV Bayer Dormagen, he was overall winner at the World Cup, topped the world ranking, was crowned German Individual Champion for the 5th time and, as part of the national team, contributed to its bronze medal win at the European Championships. What's more, he came 5th at the London Olympics. Delivering such a performance within the space of just one year certainly brightens his prospects for the next Olympics!

Bestleistung: Weltcup-Gesamtsieger im Säbelfechten
Region: Niederrhein
Ort: Dormagen

Best performance: Overall worldcup winner in fencing
Region: Lower Rhine
Place: Dormagen

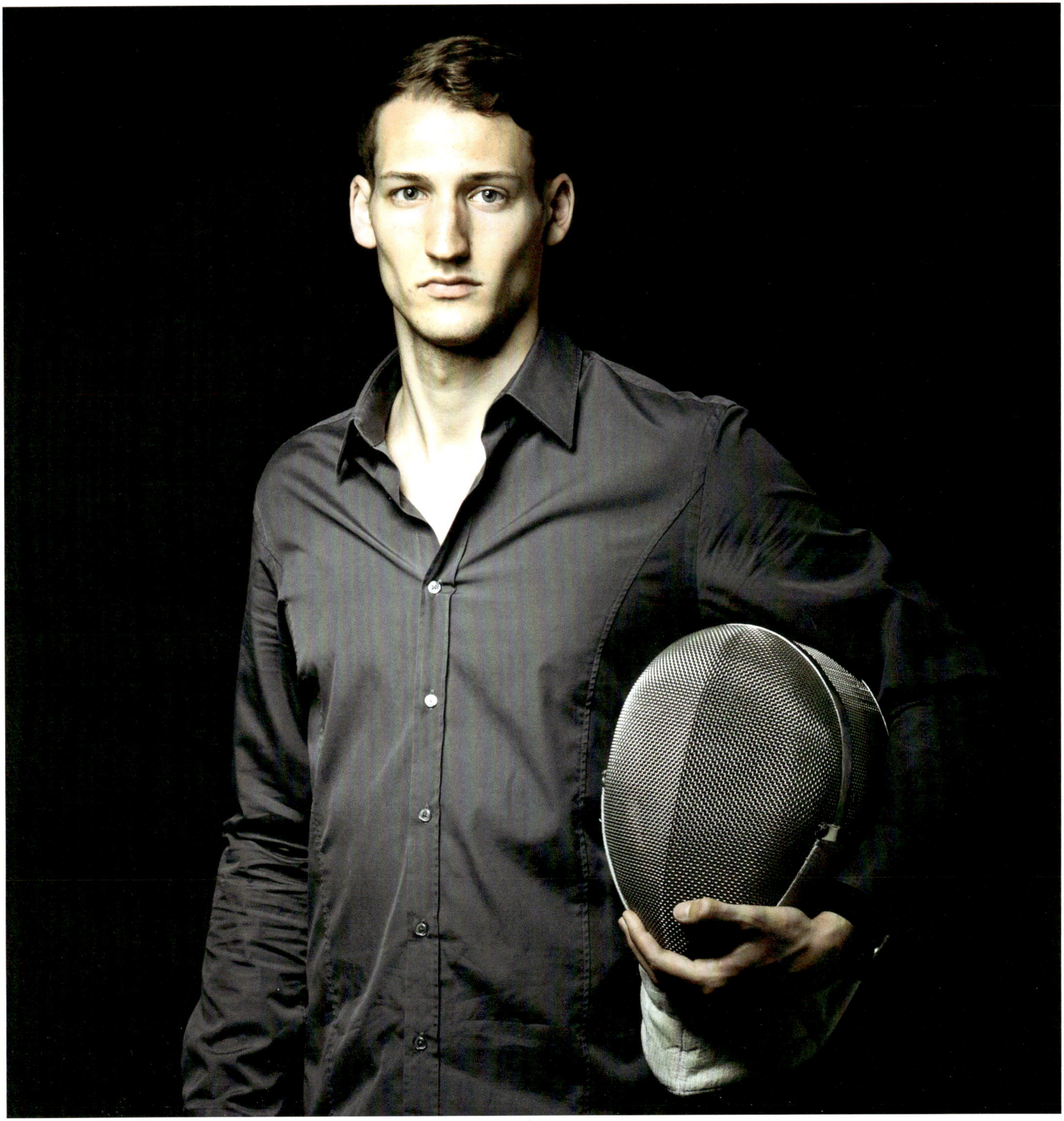

LICHT OHNE LAMPEN
LIGHT WITHOUT BULBS

OLEDS. Ein Kleiderschrank, der zugleich als Lichtquelle für das Schlafzimmer dient, oder großflächig leuchtende Tapeten, die eine freundliche Raumatmosphäre ganz ohne Lampen schaffen – dies alles könnte in ein paar Jahren Realität werden. Der Kreativität von Möbeldesignern und Innenarchitekten sind aber bereits jetzt kaum noch Grenzen gesetzt.

Hinter den innovativen Beleuchtungsideen stehen organische Leuchtdioden. Die sogenannten OLEDs sind nur wenige Millimeter dünn und erzeugen ein weiches, diffuses Licht, das sie über die gesamte Oberfläche abgeben. Wissenschaftlern der Philips Technologie GmbH in Aachen ist es gelungen, diese hauchdünnen Glasplättchen auch bei haushaltsüblichem Wechselstrom leuchten zu lassen. Damit wären dann auch die Zeiten von klobigen Netzteilen gezählt. Im Aachener Lumiblade Creative Lab sind Designer und Produzenten eingeladen, Ideen für den Einsatz der OLED-Technik auszutesten. Gut möglich, dass schon in wenigen Jahren für eine neue Tapete der Elektriker ins Haus kommt – mit einer Hightech-Folie unter dem Arm und einem Beleuchtungskonzept im Kopf.

OLEDS. A closet doubling as light source for a bedroom or wallpaper that glows over large areas, creating a warm atmosphere in a room completely devoid of light bulbs. Two ideas that might well become reality in a few years. Even now there are hardly any limitations placed on the creativity of furniture or interior designers.

These innovative lighting ideas have their source in organic light-emitting diodes (OLEDs). Just a few millimetres thin, they are capable of emitting soft, diffused lighting over entire surfaces. Scientists from Philips Technologie GmbH in Aachen have successfully applied domestic AC to light up these tiny wafer thin glass sheets. This also sounds the death knell for clunky adaptors.

Designers and manufacturers have been invited by Lumiblade Creative Lab in Aachen to test ideas based on OLED technology. In times to come, it is completely conceivable that an electrician might be called to change the wallpaper at home, with a high-tech foil tucked under his arm and a lighting concept in his head.

Bestleistung: Erste mit Wechselstrom betriebene OLED-Beleuchtung
Region: Aachen
Ort: Aachen

Best performance: The first OLED lighting run on alternating current
Region: Aachen
Place: Aachen

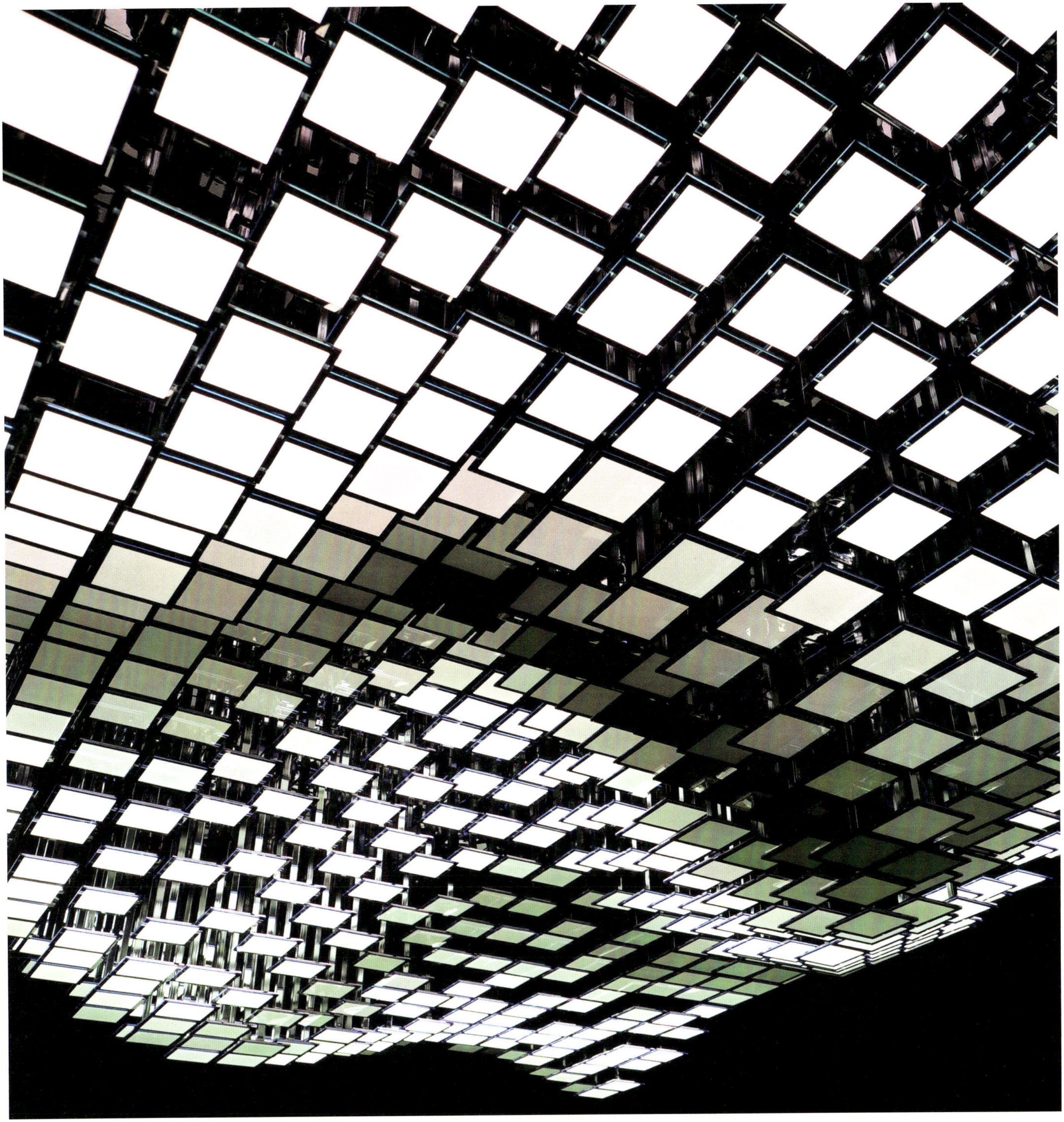

LAMINATBÖDEN INDIVIDUELL BEDRUCKT
CUSTOM PRINTED LAMINATE FLOORING

PARADOR. Zaha Hadid, Jean Nouvel, Ross Lovegrove sowie Ronan und Erwan Bouroullec haben mindestens zwei Dinge gemeinsam: Sie gehören zur internationalen Kreativelite. Und sie haben Designs für die Bodenbeläge aus Laminat von Parador entwickelt, einem der führenden Anbieter von hochwertigen Bodenbelägen für Innenräume.

Ob das Lichtspiel eines Kirchenfensters, eine entfremdete Computerplatine oder der Schattenwurf von Zedern – jegliches Motiv kann auf die Böden des Coesfelder Unternehmens gedruckt werden, wie die aktuellen Entwürfe zeigen. Dafür sorgt das einzigartige, von Parador entwickelte ArtPrint-Druckverfahren.

Die patentierte Technik legte bereits die Basis für die erste Kollektion „Edition 1", bei der Parador ebenfalls mit international bekannten Designern und Architekten zusammenarbeitete. Die dabei entstandenen Laminatdekore erhielten wichtige Designpreise, darunter den red dot award und den Interior Innovation Award.

Ab 100 Quadratmeter Fläche produziert Parador Unikate in Laminat nach individuellen Vorlagen. So kann der Kunde dank ArtPrint selbst zum Designer werden.

PARADOR. Zaha Hadid, Jean Nouvel, Ross Lovegrove, Ronan and Erwan Bouroullec have at least two things in common. They belong to the international elite in creativity. And they have created laminate flooring designs for Parador, one of the leading suppliers of top-grade indoor floorings.

Whether the play of light of a church window, a detached computer circuit board or cedars casting shadows, any motif can be printed on the floors of the company from Coesfeld, as is evident from the current designs. It is the unique printing method called ArtPrint, developed by Parador, which makes this possible.

The patented technique formed the basis for the first collection, "Edition 1", where Parador similarly collaborated with internationally renowned designers and architects. The laminate decor conceived here went on to receive important design awards, among which are the red dot award and Interior Innovation Award.

For surface areas of over 100 square metres Parador produces customised laminates as per specified design. Hence ArtPrint can even make designers out of clients!

Bestleistung: Einzigartiges Druckverfahren für Laminatböden
Region: Münsterland
Ort: Coesfeld

Best performance: Unique printing process for floor laminates
Region: Muensterland
Place: Coesfeld

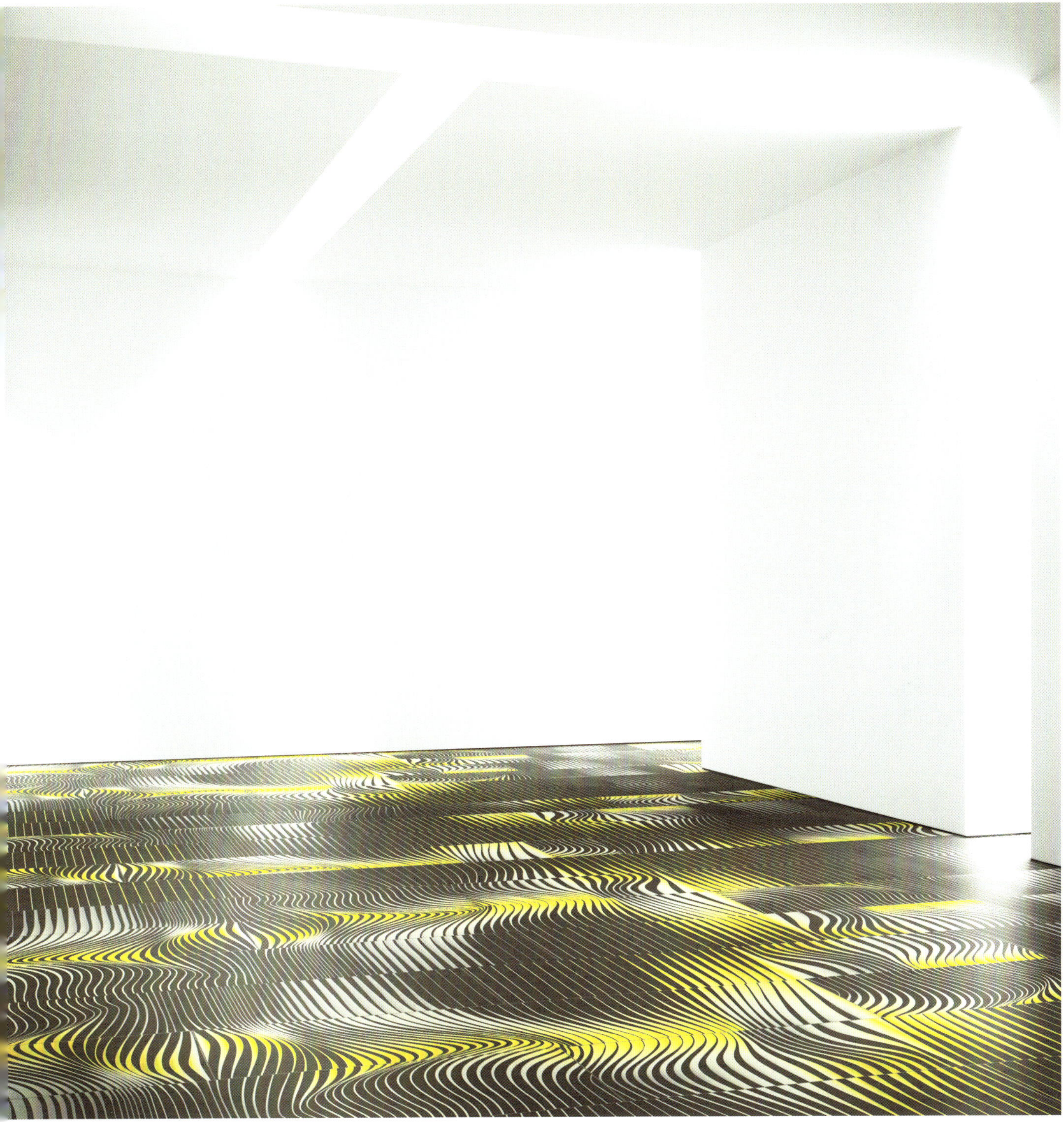

DER VATER DES GIGABYTES
FATHER OF GIGABYTES

PETER GRÜNBERG. Eine Welt ohne Gigabyte-Festplatten oder MP3-Player ist heute nicht denkbar. Die Voraussetzung dafür wurde im Forschungszentrum Jülich geschaffen. Im Dezember 1988 entdeckte dort der Physiker Peter Grünberg den Riesenmagnetowiderstandseffekt (GMR) und ließ ihn gleich patentieren. Ihm sei sofort klar gewesen, dass man mit seiner Entdeckung die Speicherkapazitäten von Festplatten enorm ausbauen könnte. Tatsächlich hat selten eine wissenschaftliche Leistung so schnell den Sprung zur industriellen Produktionsreife erreicht. Nur Monate später meldete sich IBM in Jülich, und schon 1997 wurden GMR-Leseköpfe für Computerfestplatten vorgestellt.

Nach weiteren zehn Jahren wurde Peter Grünberg mit dem Nobelpreis für Physik ausgezeichnet. Eine Ehrung, die ihn nicht völlig überrascht hat. Schließlich stand er bereits seit einigen Jahren auf der Kandidatenliste. Nach der Verkündung gab Grünberg aber unumwunden zu: „Ich war bei dem Anruf völlig überwältigt, hatte aber insgeheim gehofft, diesen Preis einmal zu bekommen." Grünberg war bis zu seinem Ruhestand 2004 ganze 32 Jahre in Jülich als Wissenschaftler tätig.

PETER GRÜNBERG. Can you conceive of a world without multi-gigabyte hard drives or MP3 players today? The foundations for these were laid at the Research Center Juelich, where physicist Peter Grünberg discovered the Giant Magnetoresistive Effect (GMR) in December 1988 and went on to patent it soon thereafter. He at once saw the potential of his discovery to expand storage capacity phenomenally. In fact, seldom has a scientific finding made a mass market debut so swiftly. Within months of its discovery, IBM showed interest in it and Juelich and by 1997 GMR read heads for computer drives were introduced.

Peter Grünberg was awarded the Nobel Prize in Physics ten years later. This did not come as a complete surprise to him as he had, after all, bided his time as a potential candidate for several years previously. After he was pronounced winner he candidly confessed, "I was completely overwhelmed by the phone call but had secretly nursed the hope that I would bag this prize one day". Grünberg had served 32 long years as scientist at Juelich by the time he retired in 2004.

Bestleistung: Nobelpreisträger für Physik
Region: Aachen
Ort: Jülich

Best performance: Nobel Prize winner in physics
Region: Aachen
Place: Juelich

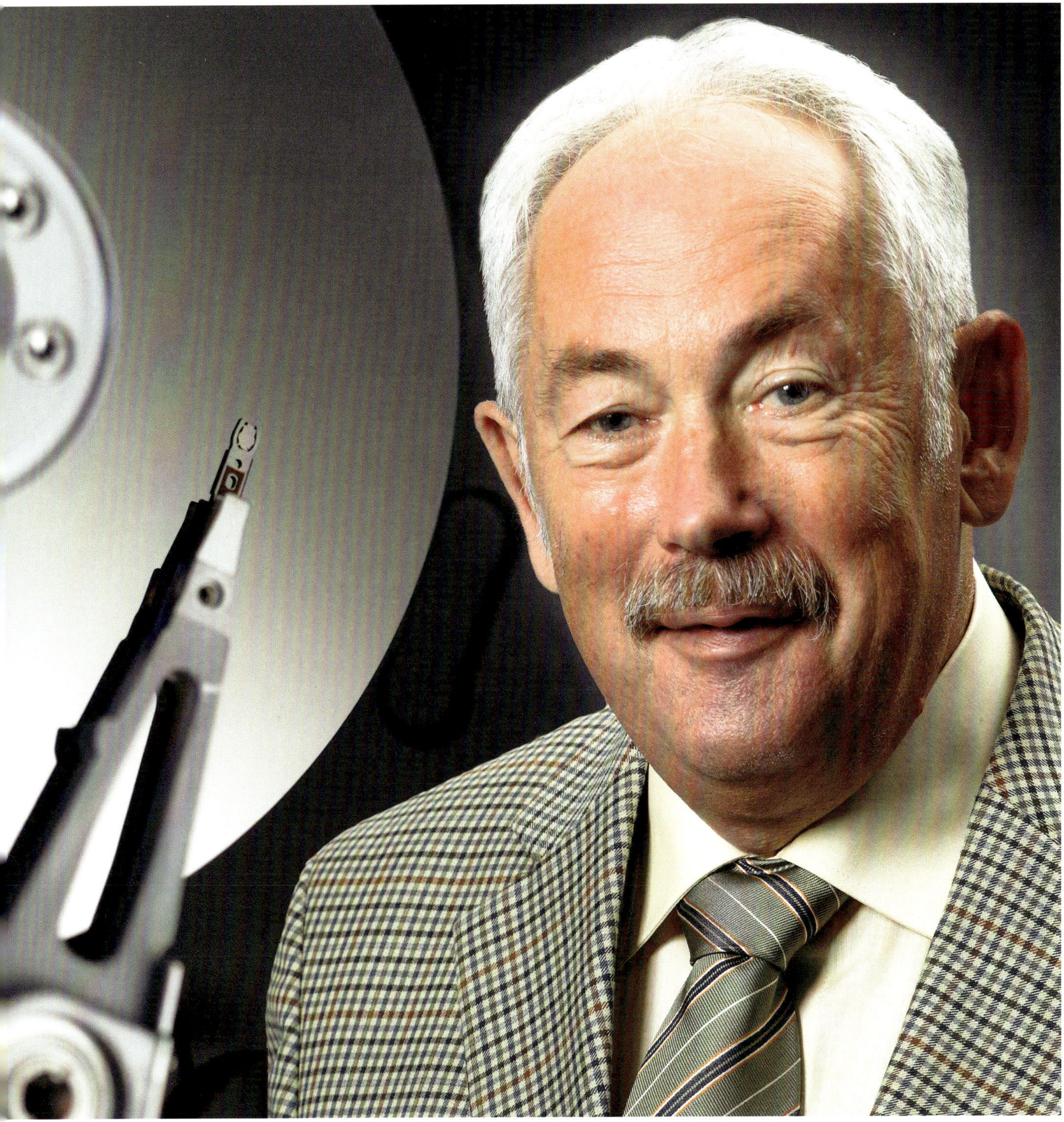

BLITZSCHNELL GEHOLFEN
HELP AT THE SPEED OF LIGHTNING

PHOENIX CONTACT. Das Hermannsdenkmal bei Detmold erinnert an die Schlacht im Teutoburger Wald im Jahr 9 nach Christus, bei der germanische Stämme die römische Legion besiegten. Mit ihrer Höhe von knapp 54 Metern zieht Deutschlands höchste Statue auch regelmäßig Blitze an. Deshalb wird genau hier untersucht, wann und in welcher Intensität Blitze in hochgelegene Ziele einschlagen. Ein Messsystem erfasst nun Blitzströme, deren Steilheit und Energie.

Entwickelt wurde das Lightning Monitoring System LM-S von dem Unternehmen Phoenix Contact, eigentlich um Windkraftanlagen kontinuierlich zu überwachen. LM-S misst die dortigen Blitzeinschläge, wertet die Daten aus und übermittelt sie per Internet an den Betreiber, der die umgehende Instandsetzung veranlassen kann. Dadurch entfallen teure vorbeugende Wartungen – gleichzeitig wird die Energieerzeugung sicherer.

Die Innovation aus dem Hause Phoenix Contact findet viel Anerkennung. So erhielt der Weltmarktführer für elektrische Verbindungstechnik aus dem ostwestfälischen Blomberg 2012 den renommierten Hermes Award der Deutschen Messe AG.

PHOENIX CONTACT. The Hermann monument near Detmold was erected in memory of the battle at the Teutoburg Forest in 9 AD, which saw Germanic tribes defeat a Roman legion. At just under 54 metres the tallest statue in Germany, it habitually attracts lightning, making it ideal for studying the time and intensity of lightning strikes on objects situated at a height. A measuring system now detects lightning strikes and analyses their steepness and energy.

The Lightning Monitoring System LM-S was developed by a company called Phoenix Contact, originally for continuous monitoring of wind turbines. LM-S measures the lightning strikes in the area, evaluates the data and informs the operator online, who can then promptly initiate corrective measures. This prevents expensive maintenance, while making power generation safer.

Phoenix Contact is gaining recognition for this innovation from many quarters. For example, Deutsche Messe AG honoured this global leader in electrical connection technology, based in Blomberg in Ost-Westfalen, with its famed Hermes Award in 2012.

Bestleistung: Hermes Award für innovatives Überwachungssystem
Region: Ostwestfalen-Lippe
Ort: Blomberg

Best performance: Hermes Award for an innovative monitoring system
Region: Ostwestfalen-Lippe
Place: Blomberg

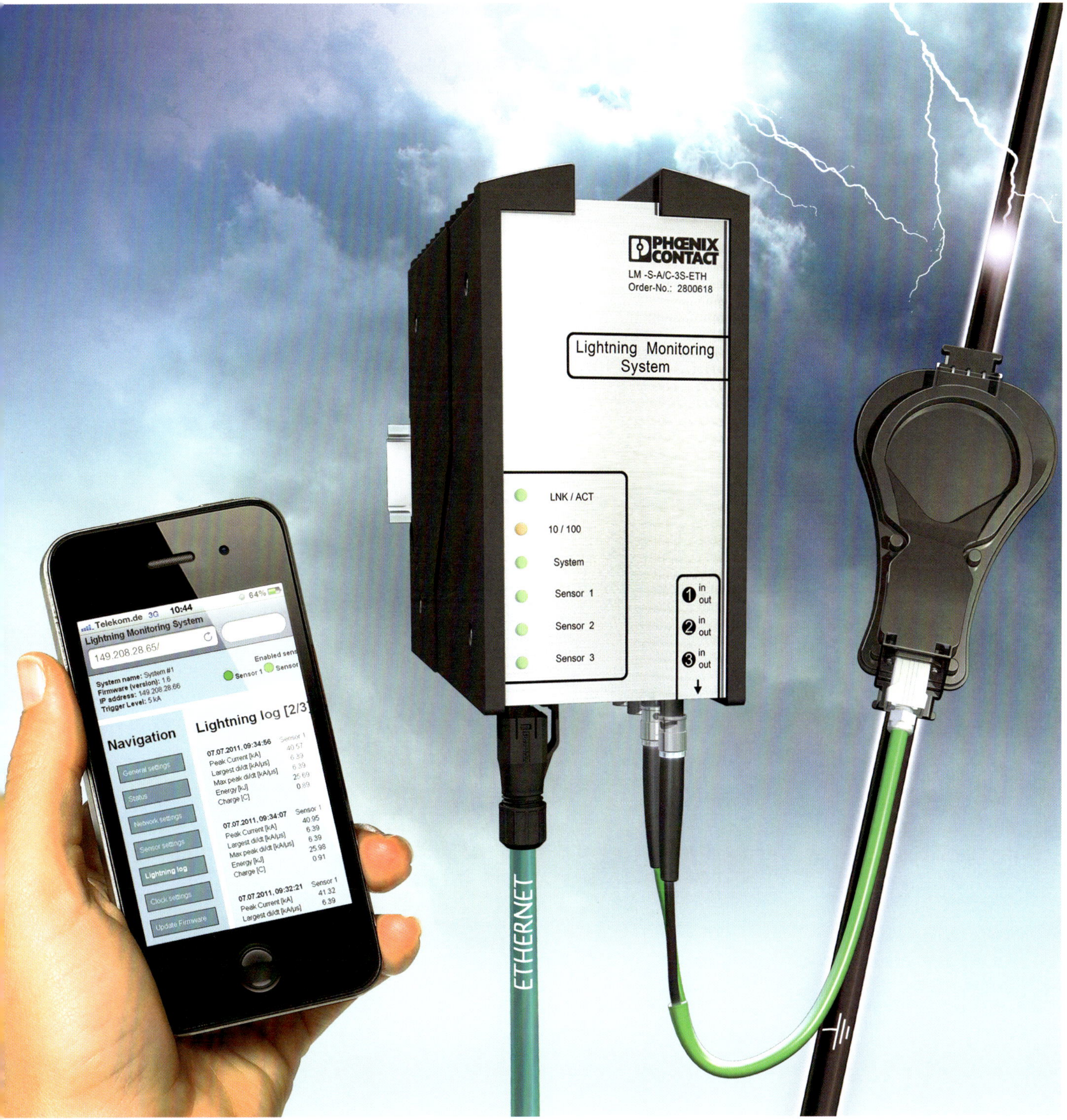
PHOENIX CONTACT
LM -S-A/C-3S-ETH
Order-No.: 2800618
Lightning Monitoring System
LNK / ACT
10 / 100
System
Sensor 1
Sensor 2
Sensor 3
in out
in out
in out
ETHERNET
Telekom.de 3G 10:44
64%
Lightning Monitoring System
149.208.28.65/
System name: System #1
Firmware (version): 1.6
IP address: 149.208.28.66
Trigger Level: 5 kA
Navigation
General settings
Status
Network settings
Sensor settings
Lightning log
Clock settings
Update Firmware
Lightning log [2/3]
07.07.2011, 09:34:56
Peak Current [kA]
Largest di/dt [kA/µs]
Max peak di/dt [kA/µs]
Energy [kJ]
Charge [C]
07.07.2011, 09:34:07
Sensor 1
Peak Current [kA] 40.95
Largest di/dt [kA/µs] 6.39
Max peak di/dt [kA/µs] 6.39
Energy [kJ] 25.98
Charge [C] 0.91
07.07.2011, 09:32:21
Sensor 1
Peak Current [kA] 41.32
Largest di/dt [kA/µs] 6.39

LEISTUNGSSCHAU DER FOTOGRAFIE
PHOTOGRAPHY ON SHOW

PHOTOKINA. Alle zwei Jahre ist Köln für einige Tage die Welthauptstadt der Fotografie. Dann nämlich treffen sich Fotobegeisterte aus aller Welt auf der photokina, der weltweit bedeutendsten Leistungsschau zum Thema Fotografie. Die Leitmesse der Foto- und Imaging-Branche bringt wie keine andere Veranstaltung Industrie, Handel, professionelle Anwender und fotobegeisterte Endverbraucher zusammen.

Die erste photokina wurde 1950 auf Initiative des Präsidenten des Fotoverbandes, Bruno Uhl, in Köln eröffnet. Bereits damals gab es als Rahmenprogramm sogenannte Bilderschauen, Ausstellungen von bekannten Fotografen und Künstlern. Diese sind auch gut 60 Jahre später noch Highlights im Rahmenprogramm der Messe.

Auf der photokina stellen rund 1.200 Anbieter aus 50 Ländern ihre Produkte und Dienstleistungen vor. Über 180.000 Besucher aus 165 Ländern finden während der gesamten Laufzeit der Messe verschiedene Vorträge und Diskussionsrunden im Kongressprogramm. Events in der gesamten Domstadt runden die internationale Leitmesse ab.

PHOTOKINA. Every two years for a few days, Cologne turns into the photography capital of the world as enthusiasts from the four corners of the earth converge at photokina, the world's best-known photography exhibition. More so than any other event, this leading trade fair for the photography and imaging sector brings together industry, trade, professional users and end consumers with a passion for photography.

Photokina was first held in Cologne in 1950 at the initiative of Bruno Uhl, president of the photography association. Even in those days the supporting programme comprised of so-called photo-shows and expositions of well-known photographers and artists. A good 60 years later these still form highlights of the programme.

1,200 suppliers from 50 countries present their products and services at photokina. The convention programme offers a diverse line-up of lectures and discussion forums to 180,000 visitors from 165 countries throughout the duration of the exhibition. Events spread out all over the cathedral city add the perfect touch to this leading international trade fair.

Bestleistung: Wichtigste Leistungsschau der Fotografie
Region: Köln / Bonn
Ort: Köln

Best performance: A seminal competitive photography exhibition
Region: Cologne / Bonn
Place: Cologne

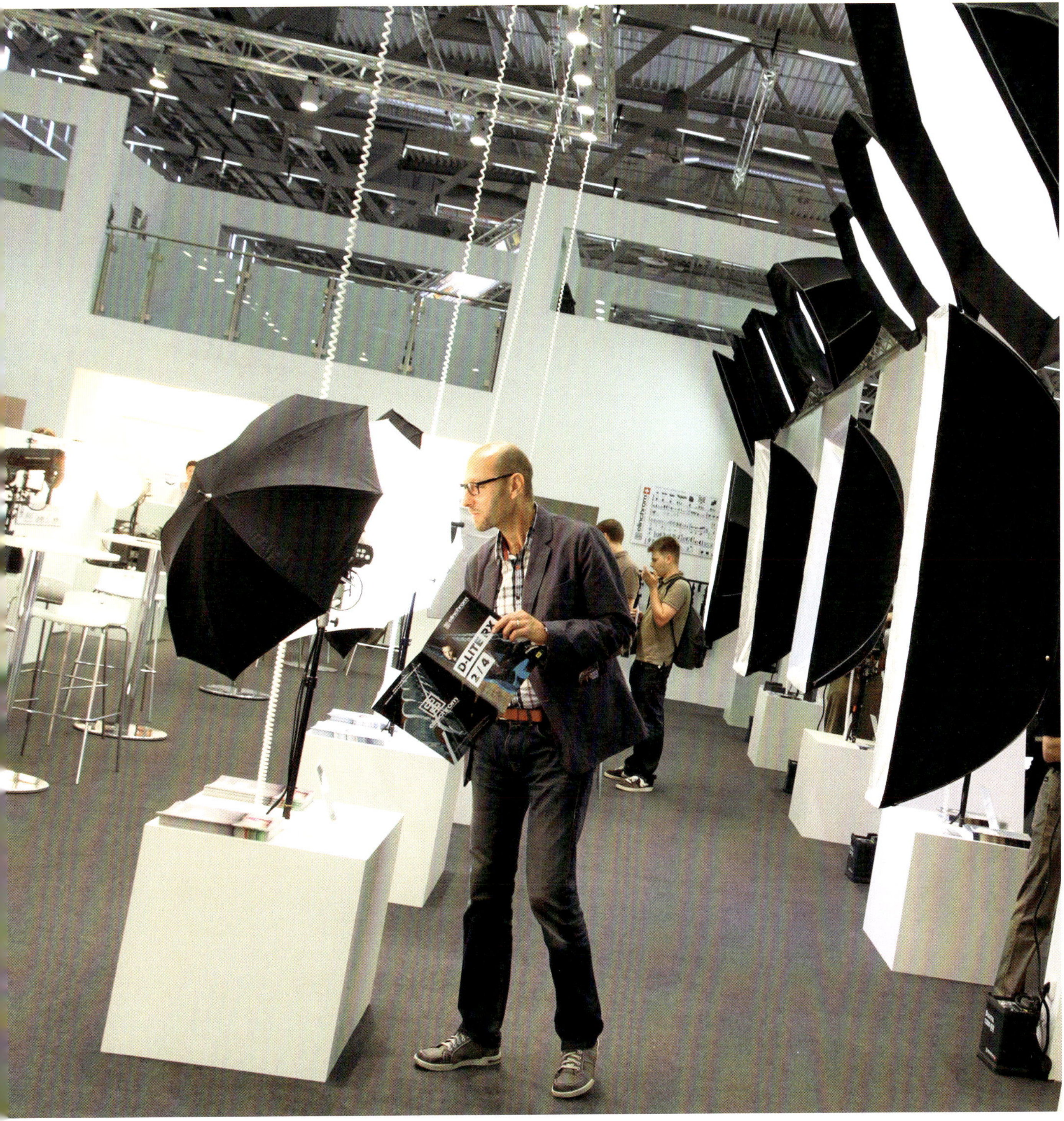
D-LITE RX
2/4

MORE DATA AT THE SPEED OF LIGHT

POLARISATION CONTROLLER EPC1000. Ever increasing quantities of videos, music, information and data are being transmitted via the internet. To cope with this vast data stream requires high-capacity fibre optic cables that transmit data by light pulses, not by electrical pulses as in copper cables. Optical fibres can cope with transmission rates around 10,000 times higher, but fibre optics have even greater potential, provided so-called polarisation controllers are also used.

The innovation from Paderborn enables both of the light's perpendicularly arranged polarisation directions in the optical fibre to be used, doubling information flow and significantly cutting the cost of data transfer.

Research on the polarisation controller for optical fibres was carried out at the Institute of Electrical and Information Technology, University of Paderborn. It is now more than a hundred times faster than the devices and research performance of global competitors. The founding of spin-off company Novoptel led to the product, now named EPC1000, being developed for full-fledged industrial use and launched on the market in 2010.

Best performance: World's fastest polarisation controller
Region: Ostwestfalen-Lippe
Place: Paderborn

Novoptel

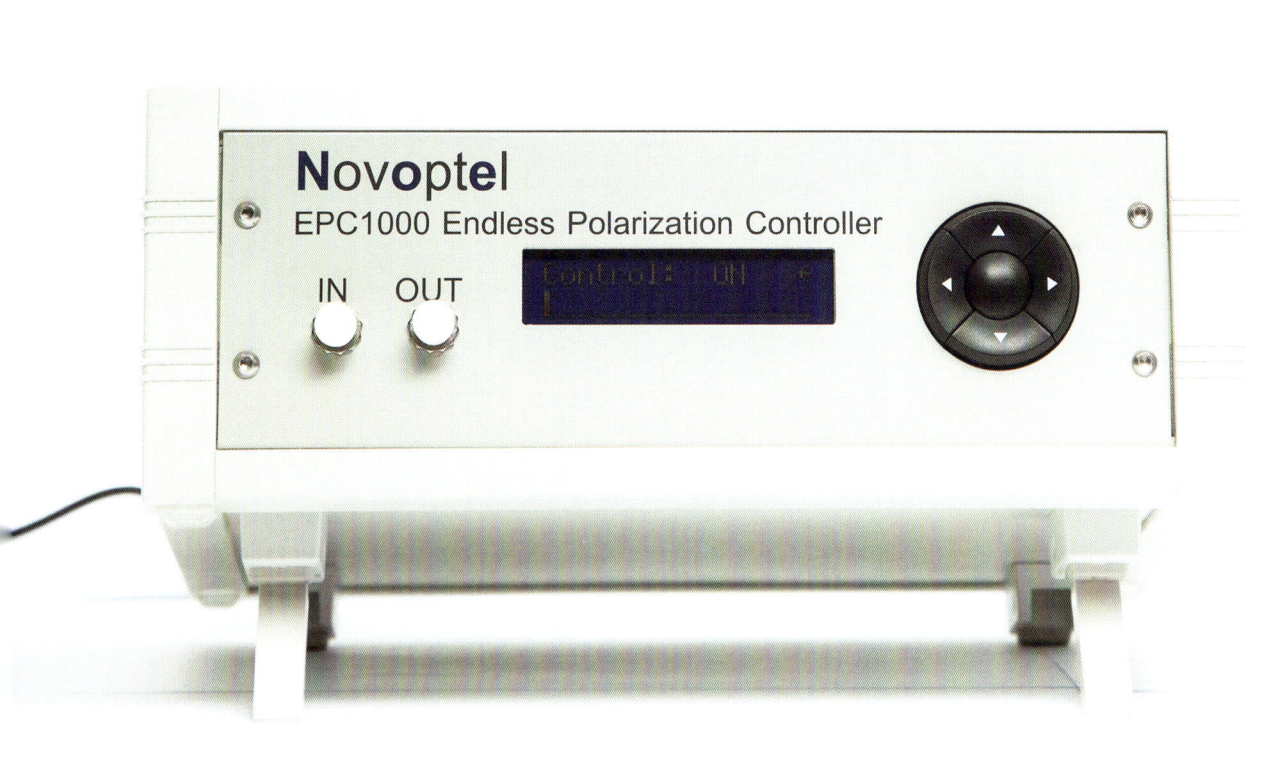

EPC1000 Endless Polarization Controller

IN OUT

Control: ON

JEDE BOHNE PERFEKT GERÖSTET
EACH BEAN PERFECTLY ROASTED

PROBAT-WERKE. Ob zum Frühstück, zum Mitnehmen oder zum Kuchen – Kaffee verbindet täglich weltweit Millionen Menschen. Für den richtigen Geschmack sorgen die Maschinen und Anlagen der PROBAT-Werke von Gimborn Maschinenfabrik GmbH aus Emmerich am Rhein. Von zehn Tassen Kaffee sind sieben mit PROBAT-Anlagen geröstet – eine klare Weltmarktführerschaft.

124 Arten Kaffeebohnen gibt es weltweit – doch erst mit der richtigen Röstung entstehen das typische Aroma und der bekannte Geschmack. Diese Kunst beherrschen die Anlagenbauer vom Niederrhein meisterhaft – und das seit 1868. Auf den richtigen Mix aus Temperatur, Dauer und Art der Röstung kommt es an. Neben dem verwendeten Rohkaffee spielen auch Verbrauchervorlieben für Röstkaffee eine Rolle: hell und mild oder dunkel und kräftig. Die Welterntemenge an Kaffee beträgt ungefähr 130 Millionen Sack à 60 Kilogramm – eine gewaltige Menge, die schnell, schonend und nachhaltig verarbeitet werden muss. Dabei setzen Kaffeeanbieter weltweit auf Probat-Anlagen, deren größte Maschine rund sechs Tonnen Röstkaffee pro Stunde verarbeitet.

PROBAT-WERKE. Whether over breakfast, as a takeaway, with cakes – every day coffee unites millions of people, throughout the world. And it's machinery and equipment made by PROBAT-Werke von Gimborn Maschinenfabrik GmbH from Emmerich am Rhein that lend their coffee just the right flavour. With seven cups out of ten being roasted by its machines, the verdict is in: PROBAT is world leader, hands down.

There are 124 types of coffee beans worldwide, but it is not until they have been properly roasted that their classic aroma and familiar taste can be unlocked. The equipment manufacturers from Lower Rhine have been masters of this fine art since 1868. In the proper blend of temperature, duration and roasting method lies the key. Light and mild or dark and strong: consumer preferences in roasted coffee, apart from the green coffee used, also have a say. The global coffee harvest yields roughly 130 million sacks, weighing 60 kilogrammes each; a staggering amount that requires quick processing, performed effectively and with care. Coffee suppliers the world over rely on Probat equipment for this. The company's largest machine can process about six tonnes of coffee per hour.

Bestleistung: Marktführer für Röstmaschinen und -anlagen
Region: Niederrhein
Ort: Emmerich am Rhein

Best performance: Market leader in roasting machines and plants
Region: Lower Rhine
Place: Emmerich am Rhein

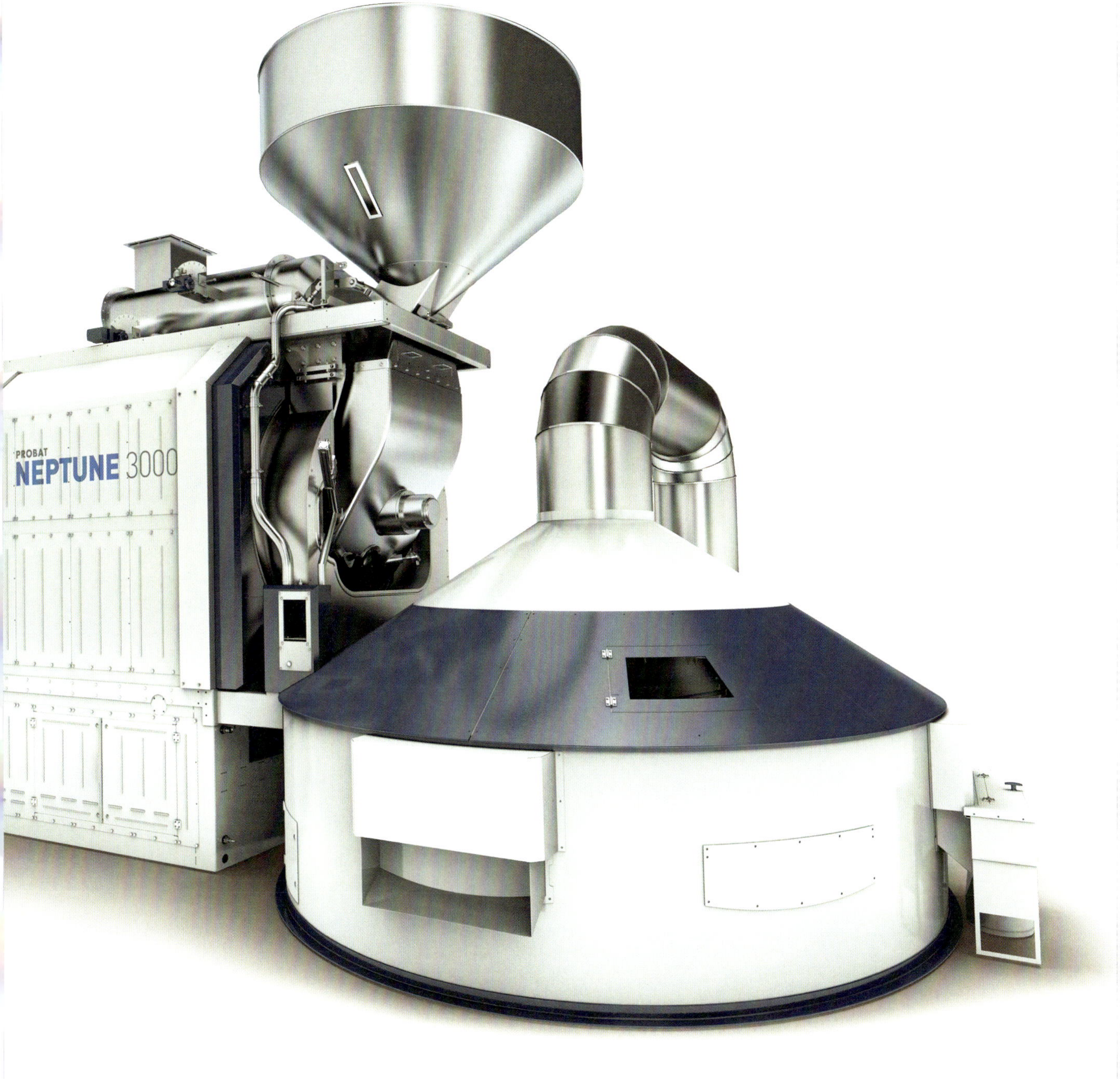
PROBAT
NEPTUNE 3000

GOLDSTANDARD DER KREBSPRÄVENTION
GOLD STANDARD FOR CANCER PREVENTION

QIAGEN. Im Mai 2011 meldete QIAGEN die Marke von 75 Millionen verkauften Digene HPV DNA Tests. Dieser Test zur Früherkennung von Gebärmutterhalskrebs ist weltweit führend und daher aktuell „Goldstandard" der Prävention. HPV – Humane Papillomaviren – gelten als Ursache für Gebärmutterhalskrebs. 75 Prozent aller Menschen haben im Laufe ihres Lebens eine HPV-Infektion. Normalerweise wird diese vom körpereigenen Immunsystem bekämpft, jedoch kann es bei Immunschwäche dauerhafte Infektionen geben, die Gebärmutterhalskrebs verursachen können.

Während der in der Vorsorge übliche Pap-Test nur bereits veränderte Zellen nachweist, stellt der Digene HPV DNA Test bereits das Risiko einer Erkrankung fest – ein routinemäßiger Abstrich genügt. Bislang wurde der HPV-Test in über 300 unabhängigen klinischen Studien auf seine Sicherheit getestet. Die flächendeckende Einführung des HPV-Tests in die routinemäßige Früherkennung wäre ein entscheidender Schritt zur weiteren Reduzierung der zweithäufigsten Krebserkrankung bei Frauen.

QIAGEN bietet zudem weitere Testverfahren und Technologien an, um auch in unterentwickelten Regionen die Gebärmutterhalskrebsprävention einführen zu können.

QIAGEN. QIAGEN reported having reached the 75 million mark of Digene HPV DNA tests marketed in May 2011. The world's leading test for early detection of cervical cancer, it is considered the "gold standard" of prevention. HPV – or human papilloma viruses – can cause cervical cancer. 75 per cent of all people will be infected with HPV in the course of their lives. Normally, the immune system succeeds in fighting them, but low immunity can result in permanent infection, leading to cervical cancer.

Standard preventative Pap smear tests only detect cell changes once they have taken place, whereas just a routine swab subjected to the Digene HPV DNA test predicts the risk of infection. To date, over 300 independent clinical studies have proven its reliability. The widespread introduction of HPV tests as part of routine early detection checks would be a decisive step in further reducing the incidence of one of the most common cancers among women.

QIAGEN also offers other test procedures and technologies to introduce cervical cancer prevention even in underdeveloped regions.

Bestleistung: Sicherster Test zur Früherkennung von Gebärmutterhalskrebs
Region: Düsseldorf
Ort: Hilden

Best performance: Most reliable test for early detection of cervical cancer
Region: Duesseldorf
Place: Hilden

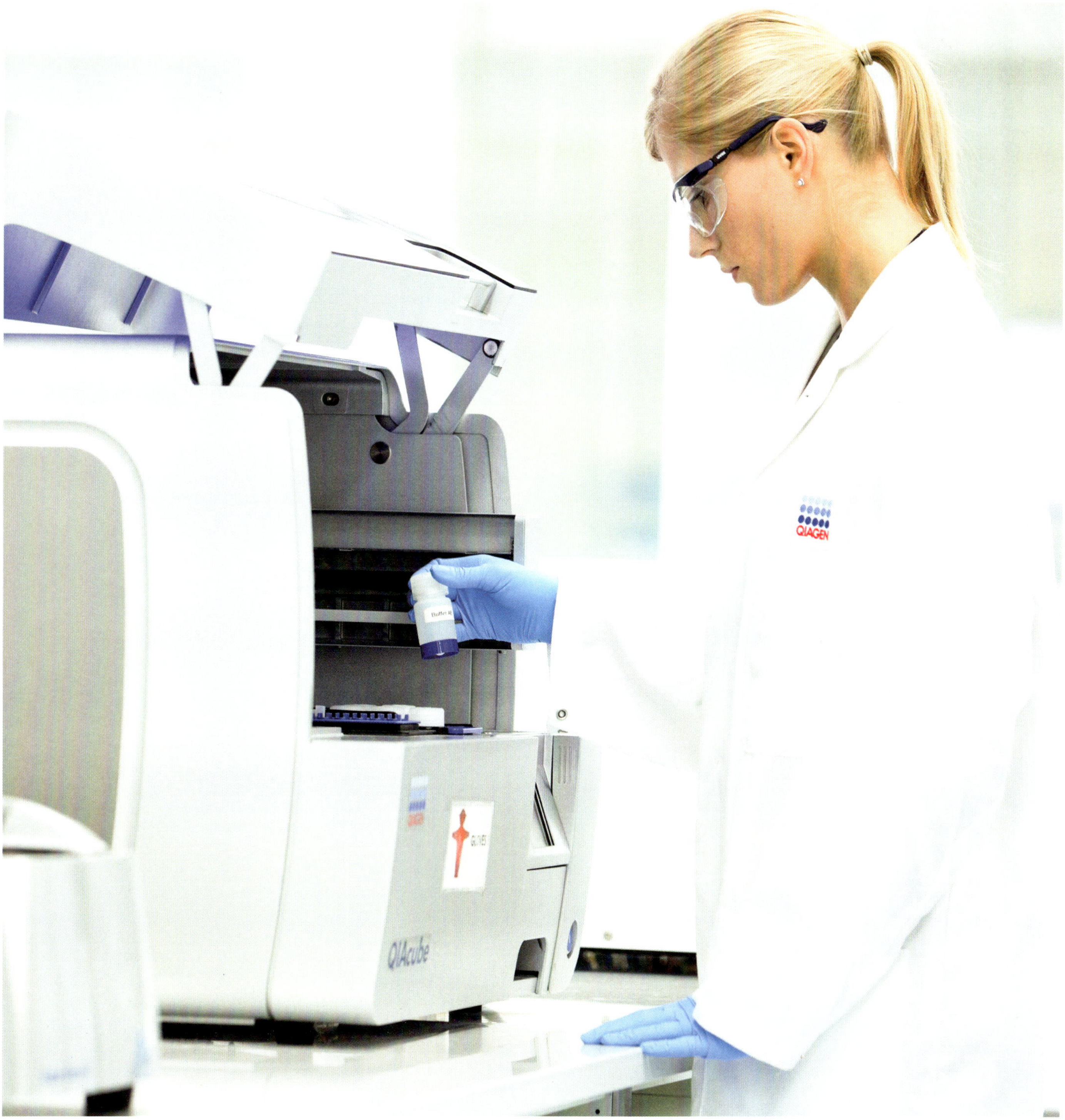
QIAGEN
QIAcube

BLICK INS WELTALL
GLIMPSE OF THE UNIVERSE

RADIOTELESKOP EFFELSBERG. Nur bedeutende Entwicklungen aus Industrie und Technik wurden in eine Briefmarkenserie der Bundesrepublik Deutschland aufgenommen. So zieren zum Beispiel der Hochofen Rheinhausen oder ein Braunkohlebagger die in den 70er und 80er Jahren erschienen Marken – aber auch das Radioteleskop Effelsberg wurde als wichtige technische Innovation berücksichtigt.

Seit 1972 erforscht das Max-Planck-Institut für Radioastronomie mit dem Radioteleskop den Weltraum. So wird es unter anderem eingesetzt, um Pulsare, Gas- und Staubwolken oder die Kerne ferner Galaxien zu beobachten. Durch das Teleskop ist es möglich, in sehr große Tiefen des Weltraums vorzudringen.

Mit 100 Metern Durchmesser ist es das größte vollbewegliche Radioteleskop Europas und gehört zu den größten weltweit. Das Gesamtgewicht der Konstruktion beträgt 3.200 Tonnen. In knapp zwölf Minuten kann der Parabolspiegel des Teleskops um 360 Grad gedreht und in knapp sechs Minuten um nahezu 90 Grad gekippt werden. So hat das Teleskop den gesamten Himmel im Blick.

RADIO TELESCOPE OF EFFELSBERG. Only the most significant industrial and technological developments have been recorded in a series of postage stamps of the Federal Republic of Germany. Thus, for instance, it is the blast furnace of Rheinhausen or a lignite excavator that adorned, the stamps appearing in the seventies and eighties; nonetheless the radio telescope of Effelsberg too was considered to be an important technological innovation.

The Max Planck Institute for Radio Astronomy has been exploring the universe with the radio telescope since 1972. It has thus been set up among other things to observe pulsars, cold gas and dust clusters or the nuclei of distant galaxies. It is possible to penetrate into remarkable depths of the universe with the telescope.

With a 100 meter diameter it is the biggest fully steerable radio telescope of Europe and ranks among the biggest worldwide. The gross weight of the construction amounts to 3,200 tonnes. It takes just under twelve minutes for the telescope's parabolic reflector to rotate around by 360 degrees and about six minutes to change its elevation angle by almost 90 degrees. The telescope has thus the whole sky within its range of vision.

Bestleistung: Größtes vollbewegliches Radioteleskop Europas
Region: Köln / Bonn
Ort: Bonn

Best performance: Europe's biggest fully steerable radio telescope
Region: Cologne / Bonn
Place: Bonn

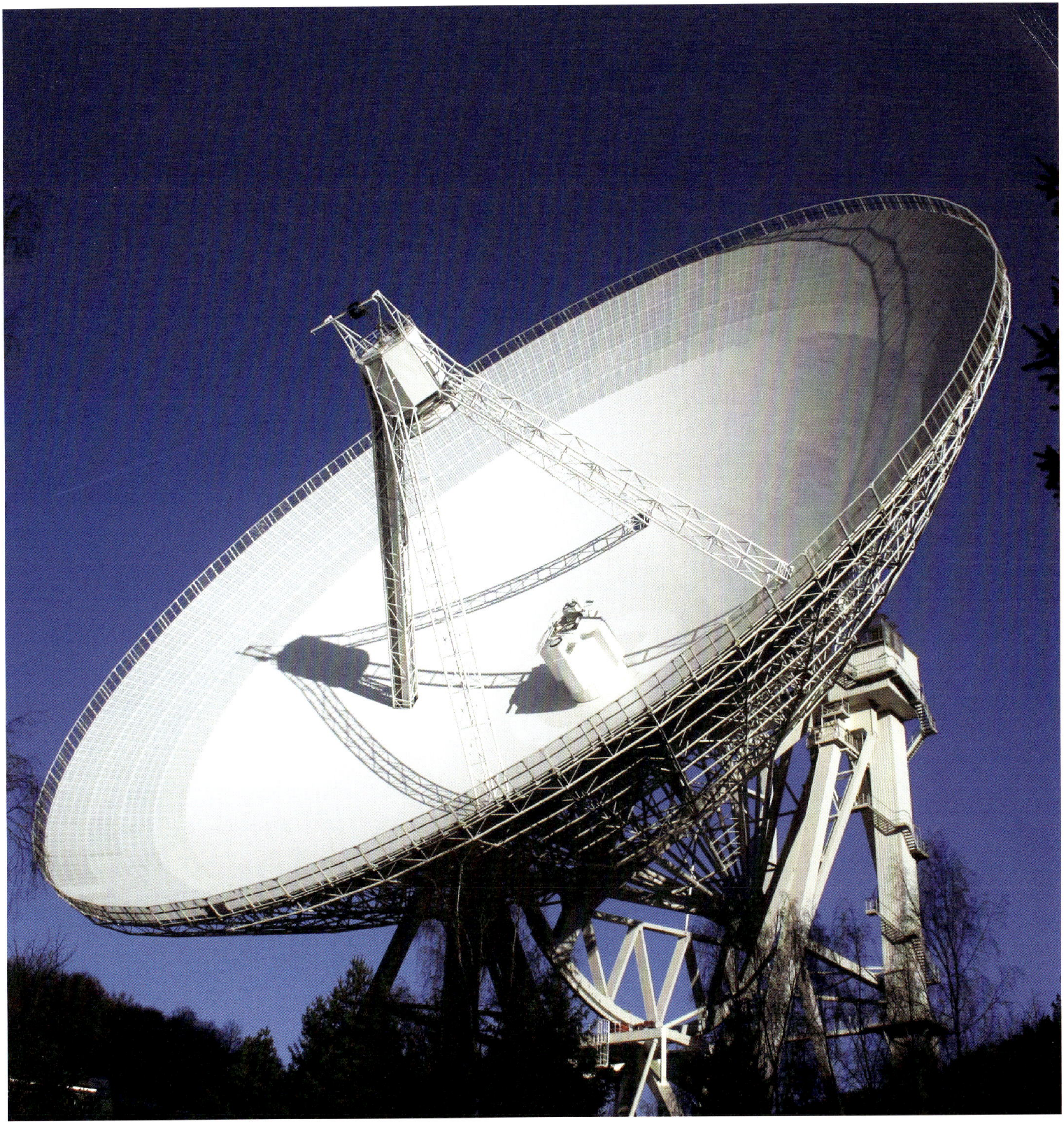

DAS WELTWEIT KLEINSTE KUNSTHERZ
THE SMALLEST ARTIFICIAL HEART IN THE WORLD

REINHEART. 2015 soll es so weit sein. Dann könnte ReinHeart, das weltweit kleinste Kunstherz, erstmals transplantiert werden. Bis dahin hat man im Institut für Angewandte Medizintechnik der Rheinisch-Westfälischen Technischen Hochschule (RWTH) Aachen genug zu tun. Die Ingenieure, Forscher und ihre medizinischen Partner vom Evangelischen Klinikum Niederrhein in Duisburg haben aber gemeinsam schon sehr viel erreicht, bis hin zu erfolgreichen Tests an Rindern.

ReinHeart wiegt 800 Gramm, ist so groß wie ein Granatapfel und für vier von fünf Patienten passend. Es wird vollimplantiert – das Kunstherz braucht keine künstlichen Ausgänge, was die Infektionsgefahr verringert. Externe Pumpen und Batterien entfallen. Um anfällige Teile zu vermeiden, arbeitet der Motor getriebelos. Den Strom liefern kleine Akkupacks am Gürtel drahtlos über die Haut. Diese kann der Patient für eine Stunde abnehmen, etwa zum Duschen.

Medizin-Hightech aus Nordrhein-Westfalen. Klar ist: Ein Spenderherz ist der beste Ersatz für ein krankes Herz, leider jedoch chronische Mangelware. Gäbe es ein kompaktes, finanzierbares Kunstherz mit langer Lebensdauer und hoher Mobilität – ReinHeart könnte Medizingeschichte schreiben.

REINHEART. 2015 could well see the smallest artificial heart ever, ReinHeart, being transplanted for the first time. Between now and then, the Institute for Applied Medical Engineering of the RWTH Aachen University still has a lot to do, but engineers, researchers and medical partners from the Evangelisches Klinikum Niederrhein in Duisburg have already conducted successful tests on animals.

ReinHeart weighs 800 grammes, is as big as a pomegranate and is a match on four out of five patients. The artificial heart is fully implantable and does not require artificial outlets, reducing the risk of infection. There are no external pumps and batteries, while operating on a direct linear motor does away with delicate parts. Small battery packs on a belt provide energy transdermally. These can be removed for an hour, for example to enable the patient to have a bath.

High-tech medical engineering from North Rhine-Westphalia. Clearly a donor heart is the best substitute for an unfit heart, but such hearts are in chronic short supply. As a compact, economically viable artificial heart with a long life and allowing for greater mobility, ReinHeart could well create medical history.

Bestleistung: Kleinstes Kunstherz der Welt
Region: Aachen
Ort: Aachen

Best performance: World's smallest artificial heart
Region: Aachen
Place: Aachen

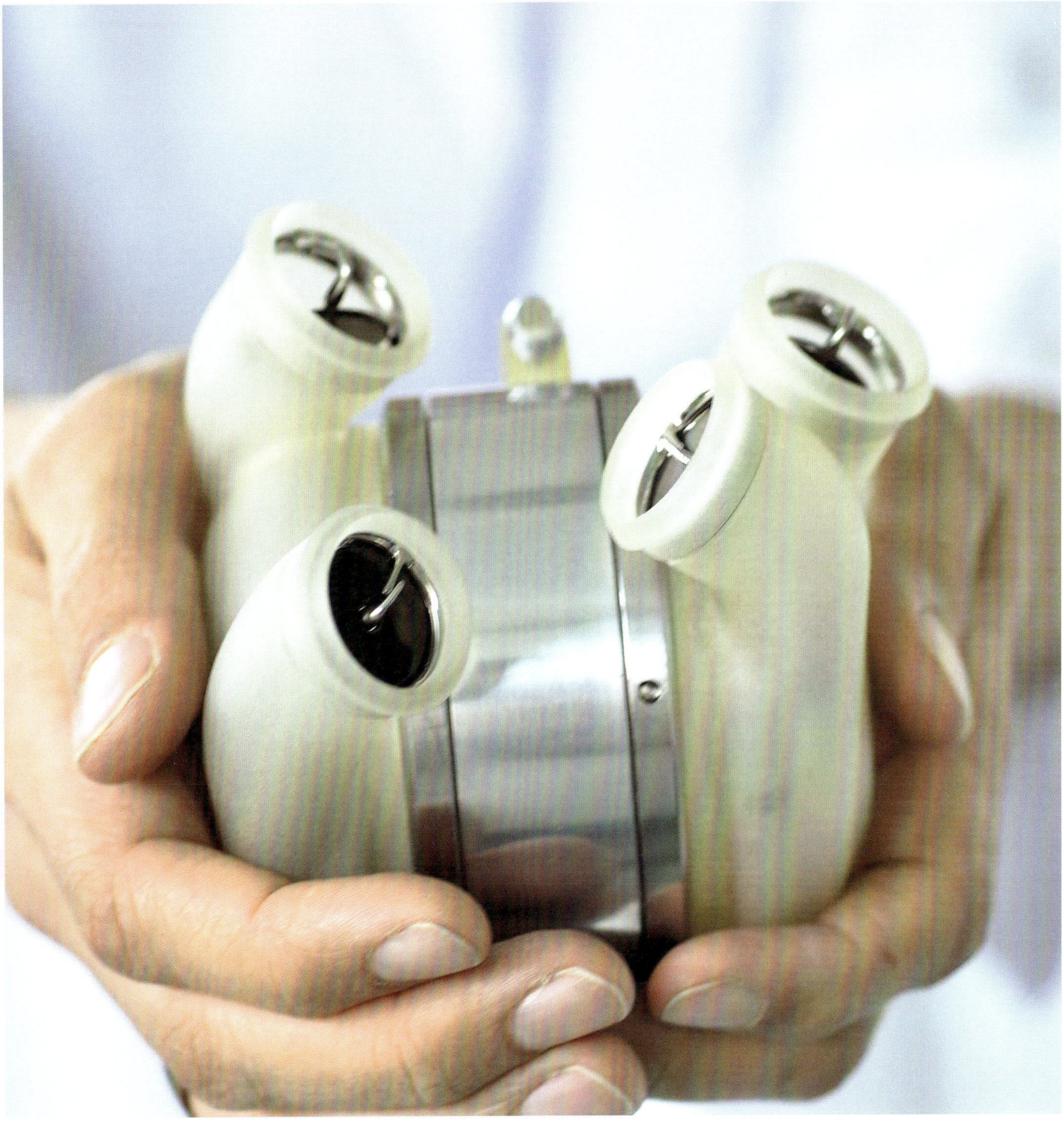

DIE KOFFER MIT DEN RILLEN
RIBBED LUGGAGE

RIMOWA. Seit über 100 Jahren stellt RIMOWA (Richard Morszeck Warenzeichen) hochwertiges Reisegepäck her. Durch die „Koffer mit den Rillen" ist das Kölner Familienunternehmen weltweit bekannt und zu Europas führendem Hersteller für Reisegepäck geworden.

1898 verließ der erste Koffer die Manufaktur in Köln, die zu diesem Zeitpunkt noch den Namen „Kofferfabrik Paul Morszeck" trug. Und auch wenn diese Serie noch traditionell aus Holz gefertigt wurde, legte die Manufaktur von Beginn an großen Wert auf eine leichte Bauweise. 1937 brachte Richard Morszeck, Sohn des Firmengründers, den ersten Koffer aus Leichtmetall auf den Markt, nun unter dem Namen RIMOWA. 1950 entstand der erste Koffer mit der bis heute typischen Rillenstruktur. „Handwerk meets Hightech" ist das Credo des Kölner Unternehmens. Seit 2000 produziert RIMOWA auch mit Polycarbonat. Die Koffer sind bei geringem Eigengewicht extrem robust und belastbar.

Dieter Morszeck, Inhaber und selbst Produktentwickler, leitet das Unternehmen heute in dritter Generation. Mit großem Erfolg bleibt er RIMOWAs Linie treu: erstklassiges Reisegepäck made in Germany.

RIMOWA. RIMOWA (Richard Morszeck's brand) has been manufacturing high quality travel bags for over 100 years. This family business from Cologne is famed all over the world for its "ribbed luggage" and has achieved a position of leadership in luggage manufacturing in Europe.

The first bag saw the light of day in 1898 in Cologne from a factory that still bore the name "Kofferfabrik Paul Morszeck". Despite wood being used for this series as per tradition, the factory set store right from the start on a lightweight form. The founder's son, Richard Morszeck, introduced the first light metal bag onto the market in 1937 under the name of RIMOWA. The signature ribbed bag was first launched in 1950. This company from Cologne goes by the credo of "Handcraft meets High-tech". It has also been producing polycarbonate bags since 2000. Despite their light weight, the bags are exceptionally tough and resilient.

Dieter Morszeck is the third generation owner and himself a product developer. The resounding success of the company lies in his commitment to RIMOWA's lineage of first class luggage, made in Germany.

Bestleistung: Führender Hersteller von Reisegepäck
Region: Köln / Bonn
Ort: Köln

Best performance: Leading manufacturer of travel bags
Region: Cologne / Bonn
Place: Cologne

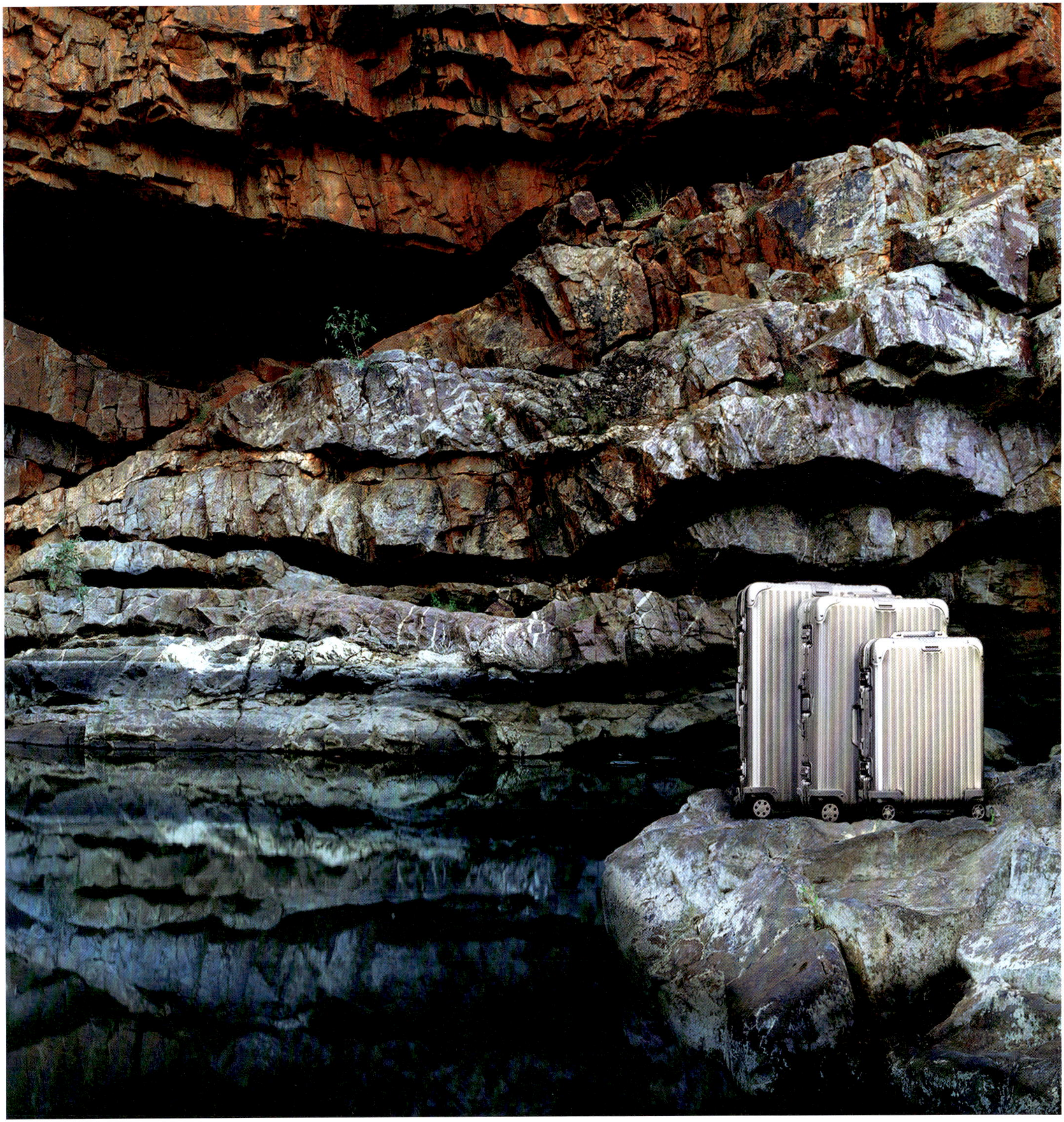

SILICON VALLEY IN AACHEN
SILICON VALLEY IN AACHEN

RWTH AACHEN. 1951 verkaufte und vermietete die kalifornische Stanford University hochschuleigene Flächen an Industrieunternehmen, verbunden mit dem Angebot, dass deren Mitarbeiter an Aus- und Weiterbildungsangeboten sowie an Studien- und Forschungsprojekten der Universität teilnehmen können. Ein Riesenerfolg und gleichzeitig der Grundstein für das Silicon Valley.

Auf dem Gelände der Rheinisch-Westfälischen Technischen Hochschule (RWTH) Aachen entsteht nach diesem Vorbild auf rund 800.000 Quadratmetern Fläche eine der größten Forschungslandschaften Europas. Hier werden bis zu 19 Forschungscluster mit ergänzender Infrastruktur ihre Arbeit aufnehmen. Unternehmen und Hochschulinstitute arbeiten dann gemeinsam in einer neuen Qualität des Austausches an definierten Forschungsschwerpunkten: ganzheitlich und interdisziplinär. Dabei erhalten sie exklusiven Zugang zu den technischen Einrichtungen sowie Bildungsangeboten des Campus. Durch diese enge Vernetzung von Experten aus Wissenschaft und Wirtschaft entstehen „Hotspots" der Forschung, die Wissen in einzigartiger Form bündeln und in die Praxis überführen.

RWTH AACHEN UNIVERSITY. In 1951, the Stanford University of California sold and leased academic spaces to industrial establishments with the offer of letting employees get training, pursue further education, and participate in studies and research projects of the university. Besides being a huge success, this decision laid the foundations for the creation of Silicon Valley.

Based on this model, one of the largest research sites in Europe is being developed on about 800,000 square metres of campus space at RWTH Aachen University. The space will provide the infrastructure for up to 19 clusters to take up research. Companies and academic institutions will then, based on a new calibre of exchange, jointly take up holistic and interdisciplinary work on defined core research areas. They will have exclusive access to the technical facilities and training offers of the campus. This networking between authorities on science and commerce will give rise to hotspots of research, providing a unique opportunity for knowledge to be pooled and put into practice.

Bestleistung: Eine der größten Forschungslandschaften
Region: Aachen
Ort: Aachen

Best performance: One of the biggest research scenarios
Region: Aachen
Place: Aachen

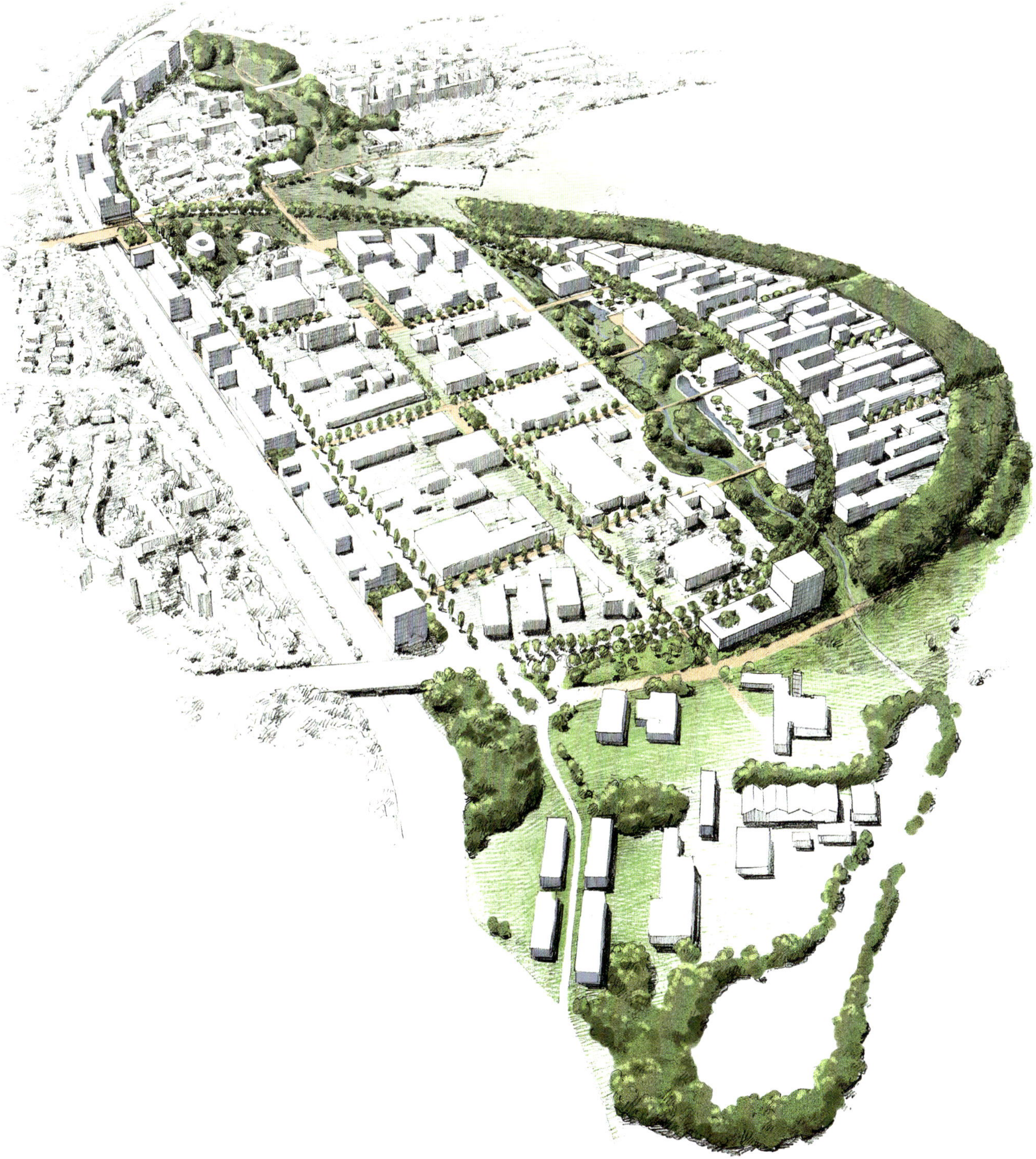

KLEINE FASERN – GROSSE KRAFT
FINE FIBRES – MASSIVE STRENGTH

SACHSENRÖDER. Ein fast zwei Tonnen schwerer Mercedes SLR wird an einem Kran nach oben gezogen. Zwischen Haken und Auto befindet sich ausschließlich ein Stück Vulkanfiber, etwa so groß wie ein DIN-A4-Blatt. Das innovative Produkt besteht die Zerreißprobe und hält den Wagen in der Höhe.

Grundstoff des Spezialpapiers sind Baumwollfasern, die das Wuppertaler Unternehmen Sachsenröder in einem besonderen Verfahren zu Vulkanfiber verarbeitet – ein fester, hornartiger Werkstoff, der verschleißfest ist und sich exzellent weiterverwenden lässt. Entsprechend vielfältig sind die Anwendungsgebiete: So eignet sich Vulkanfiber als Trägermaterial für Schleifmittel und sorgt dafür, dass sich Holzfurniere nicht ablösen. Zudem wird die Naturfaser in gestanzter Form als Dichtung verwendet oder dient als Einlage in medizinischen Geräten.

Den Grundstein für die Entwicklung zum Weltmarktführer für Vulkanfiber legte Anfang des 20. Jahrhunderts Gründer Gustav-Heinrich Sachsenröder. Er hätte sich damals wahrscheinlich nicht träumen lassen, dass der von ihm entwickelte Werkstoff einmal ein fast zwei Tonnen schweres Automobil halten würde.

SACHSENRÖDER. Imagine a Mercedes SLR weighing almost two tonnes being lifted by crane. There is nothing between the hook and car but this piece of approximately A4-sized vulcanised fibre. Yes, the innovative product passes the shear test to hold the car up with flying colours!

The basic material of the speciality paper consists of cotton fibres. By a special procedure the Wuppertal based company, Sachsenröder, processes it into vulcanised fibre, a tough, horn-like material, which is wear-resistant and excellent for further processing. The fields of application are equally varied. And so vulcanised fibre is suitable as a carrier for abrasives and ensures that wood veneers do not peel off. The natural fibre in its punched form can, moreover, be used as a gasket or serves as an insert in medical equipments.

The early 20th century saw the founder, Gustav-Heinrich Sachsenröder, pave the way for the company's emergence as a global market leader in vulcanised fibre. In all likelihood, he could not have dreamt then that the material developed by him would someday hold a car weighing nearly two tonnes.

Bestleistung: Marktführer für Vulkanfiber
Region: Bergisches Städtedreieck
Ort: Wuppertal

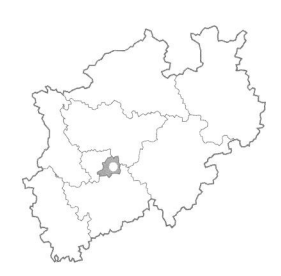

Best performance: A market leader in vulcanised fibres
Region: Bergisches Staedtedreieck
Place: Wuppertal

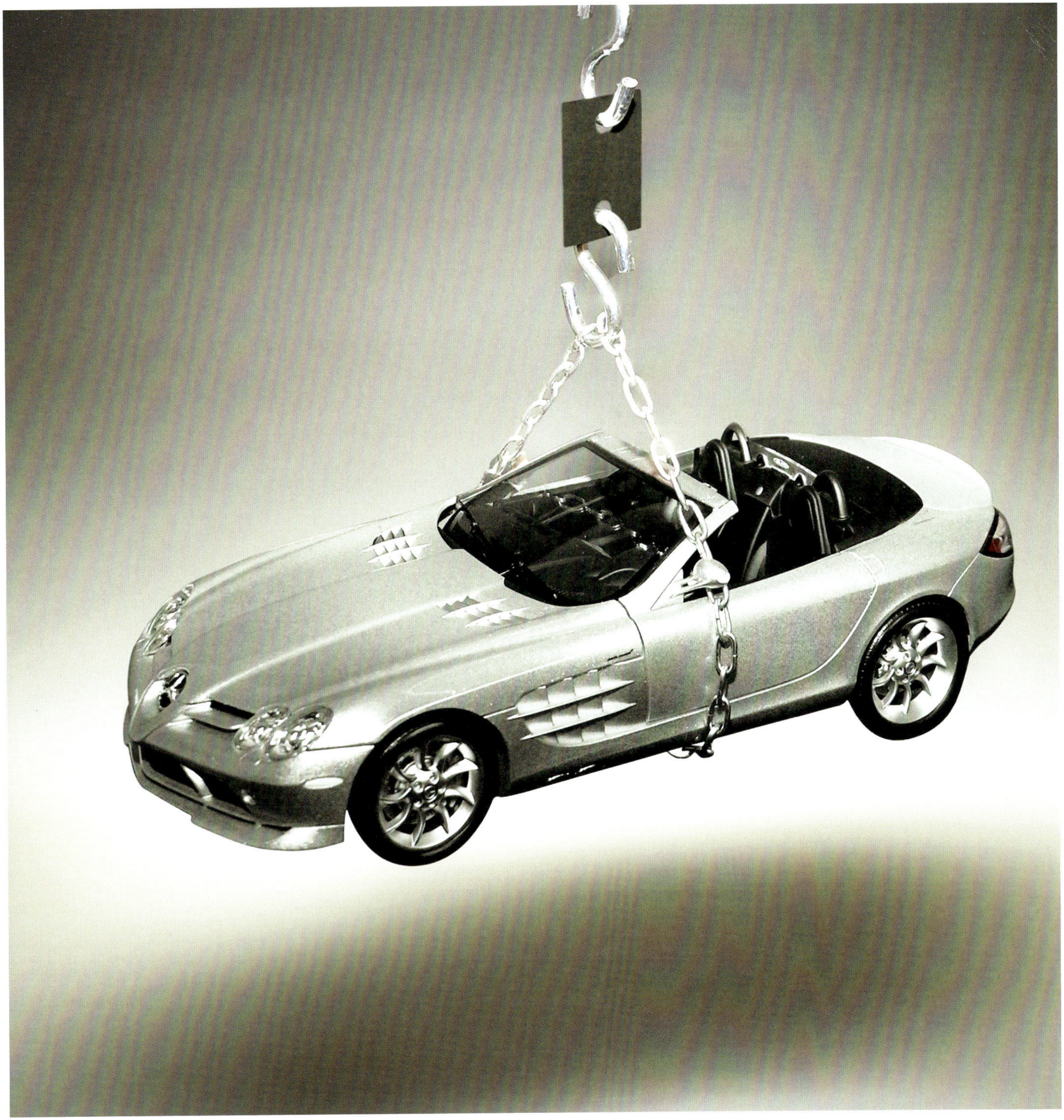

LEICHTBAU MASSGESCHNEIDERT
CUSTOMISED LIGHTWEIGHT CONSTRUCTION

SAERTEX. Die Erfolgsgeschichte des Unternehmens beginnt 1982 im westfälischen Saerbeck: SAERTEX verknüpft Produktionserfahrung von textilen Flächen mit einer wegweisenden Idee – der Entwicklung und Herstellung von Industrietextilien aus Glasfaser, Carbon und Aramid. Abhängig von den eingesetzten Fasern, deren Flächengewicht, Winkelkombination und Ausrichtung, werden unterschiedliche mechanische Festigkeiten erzielt. So entstehen Non Crimp Fabrics (NCF) für die Composite-Industrie: extrem belastbare Bauteile für Flugzeuge, Brücken, Schiffe und Autos, die deutlich leichter sind als herkömmliche Materialien.

Die innovativen Verbundwerkstoffe von SAERTEX spielen zum Beispiel in den Flügeln des größten Verkehrsflugzeugs der Welt – dem Airbus A380 – eine tragende Rolle.

Die Nachfrage wächst, auch dank der boomenden Windenergiebranche. Heute ist die SAERTEX-Gruppe ein Global Player: Das Unternehmen hat acht Niederlassungen in sieben Ländern auf vier Kontinenten. Der Stammsitz im Münsterland ist nach wie vor Schaltzentrale des Unternehmens. Von hier aus treiben die innovativen SAERTEX-Produkte weltweit ganze Branchen an.

SAERTEX. Cut to Saerbeck, Westphalia: the year is 1982 and SAERTEX is setting out to combine its production know-how on textile surfaces with a path breaking concept to develop and manufacture industrial textiles from a mix of glass fibre, carbon and aramide. What follows is a success story! Mechanical resistances differ depending on the fibre type, surface load, angle combination and direction. The Non Crimp Fabrics (NCF) obtained in this way for the composites industry to make extremely resilient components in aircrafts, bridges, ships and cars are considerably lighter than conventional materials.

Innovative composites made by SAERTEX play a key role, for instance, in the wings of the world's biggest carrier aircraft, the Airbus A380.

The growth in demand can also be put down to the booming wind energy sector. Today, the SAERTEX Group is a global player with eight subsidiaries in seven countries, spread over four continents, but the Muensterland headquarters of this pioneering company remains the centre of operations. All over the world innovative SAERTEX-products advance entire industries.

Bestleistung: Führender Hersteller für textile Verbundwerkstoffe
Region: Münsterland
Ort: Saerbeck

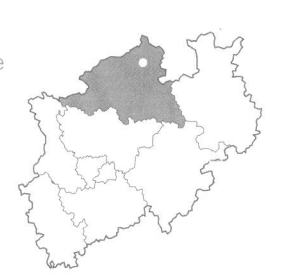

Best performance: Leading manufacturer of textile composites
Region: Muensterland
Place: Saerbeck

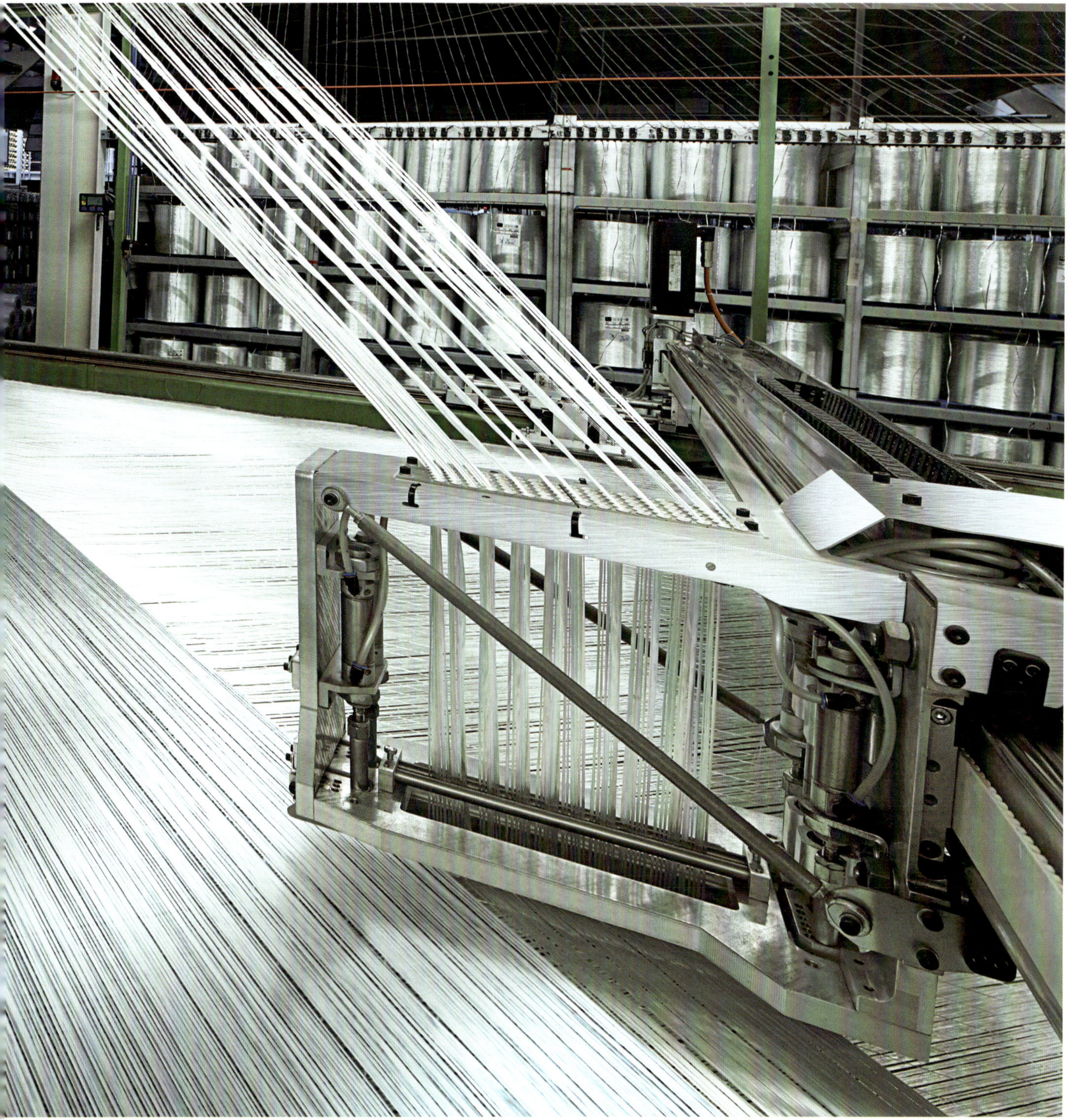

ERFOLGREICHES WANDERTHEATER
SUCCESSFUL TRAVELLING THEATRE

SCHAUSPIEL KÖLN. 2007 übernimmt eine Kölnerin: Die gefeierte Regisseurin Karin Beier wird Intendantin des Schauspiel Köln. Das Haus wurde 2010 und 2011 von Deutschlands Theaterkritikern zum Theater des Jahres gewählt. Im selben Zeitraum wurde die Bühne außerdem in den Kategorien der besten Dramaturgin, der besten Schauspielerin und der besten Inszenierung ausgezeichnet. 2012 wurde sie dann zum besten Theater in Nordrhein-Westfalen gekürt.

Als Intendantin holte Karin Beier Regie- und Schauspielgrößen in die Rheinmetropole, als Regisseurin überzeugte sie mit besonderem Programm, wie eben mit der besten Inszenierung 2011: eine Uraufführung aus der Feder von Literaturnobelpreisträgerin Elfriede Jelinek – mit dem fulminanten Dreiteiler „Das Werk/Im Bus/Ein Sturz" überzeugte Beier nicht nur die Theaterkritiker, sondern auch erneut ihre Besucher im Schauspielhaus.

Diese müssen ihr Theater zurzeit in Ausweichquartieren genießen: Das von dem renommierten Architekten Wilhelm Riphahn 1962 gebaute Haus wird nämlich aufwändig saniert, um dann ab 2015 unter neuer Intendanz in frischem Glanz zu erstrahlen.

SCHAUSPIEL KÖLN. She takes charge in 2007 and is originally from Cologne. The celebrated director Karin Beier becomes director of Schauspiel Köln (The Cologne Theatre). In 2010 and 2011 the playhouse was voted "Theatre of the Year" by critics in Germany. The same period also saw this theatre win in the Best Producer, Best Actress and Best Production categories. In 2012 it went on to be nominated the best theatre of North Rhine-Westphalia.

In her role of theatre manager Karin Beier brought star directors and theatre greats to this metropolis of the Rhine region. She impressed as a director, for her select programmes, the best production of 2011 being a case in point. This was a debut performance of the play written by Elfriede Jelinek, the Nobel Prize winner for literature. The brilliant trilogy "Das Werk/Im Bus/Ein Sturz" ("The Works/In the Bus/A Fall") left not just critics impressed with Beier, but enthused her theatre audiences anew.

At present they have little choice but to enjoy theatre at other locations. Constructed in 1962 by the famous architect Wilhelm Riphahn, the theatre is now under extensive renovation. In 2015 it will re-open in renewed splendour under a new theatre manager.

Bestleistung: Theater des Jahres 2010 und 2011
Region: Köln / Bonn
Ort: Köln

Best performance: Theater of the Year in 2010 and 2011
Region: Cologne / Bonn
Place: Cologne

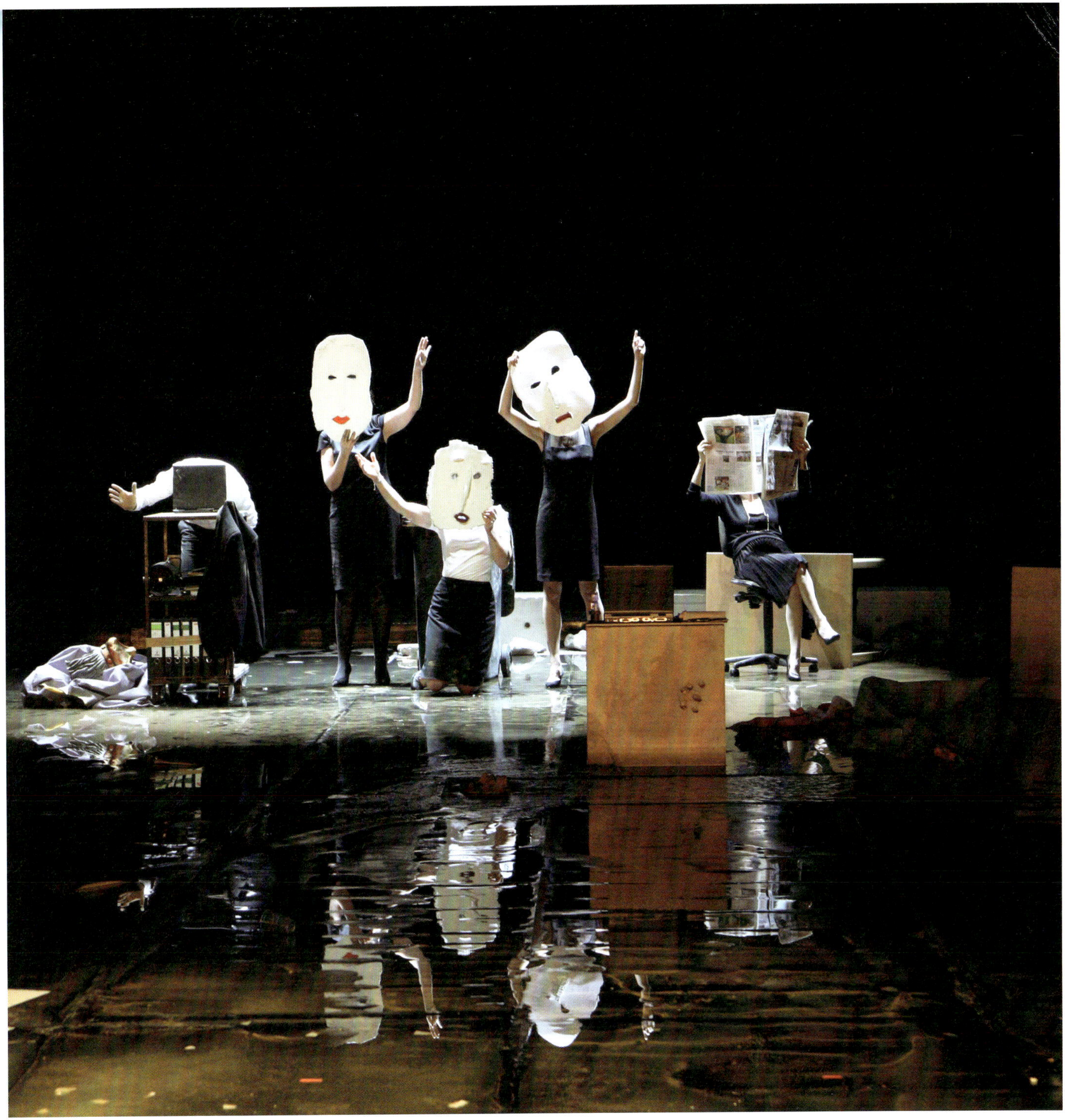

ROKOKO IM RHEINLAND
ROCOCO IN THE RHINELAND

SCHLOSS AUGUSTUSBURG. Ein prunkvolles Treppenhaus, verspielte Ornamente, üppig angelegte Gärten – um ein echtes Rokoko-Schloss zu erleben, muss man in Nordrhein-Westfalen nicht weit reisen: Schloss Augustusburg in Brühl zählt zu den ersten bedeutenden Schöpfungen dieser Stilrichtung in Deutschland.

Von 1725 bis 1768 errichteten der westfälische Baumeister Johann Conrad Schlaun und der kurbayerische Hofbaumeister François de Cuvilliés im Auftrag des Kölner Kurfürsten und Erzbischofs Clemens August dessen Sommer-Residenzschloss auf den Ruinen einer mittelalterlichen Wasserburg. Als besonderes Prunkstück beherbergt Schloss Augustusburg das berühmte Treppenhaus von Balthasar Neumann, einem der renommiertesten Architekten jener Zeit.

Die UNESCO nahm Schloss Augustusburg 1984 gemeinsam mit dem benachbarten Jagdschloss Falkenlust und den weitläufigen Parkanlagen als herausragendes Beispiel für die Schlossbaukunst des 18. Jahrhunderts in die Welterbeliste auf. Zur Zeit der Bundesregierung in Bonn wurde Augustusburg zudem als Repräsentationsschloss des Bundespräsidenten und der Bundesregierung genutzt.

SCHLOSS AUGUSTUSBURG. A magnificent staircase, dainty ornamentation, luxuriously laid out gardens – one does not have to travel too far in North Rhine-Westphalia to enjoy a genuine Rococo palace. Schloss Augustusburg (The Augustusburg Palace) in Bruehl ranks among the earliest creations of significance in this style in Germany.

The Elector and Archbishop of Cologne, Clemens August, commissioned the Westphalian masterbuilder, Johann Conrad Schlaun, and the Bavarian court architect, François de Cuvilliés, to build him a summer palace. It was built between 1725 and 1768 on the ruins of a mediaeval moated castle. This palace houses the famous staircase designed by Balthasar Neumann, one of the most renowned architects of his time, as its stunning centrepiece.

In 1984 UNESCO declared Schloss Augustusburg and the neighbouring hunting lodge, Falkenlust, with its spacious gardens, World Heritage sites for being outstanding examples of 18th century palace architecture. In addition, Schloss Augustusburg was used for representational purposes by the German president and government when Bonn was the capital.

Bestleistung: UNESCO-Welterbe
Region: Köln / Bonn
Ort: Brühl

Best performance: UNESCO World Heritage Site
Region: Cologne / Bonn
Place: Bruehl

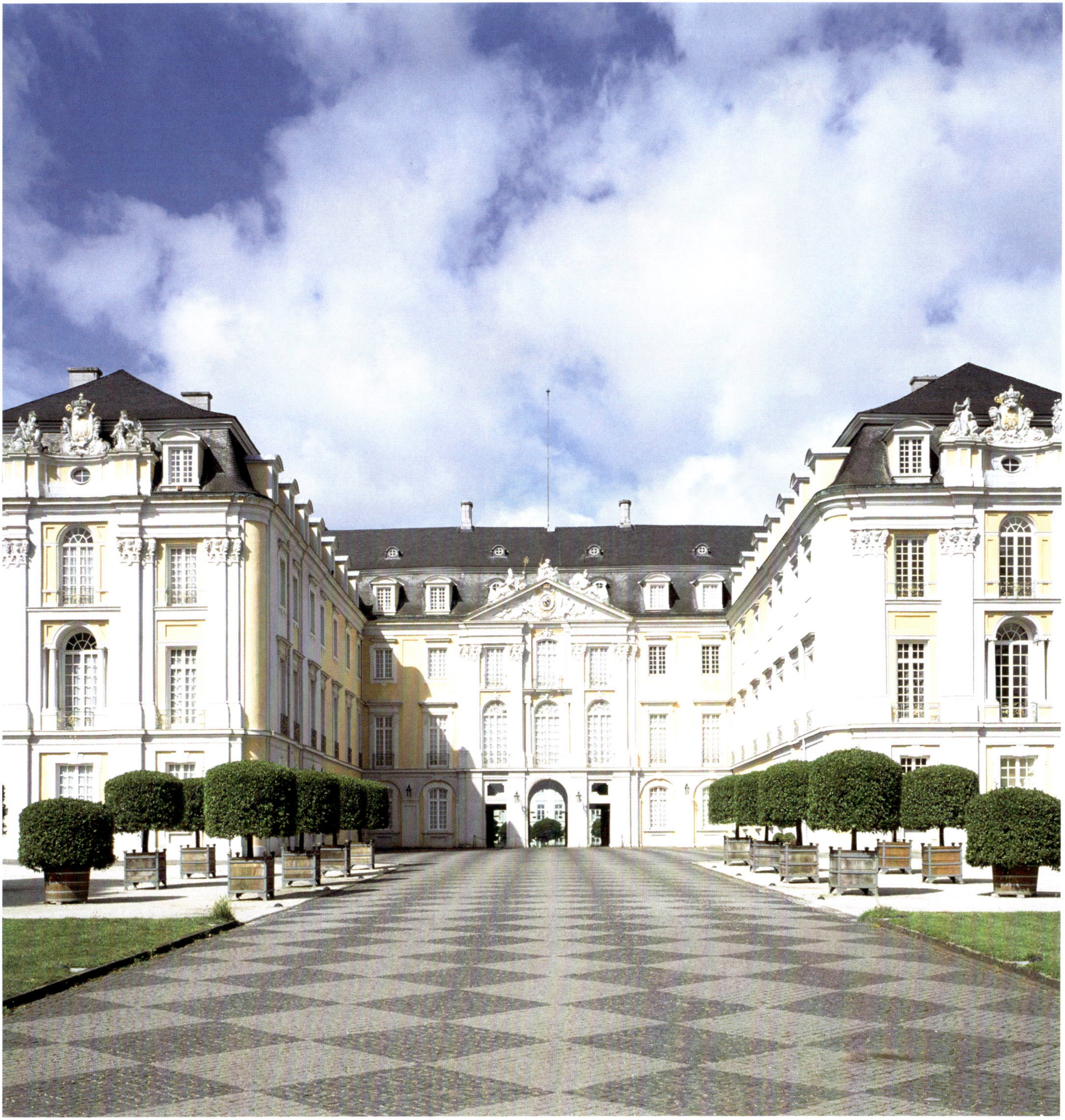

MIT DER SONNE UM DIE WELT
AROUND THE WORLD ON SOLAR POWER

SOLARCAR-TEAM HOCHSCHULE BOCHUM. Phileas Fogg schließt mit den Mitgliedern seines Londoner Klubs eine Wette ab: In 80 Tagen um die Welt – so lautet sein abenteuerliches Ziel. In dem 1873 erschienenen Buchklassiker reist Jules Vernes' Held per Schiff, mit der Eisenbahn oder auf dem Elefantenrücken. 139 Jahre später schreibt das Leben eine ähnlich spektakuläre Geschichte: Am 13. Dezember 2012 erreicht das Solarauto SolarWorld GT Adelaide in Australien, nachdem es – allein von Sonnenenergie angetrieben – die Welt umrundet hat.

Auf der fast 30.000 Kilometer langen Reise gelangte das gelbe Solarauto in 455 Tagen über Neuseeland in die USA und durchquerte den europäischen Kontinent sowie Russland, bevor es wieder am australischen Ausgangspunkt eintraf.

Ein modernes Abenteuer und ein Beweis für die führende Stellung der Hochschule Bochum in der Elektromobilität: Seit über zehn Jahren baut hier die Bochumer SolarCar-Manufaktur Solarfahrzeuge wie das SolarWorld GT, die in zahlreichen Wettbewerben ausgezeichnet wurden – zuletzt 2011 mit dem Design Award der World Solar Challenge.

SOLARCAR TEAM OF BOCHUM UNIVERSITY OF APPLIED SCIENCES. Phileas Fogg makes a wager with the members of London's Reform Club. His adventurous mission goes by the name of "Around the World in 80 Days". The classic novel published in 1873 has this Jules Verne protagonist travelling by ship, rail or on the back of an elephant. 139 years later a similarly spectacular tale rewrites history. The solar car, "SolarWorld GT", run exclusively on solar energy, reaches Adelaide, Australia on 13th December 2012 after a journey around the world.

On a journey of 455 days covering almost 30,000 kilometres, the yellow solar car reached the USA via New Zealand and crossed the European continent and Russia before returning to its Australian port of departure.

This modern adventure bears testimony to the leading position of Bochum University of Applied Sciences in the field of e-mobility. For over ten years the Bochum based manufacturer SolarCar has been building solar powered vehicles like the "Solar World GT". These have won prizes in numerous competitions, the last one being the Design Award of the World Solar Challenge in 2011.

Bestleistung: Per Solarauto um die Welt
Region: Metropole Ruhr
Ort: Bochum

Best performance: Around the world in a solar-powered car
Region: Ruhr Metropolis
Place: Bochum

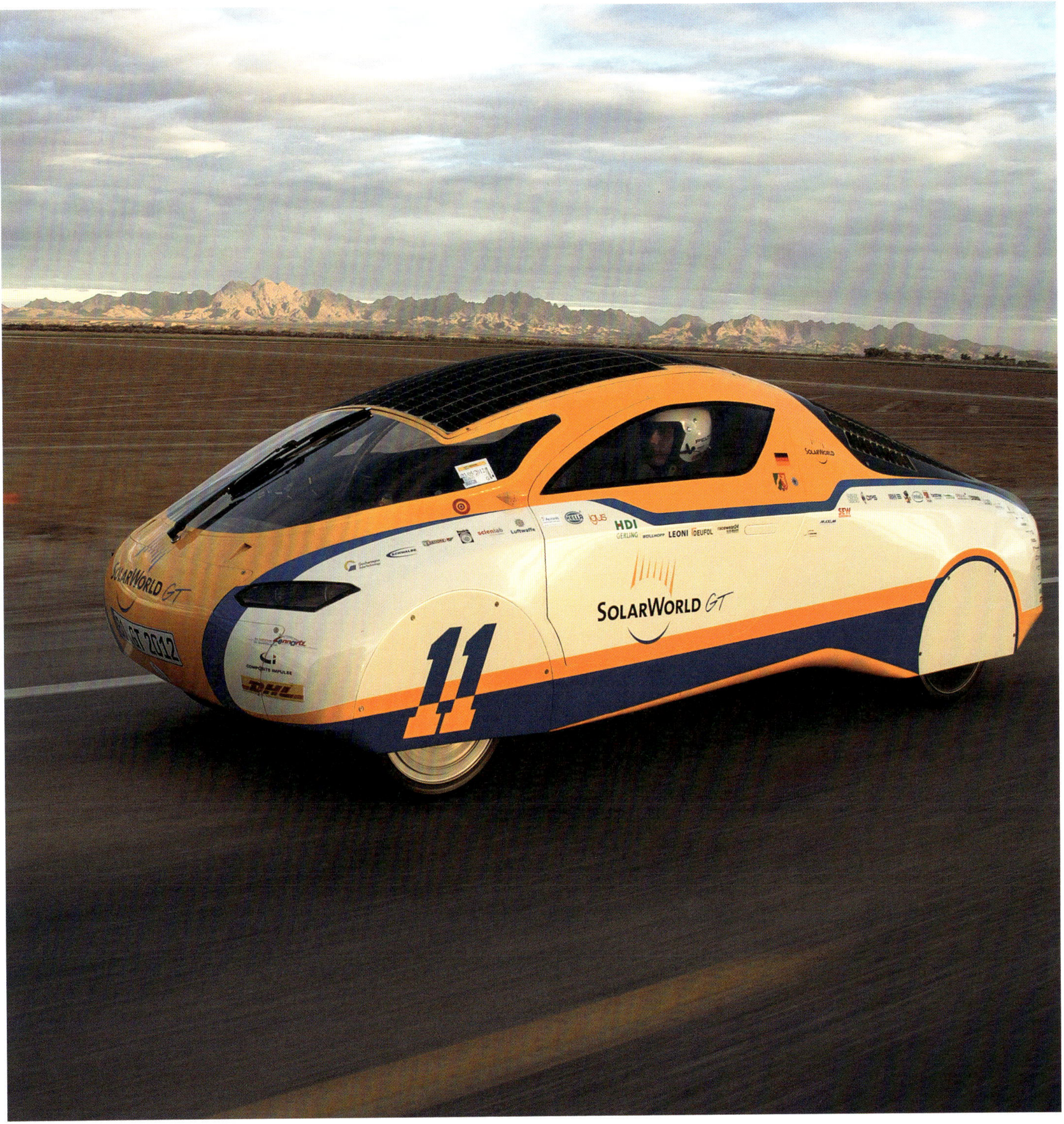
SOLARWORLD GT
11
HDI
LEONI

STROMENERGIE SATT DANK SONNENLICHT
ENOUGH POWER THANKS TO SUNLIGHT

SOLARTURM JÜLICH. 2.153 bewegliche Spiegel reihen sich auf einer Fläche von zwölf Fußballfeldern aneinander. Die sogenannten Heliostate folgen dem Lauf der Sonne, bündeln das Licht und fokussieren dieses tausendfach konzentriert auf einen 60 Meter hohen Solarturm, in dem dann Strom erzeugt wird. Kein Science-Fiction-Szenario, sondern Realität im solarthermischen Demonstrations- und Versuchskraftwerk in Jülich. Von dort kommt auch das Know-how: Die Technik des Solarturms wurde vom Solar-Institut Jülich der Fachhochschule Aachen mitentwickelt.

In der weltweit einzigartigen Anlage untersuchen Forscher des Deutschen Zentrums für Luft- und Raumfahrt (DLR), wie ein Versuchskraftwerk zum Hybridkraftwerk ausgebaut werden kann: Die Gasturbinen sollen bei fehlender Sonneneinstrahlung mit Biomasse als Energielieferant gespeist werden.

Ziel ist die Weiterentwicklung des Kraftwerks bis zur Marktreife und der internationale Vertrieb in sonnenreiche Mittelmeerregionen: Bis 2050 könnten 15 Prozent des europäischen Strombedarfs gedeckt werden – mit dem solarthermischen Kraftwerk in Jülich kommt die Menschheit dieser Vision ein Stück näher.

SOLAR TOWER JUELICH. Rows of moveable mirrors, 2,153 of them, lined up in an area the size of twelve football fields. These so-called heliostats track the sun and focus the thousand fold concentration of merged solar radiation on a receiver at the 60 metres solar tower, in which power is then generated. This is not science fiction but reality at the solar thermal demonstration and experimental plant in Juelich. The know-how for the technology behind the solar tower was developed by the Juelich Solar Institute of Aachen University of Applied Sciences.

At this facility unique in the world, researchers from the German Aerospace Centre (DLR) are working on expanding this experimental power plant into a hybrid power plant. In the absence of sunlight, biomass will be fed into the gas turbines as a substitute energy source.

The aim is to further develop the technology for marketability and sale to the sunny Mediterranean regions. By 2050, 15 per cent of Europe's power requirements could well be met. Mankind may have just inched closer to this vision with the solar thermal power plant.

Bestleistung: Einziges solarthermisches Demonstrationskraftwerk Deutschlands
Region: Aachen
Ort: Jülich

Best performance: Germany's only solar thermal demonstration power plant
Region: Aachen
Place: Juelich

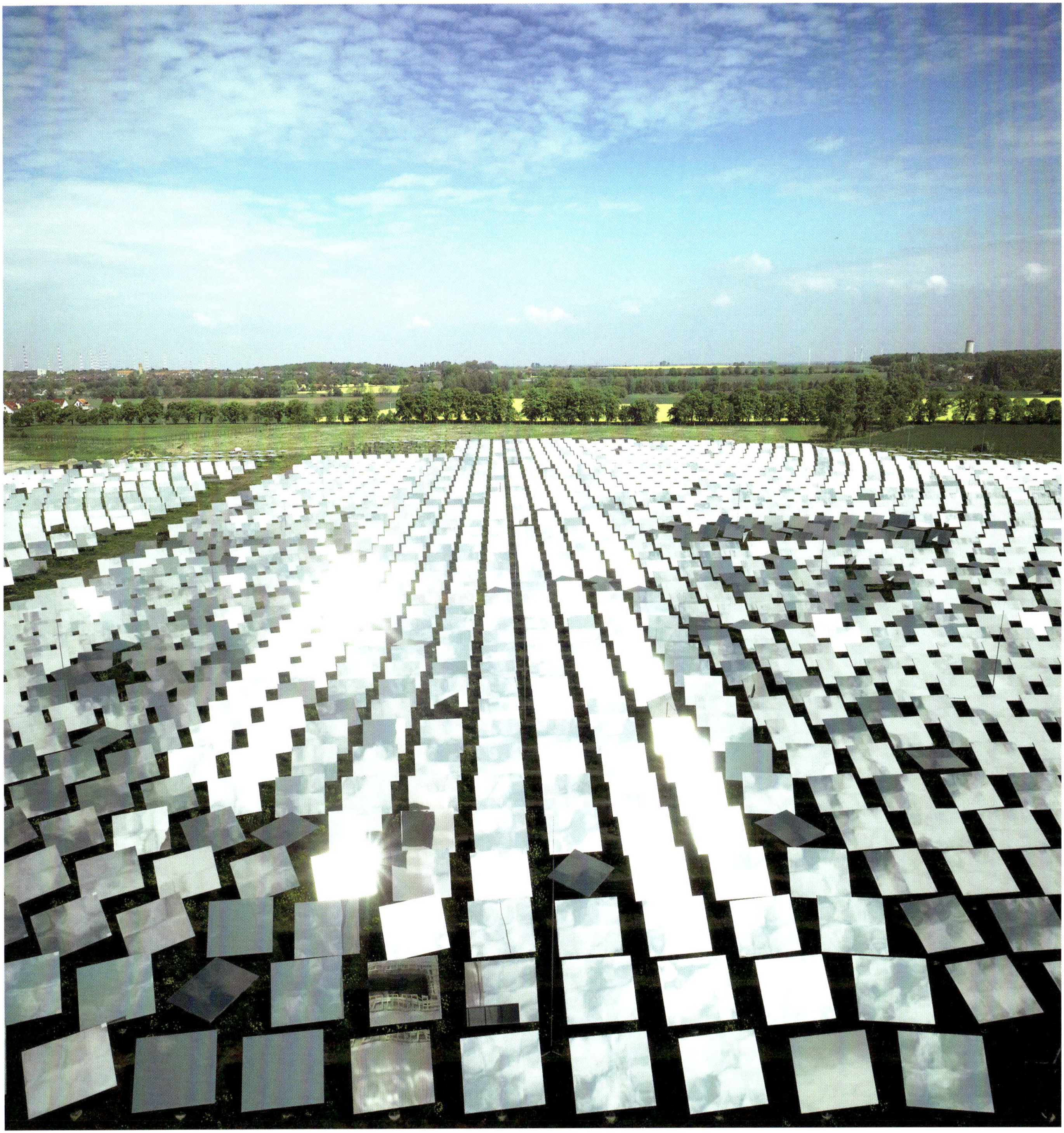

WERKSTOFFE AUS PULVER
RAW MATERIALS FROM POWDER

SPARK PLASMA CONSOLIDATION. Die Versuchsanlage erinnert an eine gewaltige Presse. Tatsächlich pressen zwei Kupferstempel eine Metallpulvermischung zusammen, doch der wichtigste Schritt der Produktion ist ein anderer: Die Forscher der Ruhr-Universität Bochum entladen Strom über die Stempel in das Pulver – die hohe Stromdichte komprimiert die speziellen Werkstoffe blitzschnell und energieeffizient zu dichten und besonders verschleißbeständigen Bauteilen.

Spark Plasma Consolidation – kurz SPC – heißt das Verfahren. Am Bochumer Lehrstuhl für Werkstofftechnik erkannte man das Potenzial: Herkömmliche Verfahren kosten viel Zeit sowie Energie und benötigen darüber hinaus immer seltener werdende Rohstoffe.

Anders bei SPC: Die verfügbare Energie wird optimal genutzt und erlaubt die ressourcenschonende Herstellung neuer Materialien mit speziellen Eigenschaften. So könnten verschleißbeständige Bauteile sozusagen auf Knopfdruck produziert werden, anstatt wie bislang bei 1.100 Grad Celsius und 100 bar Druck stundenlang im Ofen verdichtet zu werden.

SPARK PLASMA CONSOLIDATION. The test facility is reminiscent of a huge compactor. Two copper plungers literally compress a mix of metal powders, but this is not the main step in production. Researchers at the Ruhr University Bochum discharge currents through the plungers into the powder, the high electrical charge compressing the special materials within milliseconds into compact and extremely resistant components using less energy.

The procedure is called Spark Plasma Consolidation, or SPC. The Bochumer Lehrstuhl für Werkstofftechnik (Research Group for Material Engineering, Bochum) recognised its potential to replace conventional processes which require a lot of time and energy, while using up increasingly scarce raw materials.

SPC on the other hand makes optimal use of existing energy and spares resources in the production of new materials with special features. Wear-resistant components can thus be produced at the press of a button, unlike compaction of yore requiring 1,100 degrees Celsius and 100 bar pressure for hours in a furnace.

Bestleistung: Schnellstes Verfahren zur Herstellung von Bauteilen
Region: Metropole Ruhr
Ort: Bochum

Best performance: Fastest method of producing components
Region: Ruhr Metropolis
Place: Bochum

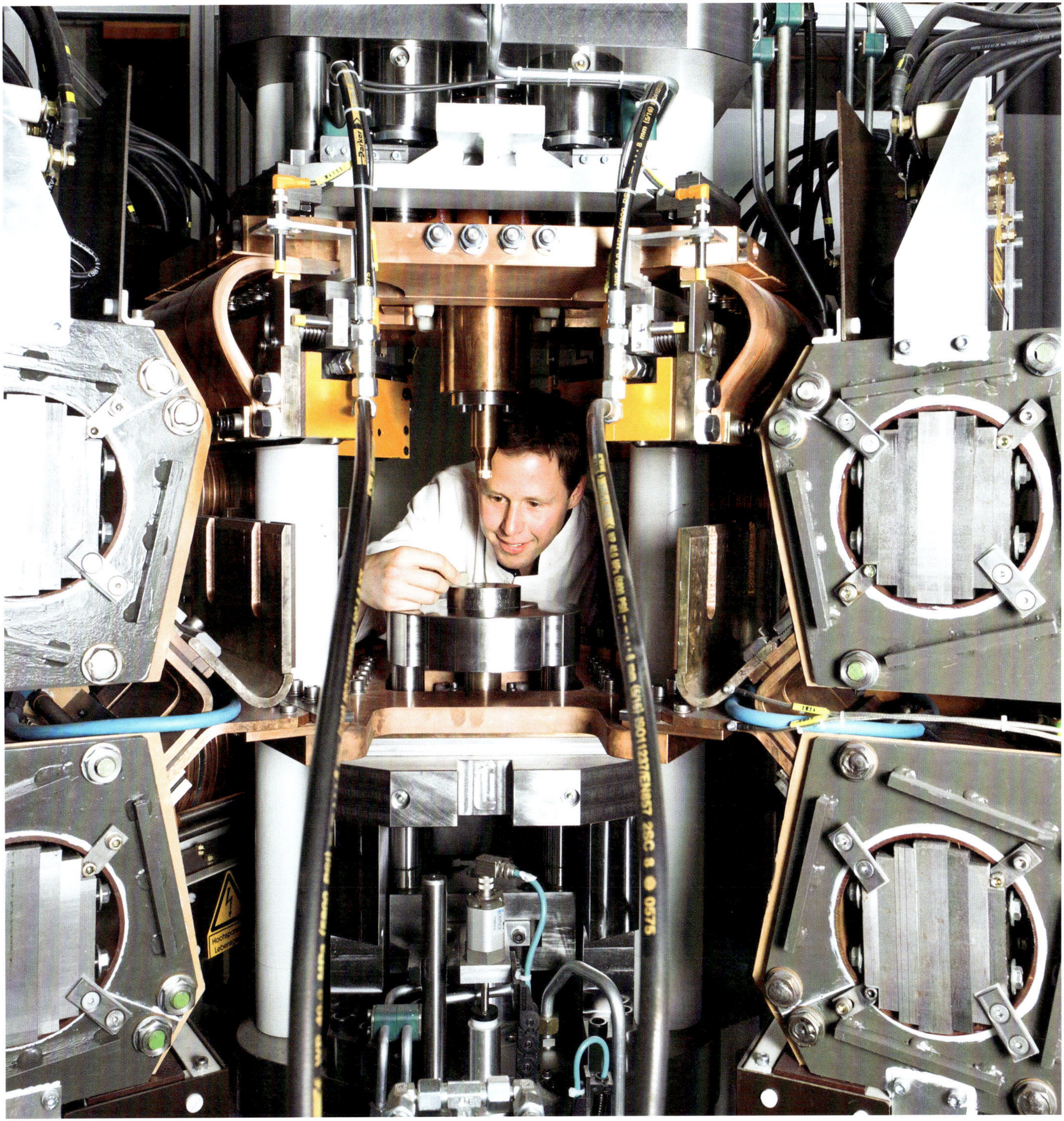

EIN SCHÖNER ALTER FLECKEN
A QUAINT OLD MARKET TOWN

STADT FREUDENBERG. Flecken sind kleine Orte, die im Mittelalter für die umliegenden Dörfer einen Mittelpunkt darstellten, etwa wegen ihres Marktes. Freudenberg, ein freundliches Städtchen im historischen Siegerland, war schon früh eine solche Ansiedlung: 1389 bereits wird es urkundlich erwähnt. „Alter Flecken" heißt seine Altstadt bis heute, die nicht nur schön anzuschauen, sondern auch ein Baudenkmal von internationaler Bedeutung ist.

Der Wilde Mann hat daran einen großen Anteil. Nicht das Waldungeheuer aus Sagen ist gemeint, sondern eine Verstrebungstechnik, die an einem der aufwändig restaurierten Fachwerkhäuser des Alten Fleckens vollständig ausgeführt zu sehen ist. Das Fachwerk besteht aus einem tragenden Holzgerüst, dessen Zwischenräume meist mit einer Holz-Lehm-Mischung gefüllt sind – so schmückt es in seinem markanten Schwarz-Weiß die Freudenberger Altstadt.

Es empfiehlt sich ein schöner Blick auf das Ensemble vom hochgelegenen Kurpark aus – genauso wie ein Besuch des Stadtmuseums und eine Wanderung auf dem Fachwerkweg in den weitläufigen Wäldern um den schönen, alten Flecken herum.

TOWN OF FREUDENBERG. The German term, Flecken, refers to small towns of local importance. In the Middle Ages these small places formed the nucleus of the surrounding villages, say because of a market. Freudenberg, a pleasant little town in the historical Siegerland region was one such early settlement and finds mention in documents dating as far back as 1389. The historical city centre even today goes by the name of "Alter Flecken" (old market town). It is not only charming to look at but is also a historical monument of international importance. The Wild Man has a large part to play in this. No, not the mythical wild man of the woods but a bracing technique that goes by that name! It is seen fully completed in one of the extensively restored timber frame houses of the old market town. The timber frame house consists of a load-bearing timber scaffolding, the interspaces of which are mostly packed with a wattle and daub mixture. And thus in its distinctive black and white it adorns the historic city centre of Freudenberg. A lovely bird's eye view of the ensemble is recommended from the heights of the spa gardens, as is a visit to the town museum. Add a walk on the timber-frame path through the rambling woods around the quaint old market town to the recommended sights!

Bestleistung: International einmaliges Fachwerkensemble
Region: Südwestfalen
Ort: Freudenberg

Best performance: Internationally unique ensemble of timbered houses
Region: Suedwestfalen
Place: Freudenberg

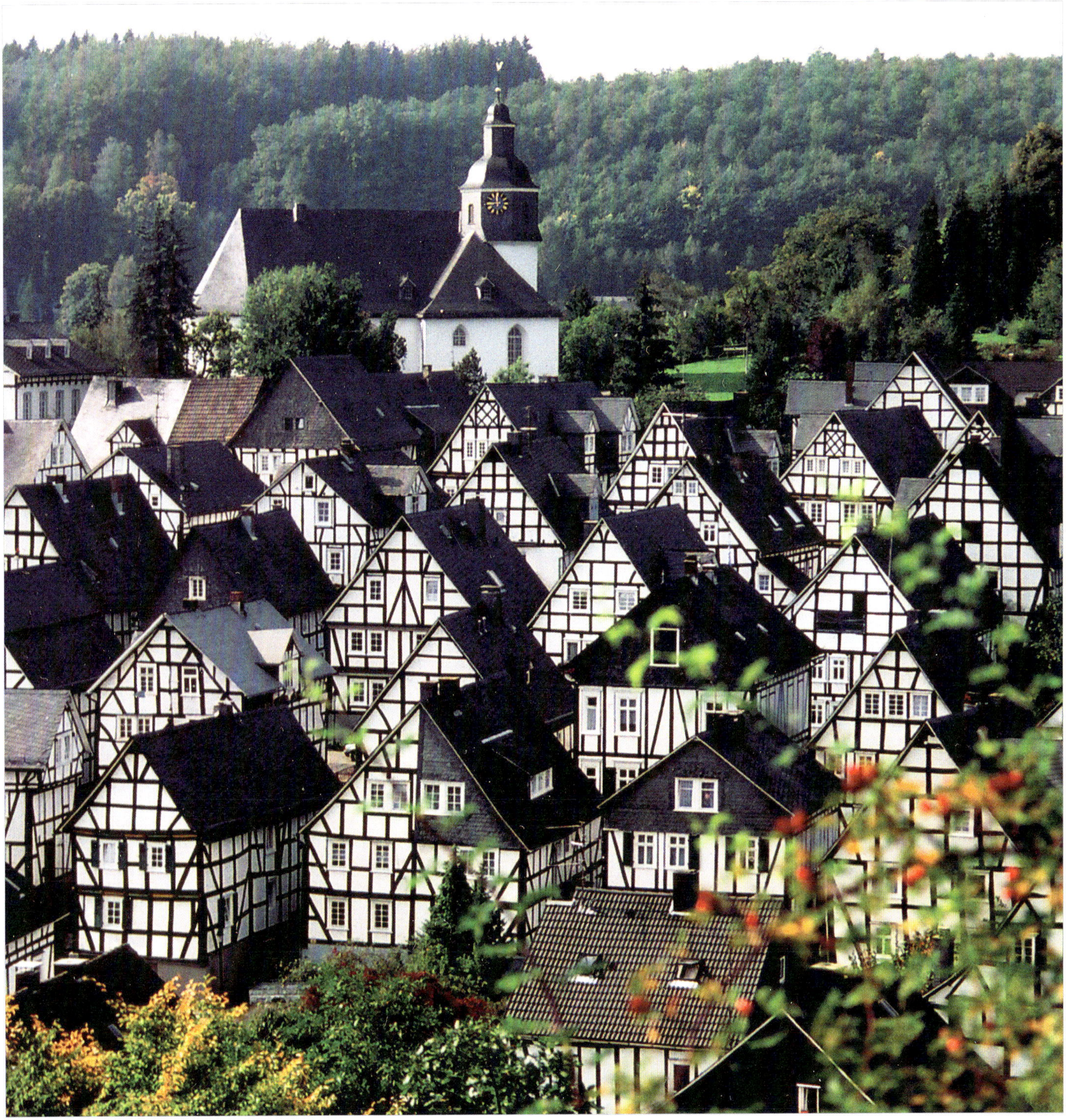

BERGISCHE STERNEKÜCHE
STAR CUISINE IN THE GRAND DUCHY OF BERG

STERNEKÖCHE. Eine Stadt, fünf Sterne, zwei Köche: Willkommen im Gourmetmekka Bergisch Gladbach! Keine zehn Autominuten sind sie voneinander entfernt, das Gourmetrestaurant Vendôme im Grandhotel Schloss Bensberg und das Gourmetrestaurant Lerbach im gleichnamigen Schlosshotel. Hier befinden sich zwei der besten deutschen Restaurants dank zweier Meister: 2-Sterne Koch Nils Henkel und 3-Sterne Koch Joachim Wissler.

Letztgenannter gilt Kritikern zufolge als bester Vertreter der „Neuen deutschen Schule", die vergessene regionale Produkte und Gerichte neu entdeckt. Wissler verbindet die klassische, traditionelle Küche mit kreativen Elementen. Im Vendôme lebt er erfolgreich seine Liebe zum Produkt und zu raffinierten Kompositionen aus: 2012 wählen ihn seine deutschen Kollegen zum „Koch der Köche".

Ein Schlosshotel weiter bietet Nils Henkel seinen Gästen „Pure Nature". Seine Kochphilosophie legt den Fokus auf Natur und Natürlichkeit, im hauseigenen Garten zieht man dazu viele Kräuter mit unterschiedlichen Aromen. Besonderes Augenmerk legt Nils Henkel auf Fisch, Meeresfrüchte und sein ausgezeichnetes Gemüsemenü – seine raffinierten Kreationen gleichen kulinarischen Kunstwerken.

STAR CHEFS. One city, five stars, two master chefs. Welcome to the gourmet mecca of Bergisch Gladbach! Less than ten minutes' drive separate the two gourmet restaurants Vendôme at Grandhotel Schloss Bensberg (the Grand Hotel of Bensberg Castle) and Lerbach housed in a castle hotel of the same name. The area is home to two of the finest German restaurants thanks to the two master chefs: 2-star chef Nils Henkel and 3-star chef Joachim Wissler.

Critics say the latter is the finest ambassador for the "Nouvelle German School of Cuisine", which rediscovers forgotten local produce and recipes. Wissler blends classic traditional cuisine with creative elements. At Vendôme he lives out his love for produce and sophisticated compositions. In 2012 he was voted "Chef of Chefs" by his peers in Germany.

At another castle hotel Nils Henkel serves "Pure Nature" to his guests. His food philosophy lays emphasis on nature and organic quality; what's more, several herbs of different aromas are grown in-house. The accent in Nils Henkel's cuisine is on fish, seafood and on his amazing vegetables fare. His sophisticated creations border on culinary artistry.

Bestleistung: 5-Michelin-Sterne im Gourmetmekka Bergisch Gladbach
Region: Köln / Bonn
Ort: Bergisch Gladbach

Best performance: 5-Michelin stars in Bergisch Gladbach's gourmet mecca
Region: Cologne / Bonn
Place: Bergisch Gladbach

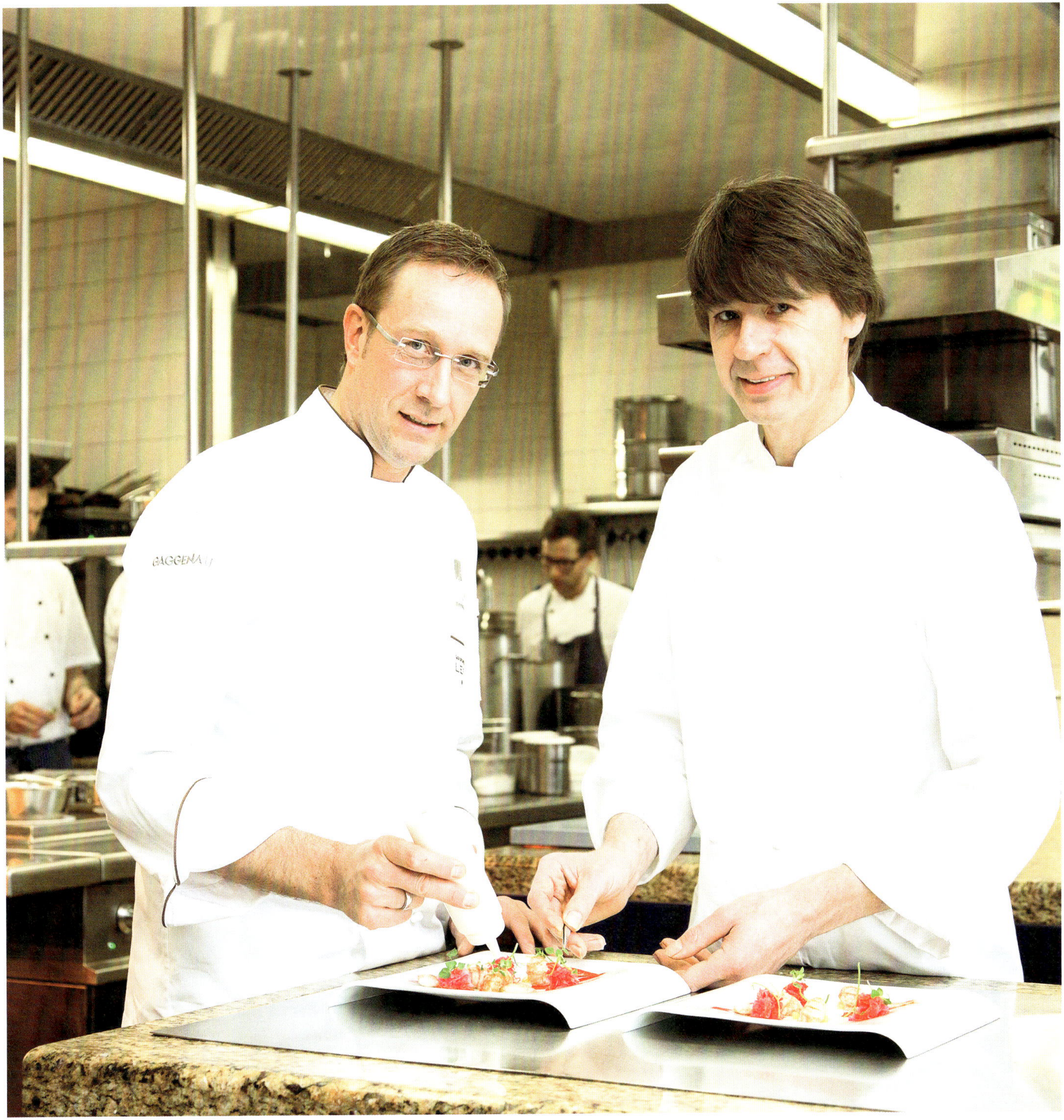

DAS EFFIZIENTE ELEKTROAUTO
THE EFFICIENT ELECTRIC CAR

STREETSCOOTER. Ein Elektroauto soll bezahlbar, umweltfreundlich, individuell und nachhaltig sein. Dies war die Zielsetzung der Rheinisch-Westfälischen Technischen Hochschule (RWTH) Aachen – und so gründete ein Verbund aus elf Unternehmen eine Firma, die mit vielen Industriepartnern und Forschern gemeinsam das Auto entwickelt und baut.

Mit einem klaren Konzept: Gemeinsam mit der Wirtschaft und unabhängig von einzelnen Konzernen wird ein E-Mobil völlig neu entwickelt. Dabei liegt der Fokus auf geringen Kosten, wiederverwendbaren Teilen und Serientauglichkeit.

Und das klappt sehr gut: Reichweiten bis 130 Kilometer, Höchstgeschwindigkeit von 120 Kilometer pro Stunde, flexibler Aufbau. Die StreetScooter GmbH hat zwei Prototypen als modulare Baukastensysteme entwickelt. Diese können als Zwei- und Viersitzer, als Cabrio oder als Lieferwagen gebaut werden.

Für letztere Variante hat sich bereits die Deutsche Post entschieden. 50 Vorserienfahrzeuge gehen bundesweit für die Brief- und Paketzustellung in den Alltagsbetrieb. Wenn dieser Praxistest gelingt, könnte der StreetScooter bald in Serie gehen.

STREETSCOOTER. An electric car should be affordable, eco-friendly, distinctive and sustainable. The RWTH Aachen University set this as its goal, which lead a group of eleven businesses to launch a company. This company then built the car in collaboration with various industry stakeholders and researchers.

On the lines of a clear concept an all new e-mobile has been developed together with industry and independent of individual companies. The focus while doing so has been on low costs, reusable parts and suitability for series production.

And it has worked out well: ranges of up to 130 kilometres, maximum speed of 120 kilometres per hour, flexible design. The StreetScooter GmbH has developed two prototypes as modular systems. These can be built as a two-seater, four-seater, convertible or delivery van.

The Deutsche Post (German postal service) has already opted for the latter version. 50 pre-series vehicles shall start daily operations all over the country for letter and parcel deliveries. If this on-road test is successful, the StreetScooter could soon go into series production.

Bestleistung: Besonders effizientes Elektroauto
Region: Aachen
Ort: Aachen

Best performance: Particularly efficient electric car
Region: Aachen
Place: Aachen

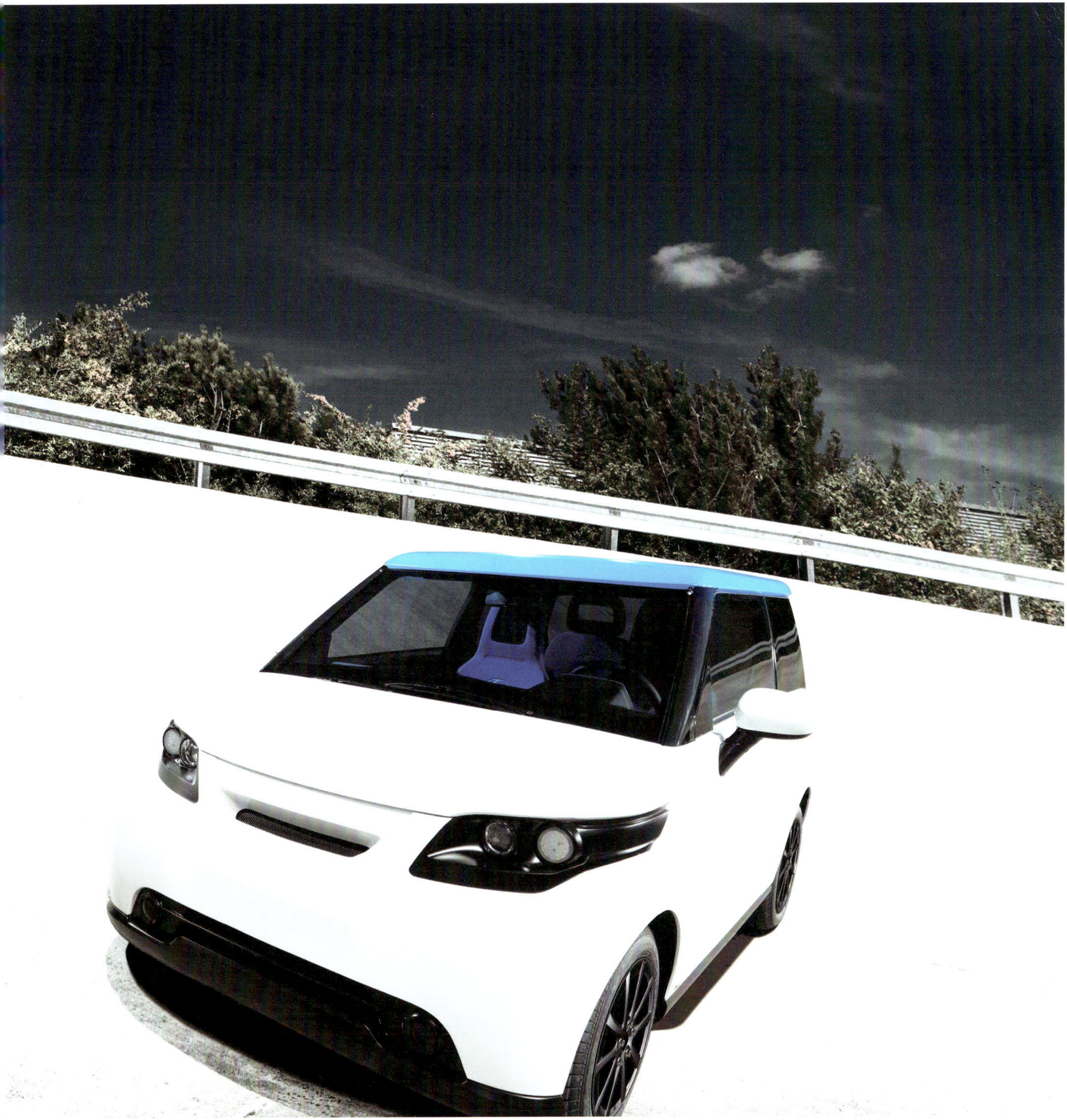

DIE LEICHTIGKEIT DES AUTOS
THE LIGHT CAR

SUPERLIGHT-CAR. Welcher Autofahrer wünscht sich nicht ein Fahrzeug, das umweltfreundlich ist, dabei Geld und Benzin spart, aber trotzdem das volle Fahrvergnügen bietet? Diesen Traum zu verwirklichen, schafft das SuperLIGHT-CAR (SLC), eine der leichtesten Autokarosserien der Welt. Als Teil eines europäischen Verbundprojekts hat das Institut für Kraftfahrzeuge (ika) der Rheinisch-Westfälischen Technischen Hochschule (RWTH) Aachen maßgeblich an der Entwicklung der neuen Leichtbauweise mitgewirkt.

Das innovative Multimaterial-Konzept sorgt für die optimale Kombination speziell ausgewählter Werkstoffe wie Aluminium, Stahl, Magnesium und faserverstärkter Kunststoffe. Hierfür hat das ika unter anderem ein Simulationsmodell entwickelt, das sich für alle relevanten Untersuchungen eignet. So wurde das Ziel einer 30-prozentigen Gewichtseinsparung sogar übertroffen. Das Auto ist um 35 Prozent bzw. 180 Kilogramm leichter als das auf dem VW Golf V basierende Referenzfahrzeug. Das Konzept des SuperLIGHT-CAR ist nicht nur bei konventionellen Antrieben zukunftsweisend, sondern eignet sich auch für Elektrofahrzeuge.

SUPERLIGHT-CAR. Is there a motorist who does not want a car that is eco-friendly, saves money and fuel, but still affords driving pleasure? To satisfy this desire "SuperLIGHT-CAR" (SLC) has come up with the lightest car body in the world. The Institut für Kraftfahrzeuge (ika) of the RWTH Aachen University is working in a big way on the development of a new lightweight design within the framework of a joint European research project.

The pioneering multi-material concept is based on the optimal combination of specially chosen materials such as aluminium, steel, magnesium and fibre-reinforced plastics. ika has created a simulation model suited to run all the relevant tests for this. They have, in fact, surpassed the target of a 30 per cent reduction in weight. The car is now 35 per cent, i.e. 180 kilogrammes lighter than the reference vehicle, a VW Golf V. The SuperLIGHT-CAR concept is not only a trend-setting one with regard to conventional drives but is also geared to supporting electric cars.

Bestleistung: Weltweit eine der leichtesten Autokarosserien
Region: Aachen
Ort: Aachen

Best performance: One of the world's lightest car bodies
Region: Aachen
Place: Aachen

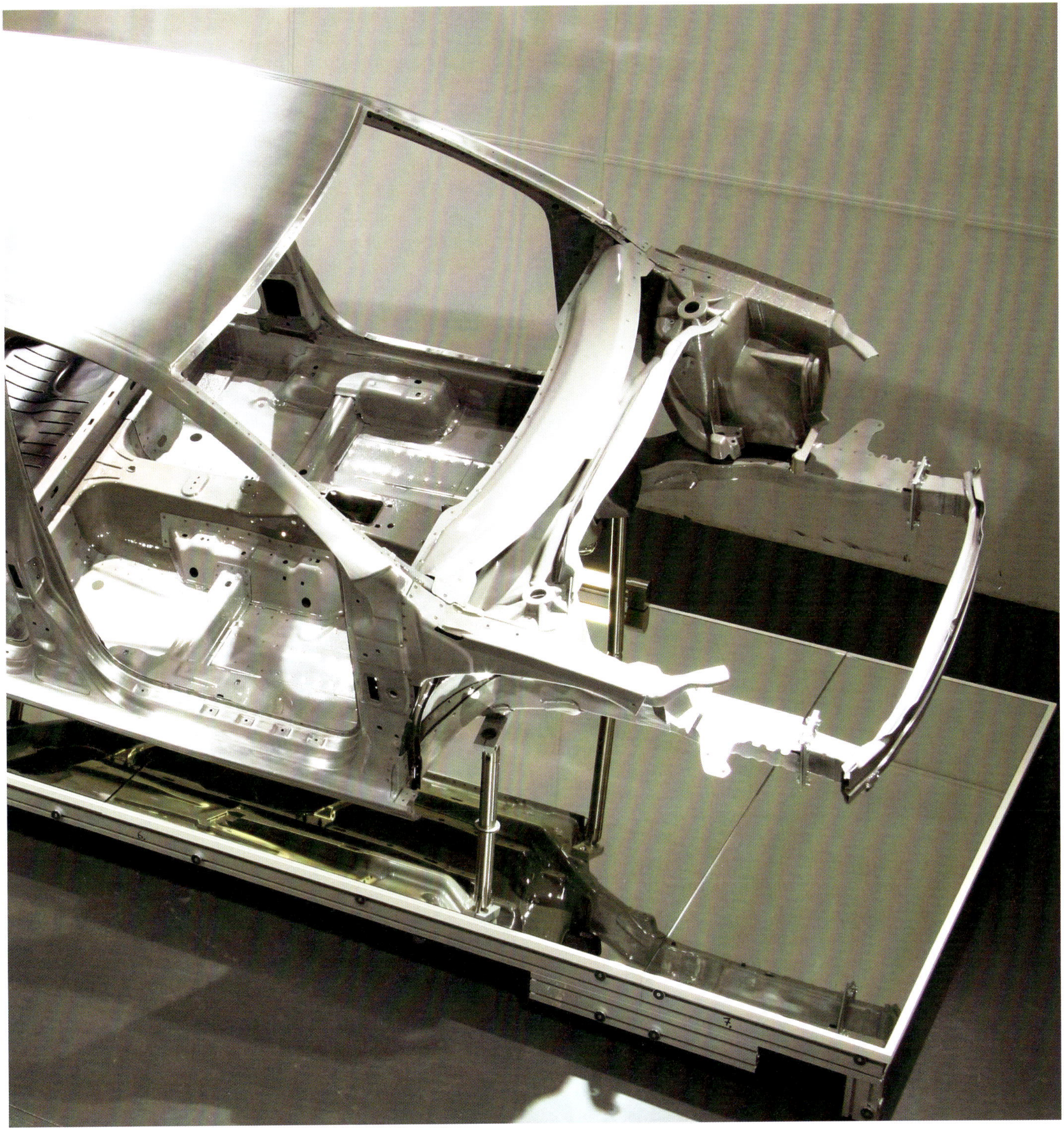

DIE INNOVATIONSSCHMIEDE IM RUHRGEBIET
THE HUB OF INNOVATION IN THE RUHR REGION

TECHNOLOGIEZENTRUMDORTMUND. Die westfälische Metropole Dortmund ist die größte Stadt des Ruhrgebiets, Nordrhein-Westfalens Logistikstandort des Jahres 2012 und mehrmaliger Deutscher Fußballmeister. Doch das ist noch nicht alles.

Mit dem TechnologieZentrumDortmund ist hier die größte Einrichtung seiner Art in Deutschland auf mehr als 100.000 Quadratmetern Fläche beheimatet. Technologieorientierten Unternehmen und Existenzgründern bietet das Zentrum Flächen, Infrastruktur und umfangreiche Unterstützung, ihre Geschäftsideen zu verwirklichen. Rund 280 Firmen mit über 8.500 Beschäftigten haben sich hier bis heute angesiedelt – darunter in ihren Branchen bekannte Namen wie ELMOS Semiconductor oder Vestas Wind Systems.

Die Technologiefelder in den zehn Kompetenzzentren des 1985 gegründeten TechnologieZentrumDortmund reichen von der Informationstechnologie und Logistik über die Biomedizin sowie Mikro- und Nanotechnologie. Aber auch Produktions- und Fertigungstechnik sowie Elektromobilität sind vertreten. In einzelnen Bereichen, wie der Mikrostruktur- oder der Lasertechnologie, zählen die Dortmunder Technologieunternehmen weltweit zu den Innovationstreibern.

TECHNOLOGIEZENTRUMDORTMUND. The Westphalian metropolis of Dortmund is the biggest city of the Ruhr region, the logistical location of the year 2012 of North Rhine-Westphalia, and German Bundesliga champions many times over. And yet the list of laurels does not end here. The TechnologieZentrumDortmund (Dortmund Technology Centre) that is housed here on more than 100,000 square metres of area makes it the biggest facility of its kind in Germany. The centre provides space, infrastructure and comprehensive support to technology-oriented companies and entrepreneurs to develop their business ideas. To date about 280 companies with over 8,500 employees have been set up here – among them ELMOS Semiconductors or Vestas Wind Systems, famous names in their respective fields. The fields of technology in the ten centres of excellence of the TechnologieZentrumDortmund, founded in 1985, range from information technology and logistics to biomedicine, including microtechnology and nanotechnology. Production and manufacturing technology and electromobility are also represented here. Technological companies of Dortmund from unique fields like microstructure or laser technology are regarded as drivers of innovation globally.

Bestleistung: Größtes Technologiezentrum Deutschlands
Region: Metropole Ruhr
Ort: Dortmund

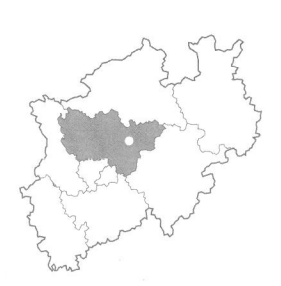

Best performance: The biggest technology centre of Germany
Region: Ruhr Metropolis
Place: Dortmund

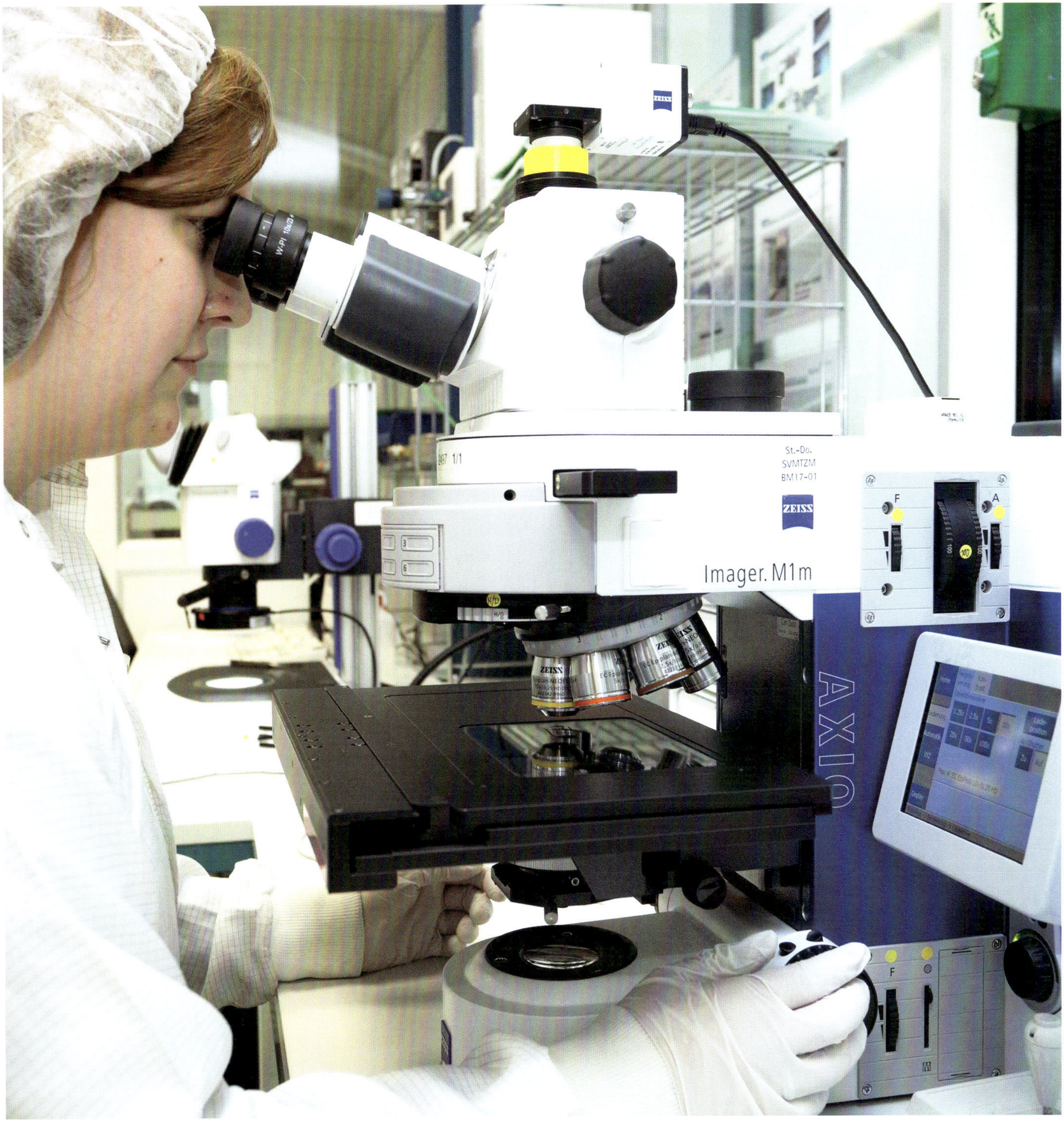
St.-Do.
SVMTZM
BM17-01
ZEISS
Imager. M1m
AXIO

FEINSTE OBERFLÄCHEN AUS WUPPERTAL
THE SMOOTHEST SURFACES FROM WUPPERTAL

THIELENHAUS TECHNOLOGIES. Was haben Kugel- und Rollenlager in der Industrie, die Messerköpfe von elektrischen Rasierapparaten sowie Kurbelwellen und Einspritztechnik in Autos gemeinsam? Bei allen drei Anwendungen kommt es auf besonders feine Oberflächen an. Überall dort, wo Teile unter hoher Belastung rotieren, gleiten oder abdichten, entscheidet die Beschaffenheit der Oberfläche über Lebensdauer oder Energieverbrauch.

Das Traditionsunternehmen Thielenhaus Technologies entwickelt genau hierfür Präzisionswerkzeugmaschinen, die das sogenannte Microfinish-Verfahren anwenden. Damit können Oberflächen geschaffen werden, deren Formgenauigkeiten unter einem zehntausendstel Millimeter liegen. Dies macht das 1909 in Wuppertal-Barmen gegründete Unternehmen zum Weltmarktführer in der Oberflächenfeinstbearbeitung sowie zum gefragten Spezialisten für die Industrie – aber auch für die Medizintechnik. Denn künstliche Hüftgelenke profitieren ebenfalls von den Feinstoberflächen aus Wuppertal: Sie weisen eine höhere Belastbarkeit und längere Lebensdauer auf.

THIELENHAUS TECHNOLOGIES. What do industrial ball and roller bearings have in common with the cutter heads in electrical shavers and crankshafts, and fuel injection technology in automobiles? Exceptionally smooth surfaces are key to all three applications. All parts rotating under heavy load, with spinning or sealing functions, rely on surface properties for longevity and energy consumption.

With precisely this in mind, Thielenhaus Technologies, a company with a long tradition, develops machinery for precision tools that employ the so-called microfinishing process, allowing smooth surfaces to be created with whose dimensions and shapes are accurate down to less than a thousandth of a millimetre. This makes the company founded in 1909, in Wuppertal-Barmen, the global market leader in microfinishing and a much sought-after specialist both in industry and in medical engineering. After all, artificial hip joints also benefit from the microfinished surfaces made in Wuppertal, which give them a higher load-carrying capacity and longer life.

Bestleistung: Marktführer in der Oberflächenfeinstbearbeitung
Region: Bergisches Städtedreieck
Ort: Wuppertal

Best performance: Market leader in microfinish surface processing
Region: Bergisches Staedtedreieck
Place: Wuppertal

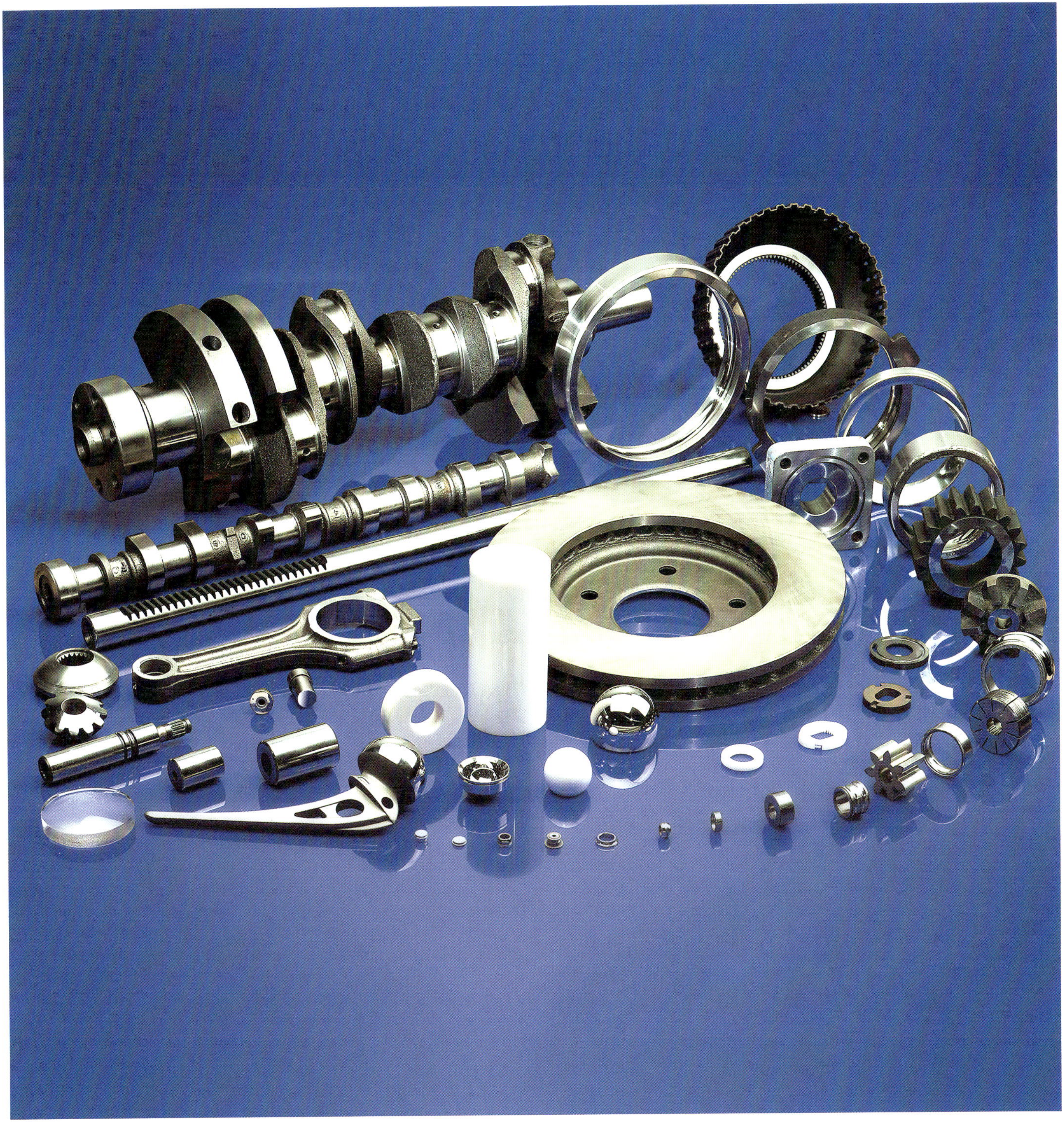

DER HERR DER BÄLLE
MASTER OF THE GAME

TIMO BOLL. Bis April 2011 Nummer eins der Weltrangliste, Weltmeisterschafts-Dritter, zweifacher Olympischer Medaillengewinner, zweifacher World-Cup-Sieger, sechsfacher Europameister, neunfacher deutscher Meister – die Liste der sportlichen Erfolge von Timo Boll ließe sich lange fortsetzen. Hat der Tischtennisprofi von Borussia Düsseldorf doch schon mit vier Jahren zum Schläger gegriffen. Das Ausnahmetalent begeistert seine Fans durch Schnelligkeit und Flexibilität. Gegner fürchten den Linkshänder für sein nur schwer auszurechnendes Spiel. Selbst Chinas Nationalcoach Liu Guoliang hat zugegeben, dass er nicht ruhig schlafen könne, solange Boll noch spiele. Der bescheiden auftretende Boll ist in China sehr beliebt. Unvergessen ist sein Fairplay bei der WM 2005 in Shanghai. Bei einem Matchball für ihn ließ Boll eine Fehlentscheidung des Schiedsrichters zugunsten seines Gegners korrigieren und verlor anschließend. „Wofür macht man den Sport das ganze Leben lang? Natürlich auch, um Geld zu verdienen. Aber es ist vor allem eine große Liebe, und die betrügt man nicht." Die Verleihung des Fair-Play-Preises 2007 an Boll ist die verdiente Anerkennung einer sportlichen Lebenshaltung.

TIMO BOLL. Long is the list of sporting successes of Timo Boll: by April 2011 number one in the world ranking, third in the world championships, twice Olympic medal winner, twice World Cup winner, six times European champion, nine times German champion. It is but to be expected of this table tennis professional playing for Borussia Duesseldorf, that he took to the bat at the tender age of four. The speed and flexibility of this exceptionally talented player impresses his fans. Opponents fear the left-handed player for his game that is difficult to figure out. Even China's national coach, Liu Guoliang, has confessed that he cannot sleep easy while Boll is still playing.
Boll with his modest demeanour is very popular in China. His sense of fair play at the World Cup 2005 in Shanghai lives on in memory. At a match point called in his favour Boll corrected the referee's wrong decision in favour of his opponent. He went on to lose this match. "Why does one pursue sports his whole life long? Obviously to earn money. But above all it is true love and one does not cheat on that." The "Fair Play Award" given to Boll in 2007 is a well deserved recognition of a life led in the spirit of true sportsmanship.

Bestleistung: Bester deutscher Tischtennisspieler
Region: Düsseldorf
Ort: Düsseldorf

Best performance: The best German table tennis player
Region: Duesseldorf
Place: Duesseldorf

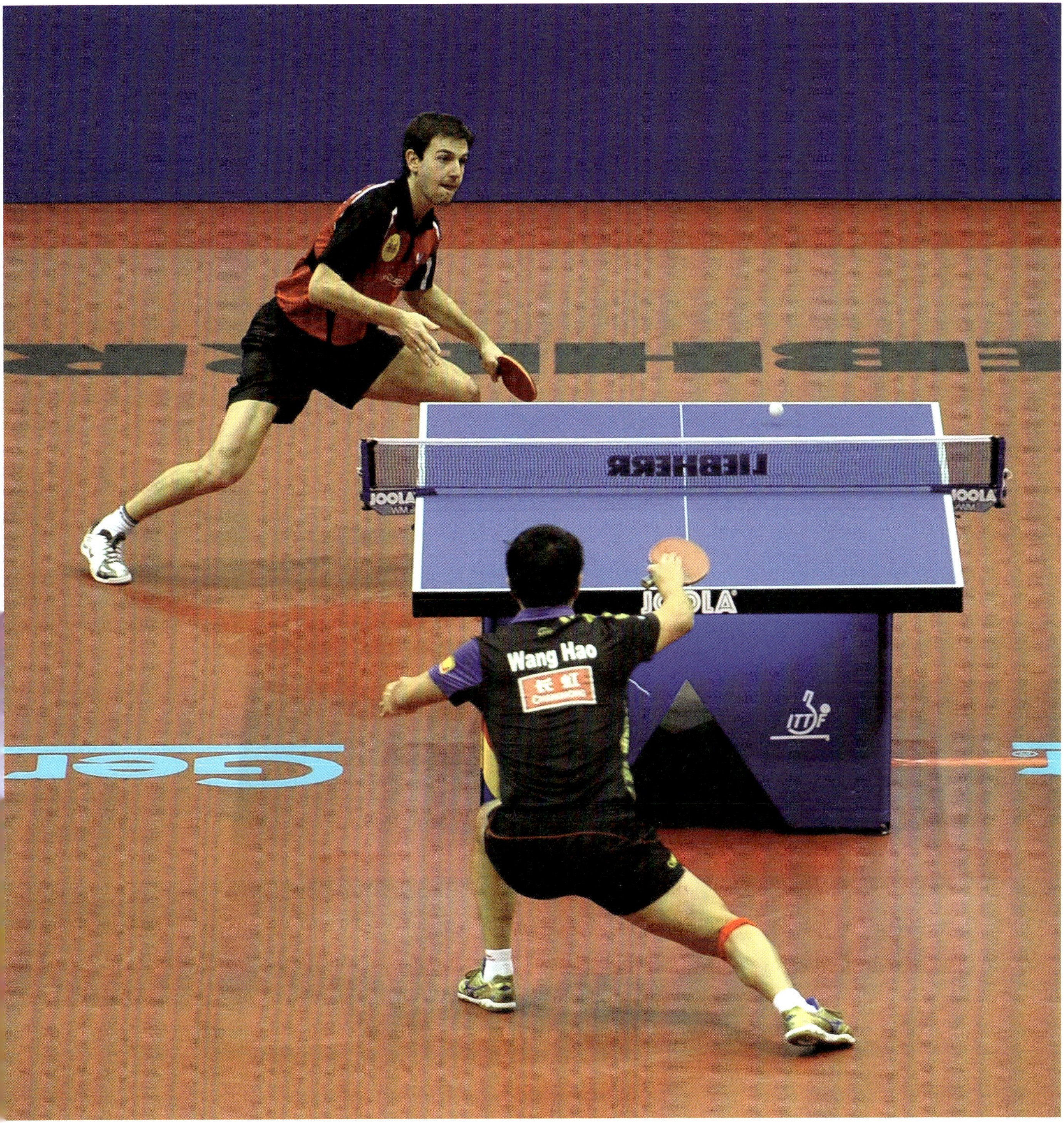
JOOLA
Wang Hao
ITTF

WUPPERTALER WELTBÜRGER
WORLD CITIZEN OF WUPPERTAL

TONY CRAGG. Nur für ein Jahr wollte der britische Bildhauer 1977 in Wuppertal bleiben. Dass die Stadt seine neue Heimat werden sollte, hätte den heutigen Kunstprofessor und Rektor der Düsseldorfer Kunstakademie damals bestimmt überrascht. Hier, in seiner Wahlheimat Wuppertal, schuf er ein ganz besonderes Kunstwerk: einen Wald voller Skulpturen. Den Skulpturenpark Waldfrieden eröffnete Anthony „Tony" Douglas Cragg 2008 auf den grünen Höhen der einstigen Industriestadt. Auf Lichtungen inmitten eines einzigartig vielfältigen Baumbestands stehen seine teils monumentalen Skulpturen. Sie bilden den Kern – in einem Glaspavillon zeigt er in Wechselausstellungen Werke bedeutender Bildhauerkollegen, beispielsweise von Jean Tinguely, Richard Long und Eduardo Chillida.

Cragg ist unermüdlicher Formenerfinder: Seine Figuren suchen sich ihren Platz im Raum, ihre geschichteten oder verdrehten Formen fließen scheinbar. Er spielt mit Materialien, entwirft unkonventionelle Oberflächen und experimentiert mit räumlicher Tiefe wie Perspektive. In Wuppertal wird ein Waldspaziergang im Skulpturenpark mit Sicherheit zu einem ganz besonderen Erlebnis.

TONY CRAGG. In 1977 this British sculptor meant to stay only a year in Wuppertal. Today a professor and director of the Arts Academy of Duesseldorf little did he know then that he would ultimately settle down here. This resident sculptor of Wuppertal has given his adopted home an exceptional work of art: the sculpture park.

Anthony "Tony" Douglas Cragg opened the Waldfrieden sculpture park in 2008 in the wooded heights of the former industrial city. His sculptures, some of them massive, are placed here on glades in a grove of uniquely varied trees. While these form the focal point, he has temporary exhibits in a glass pavilion of the works of eminent peers, such as Jean Tinguely, Richard Long und Eduardo Chillida.

Cragg works tirelessly on devising forms. His figures seek their place out in space, their stacked or randomly twisted silhouettes conveying motion and fluidity. He manipulates materials, creates unconventional textures and experiments with spatial depth such as perspective. A walk in the woods of Wuppertal's sculpture park holds the promise of a very special experience.

Bestleistung: Einer der bedeutendsten Bildhauer
Region: Bergisches Städtedreieck
Ort: Wuppertal

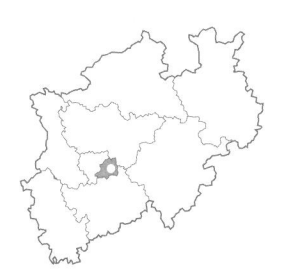

Best performance: One of the most famous sculptors
Region: Bergisches Staedtedreieck
Place: Wuppertal

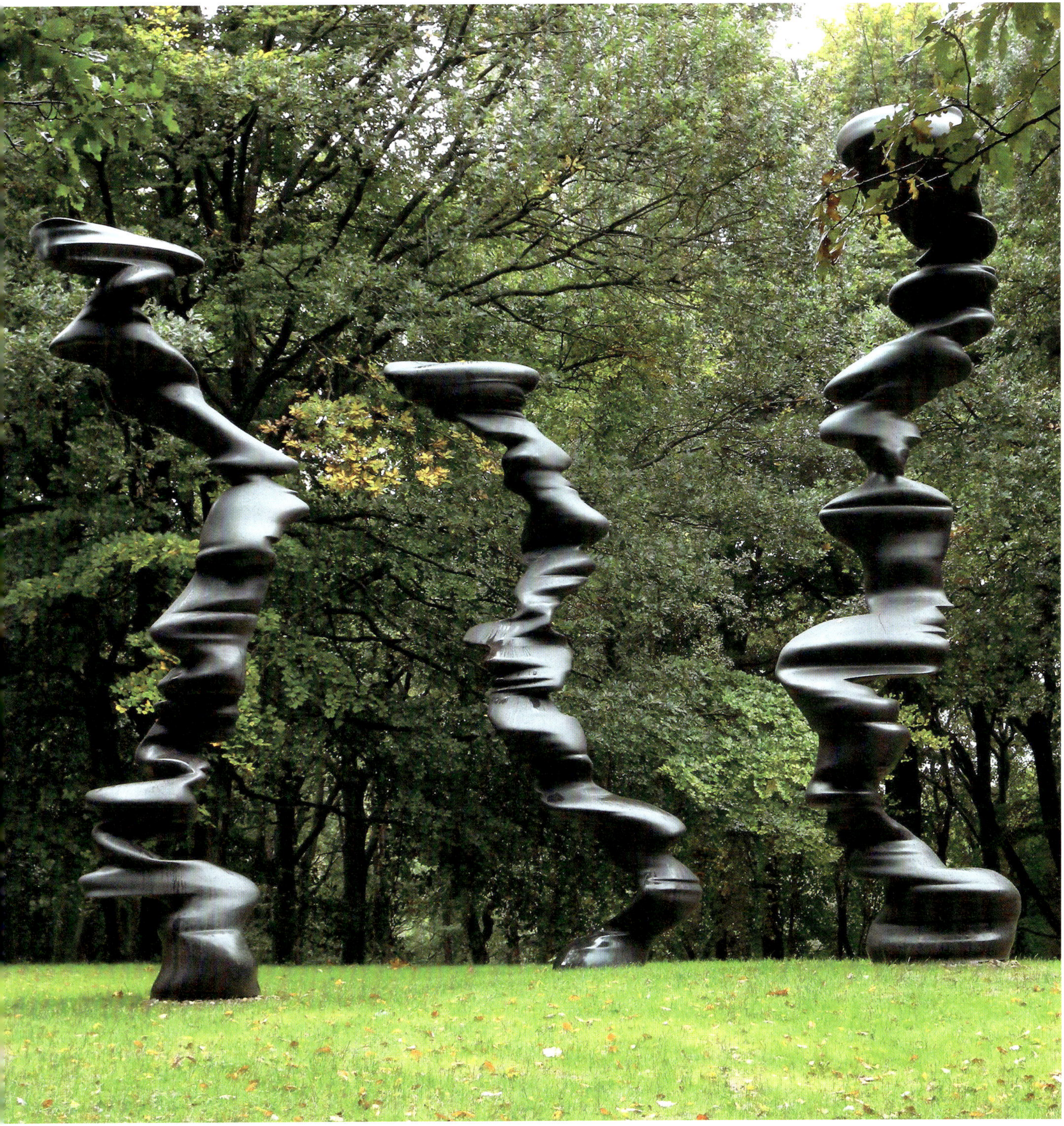

DURCHBLICK DANK SPEICHERRING
INSIGHT BY VIRTUE OF THE STORAGE RING

TU DORTMUND. Korrosionsprozesse verstehen, Metallschichten charakterisieren, Katalysatoren untersuchen – der Elektronenspeicherring DELTA an der Technischen Universität Dortmund gibt einen Einblick in die Struktur von Materie. Die Synchrotronlichtquelle ist weltweit eine von wenigen Anlagen dieser Art, die von einer Hochschule betrieben wird – und von ihr profitieren verschiedene Forschungseinrichtungen aus Physik, Chemie, Biologie oder den Materialwissenschaften.

In der Beschleunigeranlage werden Elektronen fast bis auf Lichtgeschwindigkeit beschleunigt und in einen 115 Meter langen Ring eingeschleust. Entlang des Rings lenken Magnetfelder die Elektronen ab, die dabei elektromagnetische Wellen aussenden – die Synchrotronstrahlung. Aufgrund ihrer besonderen Eigenschaften eignet sich diese hervorragend, um verschiedenste Materialien zerstörungsfrei zu durchleuchten. Wie mit einem unvorstellbar schnellen Stroboskop kann DELTA Veränderungen bis in den Pikosekundenbereich hinein beobachten – dagegen dauert ein Wimpernschlag eine Ewigkeit.

TU DORTMUND. Need an insight into the structure of matter? "DELTA", the electron storage ring at Technical University Dortmund helps to understand corrosion processes, characterise metal layers and analyse catalysers, among other uses. The synchrotron light source system is one of the few pieces of equipment of its kind to be operated by a university anywhere in the world. Various research institutes for physics, chemistry or material sciences now stand to gain from it.

Electrons are accelerated to just short of the speed of light in the accelerator and fed into a 115 metre-long ring. Magnetic fields along the ring deflect the electrons, which then emit electromagnetic waves, i.e. ultra bright synchrotron radiation. The ring's extraordinary features make it ideal for the non-destructive x-ray penetration of the most diverse materials. As with an inconceivably fast stroboscope, DELTA can observe changes right down to picoseconds. Compared to that, the blink of an eyelid seems to last an eternity!

Bestleistung: Deutschlands einzige von einer Universität betriebene Synchrotronlichtquelle
Region: Metropole Ruhr
Ort: Dortmund

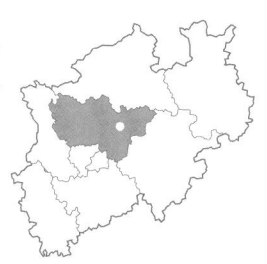

Best performance: Germany's only synchrotron light source run by a university
Region: Ruhr Metropolis
Place: Dortmund

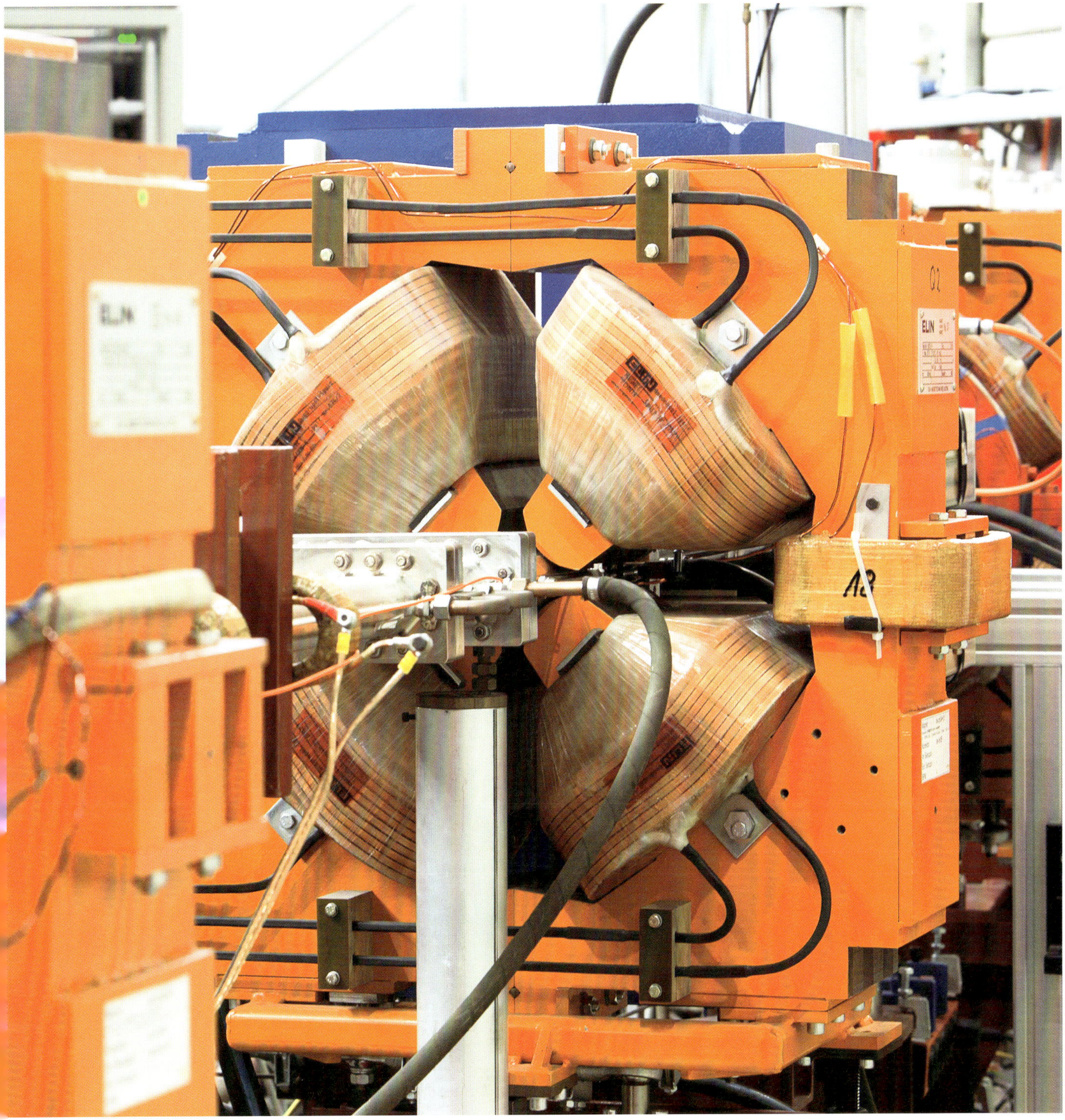
ELIN
Q2
ELIN

ZERTIFIZIERUNG OHNE GRENZEN
CERTIFICATION BEYOND BORDERS

TÜV RHEINLAND. Nichts ist für die Ewigkeit geschaffen. Das gilt auch für umweltfreundliche Solarsysteme – unabhängig davon, ob sie mit Photovoltaik-Modulen, thermischen Solarkollektoren oder einer Kombination aus beidem ausgestattet sind. Aber wie lange halten sie? Lohnt sich eine Anschaffung? Um bei der Beantwortung solcher Fragen zu helfen, hat der TÜV Rheinland in Köln das weltweit modernste Prüfzentrum für Solarsysteme geschaffen.

Auf einer Fläche von 1.800 Quadratmetern sind hochmoderne technische Einrichtungen zur Untersuchung von Solarsystemen jeglicher Art installiert. Abgesehen von der Prüfzeithalbierung bei den Sicherheits-, Qualitäts- und Effizienzkontrollen kann der TÜV Rheinland dort zwei der weltweit größten Prüfkammern vorweisen, mit denen auch Korrosionstests für größere Komponenten von Offshore-Windanlagen durchgeführt werden. Außerdem wird die technische Ausrüstung unter anderem durch sechs Klimakammern und fünf Sonnensimulatoren komplettiert. Einen Spektralmessplatz wie hier gibt es sonst nirgends. Über 500 internationale Hersteller von Solarsystemen lassen ihre Produkte vom TÜV Rheinland prüfen und zertifizieren.

TÜV RHEINLAND. Nothing lasts forever. Not even eco-friendly solar energy systems, be they photovoltaic modules, solar thermal collectors or should they consist of a combination of both. Help is now at hand, though, to resolve issues regarding their longevity and cost effectiveness thanks to TÜV Rheinland (Technical Control Board Rhineland), which has created the world's most advanced testing centre for solar energy systems in Cologne.

Ultra-modern equipment to test solar energy systems of all kinds has been set up over an area measuring 1,800 square metres. Apart from halving the testing time for efficiency, quality and security checks, TÜV Rheinland can boast the two largest testing chambers in the world. Even corrosion tests of bigger offshore wind turbine components can be carried out in these. Six climate chambers and five solar simulators add to the installation and the spectral measuring station here is simply beyond compare. Is it of any surprise, then, that over 500 international manufacturers of solar energy systems have their products tested and certified by TÜV Rheinland?

Bestleistung: Modernstes Prüfzentrum für Solarsysteme
Region: Köln / Bonn
Ort: Köln

Best performance: The most advanced testing centre for solar energy systems
Region: Cologne / Bonn
Place: Cologne

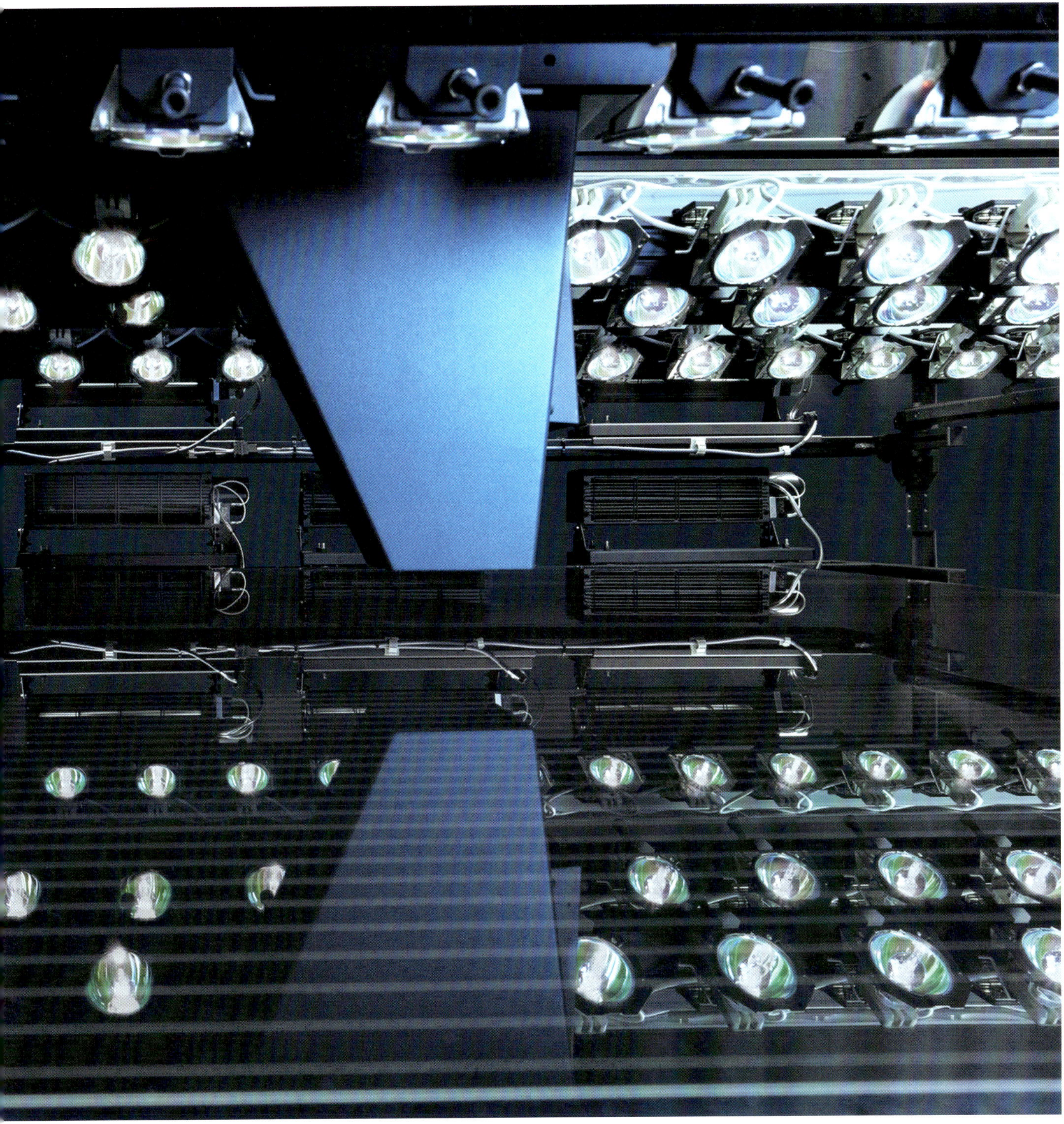

BETTEN FÜR DIE JUGEND
LODGING FOR THE YOUTH

WELTJUGENDHERBERGE BURG ALTENA. Erst hatte Richard Schirrmann schlechte Laune, dann eine Idee. 1909 befand sich der Lehrer aus Altena mit seinen Schülern auf einer Wanderung, als sie ein Gewitter überraschte und ihnen niemand Unterkunft gewähren wollte. Am Ende hatten sie es schließlich in eine leere Schule geschafft – dort kam ihm der simple, aber geniale Einfall: Es bräuchte ein Netz preisgünstiger Übernachtungsmöglichkeiten im Abstand einer Tageswanderung. Die Idee der Jugendherberge war geboren, und etwas mehr als 100 Jahre später gibt es weltweit etwa 4.500 Filialen in 80 Ländern.

1914 wurde schließlich die erste ständige Jugendherberge der Welt ausgerechnet in einer der schönsten deutschen Höhenburgen eröffnet – der Burg Altena. In ihrer großartigen Kulisse gab es anfangs 48 Betten, nach dem Krieg war sie auch Ort der Wiedergründung des Deutschen Jugendherbergswerks. Mit ihrer fast 1.000-jährigen, bewegten Geschichte bietet die Prachtburg im Märkischen Kreis inzwischen ein großes Museum, inklusive der alten Jugendherberge.

WORLD YOUTH HOSTEL BURG ALTENA. What began as a bad mood for Richard Schirrmann turned into a moment of epiphany. One day in 1909, this teacher from Altena set out with his students on a hike when they ran unexpectedly into a storm and nobody would give them shelter. All they were left with was an empty school, and there he hit upon this simple but brilliant idea: the formation of a network of low-priced lodging for a one-day hike. The concept of a youth hostel was born. A little over 100 years later there are more than 4,500 branches in 80 countries all over the world.

Eventually in 1914 the world's first permanent youth hostel opened in Burg Altena, one of the most beautiful hilltop castles of Germany. Set in this magnificent locale, it had 48 beds to begin with. Post war this also became the seat of the reinstated German Youth Hostel Association. This glorious castle in Maerkischer Kreis – central North Rhine-Westphalia – with its momentous past of almost 1,000 years, now houses a large museum including the old youth hostel.

Bestleistung: Die erste ständige Jugendherberge der Welt
Region: Südwestfalen
Ort: Altena

Best performance: The first permanent youth hostel of the world
Region: Suedwestfalen
Place: Altena

DJH-MUTTERHAUS

19 — HEIMATLIEBE · VÖLKERFRIEDEN · JUGENDFREUDE · / D JH — 09

WELT JUGENDHERBER[GE]

HEIZEN MIT HOLZ UND GUTEM GEWISSEN
HEATING WITH WOOD AND A CLEAR CONSCIENCE

WESTFEUER. Ein Winterabend am Kamin – kaum etwas ist gemütlicher als die wohlige Wärme und das Knistern der brennenden Scheite. Aus gutem Grund heizen daher viele Deutsche mit Holz, hierzulande nach der Windenergie einer der wichtigsten erneuerbaren Energieträger. Gerade bei älteren Heizsystemen entsteht jedoch bei der Verbrennung Feinstaub. Dieser muss auf ein Minimum reduziert werden.

Das Coesfelder Unternehmen WESTFEUER bietet dazu die erste ideale Lösung zur Bekämpfung von Feinstaub bei der Holzverbrennung. Der Filter OekoTube wird ohne großen Aufwand auf den Schornsteinkopf montiert. Mit seinem sogenannten elektrostatischen Prinzip sorgt er dafür, dass sich die feinen Staubpartikel als Grobruß an der Innenwand des Schornsteins ablagern und so ganz einfach vom Schornsteinfeger beseitigt werden können.

Auf diese Weise reduziert OekoTube den Feinstaub um bis zu 95 Prozent. Und so lassen sich die Stunden am Kamin mit dem Wissen genießen, gleichzeitig einen wichtigen Beitrag zum Umweltschutz geleistet zu haben.

WESTFEUER. What could be cosier than the comforting warmth of a fireplace and the crackle of burning log pieces on a wintry evening? Germans prefer to use wood for heating and with good reason. In this country, next to wind power, it is one of the most important sources of renewable energy. But burning wood, especially in old heating systems, generates particulate matter, which has to be kept at a minimum.

WESTFEUER, based in Coesfeld, offers an ideal solution to deal with fine dust from wood fire. The OekoTube filter is easily mounted on chimney tops. Its so-called electrostatic principle ensures that dust particles accumulate on the inside walls of the chimney and clump there in coarse flakes. These deposits are easily removed by chimney sweeps.

OekoTube helps thus to reduce fine dust by 95 per cent. The joy of hours spent before the fireplace also lies in having made a major contribution to environmental protection.

Bestleistung: Effektivste Reduzierung von Feinstaub bei Holzverbrennung
Region: Münsterland
Ort: Coesfeld

Best performance: The most effective way of reducing fine dust from wood fire
Region: Muensterland
Place: Coesfeld

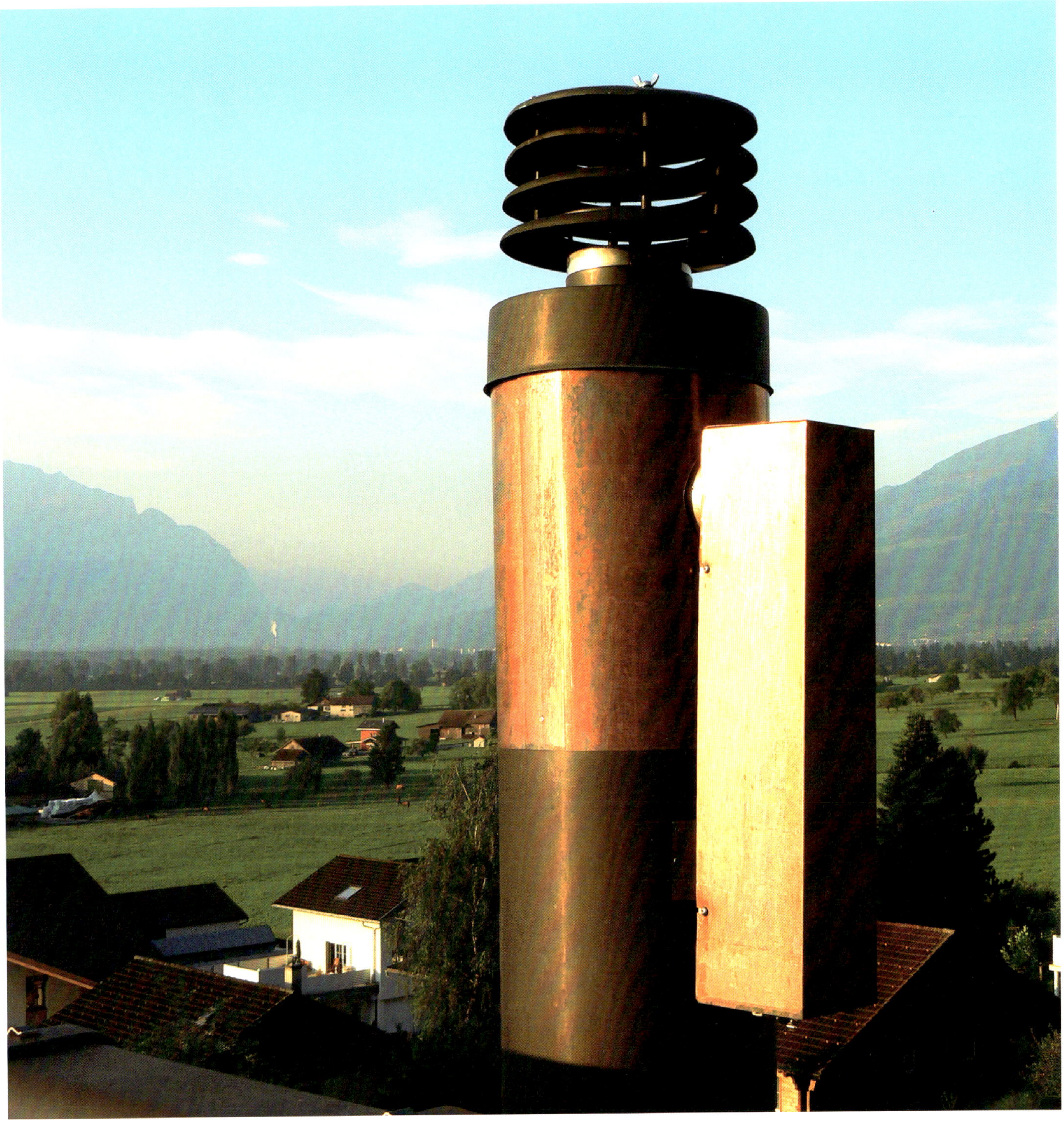

AUTOMOBILES KULTURGUT
AUTOMOBILES AS CULTURAL ASSETS

WIESMANN. Exklusive Autos, die wirklich rar sind im Straßenbild, findet man in Dülmen im Münsterland: Hier sind zwei Brüder groß geworden, die sich ihren Traum erfüllt haben, faszinierende Sportwagen zu bauen, die zeitloses Design und modernste Technik kombinieren. 1988 gründeten der Kaufmann Friedhelm und der Ingenieur Martin Wiesmann hier ihre Firma mit dem Gecko im Logo.

Über 1.600 handgefertigte Wagen sind seitdem in der führenden deutschen Manufaktur für puristische und individuelle Sportwagen produziert worden. Schnelle, schöne und seltene Fahrzeuge – hinter jedem Wagen stecken rund 110 hoch spezialisierte Mitarbeiter und über 350 Stunden Handarbeit, ausgestattet mit PS-starken Motoren aus dem Hause BMW. Aufgrund der hohen Fertigungstiefe kann Wiesmann nahezu jeden individuellen Kundenwunsch erfüllen – alleine die hauseigene Sattlerei bietet 400 Ledersorten an. Somit wird jeder Sportwagen mit dem Gecko auch zu einem echten Unikat.

Wiesmann steht für den klassischen Fahrzeugtyp – den Sportwagen. Emotionale Autos mit unvergleichlicher Fahrdynamik – dies spricht sich herum: Rund 200 Autos werden jährlich verkauft. Tendenz steigend.

WIESMANN. Looking for exclusive cars truly rare on roads? Then go to Duelmen in Muensterland. Two brothers grew up here to fulfil their dream of making fascinating sports cars that combine timeless design with state-of-the-art technology. Friedhelm, a businessman and Martin Wiesmann, an engineer formed their company here in 1988 using a gecko as their logo. Since then over 1,600 handcrafted cars have rolled out from this leading German manufacturing facility for purist, customised sports cars. These are fast and rare beauties equipped with powerful BMW engines, created by about 110 highly specialised employees and over 350 hours of workmanship. Vertically integrated production enables Wiesmann to fulfil virtually every customisation wish of its clients. The in-house car seat upholstery division alone offers 400 leather varieties, meaning that each sports car bearing the gecko logo truly is one of its kind.

Wiesmann stands for the classic sports car, and word about cars that combine sheer emotion with incomparable driving dynamics soon spreads around. About 200 cars sell annually and the trend is definitely rising.

Bestleistung: Führende Manufaktur für puristische Sportwagen
Region: Münsterland
Ort: Dülmen

Best performance: Leading manufacturer of puristic sports cars
Region: Muensterland
Place: Duelmen

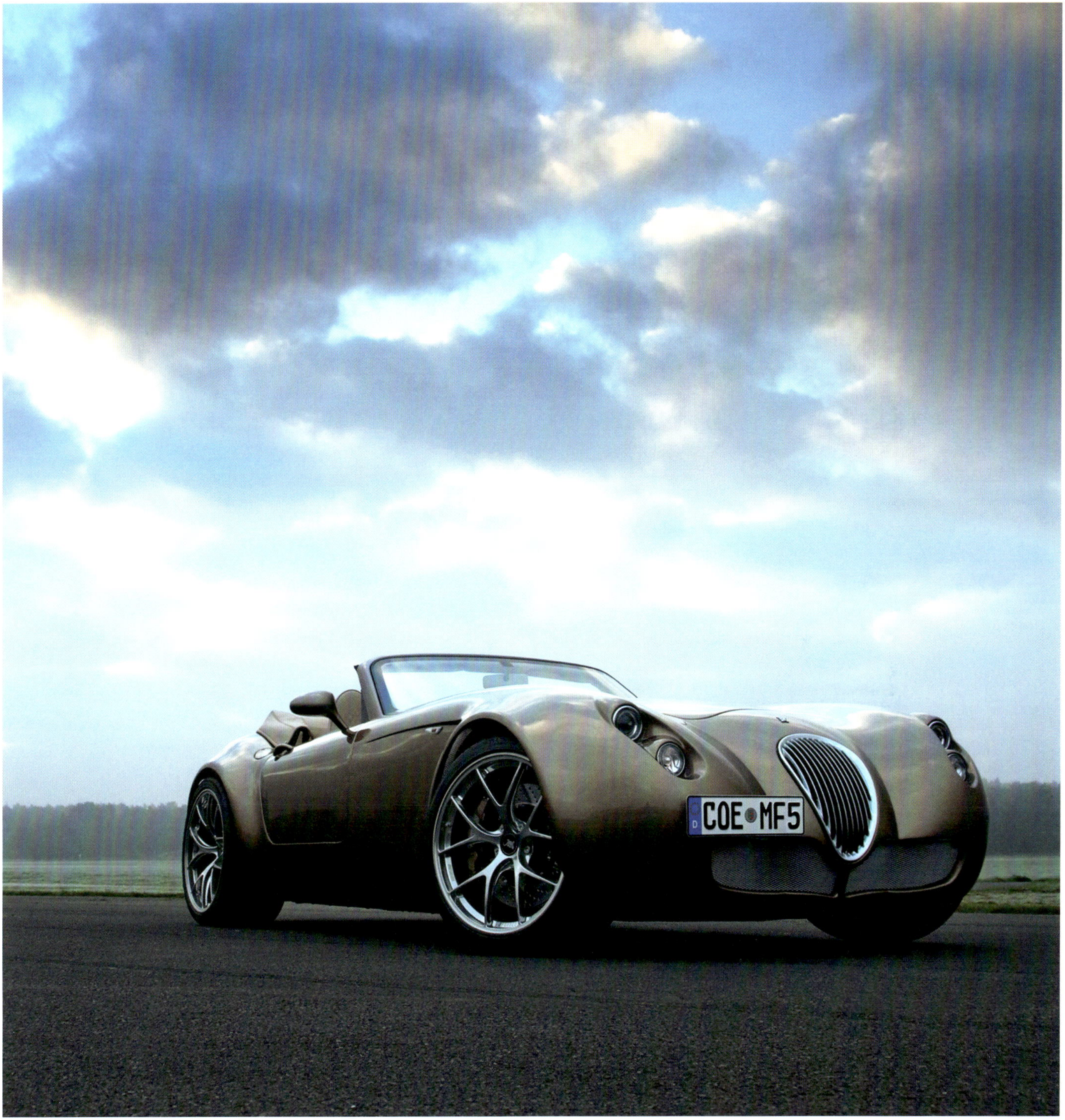
COE MF5

WILDPFERDE AUF FREIER BAHN
WILD HORSES ON A NATURAL RESERVE

WILDBAHN MERFELDER BRUCH. Sie tragen Hängemähnen und Stirnschopf, ihr mausgraues oder falbes Fell verdanken sie ihren Urahnen: Falben, mongolischen Urwildpferden und südrussischen Tarpanen. Ein Naturdenkmal – die Dülmener Wildpferde leben auf Europas einzig verbliebener Wildbahn. Betrieben wird sie von Rudolph Herzog von Croÿ, dessen Urururgroßvater die Herde 1845 unter Schutz stellen ließ. Die sogenannten Wildlinge sind in der Dülmener Region seit vielen Jahrhunderten ansässig. Die Bahn bietet ihnen auf 3,6 eingezäunten Quadratkilometern einen guten Lebensraum mit Weiden, Moor und Wald. An die 350 Tiere finden hier Nahrung, Deckung und Schutz – die Herde ist ganz sich selbst überlassen.

Es gibt nur zwei Ausnahmen: Einmal wird beispielsweise bei Schneelage Heu beigefüttert, und dann kommt es im Mai zum traditionellen Wildpferdefang. Dabei fangen mutige Männer einjährige Hengste ganz altmodisch und mit eigener Hand aus der Herde heraus – ein Muss, da das Reservat bei unbegrenztem Herdenwachstum schnell zu klein werden würde. Die Junghengste werden versteigert und finden als begehrte Reit- oder Zugtiere ein gutes Auskommen – und tragen somit zum Erhalt der Wildlinge bei.

THE MERFELDER BRUCH NATURE RESERVE. The horses here have floppy manes and a tuft on the forehead and owe their mouse grey or dun coats to their ancestors: dun horses, Mongolian Przewalski horses and South Russian Tarpan horses. This natural monument is home to the Duelmen ponies, Europe's only surviving breed of native horses living in the wild. The reserve is run by Duke Rudolph of Croÿ. In 1845 his great-great-great grandfather granted this herd of horses protected status. The so-called wild horses have been indigenous to the Duelmen region for centuries. The reserve provides them with a good habitat with meadows, moors and woodlands in a fenced area measuring 3.6 square kilometres. Roughly 350 animals find food, shelter and protection here. The herd is left to fend completely for itself. Only two exceptions are made: for one, when it snows heavily they are fed hay, and then in May there is the traditional trapping of wild horses by hand. Brave men catch one-year-old stallions by hand from the herds in the old-fashioned way. This is a necessity since the reserve would in no time become too small if left to breed rampantly. The young stallions are auctioned and do well as coveted mounts or draught animals and thus contribute to the conservation of the wild horses.

Bestleistung: Europas einzig verbliebenes Wildpferdegestüt
Region: Münsterland
Ort: Dülmen

Best performance: Europes only surviving stud farm of horses living in the wild
Region: Muensterland
Place: Duelmen

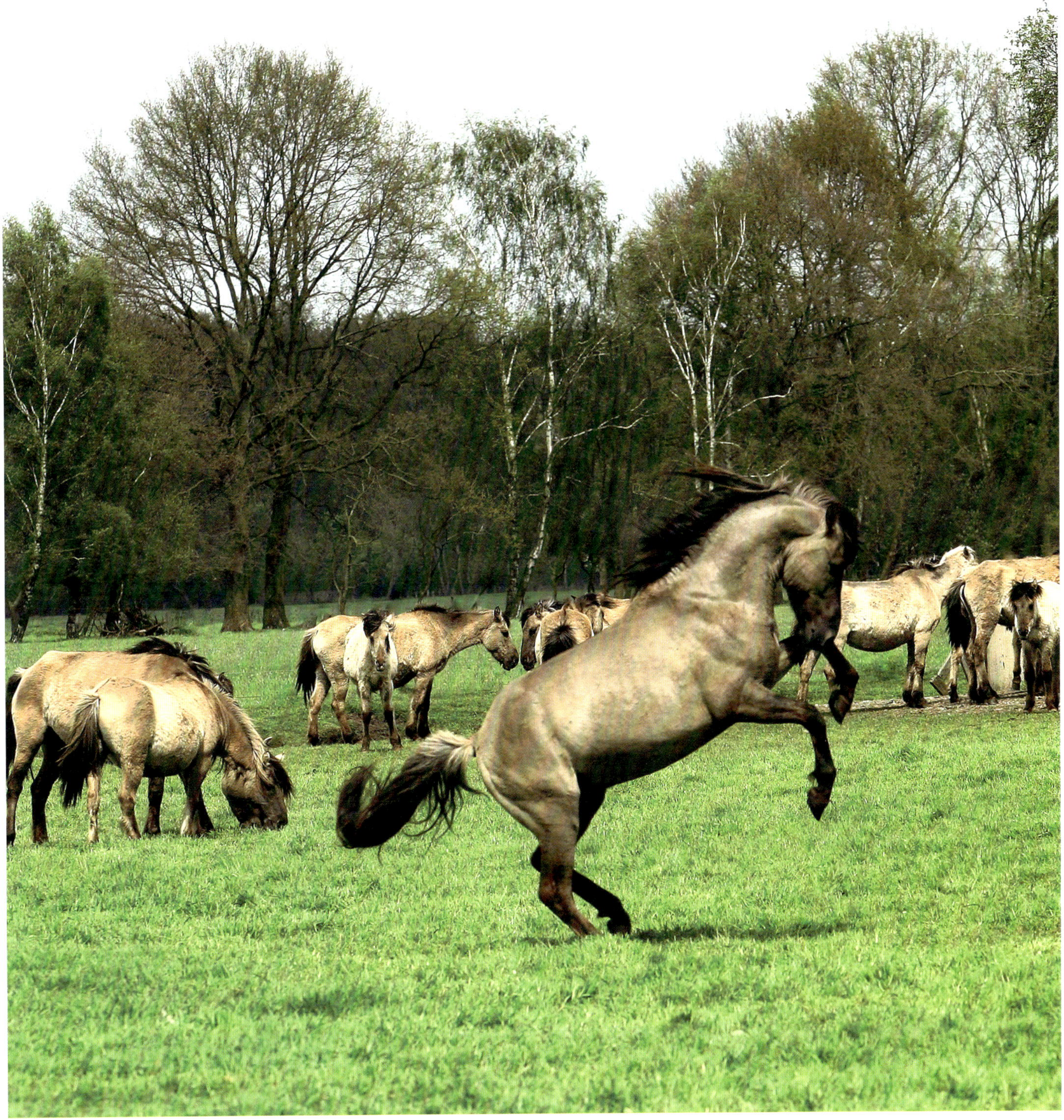

MIT HOCHLEISTUNG PUMPEN UND ENERGIE SPAREN
HIGH PERFORMANCE AND POWER-SAVING PUMPS

WILO SE. Jordanien gehört zu den wasserärmsten Ländern der Welt. Neben der Knappheit stellt der Transport die größte Herausforderung dar: Über einen Kilometer hoch muss das Wasser aus dem Jordantal in die Städte gepumpt werden. Das kostet viel Strom, und noch dazu geht auf diesem Weg viel Wasser verloren.

Anders in der Pumpstation Ebquoreyeh, gelegen in der Nähe des jordanischen Salt: Hier versorgen zwei Pumpen aus Dortmund 50.000 Menschen reibungslos mit Trinkwasser. Doch das ist längst noch nicht alles: Die Hochleistungspumpen der Firma WILO SE sparen jährlich mehr als 1,5 Millionen Kilowattstunden Energie und 1.100 Tonnen Kohlendioxid ein.

Die Produkte des weltweit führenden Herstellers von Pumpen und Pumpsystemen erbringen eine maximale Leistung – und das bei möglichst geringem Einsatz von Energie. WILO SE beschäftigt ungefähr 7.000 Mitarbeiter weltweit, und die Hochleistungspumpen des Dortmunder Unternehmens sorgen europaweit für Stromeinsparungen von bis zu 90 Prozent im Jahr – und natürlich auch für deutliche Kostenvorteile.

WILO SE. Jordan is among the nations facing the most acute water shortage in the world. Besides the scarce water supplies themselves, the greatest challenge lies in their transportation. Water from the Jordan river has to be pumped to a height of one kilometre to supply to the cities. This is extremely energy consuming and a lot of water is lost en route.

The story is rather different, though, at the Ebquoreyeh pumping station, located near the city of Salt, where two pumps made in Dortmund provide for an uninterrupted supply of potable water to 50,000 people. But that's not the end of the story by far. The high performance pumps from WILO SE have enabled energy consumption to be cut by more than 1.5 million kilowatt-hours per year and carbon dioxide emissions to be reduced by 1,100 tonnes.

The products of this world leading manufacturer of pumps and pumping systems offer maximum performance coupled with minimal energy consumption. WILO SE, which is based in Dortmund, has about 7,000 employees worldwide. Its pumps can deliver energy savings of up to 90 per cent per year and, not surprisingly, significant cost benefits too.

Bestleistung: Führender Hersteller von Pumpen
Region: Metropole Ruhr
Ort: Dortmund

Best performance: Leading manufacturer of pumps
Region: Ruhr Metropolis
Place: Dortmund

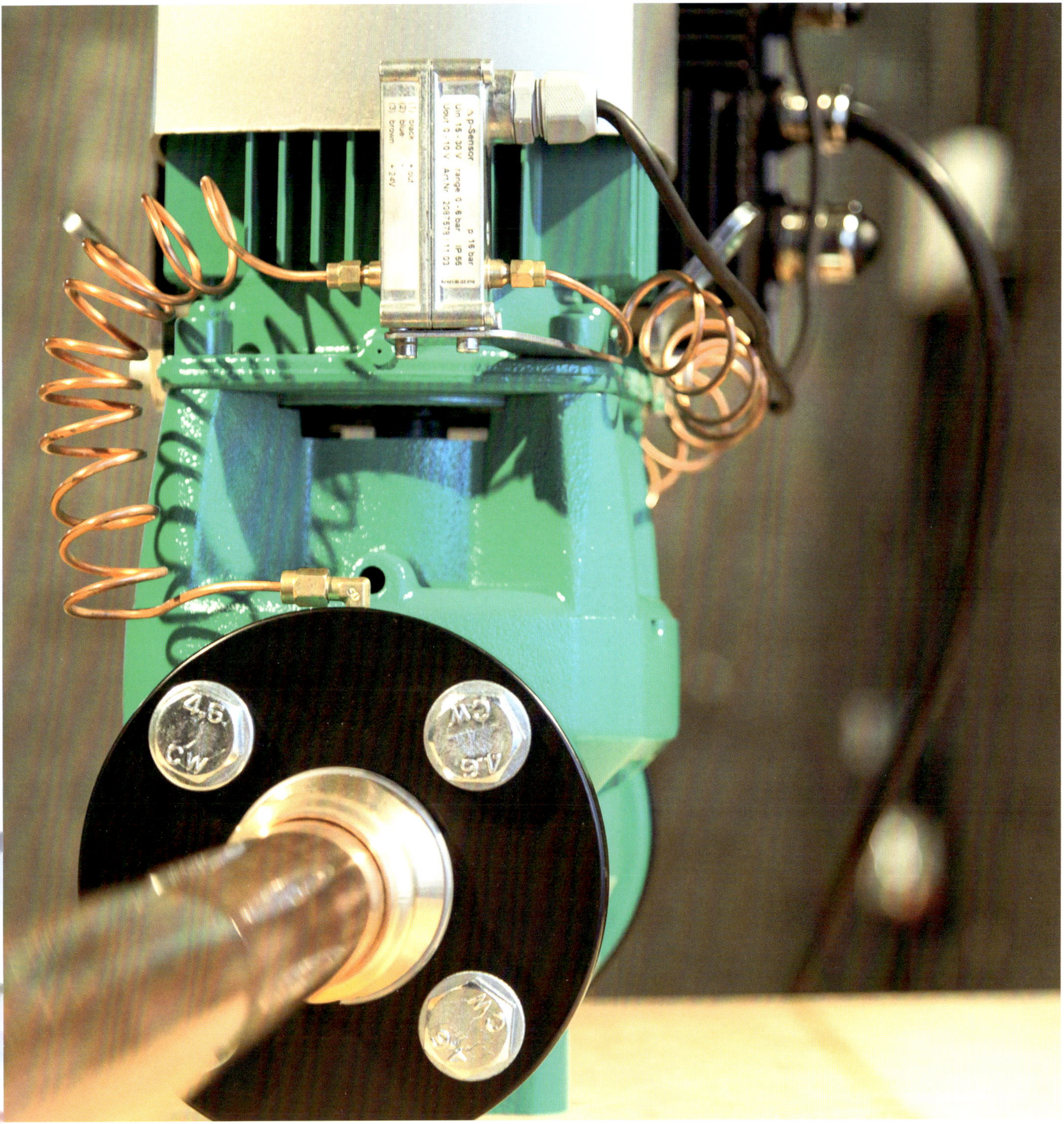

WILLKOMMEN IM WINTERWUNDERLAND
WELCOME TO THE WINTER WONDERLAND

WINTERSPORT-ARENA SAUERLAND. Kaum bewegen sich die Außentemperaturen auf den Gefrierpunkt zu, schon geht es los: Ein Netz modernster Beschneiungsanlagen sorgt auf der 280 Hektar großen Pistenfläche und den insgesamt 80 Kilometern Abfahrten für perfekte Skiverhältnisse – und das von Mitte Dezember bis Mitte März. Wir befinden uns im größten Skizirkus nördlich der Alpen: Ski Heil in der Wintersport-Arena Sauerland.

Ist es nur kalt genug, zahlen sich die getätigten Investitionen der letzten Jahre aus – in Zahlen: 148 Liftanlagen, 500 Kilometer Qualitätsloipennetz und Abfahrten von bis zu zwei Kilometern Länge bieten alles, was das Wintersportherz höherschlagen lässt – das Sauerland macht den Alpen ernsthafte Konkurrenz. Die zentrale Lage hilft: Von Rhein, Main und Ruhr, aber auch aus den Niederlanden reisen überzeugte Ski- wie auch Natur-Fans an. Dank ihrer hervorragenden Ausstattung zieht die Arena auch die internationale Sportwelt mit Weltcup-Veranstaltungen an, sei es im Skispringen, Snowboarden oder Bobfahren. Für Groß und Klein, Anfänger und Profi – hier fehlt es an nichts. Mitten im Westen, zwischen Bremen und Frankfurt/Main, ist im Sauerland ein wahres Winterwunderland entstanden.

WINTER SPORT ARENA SAUERLAND. No sooner do outside temperatures nudge towards freezing point than things begin to move. A network of the most modern snow blowing equipments are brought into service to create optimal skiing conditions on the piste with an area of 280 hectares and 80 kilometres of downhill ski-run, from mid-December to mid-March at that. We are in the thick of the greatest skiing extravaganza north of the Alps: a ski getaway at the winter sport arena of Sauerland.

It only needs to be cold enough for investments made in the last few years to begin to pay off, in actual figures: 148 ski lifts, 500 kilometres of quality network of cross-country ski runs and downhill runs with distances of up to two kilometres, offering everything that a winter sport enthusiast desires – the Sauerland is becoming a serious rival to the Alps. Being centrally located helps: it brings skiing enthusiasts as much as nature lovers from the Rhine, Main and Ruhr areas and from the Netherlands as well. By its excellent facilities the arena also draws international sport-events, World Cup championships be it in ski jump, snowboarding or bobsled. For the young and old, beginners and professionals, everyone is catered for. Emerging in the heart of the Western region, between Bremen and Frankfurt/Main here in Sauerland is a veritable winter wonderland.

Bestleistung: Größtes deutsches Skigebiet nördlich der Alpen
Region: Südwestfalen
Ort: Winterberg

Best performance: The biggest skiing region in Germany north of the Alps
Region: Suedwestfalen
Place: Winterberg

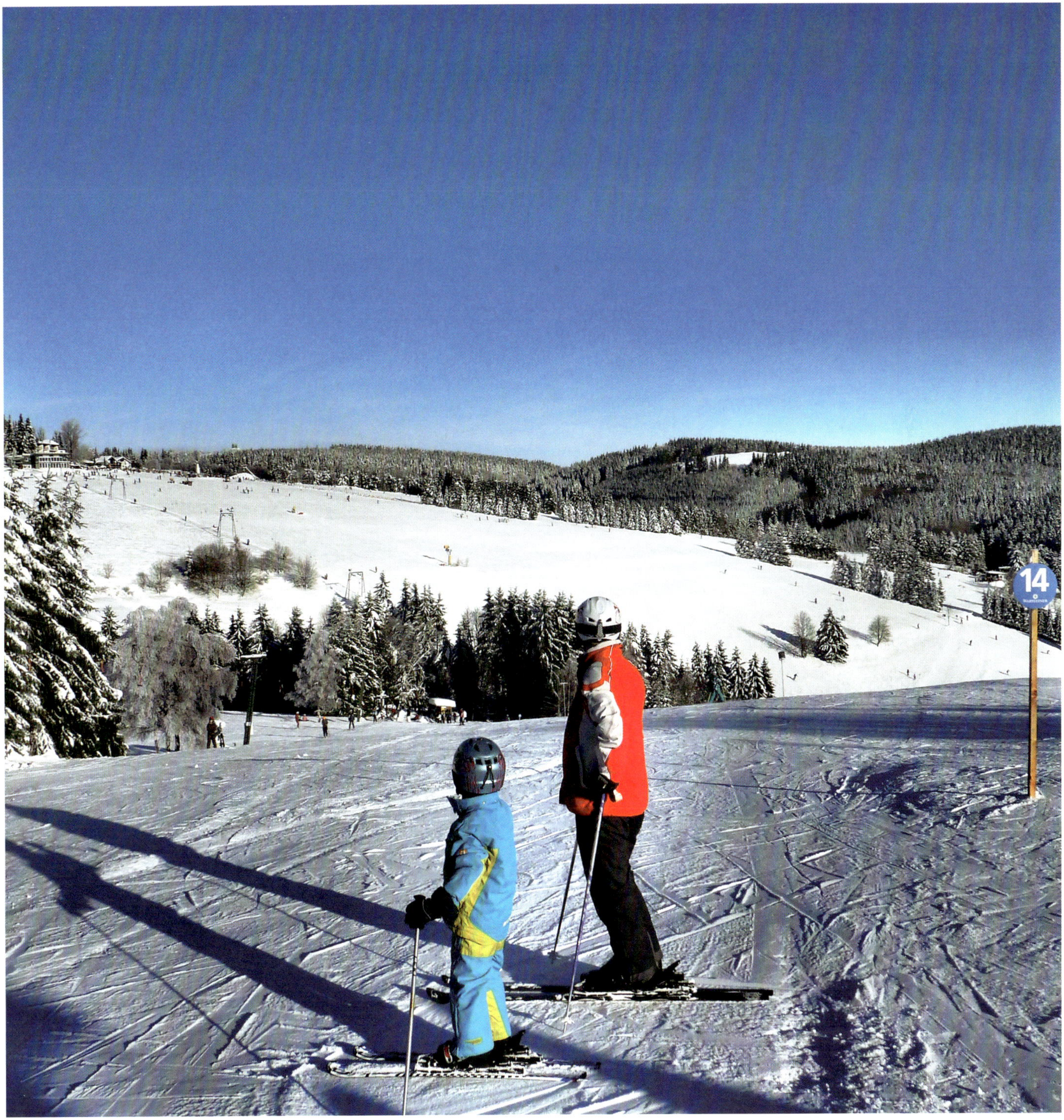
14

ORT DER ERINNERUNG
THE MEMORIAL

WOLFGANG BATTERMANN. Der pensionierte Gymnasiallehrer Wolfgang Battermann hat viel geschafft: Seinem Engagement verdankt die Stadt Petershagen den Erhalt eines historischen Synagogenensembles. 2012 bekommt Battermann dafür den international renommierten Obermayer German Jewish History Award verliehen.

Bereits in der Nachkriegszeit beginnt er als Schüler Fragen zur deutschen Vergangenheit und zum Holocaust zu stellen – und Antworten zu suchen. Als sein Lehrerberuf ihn nach Petershagen führt, engagiert er sich dort für die deutsch-jüdische Erinnerungskultur – bis heute. Das hat die den Preis ausschreibende Stiftung aus den USA überzeugt. Und natürlich das Ergebnis seiner beherzten Initiative: Die Wiederentdeckung und -herstellung einer in der NS-Zeit geschändeten Synagoge, einer jüdischen Schule und eines rituellen Tauchbads von 1796. Sie sind heute zugleich Gedenk- und Informationsstätte. Ausstellungen und Veranstaltungen ziehen Tausende Besucher an, die mehr erfahren möchten von der über 450 Jahre zurückreichenden jüdischen Lokal- und Regionalgeschichte. Ein Lernort ist entstanden, der die Erinnerung an die jüdischen Mitbürger aufrechterhält.

WOLFGANG BATTERMANN. Wolfgang Battermann, the retired grammar school teacher has a lot to be proud of. The town of Petershagen has his dedication to thank for preserving a historical synagogue ensemble. Batterman received the prestigious international "Obermayer German Jewish History Award" for his efforts in 2012.

Even as a schoolboy in the post-war era, he took an interest in Germany's past and the Holocaust. Teaching took him to Petershagen, where his lifelong involvement with the German-Jewish Culture of Remembrance took root. A just cause for the US-based award foundation; not any the less the fruits of his valiant efforts to rediscover and reinstate a synagogue defiled in the Nazi era, a Jewish school and a mikvah (ritual immersion bath) dating from 1796. This ensemble is today both a memorial and information space. Exhibitions and events draw thousands of visitors keen to learn more about the local and regional Jewish history going back over 450 years. Indeed the genesis of a true centre of learning, above all, in eternal memory of fellow Jewish citizens!

Bestleistung: Bewahrer eines einmaligen Erinnerungs- und Lernortes
Region: Ostwestfalen-Lippe
Ort: Petershagen

Best performance: Preserver of a unique memorial and centre of learning
Region: Ostwestfalen-Lippe
Place: Petershagen

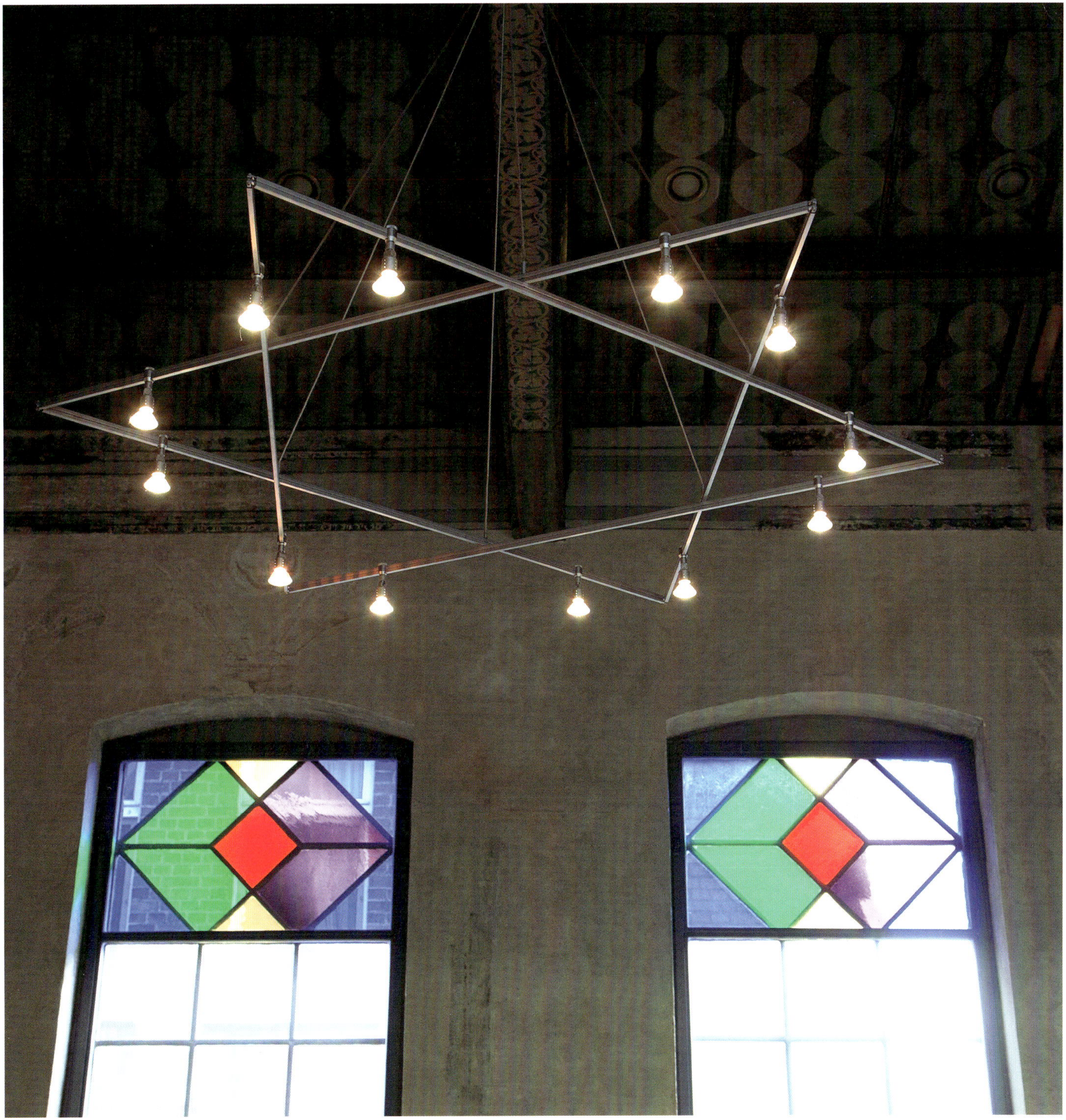

ÜBER DER WUPPER SCHWEBEN
FLOATING OVER THE WUPPER

WUPPERTALER SCHWEBEBAHN. Es schaukelt deutlich beim Einsteigen. Ist dies der Bahnsteig einer normalen Straßenbahn? Aber nein, hier ist alles anders. Was sonst unten ist – Räder, Getriebe, Bremsen ist nun oben. Einsteigen und staunen: eine Fahrt im denkmalgeschützten Wahrzeichen, der Wuppertaler Schwebebahn.

Seit 1901 schon fährt, nein schwebt die einmalige Bahn über der Wupper. Streng genommen hängen die Waggons der Einschienenbahn an ihrem seegrünen Stahltragwerk, dessen 468 Stützrahmen sich wie ein Tausendfüßler über 13 Kilometer durch die schmale, langgezogene Stadt an der Wupper winden.

Ein gigantisches Karussell: An den Endhaltestellen drehen die wendigen Bahnen und fahren retour. 20 Bahnhöfe, einmal rum in 30 Minuten – täglich 85.000 Fahrgäste. Kreuzungs- und staufrei hat die Schwebebahn zwölf Meter über dem Fluss eine eigene Hochebene erhalten. Platzsparend, schnell und sicher – auch in Zukunft: Dank der Modernisierung des praktischen und schönen Wahrzeichens kann man auch weiterhin „einmal im Leben durch Wuppertal schweben".

SUSPENSION MONORAIL OF WUPPERTAL. It sways unmistakably as you get in. Nothing about it is normal; not the platform, nor wheels, gears or brakes – all of them are on the top rather than below. Hop on for an amazing ride in this listed landmark, the suspension monorail of Wuppertal!

This unique tram has been running, nay floating since 1901 over the river Wupper. Technically speaking, the cars are suspended from the single rail underneath a teal steel frame. 13 kilometres of 468 supporting frames snake through the narrow, drawn out city on the banks of the Wupper like a centipede.

It is like a gigantic carousel of sinuous tracks that run back and forth between terminal stops. 20 stations, 85,000 commuters daily, an entire trip lasts 30 minutes. Meeting no junction or traffic, space-saving, speedy and safe for good, the monorail sustains an elevated plain of operations of its own, twelve metres above the river. Modernisation of this practical and wonderful landmark ensures that you continue to "Once in your life float over Wuppertal".

Bestleistung: Sicherstes Verkehrsmittel
Region: Bergisches Städtedreieck
Ort: Wuppertal

Best performance: The safest means of transport
Region: Bergisches Staedtedreieck
Place: Wuppertal

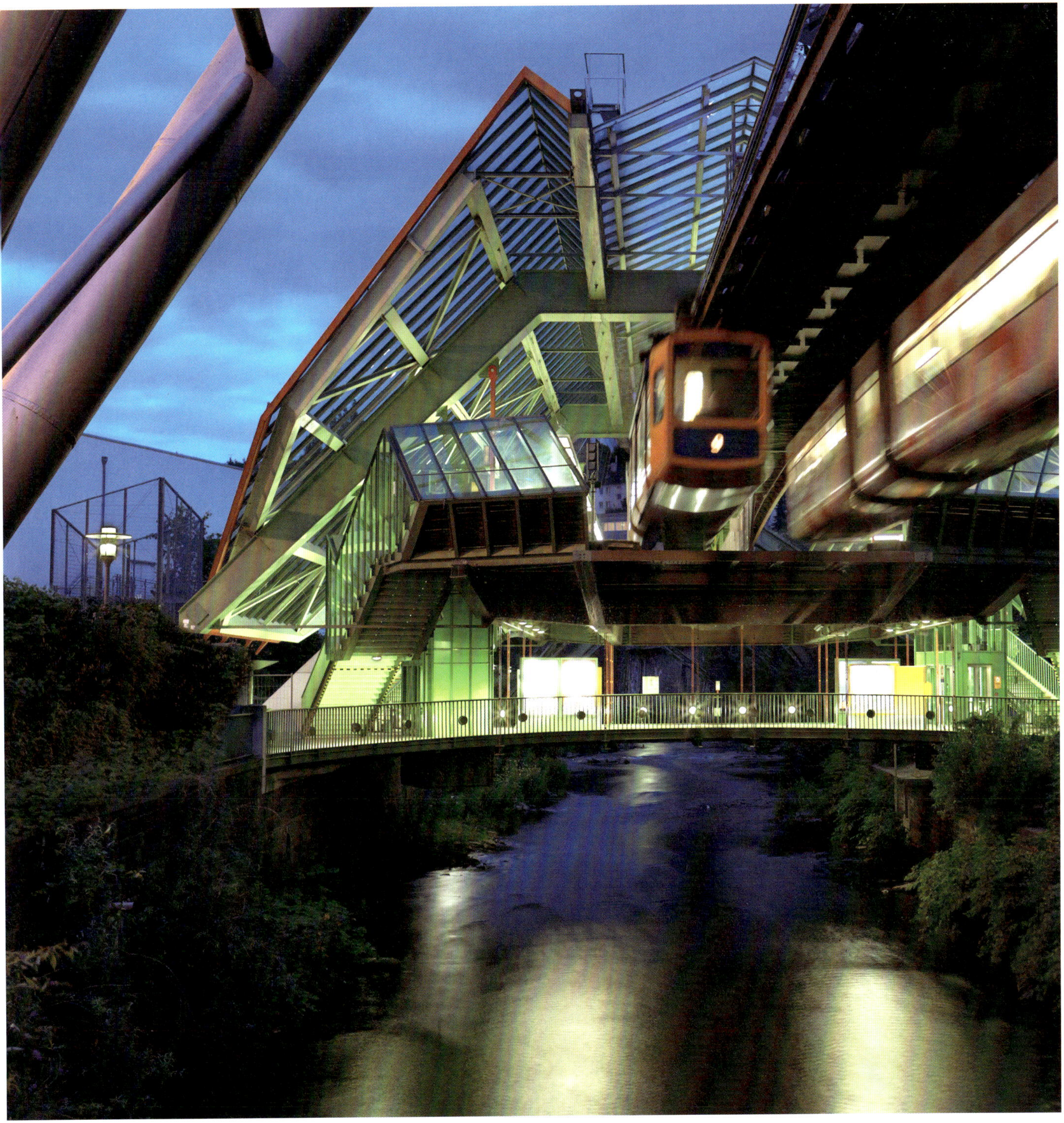

DIE SCHÖNSTE ZECHE DER WELT
THE FINEST COLLIERY IN THE WORLD

ZECHE ZOLLVEREIN. Viele Millionen Tonnen Steinkohle hat sie gefördert, die ehemals größte und modernste Zeche Europas. 1932 wurde im Essener Norden der Schacht XII in Betrieb genommen. Gebaut im Stil der Neuen Sachlichkeit, ist seine symmetrische und harmonisch gestaltete Silhouette das Gesicht der Zeche Zollverein. Vielen gilt sie als schönste Zeche der Welt, seit 2001 ist sie UNESCO-Welterbe.

Ihre Architektur erstrahlt heute – viele Jahre nach der Werksschließung – in neuem Glanz. Die Zeche ist ein Paradebeispiel für die erfolgreiche Umnutzung einer industriellen Anlage: Kunst, Kultur und Design werden nun statt Kohle in den monumentalen Gebäuden gefördert. Ein Zentrum für Kreativwirtschaft ist entstanden – Kulturschaffende lassen sich zwischen Förderturm und Kokerei ebenso inspirieren. Zudem locken Führungen, Tanz, Konzerte, Ausstellungen und Einrichtungen wie das Ruhr Museum, der Denkmalpfad ZOLLVEREIN® oder das red dot design museum jährlich ca. 1,5 Millionen Besucher an. Insgesamt stehen die Zeche und die Kokerei Zollverein für vielfältige, große Kulturprojekte vor einzigartiger Architekturkulisse.

ZECHE ZOLLVEREIN. Once the biggest and most modern colliery in Europe, it yielded millions of tonnes of coal. Shaft (or "Schacht") XII, to the north of Essen, was put into operation in 1932. Built on the elements of New Objectivity (Neue Sachlichkeit), its symmetrically and harmoniously formed contours are the face of the Zollverein colliery. For many it is the world's finest colliery; since 2001 a UNESCO World Heritage Site.

Its architecture stands out today in renewed splendour decades after closure. The colliery exemplifies the successful conversion of an industrial site, the call for art, culture and design now replacing that of coal in these epic monoliths. A hotspot for the creative industry has evolved leaving creative artists no less inspired amid shaft tower and coking plant. Guided tours, dance recitals, concerts, exhibitions and features like the Ruhr museum, Denkmalpfad ZOLLVEREIN® (heritage trail) or the red dot design museum too attract 1.5 million visitors annually. The Zollverein stands collectively for a kaleidoscope of cultural mega-projects in a unique architectural setting.

Bestleistung: UNESCO-Welterbe
Region: Metropole Ruhr
Ort: Essen

Best performance: UNESCO World Heritage Site
Region: Ruhr Metropolis
Place: Essen

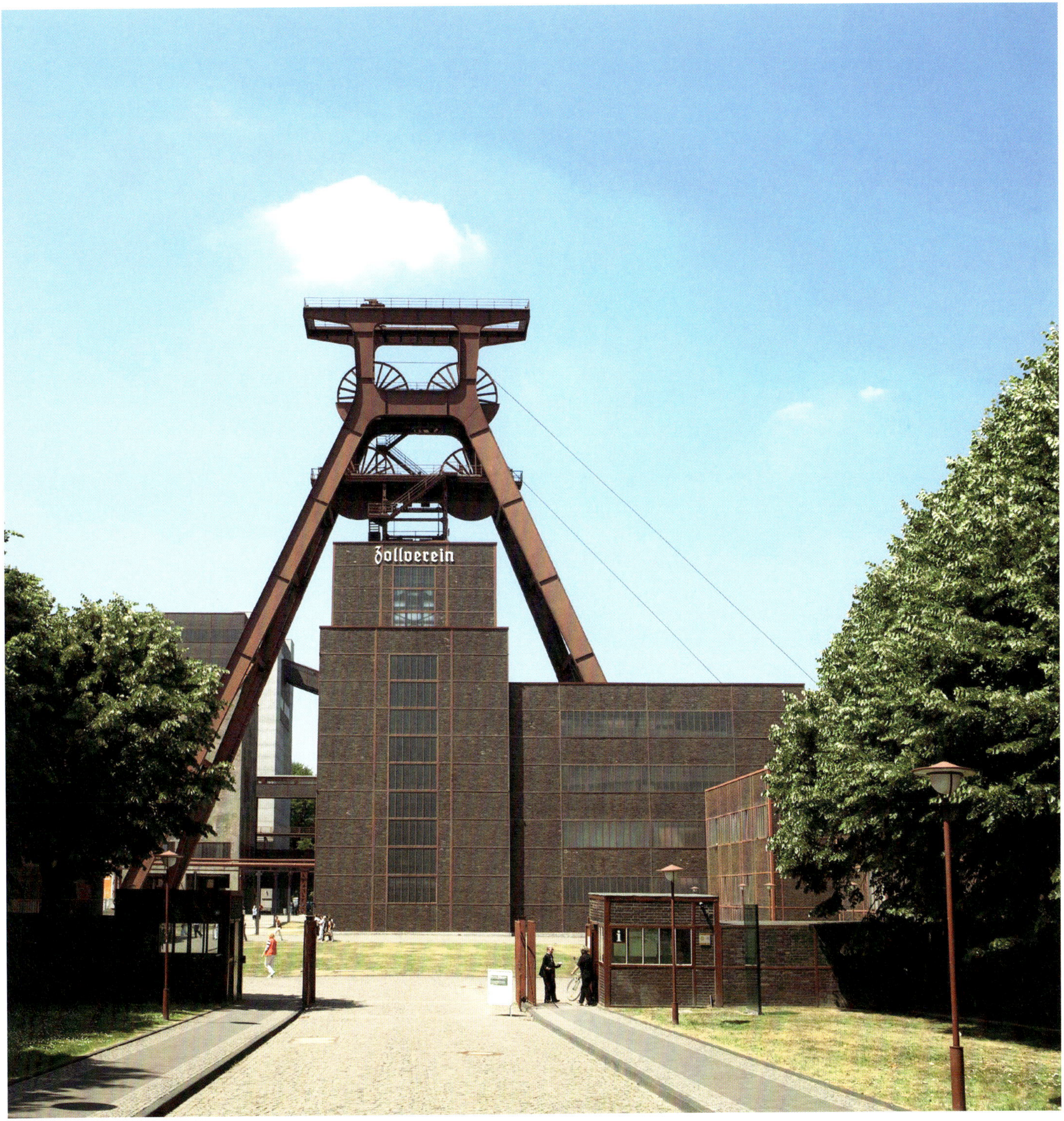
Zollverein

IM ZEICHEN DES ZWILLING
UNDER THE ZODIAC SIGN

ZWILLING J.A. HENCKELS. Im Bergischen Land liegt Solingen – die 160.000-Einwohnerstadt ist das Zentrum der deutschen Klingen-, Messer- und Schneidwarenindustrie und führt seit März 2012 den offiziellen Beinamen „Klingenstadt". Maßgeblich dazu beigetragen hat die Firma ZWILLING J.A. Henckels. Einer der weltweit führenden Hersteller hochwertiger Markenartikel in den Bereichen Küche, Gedeckter Tisch und Beauty hat hier seinen Stammsitz und seine Ursprünge.

Am 13. Juni 1731 – im Sternzeichen Zwillinge gegründet – ließ der Messermacher Peter Henckels diese als Schutzmarke in die Solinger Messermacher-Rolle eintragen. Damit ist ZWILLING eine der ältesten Marken der Welt. Das Traditionsunternehmen ist heute in den wichtigsten Industrieländern mit Tochtergesellschaften vertreten und vertreibt seine Produkte in über 100 Ländern. Erzeugnisse aus dem Hause ZWILLING stehen für höchste Qualität und Funktionalität. So hat das Unternehmen unter anderem rostfreien Stahl für die Schneidwarenindustrie perfektioniert, mit optimalen Legierungen und Spezialverfahren zur Veredelung.

ZWILLING J.A. HENCKELS. With a population of 160,000, the city of Solingen nestles in the Bergisches Land (Land of Berg). The hub of the German blade, knife and cutlery industry, since March 2012 it has gone by the official sobriquet of "City of Blades". With its origins and headquarters here, ZWILLING J.A. Henckels has had a big hand in that. The firm is one of the world's leading manufacturers of premium branded ware in the kitchen, tableware and beauty segments.

It was formed on 13th June 1731, i.e. under the zodiac sign Gemini or "Zwilling" (twins). This led the knife maker, Peter Henckels, to register this as a brand with the Cutler's Guild of Solingen, making ZWILLING one of the oldest trademarks in the world. With a proud tradition, the company now has subsidiaries in most of the major industrialised nations and markets its products in over 100 countries. ZWILLING products stand for the finest quality and functionality. Among other things it has honed stainless steel for the tableware industry by superlative blending and a special curing process.

Bestleistung: Ein führender Hersteller von Küchenbesteck
Region: Bergisches Städtedreieck
Ort: Solingen

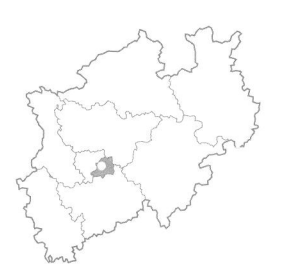

Best performance: A leading manufacturer of cutlery
Region: Bergisches Staedtedreieck
Place: Solingen

ZWILLING
J.A.HENCKELS
ZWILLING® PRO
FRIODUR ICE HARDENED
NO STAIN
38401-200 (8")
MADE IN
GERMANY

REGISTER UND BILDNACHWEISE

REGISTER AND PHOTO CREDITS

REGISTER A BIS Z
REGISTER A TO Z

NAME	BESTLEISTUNG / TOP ACHIEVEMENT	REGION	
123			
3M	Weltrekord im Kleben	Niederrhein	12
3M	World record in adhesion	Lower Rhine	12
3S Simons Security Systems	Kleinste Mikro-Farbcodepartikel zum Schutz vor Plagiaten	Münsterland	14
3S Simons Security Systems	Smallest anti-forgery micro-colour code particles	Muensterland	14
A			
Aachener Dom	UNESCO-Welterbe	Aachen	16
Aachen Cathedral	UNESCO World Heritage Site	Aachen	16
AC Schnitzer	Schnellstes Flüssiggasauto der Welt	Aachen	18
AC Schnitzer	The fastest LPG car of the world	Aachen	18
Aker Wirth	Marktführer für Bohrsysteme	Niederrhein	20
Aker Wirth	Market leader in drilling systems	Lower Rhine	20
Aloys F. Dornbracht	Führender Hersteller von Premiumarmaturen	Südwestfalen	22
Aloys F. Dornbracht	Leading manufacturer of premium taps	Suedwestfalen	22
Aluminium Norf	Das weltgrößte Walz- und Schmelzwerk	Niederrhein	24
Aluminium Norf	World's biggest rolling and smelting plant	Lower Rhine	24
Archäologischer Park Xanten	Deutschlands größtes Freilichtmuseum	Niederrhein	26
Archaeological Park Xanten	Germany's biggest open air museum	Lower Rhine	26
ART COLOGNE	Älteste Kunstmesse der Welt	Köln/Bonn	28
ART COLOGNE	World's oldest trade fair on art	Cologne/Bonn	28
AUNDE GRUPPE	Führender Hersteller von Automobiltextilien	Niederrhein	30
AUNDE GROUP	Leading manufacturer of automobile textiles	Lower Rhine	30
B			
Bayer MaterialScience	High-Tech-Kunststoff für innovativen Roboteranzug	Köln/Bonn	32
Bayer MaterialScience	High-tech synthetic material for innovative robot suit	Cologne/Bonn	32
BEA-tricks	Größte Reichweite eines E-Mobils	Metropole Ruhr	34
BEA-tricks	The biggest cruising range for an electric car	Ruhr Metropolis	34
Bergische Universität Wuppertal	Entdeckung des Higgs-Teilchens	Bergisches Städtedreieck	36
University of Wuppertal	Discovery of the Higgs particle	Bergisches Staedtedreieck	36
Bergische Universität Wuppertal	Wunderbox gegen Stromausfall	Bergisches Städtedreieck	38
University of Wuppertal	Wonder kit to prevent outages	Bergisches Staedtedreieck	38

NAME	BESTLEISTUNG / TOP ACHIEVEMENT	REGION

C

CITEC (Universität Bielefeld)	Entwicklung der intelligentesten künstlichen Systeme	Ostwestfalen-Lippe	40
CITEC (Bielefeld University)	Development of the most intelligent artificial systems	Ostwestfalen-Lippe	40
CLAAS	Weltrekord in Mähdrusch	Ostwestfalen-Lippe	42
CLAAS	World record in threshing	Ostwestfalen-Lippe	42

D

Die Sendung mit der Maus	Bekannteste und beliebteste Kindersendung Deutschlands	Köln/Bonn	44
The Programme with the Mouse	Germany's most renowned and most popular children's programme	Cologne/Bonn	44
Dream Production (Bayer MaterialScience)	Erste Pilotanlage zur Herstellung von Kunststoff aus CO_2	Köln/Bonn	46
Dream Production (Bayer MaterialScience)	The first pilot plant for production of synthetic material from CO_2	Cologne/Bonn	46
Düsseldorf	Die meisten ausländischen Neuinvestitionen in einer deutschen Stadt	Düsseldorf	48
Duesseldorf	The highest number of new investments made in a German city	Duesseldorf	48
Düsseldorf Airport	Drehkreuz der beiden größten deutschen Fluggesellschaften	Düsseldorf	50
Duesseldorf Airport	Hub of Germany's two biggest airlines	Duesseldorf	50

E

E.ON Westfalen Weser	Nutzung von Grundwasser zur Energieerzeugung	Ostwestfalen-Lippe	52
E.ON Westfalen Weser	Harnessing energy from ground water	Ostwestfalen-Lippe	52
Edirom (Universität Paderborn)	Einzigartige Software zur Indizierung von Musikkompositionen	Ostwestfalen-Lippe	54
Edirom (University of Paderborn)	Unique software to index music compositions	Ostwestfalen-Lippe	54
EMIL Sparlampen (Ruhr-Universität Bochum)	Umweltfreundlichste Energiesparlampe	Metropole Ruhr	56
EMIL Energy Efficient Bulbs (Ruhr University Bochum)	The most eco-friendly energy efficient bulbs	Ruhr Metropolis	56
Evonik Industries	Längste Strecke eines Windkraft-Fahrzeugs	Metropole Ruhr	58
Evonik Industries	The longest distance covered by a wind powered vehicle	Ruhr Metropolis	58
Extraschicht	Kulturfestival der Superlative	Metropole Ruhr	60
Extraschicht	A cultural festival of superlatives	Ruhr Metropolis	60

F

FALKE	Führender Hersteller von Markenstrumpfwaren	Südwestfalen	62
FALKE	Leading manufacturer of branded hosiery	Suedwestfalen	62
Feinbrennerei SASSE	Einzige deutsche „World-Class Distillery"	Münsterland	64
SASSE Distillery	The only German "World Class Distillery"	Muensterland	64

215

NAME	BESTLEISTUNG / TOP ACHIEVEMENT	REGION	
FG-INNOVATION	Weltweit leichtestes Aktorsystem	Metropole Ruhr	66
FG-INNOVATION	The lightest actuator of the world	Ruhr Metropolis	66
Forschungsverbund „The Reacting Atmosphere" (Bergische Universität Wuppertal)	Innovatives Stickstoffdioxid-Messgerät	Bergisches Städtedreieck	68
Research Association "The Reacting Atmosphere" (University of Wuppertal)	Innovative device to gauge nitrogen dioxide	Bergisches Staedtedreieck	68
Forschungszentrum Jülich & RWTH Aachen	Stärkstes Elektronenmikroskop Europas	Aachen	70
Research Center Juelich & RWTH Aachen University	Europe's most powerful electron microscope	Aachen	70

G

Gildemeister	Weltweit führender Hersteller von Dreh- und Fräsmaschinen	Ostwestfalen-Lippe	72
Gildemeister	World's leading manufacturer of lathes and milling machines	Ostwestfalen-Lippe	72
Gütesiegel RAL Barrierefrei	Ältestes Gütesicherungsverfahren in Europa	Aachen	74
RAL certificate barrier-free	Europe's oldest system of quality control	Aachen	74

H

HEAD acoustics	Führender Anbieter für Geräuschoptimierung	Aachen	76
HEAD acoustics	Leading suppliers of sound optimisation devices	Aachen	76
Heinrich Heine	Meistvertonter Dichter der Weltliteratur	Düsseldorf	78
Heinrich Heine	The maximum number of works by an author set to music in the literary world	Duesseldorf	78
HELLA	Innovativstes Unternehmen für Kfz-Lichttechnologie	Südwestfalen	80
HELLA	A pioneering company for automobile lighting technology	Suedwestfalen	80
Historisches Zentrum Wuppertal	Größtes Museum für Frühindustrialisierung	Bergisches Städtedreieck	82
Historical Centre Wuppertal	The biggest museum for early industrialisation	Bergisches Staedtedreieck	82
Hydro Aluminium	Walz-Weltmeister bei Aluminiumfolien	Niederrhein	84
Hydro Aluminium	A champion in the field of rolling aluminium sheets	Lower Rhine	84

I

InnovationsAllianz	Größtes Hochschulbündnis in Deutschland	Düsseldorf	86
Innovation Alliance	Germany's biggest alliance of universities	Duesseldorf	86
Internationaler Karlspreis zu Aachen	Eine der bedeutendsten europäischen Auszeichnungen	Aachen	88
International Charlemagne Prize of Aachen	One of Europe's most significant awards	Aachen	88
IQfy	Innovative Energiesteuerung im Büro	Südwestfalen	90
IQfy	Innovative energy control in an office	Suedwestfalen	90

NAME	BESTLEISTUNG / TOP ACHIEVEMENT	REGION	
Irrland	Größte Spielfläche Deutschlands	Niederrhein	92
Irrland	Biggest playground of Germany	Lower Rhine	92

J

Joseph Beuys	Einer der bedeutendsten Künstler	Düsseldorf	94
Joseph Beuys	One of the most distinguished artists	Duesseldorf	94
Julius Brink und Jonas Reckermann	Erste deutsche Olympiasieger im Beach-Volleyball	Münsterland	96
Julius Brink and Jonas Reckermann	The first Olympic winners in beach volleyball from Germany	Muensterland	96

K

Kölner Dom	Meistbesuchte Sehenswürdigkeit Deutschlands	Köln/Bonn	98
Cologne Cathedral	The most visited monument of Germany	Cologne/Bonn	98
Kölner Rosenmontagszug	Europas größter Rosenmontagszug	Köln/Bonn	100
The Shrove Monday Parade in Cologne	Europe's biggest Shrove Monday Parade	Cologne/Bonn	100
Konditorei Heinemann	Die besten Champagnertrüffel der Welt	Düsseldorf	102
Confectionery Heinemann	World's best champagne truffles	Duesseldorf	102
Krombacher Brauerei	Meistverkauftes Pilsener Bier Deutschlands	Südwestfalen	104
Krombacher Brewery	The largest selling Pilsener of Germany	Suedwestfalen	104
Kuchenmeister	Führender Anbieter von Baumkuchen und Stollen	Südwestfalen	106
Kuchenmeister	The biggest supplier of pyramid cakes and stollen	Suedwestfalen	106
Kunstakademie Düsseldorf	Eine der renommiertesten Ausbildungsstätten für bildende Kunst in Europa	Düsseldorf	108
Art Academy Duesseldorf	One of Europe's most renowned institution for instruction in fine arts	Duesseldorf	108

L

LaVision BioTec	Innovatives 3-D-Lichtblattmikroskop	Ostwestfalen-Lippe	110
LaVision BioTec	Innovative 3D light sheet microscope	Ostwestfalen-Lippe	110
Logistics Mall (Fraunhofer Institut für Materialfluss und Logistik IML)	Innovative Cloud-Computing-Software	Metropole Ruhr	112
Logistics Mall (Fraunhofer Institute for Material Flow and Logistics IML)	Innovative Cloud Computing Software	Ruhr Metropolis	112

M

MEDICA	Weltgrößte Medizinfachmesse	Düsseldorf	114
MEDICA	The biggest trade fair on medicine in the world	Duesseldorf	114

NAME	BESTLEISTUNG / TOP ACHIEVEMENT	REGION	
MEET – Münster Electrochemical Energy Technology	Innovative Batterieforschung.	Münsterland	116
MEET – Münster Electrochemical Energy Technology	Innovative battery research.	Muensterland	116
Mehmetcan Örücü	Weltrekordler im Fußball-Freestyle	Niederrhein	118
Mehmetcan Örücü	World record holder in freestyle football	Lower Rhine	118
MENNEKES Elektrotechnik	Führender Hersteller von Steckvorrichtungen	Südwestfalen	120
MENNEKES Electrical Engineering	Leading manufacturer of plug connections	Suedwestfalen	120
Miltenyi Biotec	Führend bei Produkten zur magnetischen Zellsortierung	Köln/Bonn	122
Miltenyi Biotec	Leader in products for magnetic sorting of cells	Cologne/Bonn	122
Museumskoffer (Universität Paderborn)	Weltweit kleinstes Museum	Ostwestfalen-Lippe	124
Suitcase museums (University of Paderborn)	The smallest museum of the world	Ostwestfalen-Lippe	124
Museum Ludwig	Größte Sammlung amerikanischer Pop Art außerhalb der USA	Köln/Bonn	126
Museum Ludwig	Biggest collection of American Pop Art outside the USA	Cologne/Bonn	126
Museum Plagiarius	Größte Plagiat-Sammlung	Bergisches Städtedreieck	128
Museum Plagiarius	The biggest collection of copies	Bergisches Staedtedreieck	128

N

Netzwerk Zuhause sicher	Innovative Initiative für Einbruch- und Brandschutz	Münsterland	130
Network for home security	An innovative initiative to prevent break-ins and fires	Muensterland	130
Nicolas Limbach	Weltcup-Gesamtsieger im Säbelfechten	Niederrhein	132
Nicolas Limbach	Overall worldcup winner in fencing	Lower Rhine	132

O

OLEDs (Philips)	Erste mit Wechselstrom betriebene OLED-Beleuchtung	Aachen	134
OLEDs (Philips)	The first OLED lighting run on alternating current	Aachen	134

P

Parador	Einzigartiges Druckverfahren für Laminatböden	Münsterland	136
Parador	Unique printing process for floor laminates	Muensterland	136
Peter Grünberg	Nobelpreisträger für Physik	Aachen	138
Peter Grünberg	Nobel Prize winner in physics	Aachen	138
Phoenix Contact	Hermes Award für innovatives Überwachungssystem	Ostwestfalen-Lippe	140
Phoenix Contact	Hermes Award for an innovative monitoring system	Ostwestfalen-Lippe	140
PHOTOKINA	Wichtigste Leistungsschau der Fotografie	Köln/Bonn	142
PHOTOKINA	A seminal competitive photography exhibition	Cologne/Bonn	142

NAME	BESTLEISTUNG / TOP ACHIEVEMENT	REGION	
Polarisationsregler EPC1000 (Universität Paderborn)	Weltweit schnellster Polarisationsregler	Ostwestfalen-Lippe	144
Polarisation Controller EPC1000 (University of Paderborn)	World's fastest polarisation controller	Ostwestfalen-Lippe	144
PROBAT-Werke	Marktführer für Röstmaschinen und -anlagen	Niederrhein	146
PROBAT-Werke	Market leader in roasting machines and plants	Lower Rhine	146

Q

QIAGEN	Sicherster Test zur Früherkennung von Gebärmutterhalskrebs	Düsseldorf	148
QIAGEN	Most reliable test for early detection of cervical cancer	Duesseldorf	148

R

Radioteleskop Effelsberg	Größtes vollbewegliches Radioteleskop Europas	Köln/Bonn	150
Radio telescope of Effelsberg	Europe's biggest fully steerable radio telescope	Cologne/Bonn	150
ReinHeart (RWTH Aachen)	Kleinstes Kunstherz der Welt	Aachen	152
ReinHeart (RWTH Aachen University)	World's smallest artificial heart	Aachen	152
RIMOWA	Führender Hersteller von Reisegepäck	Köln/Bonn	154
RIMOWA	Leading manufacturer of travel bags	Cologne/Bonn	154
RWTH Aachen	Eine der größten Forschschungslandschaften	Aachen	156
RWTH Aachen University	One of the biggest research scenarios	Aachen	156

S

Sachsenröder	Marktführer für Vulkanfiber	Bergisches Städtedreieck	158
Sachsenröder	Market leader in vulcanised fibres	Bergisches Staedtedreieck	158
SAERTEX	Führender Hersteller für textile Verbundwerkstoffe	Münsterland	160
SAERTEX	Leading manufacturer of textile composites	Muensterland	160
Schauspiel Köln	Theater des Jahres 2010 und 2011	Köln/Bonn	162
Schauspiel Köln	Theater of the Year in 2010 and 2011	Cologne/Bonn	162
Schloss Augustusburg	UNESCO-Welterbe	Köln/Bonn	164
Augustusburg Castle	UNESCO World Heritage Site	Cologne/Bonn	164
SolarCar-Team (Hochschule Bochum)	Per Solarauto um die Welt	Metropole Ruhr	166
SolarCar Team (Bochum University of Applied Sciences)	Around the world in a solar-powered car	Ruhr Metropolis	166
Solarturm Jülich	Einziges solarthermisches Demonstrationskraftwerk Deutschlands	Aachen	168
Solar Tower Juelich	Germany's only solar thermal demonstration power plant	Aachen	168

NAME	BESTLEISTUNG / TOP ACHIEVEMENT	REGION	
Spark Plasma Consolidation (Ruhr-Universität Bochum)	Schnellstes Verfahren zur Herstellung von Bauteilen	Metropole Ruhr	170
Spark Plasma Consolidation (Ruhr University Bochum)	Fastest method of producing components	Ruhr Metropolis	170
Stadt Freudenberg	International einmaliges Fachwerkensemble	Südwestfalen	172
Town of Freudenberg	Internationally unique ensemble of timbered houses	Suedwestfalen	172
Sterneköche	5-Michelin-Sterne im Gourmetmekka Bergisch Gladbach	Köln/Bonn	174
Star Chefs	5-Michelin stars in Bergisch Gladbach's gourmet mecca	Cologne/Bonn	174
StreetScooter (RWTH Aachen)	Besonders effizientes Elektroauto	Aachen	176
StreetScooter (RWTH Aachen University)	Particularly efficient electric car	Aachen	176
SuperLIGHT-CAR (RWTH Aachen)	Weltweit eine der leichtesten Autokarosserien	Aachen	178
SuperLIGHT-CAR (RWTH Aachen University)	One of the world's lightest car bodies	Aachen	178

T

TechnologieZentrumDortmund	Größtes Technologiezentrum Deutschlands	Metropole Ruhr	180
TechnologieZentrumDortmund	The biggest technology centre of Germany	Ruhr Metropolis	180
Thielenhaus Technologies	Marktführer in der Oberflächenfeinstbearbeitung	Bergisches Städtedreieck	182
Thielenhaus Technologies	Market leader in microfinish surface processing	Bergisches Staedtedreieck	182
Timo Boll	Bester deutscher Tischtennisspieler	Düsseldorf	184
Timo Boll	The best German table tennis player	Duesseldorf	184
Tony Cragg	Einer der bedeutendsten Bildhauer	Bergisches Städtedreieck	186
Tony Cragg	One of the most famous sculptors	Bergisches Staedtedreieck	186
TU Dortmund	Deutschlands einzige von einer Universität betriebene Synchrotronlichtquelle	Metropole Ruhr	188
TU Dortmund	Germany's only synchrotron light source run by a university	Ruhr Metropolis	188
TÜV Rheinland	Modernstes Prüfzentrum für Solarsysteme	Köln/Bonn	190
TÜV Rheinland	The most advanced testing centre for solar energy systems	Cologne/Bonn	190

W

Weltjugendherberge Burg Altena	Die erste ständige Jugendherberge der Welt	Südwestfalen	192
World Youth Hostel Burg Altena	The first permanent youth hostel of the world	Suedwestfalen	192
WESTFEUER	Effektivste Reduzierung von Feinstaub bei Holzverbrennung	Münsterland	194
WESTFEUER	The most effective way of reducing fine dust from wood fire	Muensterland	194
Wiesmann	Führende Manufaktur für puristische Sportwagen	Münsterland	196
Wiesmann	Leading manufacturer of puristic sports cars	Muensterland	196

NAME	BESTLEISTUNG / TOP ACHIEVEMENT	REGION	
Wildbahn Merfelder Bruch	Europas einzig verbliebenes Wildpferdegestüt	Münsterland	198
The Merfelder Bruch Nature Reserve	Europes only surviving stud farm of horses living in the wild	Muensterland	198
WILO SE	Führender Hersteller von Pumpen.	Metropole Ruhr	200
WILO SE	Leading manufacturer of pumps.	Ruhr Metropolis	200
Wintersport-Arena Sauerland	Größtes deutsches Skigebiet nördlich der Alpen	Südwestfalen	202
Winter sport Arena Sauerland	The biggest skiing region in Germany north of the Alps	Suedwestfalen	202
Wolfgang Battermann	Bewahrer eines einmaligen Erinnerungs- und Lernortes	Ostwestfalen-Lippe	204
Wolfgang Battermann	Preserver of a unique memorial and centre of learning	Ostwestfalen-Lippe	204
Wuppertaler Schwebebahn	Sicherstes Verkehrsmittel	Bergisches Städtedreieck	206
Suspension Monorail of Wuppertal	The safest means of transport	Bergisches Staedtedreieck	206

Z

Zeche Zollverein	UNESCO-Welterbe	Metropole Ruhr	208
Zeche Zollverein	UNESCO World Heritage Site	Ruhr Metropolis	208
ZWILLING J.A. Henckels	Ein führender Hersteller von Küchenbesteck	Bergisches Städtedreieck	210
ZWILLING J.A. Henckels	A leading manufacturer of cutlery	Bergisches Staedtedreieck	210

REGISTER NACH KATEGORIEN
REGISTER SORTED BY CATEGORIES

NAME	BESTLEISTUNG / TOP ACHIEVEMENT	REGION	

FREIZEIT & LEBEN
LEISURE & QUALITY OF LIFE

Gütesiegel RAL Barrierefrei	Ältestes Gütesicherungsverfahren in Europa	Aachen	74
RAL certificate barrier-free	Europe's oldest system of quality control	Aachen	74
Irrland	Größte Spielfläche Deutschlands	Niederrhein	92
Irrland	Biggest playground of Germany	Lower Rhine	92
MEDICA	Weltgrößte Medizinfachmesse	Düsseldorf	114
MEDICA	The biggest trade fair on medicine in the world	Duesseldorf	114
Netzwerk Zuhause sicher	Innovative Initiative für Einbruch- und Brandschutz	Münsterland	130
Network for home security	An innovative initiative to prevent break-ins and fires	Muensterland	130
Stadt Freudenberg	International einmaliges Fachwerkensemble	Südwestfalen	172
Town of Freudenberg	Internationally unique ensemble of timbered houses	Suedwestfalen	172
Sterneköche	5-Michelin-Sterne im Gourmetmekka Bergisch Gladbach	Köln/Bonn	174
Star Chefs	5-Michelin stars in Bergisch Gladbach's gourmet mecca	Cologne/Bonn	174
Wildbahn Merfelder Bruch	Europas einzig verbliebenes Wildpferdegestüt	Münsterland	198
The Merfelder Bruch Nature Reserve	Europes only surviving stud farm of horses living in the wild	Muensterland	198
Wintersport-Arena Sauerland	Größtes deutsches Skigebiet nördlich der Alpen	Südwestfalen	202
Winter sport Arena Sauerland	The biggest skiing region in Germany north of the Alps	Suedwestfalen	202

KULTUR & KUNST
CULTURE & ART

Aachener Dom	UNESCO-Welterbe	Aachen	16
Aachen Cathedral	UNESCO World Heritage Site	Aachen	16
Archäologischer Park Xanten	Deutschlands größtes Freilichtmuseum	Niederrhein	26
Archaeological Park Xanten	Germany's biggest open air museum	Lower Rhine	26
ART COLOGNE	Älteste Kunstmesse der Welt	Köln/Bonn	28
ART COLOGNE	World's oldest trade fair on art	Cologne/Bonn	28
Die Sendung mit der Maus	Bekannteste und beliebteste Kindersendung Deutschlands	Köln/Bonn	44
The Programme with the Mouse	Germany's most renowned and most popular children's programme	Cologne/Bonn	44
Extraschicht	Kulturfestival der Superlative	Metropole Ruhr	60
Extraschicht	A cultural festival of superlatives	Ruhr Metropolis	60

NAME	BESTLEISTUNG / TOP ACHIEVEMENT	REGION	
Heinrich Heine	Meistvertonter Dichter der Weltliteratur	Düsseldorf	78
Heinrich Heine	The maximum number of works by an author set to music in the literary world	Duesseldorf	78
Historisches Zentrum Wuppertal	Größtes Museum für Frühindustrialisierung	Bergisches Städtedreieck	82
Historical Centre Wuppertal	The biggest museum for early industrialisation	Bergisches Staedtedreieck	82
Internationaler Karlspreis zu Aachen	Eine der bedeutendsten europäischen Auszeichnungen	Aachen	88
International Charlemagne Prize of Aachen	One of Europe's most significant awards	Aachen	88
Joseph Beuys	Einer der bedeutendsten Künstler	Düsseldorf	94
Joseph Beuys	One of the most distinguished artists	Duesseldorf	94
Kölner Dom	Meistbesuchte Sehenswürdigkeit Deutschlands	Köln/Bonn	98
Cologne Cathedral	The most visited monument of Germany	Cologne/Bonn	98
Kölner Rosenmontagszug	Europas größter Rosenmontagszug	Köln/Bonn	100
The Shrove Monday Parade in Cologne	Europe's biggest Shrove Monday Parade	Cologne/Bonn	100
Konditorei Heinemann	Die besten Champagnertrüffel der Welt	Düsseldorf	102
Confectionery Heinemann	World's best champagne truffles	Duesseldorf	102
Kunstakademie Düsseldorf	Eine der renommiertesten Ausbildungsstätten für bildende Kunst in Europa	Düsseldorf	108
Art Academy Duesseldorf	One of Europe's most renowned institution for instruction in fine arts	Duesseldorf	108
Museumskoffer (Universität Paderborn)	Weltweit kleinstes Museum	Ostwestfalen-Lippe	124
Suitcase museums (University of Paderborn)	The smallest museum of the world	Ostwestfalen-Lippe	124
Museum Ludwig	Größte Sammlung amerikanischer Pop Art außerhalb der USA	Köln/Bonn	126
Museum Ludwig	Biggest collection of American Pop Art outside the USA	Cologne/Bonn	126
Museum Plagiarius	Größte Plagiat-Sammlung	Bergisches Städtedreieck	128
Museum Plagiarius	The biggest collection of copies	Bergisches Staedtedreieck	128
PHOTOKINA	Wichtigste Leistungsschau der Fotografie	Köln/Bonn	142
PHOTOKINA	A seminal competitive photography exhibition	Cologne/Bonn	142
Schauspiel Köln	Theater des Jahres 2010 und 2011	Köln/Bonn	162
Schauspiel Köln	Theater of the Year in 2010 and 2011	Cologne/Bonn	162
Schloss Augustusburg	UNESCO-Welterbe	Köln/Bonn	164
Augustusburg Castle	UNESCO World Heritage Site	Cologne/Bonn	164
Tony Cragg	Einer der bedeutendsten Bildhauer	Bergisches Städtedreieck	186
Tony Cragg	One of the most famous sculptors	Bergisches Staedtedreieck	186
Weltjugendherberge Burg Altena	Die erste ständige Jugendherberge der Welt	Südwestfalen	192
World Youth Hostel Burg Altena	The first permanent youth hostel of the world	Suedwestfalen	192

NAME	BESTLEISTUNG / TOP ACHIEVEMENT	REGION	

PERSÖNLICHKEITEN / PERSONALITIES

Peter Grünberg	Nobelpreisträger für Physik	Aachen	138
Peter Grünberg	Nobel Prize winner in physics	Aachen	138
Wolfgang Battermann	Bewahrer eines einmaligen Erinnerungs- und Lernortes	Ostwestfalen-Lippe	204
Wolfgang Battermann	Preserver of a unique memorial and centre of learning	Ostwestfalen-Lippe	204

SPORT / SPORTS

Julius Brink und Jonas Reckermann	Erste deutsche Olympiasieger im Beach-Volleyball	Münsterland	96
Julius Brink and Jonas Reckermann	The first Olympic winners in beach volleyball from Germany	Muensterland	96
Mehmetcan Örücü	Weltrekordler im Fußball-Freestyle	Niederrhein	118
Mehmetcan Örücü	World record holder in freestyle football	Lower Rhine	118
Nicolas Limbach	Weltcup-Gesamtsieger im Säbelfechten	Niederrhein	132
Nicolas Limbach	Overall worldcup winner in fencing	Lower Rhine	132
Timo Boll	Bester deutscher Tischtennisspieler	Düsseldorf	184
Timo Boll	The best German table tennis player	Duesseldorf	184

TECHNOLOGIE & INNOVATION / TECHNOLOGY & INNOVATION

3M	Weltrekord im Kleben	Niederrhein	12
3M	World record in adhesion	Lower Rhine	12
3S Simons Security Systems	Kleinste Mikro-Farbcodepartikel zum Schutz vor Plagiaten	Münsterland	14
3S Simons Security Systems	Smallest anti-forgery micro-colour code particles	Muensterland	14
AC Schnitzer	Schnellstes Flüssiggasauto der Welt	Aachen	18
AC Schnitzer	The fastest LPG car of the world	Aachen	18
Aker Wirth	Marktführer für Bohrsysteme	Niederrhein	20
Aker Wirth	Market leader in drilling systems	Lower Rhine	20
Aloys F. Dornbracht	Führender Hersteller von Premiumarmaturen	Südwestfalen	22
Aloys F. Dornbracht	Leading manufacturer of premium taps	Suedwestfalen	22
Bayer MaterialScience	High-Tech-Kunststoff für innovativen Roboteranzug	Köln/Bonn	32
Bayer MaterialScience	High-tech synthetic material for innovative robot suit	Cologne/Bonn	32
BEA-tricks	Größte Reichweite eines E-Mobils	Metropole Ruhr	34
BEA-tricks	The biggest cruising range for an electric car	Ruhr Metropolis	34
E.ON Westfalen Weser	Nutzung von Grundwasser zur Energieerzeugung	Ostwestfalen-Lippe	52
E.ON Westfalen Weser	Harnessing energy from ground water	Ostwestfalen-Lippe	52
Evonik Industries	Längste Strecke eines Windkraft-Fahrzeugs	Metropole Ruhr	58
Evonik Industries	The longest distance covered by a wind powered vehicle	Ruhr Metropolis	58

NAME	BESTLEISTUNG / TOP ACHIEVEMENT	REGION	
FG-INNOVATION	Weltweit leichtestes Aktorsystem	Metropole Ruhr	66
FG-INNOVATION	The lightest actuator of the world	Ruhr Metropolis	66
HEAD acoustics	Führender Anbieter für Geräuschoptimierung	Aachen	76
HEAD acoustics	Leading suppliers of sound optimisation devices	Aachen	76
HELLA	Innovativstes Unternehmen für Kfz-Lichttechnologie	Südwestfalen	80
HELLA	A pioneering company for automobile lighting technology	Suedwestfalen	80
InnovationsAllianz	Größtes Hochschulbündnis in Deutschland	Düsseldorf	86
Innovation Alliance	Germany's biggest alliance of universities	Duesseldorf	86
IQfy	Innovative Energiesteuerung im Büro	Südwestfalen	90
IQfy	Innovative energy control in an office	Suedwestfalen	90
LaVision BioTec	Innovatives 3-D-Lichtblattmikroskop	Ostwestfalen-Lippe	110
LaVision BioTec	Innovative 3D light sheet microscope	Ostwestfalen-Lippe	110
Logistics Mall (Fraunhofer Institut für Materialfluss und Logistik IML)	Innovative Cloud-Computing-Software	Metropole Ruhr	112
Logistics Mall (Fraunhofer Institute for Material Flow and Logistics IML)	Innovative Cloud Computing Software	Ruhr Metropolis	112
Miltenyi Biotec	Führend bei Produkten zur magnetischen Zellsortierung	Köln/Bonn	122
Miltenyi Biotec	Leader in products for magnetic sorting of cells	Cologne/Bonn	122
OLEDs (Philips)	Erste mit Wechselstrom betriebene OLED-Beleuchtung	Aachen	134
OLEDs (Philips)	The first OLED lighting run on alternating current	Aachen	134
Parador	Einzigartiges Druckverfahren für Laminatböden	Münsterland	136
Parador	Unique printing process for floor laminates	Muensterland	136
Phoenix Contact	Hermes Award für innovatives Überwachungssystem	Ostwestfalen-Lippe	140
Phoenix Contact	Hermes Award for an innovative monitoring system	Ostwestfalen-Lippe	140
Polarisationsregler EPC1000 (Universität Paderborn)	Weltweit schnellster Polarisationsregler	Ostwestfalen-Lippe	144
Polarisation Controller EPC1000 (University of Paderborn)	World's fastest polarisation controller	Ostwestfalen-Lippe	144
Sachsenröder	Marktführer für Vulkanfiber	Bergisches Städtedreieck	158
Sachsenröder	Market leader in vulcanised fibres	Bergisches Staedtedreieck	158
SAERTEX	Führender Hersteller für textile Verbundwerkstoffe	Münsterland	160
SAERTEX	Leading manufacturer of textile composites	Muensterland	160
SolarCar-Team (Hochschule Bochum)	Per Solarauto um die Welt	Metropole Ruhr	166
SolarCar Team (Bochum University of Applied Sciences)	Around the world in a solar-powered car	Ruhr Metropolis	166
StreetScooter (RWTH Aachen)	Besonders effizientes Elektroauto	Aachen	176
StreetScooter (RWTH Aachen University)	Particularly efficient electric car	Aachen	176

NAME	BESTLEISTUNG / TOP ACHIEVEMENT	REGION	
SuperLIGHT-CAR (RWTH Aachen)	Weltweit eine der leichtesten Autokarosserien	Aachen	178
SuperLIGHT-CAR (RWTH Aachen University)	One of the world's lightest car bodies	Aachen	178
TechnologieZentrumDortmund	Größtes Technologiezentrum Deutschlands	Metropole Ruhr	180
TechnologieZentrumDortmund	The biggest technology centre of Germany	Ruhr Metropolis	180
Thielenhaus Technologies	Marktführer in der Oberflächenfeinstbearbeitung	Bergisches Städtedreieck	182
Thielenhaus Technologies	Market leader in microfinish surface processing	Bergisches Staedtedreieck	182
TÜV Rheinland	Modernstes Prüfzentrum für Solarsysteme	Köln/Bonn	190
TÜV Rheinland	The most advanced testing centre for solar energy systems	Cologne/Bonn	190
WESTFEUER	Effektivste Reduzierung von Feinstaub bei Holzverbrennung	Münsterland	194
WESTFEUER	The most effective way of reducing fine dust from wood fire	Muensterland	194
WILO SE	Führender Hersteller von Pumpen	Metropole Ruhr	200
WILO SE	Leading manufacturer of pumps	Ruhr Metropolis	200
Wuppertaler Schwebebahn	Sicherstes Verkehrsmittel	Bergisches Städtedreieck	206
Suspension Monorail of Wuppertal	The safest means of transport	Bergisches Staedtedreieck	206
Zeche Zollverein	UNESCO-Welterbe	Metropole Ruhr	208
Zeche Zollverein	UNESCO World Heritage Site	Ruhr Metropolis	208

WIRTSCHAFT
ECONOMY

Aluminium Norf	Das weltgrößte Walz- und Schmelzwerk	Niederrhein	24
Aluminium Norf	World's biggest rolling and smelting plant	Lower Rhine	24
AUNDE Gruppe	Führender Hersteller von Automobiltextilien	Niederrhein	30
AUNDE Group	Leading manufacturer of automobile textiles	Lower Rhine	30
CLAAS	Weltrekord in Mähdrusch	Ostwestfalen-Lippe	42
CLAAS	World record in threshing	Ostwestfalen-Lippe	42
Düsseldorf	Die meisten ausländischen Neuinvestitionen in einer deutschen Stadt	Düsseldorf	48
Duesseldorf	The highest number of new investments made in a German city	Duesseldorf	48
Düsseldorf Airport	Drehkreuz der beiden größten deutschen Fluggesellschaften	Düsseldorf	50
Duesseldorf Airport	Hub of Germany's two biggest airlines	Duesseldorf	50
Edirom (Universität Paderborn)	Einzigartige Software zur Indizierung von Musikkompositionen	Ostwestfalen-Lippe	54
Edirom (University of Paderborn)	Unique software to index music compositions	Ostwestfalen-Lippe	54
FALKE	Führender Hersteller von Markenstrumpfwaren	Südwestfalen	62
FALKE	Leading manufacturer of branded hosiery	Suedwestfalen	62

NAME	BESTLEISTUNG / TOP ACHIEVEMENT	REGION	
Feinbrennerei SASSE	Einzige deutsche „World-Class Distillery"	Münsterland	64
SASSE Distillery	The only German "World Class Distillery"	Muensterland	64
Gildemeister	Weltweit führender Hersteller von Dreh- und Fräsmaschinen	Ostwestfalen-Lippe	72
Gildemeister	World's leading manufacturer of lathes and milling machines	Ostwestfalen-Lippe	72
Hydro Aluminium	Walz-Weltmeister bei Aluminiumfolien	Niederrhein	84
Hydro Aluminium	A champion in the field of rolling aluminium sheets	Lower Rhine	84
Krombacher Brauerei	Meistverkauftes Pilsener Bier Deutschlands	Südwestfalen	104
Krombacher Brewery	The largest selling Pilsener of Germany	Suedwestfalen	104
Kuchenmeister	Führender Anbieter von Baumkuchen und Stollen	Südwestfalen	106
Kuchenmeister	The biggest supplier of pyramid cakes and stollen	Suedwestfalen	106
MENNEKES Elektrotechnik	Führender Hersteller von Steckvorrichtungen	Südwestfalen	120
MENNEKES Electrical Engineering	Leading manufacturer of plug connections	Suedwestfalen	120
PROBAT-Werke	Marktführer für Röstmaschinen und -anlagen	Niederrhein	146
PROBAT-Werke	Market leader in roasting machines and plants	Lower Rhine	146
RIMOWA	Führender Hersteller von Reisegepäck	Köln/Bonn	154
RIMOWA	Leading manufacturer of travel bags	Cologne/Bonn	154
Wiesmann	Führende Manufaktur für puristische Sportwagen	Münsterland	196
Wiesmann	Leading manufacturer of puristic sports cars	Muensterland	196
ZWILLING J.A. Henckels	Ein führender Hersteller von Küchenbesteck	Bergisches Städtedreieck	210
ZWILLING J.A. Henckels	A leading manufacturer of cutlery	Bergisches Staedtedreieck	210

WISSENSCHAFT / SCIENCE

Bergische Universität Wuppertal	Entdeckung des Higgs-Teilchens	Bergisches Städtedreieck	36
University of Wuppertal	Discovery of the Higgs particle	Bergisches Staedtedreieck	36
Bergische Universität Wuppertal	Wunderbox gegen Stromausfall	Bergisches Städtedreieck	38
University of Wuppertal	Wonder kit to prevent outages	Bergisches Staedtedreieck	38
CITEC (Universität Bielefeld)	Entwicklung der intelligentesten künstlichen Systeme	Ostwestfalen-Lippe	40
CITEC (Bielefeld University)	Development of the most intelligent artificial systems	Ostwestfalen-Lippe	40
Dream Production (Bayer MaterialScience)	Erste Pilotanlage zur Herstellung von Kunststoff aus CO_2	Köln/Bonn	46
Dream Production (Bayer MaterialScience)	The first pilot plant for production of synthetic material from CO_2	Cologne/Bonn	46
EMIL Sparlampen (Ruhr-Universität Bochum)	Umweltfreundlichste Energiesparlampe	Metropole Ruhr	56
EMIL Energy Efficient Bulbs (Ruhr University Bochum)	The most eco-friendly energy efficient bulbs	Ruhr Metropolis	56

NAME	BESTLEISTUNG / TOP ACHIEVEMENT	REGION	
Forschungsverbund „The Reacting Atmosphere" (Bergische Universität Wuppertal)	Innovatives Stickstoffdioxid-Messgerät	Bergisches Städtedreieck	68
Research Association "The Reacting Atmosphere" (University of Wuppertal)	Innovative device to gauge nitrogen dioxide	Bergisches Staedtedreieck	68
Forschungszentrum Jülich & RWTH Aachen	Stärkstes Elektronenmikroskop Europas	Aachen	70
Research Center Juelich & RWTH Aachen University	Europe's most powerful electron microscope	Aachen	70
MEET – Münster Electrochemical Energy Technology	Innovative Batterieforschung	Münsterland	116
MEET – Münster Electrochemical Energy Technology	Innovative battery research	Muensterland	116
QIAGEN	Sicherster Test zur Früherkennung von Gebärmutterhalskrebs	Düsseldorf	148
QIAGEN	Most reliable test for early detection of cervical cancer	Duesseldorf	148
Radioteleskop Effelsberg	Größtes vollbewegliches Radioteleskop Europas	Köln/Bonn	150
Radio telescope of Effelsberg	Europe's biggest fully steerable radio telescope	Cologne/Bonn	150
ReinHeart (RWTH Aachen)	Kleinstes Kunstherz der Welt	Aachen	152
ReinHeart (RWTH Aachen University)	World's smallest artificial heart	Aachen	152
RWTH Aachen	Eine der größten Forschschungslandschaften	Aachen	156
RWTH Aachen University	One of the biggest research scenarios	Aachen	156
Solarturm Jülich	Einziges solarthermisches Demonstrationskraftwerk Deutschlands	Aachen	168
Solar Tower Juelich	Germany's only solar thermal demonstration power plant	Aachen	168
Spark Plasma Consolidation (Ruhr-Universität Bochum)	Schnellstes Verfahren zur Herstellung von Bauteilen	Metropole Ruhr	170
Spark Plasma Consolidation (Ruhr University Bochum)	Fastest method of producing components	Ruhr Metropolis	170
TU Dortmund	Deutschlands einzige von einer Universität betriebene Synchrotronlichtquelle	Metropole Ruhr	188
TU Dortmund	Germany's only synchrotron light source run by a university	Ruhr Metropolis	188

BILDNACHWEIS
PHOTO CREDITS

4/5	Düsseldorf Marketing & Tourismus GmbH
6/7	NRW.INVEST
8/9	Oliver Franke / Tourismus NRW e.V.
13	3M
15	3S Simons Security Systems GmbH
17	2012 Braatz / 360pixel.de
19	AC Schnitzer automobile Technik
21	Aker Wirth
23	Dornbracht / Thomas Popinger
25	Alunorf
27	Axel Thünker
29	Koelnmesse GmbH / ART COLOGNE
31	AUNDE
33	Prof. Sankai / CYBERDYNE, Inc. / Univ. of Tsukuba
35	NRW.INVEST
37	Brice Maximilien / CERN
39	SAG GmbH / Dortmund
41	Universität Bielefeld / CITEC
43	CLAAS
45	WDR / Schmitt Menzel / Streich
47	NRW.INVEST
49	davis / Fotolia.com
51	Düsseldorf Airport
53	E.ON Westfalen Weser
55	NRW.INVEST
57	NRW.INVEST
59	Evonik Industries
61	Ruhrtourismus GmbH / Nielinger
63	FALKE KGaA
65	Feinbrennerei SASSE
67	NRW.INVEST
69	Kobes / Fotolia.com
71	NRW.INVEST
73	Gildemeister
75	Javier Larrea / AGE / F1online
77	NRW.INVEST
79	Heinrich-Heine-Institut Düsseldorf
81	NRW.INVEST
83	Peter Frese / Wuppertal
85	Hydro / Udo Hüneburg
87	iStockphoto.com / bagi1998
89	Picture Alliance / Sven Simon
91	IQFY GmbH / PALMBERG GmbH
93	Freizeitpark Irrland
95	Studio Schaub – Köln
97	Red Bull Media House
99	Köln-Tourismus GmbH
101	J. Rieger / Köln / Festkomitee Kölner Karneval
103	Heinemann GmbH & Co.
105	Krombacher Brauerei
107	Kuchenmeister GmbH
109	Hye-Mi Kim
111	LaVision BioTec GmbH
113	Fraunhofer-Institut für Materialfluss und Logistik IML
115	Messe Düsseldorf GmbH
117	WWU / MEET
119	FUSSBALLMARKT.COM
121	MENNEKES Elektrotechnik GmbH & Co. KG
123	Miltenyi Biotec GmbH
125	Eva Koch
127	Thomas Riehle / arturimages
129	Aktion Plagiarius e.V.
131	Netzwerk Zuhause sicher
133	Kevin Schmitz
135	Philips Lumiblade / Whitevoid
137	Parador GmbH & Co. KG
139	Forschungszentrum Jülich
141	Phoenix Contact
143	Koelnmesse GmbH
145	NRW.INVEST
147	PROBAT-Werke von Gimborn Maschinenfabrik GmbH
149	NRW.INVEST
151	MPIfR / N. Junkes
153	Institut für Angewandte Medizintechnik / RWTH Aachen
155	RIMOWA
157	rha / reicher haase architekten / Aachen
159	PixelProduction
161	NRW.INVEST
163	Klaus Lefebvre
165	Florian Monheim
167	SolarCar-Team Hochschule Bochum
169	Kraftanlagen München
171	Christian Nielinger / RUB RUBIN
173	Stadt Freudenberg
175	NRW.INVEST
177	ADAC Motorwelt / Andreas Fechner
179	Superlight-Car-Konsortium / Institut für Kraftfahrzeuge / RWTH Aachen
181	Bartels Mikrotechnik GmbH
183	Thielenhaus Technologies GmbH
185	Dr. Stephan Roscher
187	Charles Duprat / Cragg Foundation
189	NRW.INVEST
191	NRW.INVEST
193	Stephan Sensen
195	WESTFEUER GmbH & Co. KG
197	Wiesmann GmbH
199	Gitta Gesing

201	NRW.INVEST
203	Wintersport-Arena Sauerland
205	NRW.INVEST
207	iStockphoto.com / Thomas Saupe
209	Thomas Willemsen / Stiftung Zollverein
211	ZWILLING J.A. Henckels